BENCHMARK SERIES

Microsoft® EXCEL® 2013

LEVEL 2

DENISE SEGUIN
Fanshawe College
London, Ontario

JAN DAVIDSON
Lambton College
Sarnia, Ontario

Paradigm PUBLISHING

St. Paul

Director of Editorial	Christine Hurney
Director of Production	Timothy W. Larson
Production Editor	Sarah Kearin
Cover Designer	Leslie Anderson
Text Designers	Leslie Anderson, Jaana Bykonich
Copy Editor	Communicáto, Ltd.
Desktop Production	Jaana Bykonich, Julie Johnston, Valerie King, Timothy W. Larson, Jack Ross, Sara Schmidt Boldon
Proofreader	Katherine Lee
Indexer	Terry Casey
VP & Director of Digital Projects	Chuck Bratton
Digital Projects Manager	Tom Modl

Acknowledgements: The authors, editors, and publisher thank the following instructors for their helpful suggestions during the planning and development of the books in the Benchmark Office 2013 Series: Olugbemiga Adekunle, Blue Ridge Community College, Harrisonburg, VA; Letty Barnes, Lake WA Institute of Technology, Kirkland, WA; Erika Nadas, Wilbur Wright College, Chicago, IL; Carolyn Walker, Greenville Technical College, Greenville, SC; Carla Anderson, National College, Lynchburg, VA; Judy A. McLaney, Lurleen B. Wallace Community College, Opp, AL; Sue Canter, Guilford Technical Community College, Jamestown, NC; Reuel Sample, National College, Knoxville, TN; Regina Young, Wiregrass Georgia Technical College, Valdosta, GA; William Roxbury, National College, Stow, OH; Charles Adams, II, Danville Community College, Danville, VA; Karen Spray, Northeast Community College, Norfolk, NE; Deborah Miller, Augusta Technical College, Augusta, GA; Wanda Stuparits, Lanier Technical College, Cumming, GA; Gale Wilson, Brookhaven College, Farmers Branch, TX; Jocelyn S. Pinkard, Arlington Career Institute, Grand Prairie, TX; Ann Blackman, Parkland College, Champaign, IL; Fathia Williams, Fletcher Technical Community College, Houma, LA; Leslie Martin, Gaston College, Dallas, NC; Tom Rose, Kellogg Community College, Battle Creek, MI; Casey Thompson, Wiregrass Georgia Technical College, Douglas, GA; Larry Bush, University of Cincinnati, Clermont College, Amelia, OH; Tim Ellis, Schoolcraft College, Liconia, MI; Miles Cannon, Lanier Technical College, Oakwood, GA; Irvin LaFleur, Lanier Technical College, Cumming, GA; Patricia Partyka, Schoolcraft College, Prudenville, MI.

The authors and publishing team also thanks the following individuals for their contributions to this project: checking the accuracy of the instruction and exercises—Traci Post and Janet Blum, Fanshawe College, London, Ontario; creating annotated model answers and developing lesson plans—Ann Mills, Ivy Tech Community College, Evansville, Indiana; developing rubrics—Marjory Wooten, Laneir Techncial College, Cumming, Georgia.

Trademarks: Access, Excel, Internet Explorer, Microsoft, PowerPoint, and Windows are trademarks or registered trademarks of Microsoft Corporation in the United States and/or other countries. Some of the product names and company names included in this book have been used for identification purposes only and may be trademarks or registered trade names of their respective manufacturers and sellers. The authors, editors, and publisher disclaim any affiliation, association, or connection with, or sponsorship or endorsement by, such owners.

We have made every effort to trace the ownership of all copyrighted material and to secure permission from copyright holders. In the event of any question arising as to the use of any material, we will be pleased to make the necessary corrections in future printings. Thanks are due to the aforementioned authors, publishers, and agents for permission to use the materials indicated.

Paradigm Publishing is independent from Microsoft Corporation, and not affiliated with Microsoft in any manner. While this publication may be used in assisting individuals to prepare for a Microsoft Office Specialist certification exam, Microsoft, its designated program administrator, and Paradigm Publishing do not warrant that use of this publication will ensure passing a Microsoft Office Specialist certification exam.

ISBN 978-0-76385-348-8 (Text)
ISBN 978-0-76385-391-4 (Text + CD)

© 2014 by Paradigm Publishing, Inc.
875 Montreal Way
St. Paul, MN 55102
Email: educate@emcp.com
Website: www.emcp.com

Printed in the United States of America

22 21 20 19 18 17 16 15 14 13   2 3 4 5 6 7 8 9 10

Contents

Benchmark Series Microsoft Excel 2013 is designed for students who want to learn how to use this powerful spreadsheet program to manipulate numerical data in resolving issues related to finances or other numbers-based information. No prior knowledge of spreadsheets is required. After successfully completing a course using this textbook, students will be able to

- Create and edit spreadsheets of varying complexity
- Format cells, columns, and rows as well as entire workbooks in a uniform, attractive style
- Analyze numerical data and project outcomes to make informed decisions
- Plan, research, create, revise, and publish worksheets and workbooks to meet specific communication needs
- Given a workplace scenario requiring a numbers-based solution, assess the information requirements and then prepare the materials that achieve the goal efficiently and effectively

In addition to mastering Excel skills, students will learn to import and export files between Excel and other programs in the Office 2013 suite. Upon completing the text, they can expect to be proficient in using Excel to organize, analyze, and present information.

Well-designed textbook pedagogy is important, but students learn technology skills from practice and problem solving. Technology provides opportunities for interactive learning as well as excellent ways to quickly and accurately assess student performance. To this end, this textbook is supported with SNAP, Paradigm Publishing's web-based training and assessment learning management system. Details about SNAP as well as additional student courseware and instructor resources can be found on page xiv.

Achieving Proficiency in Excel 2013 ■■■■■■■■■

Since its inception several Office versions ago, the Benchmark Series has served as a standard of excellence in software instruction. Elements of the book function individually and collectively to create an inviting, comprehensive learning environment that produces successful computer users. The following visual tour highlights the text's features.

UNIT OPENERS display the unit's four chapter titles. Each level has two units, which conclude with a comprehensive unit performance assessment.

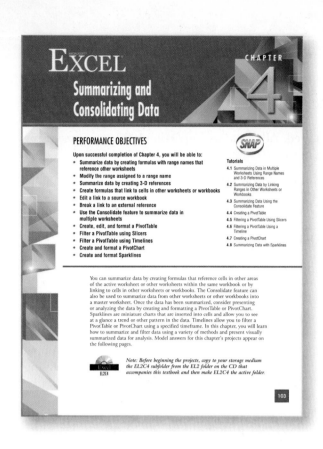

CHAPTER OPENERS present the performance objectives and an overview of the skills taught.

SNAP interactive tutorials are available to support chapter-specific skills at snap2013.emcp.com.

DATA FILES are provided for each chapter. A prominent note reminds students to copy the appropriate chapter data folder and make it active.

PROJECT APPROACH: Builds Skill Mastery within Realistic Context

MODEL ANSWERS provide a preview of the finished chapter projects and allow students to confirm they have created the materials accurately.

MULTIPART PROJECTS provide a framework for the instruction and practice on software features. A project overview identifies tasks to accomplish and key features to use in completing the work.

Between project parts, the text presents instruction on the features and skills necessary to accomplish the next section of the project.

STEP-BY-STEP INSTRUCTIONS guide students to the desired outcome for each project part. Screen captures illustrate what the student's screen should look like at key points.

Typically, a file remains open throughout all parts of the project. Students save their work incrementally.

Project 2 — Use Data Tools to Split Data and Ensure Data Integrity — 6 Parts

You will use Excel's data tools to split the client's first and last names into two separate columns, combine two columns, remove duplicate records, and restrict the type of data that can be entered into a field.

Quick Steps

Split Text into Multiple Columns
1. Insert blank column(s) next to source data.
2. Select data to be split.
3. Click DATA tab.
4. Click Text to Columns button.
5. Click Next at first dialog box.
6. Select delimiter check box for character that separates data.
7. Click Next.
8. Click Finish.
9. Deselect range.

Working with Data Tools

The Data Tools group on the DATA tab, shown in Figure 3.3, includes useful features for working with data in tables. A worksheet in which more than one field has been entered into the same column can be separated into multiple columns using the Text to Columns feature. For example, a column that has first and last names in the same cell can be split so that the first name appears in one column and the last name appears in a separate column. Breaking up the data into separate columns better facilitates sorting and other data management tasks.

Before using the Text to Columns feature, insert the number of blank columns you will need to separate the data immediately to the right of the column to be split. Next, select the column to be split and then click the Text to Columns button to start the Convert Text to Columns Wizard. The wizard contains three dialog boxes to guide you through the steps of separating the data.

Figure 3.3 Data Tools Group on the DATA Tab

Text to Columns

Project 2a — Separating Client Names into Two Columns — Part 1 of 6

1. Open **EL2-C3-P1-BillSumOctWk1.xlsx**.
2. Save the workbook and name it **EL2-C3-P2-BillSumOctWk1**.
3. Position the active cell anywhere within the table, click the Sort & Filter button in the Editing group on the HOME tab, and then click *Clear* at the drop-down list to clear the existing sort criteria.
4. Create a custom sort to sort the table first by date (oldest to newest) and then by client (smallest to largest). Refer to Project 1d, Step 3, if you need assistance with this step.
5. Split the client first and last names in column D into two columns by completing the following steps:
   a. Right-click column letter E at the top of the worksheet area and then click *Insert* at the shortcut menu to insert a blank column between the *Client Name* and *Attorney FName* columns in the table.
   b. Select D5:D25.
   c. Click the DATA tab.
   d. Click the Text to Columns button in the Data Tools group.

---

   e. At the Convert Text to Columns Wizard - Step 1 of 3 dialog box, with *Delimited* selected in the *Choose the file type that best describes your data* section, click Next.
   f. In the *Delimiters* section of the Convert Text to Columns Wizard - Step 2 of 3 dialog box, click the *Space* check box to insert a check mark and then click Next. The *Data preview* section of the dialog box updates after you click the *Space* check box to show the names split into two columns.

   g. Click Finish at the last Convert Text to Columns Wizard dialog box to accept the default General data format for both columns.
   h. Deselect the range.
6. Make cell D4 active, change the label to *Client FName*, and then AutoFit the column width.
7. Make cell E4 active, change the label to *Client LName*, and then AutoFit the column width.
8. Save **EL2-C3-P2-BillSumOctWk1.xlsx**.

Client first and last names are split into two columns in Steps 5a–5g.

Populating Data Using Flash Fill

Flash Fill is a new feature added to Excel 2013 that extracts, joins, and inserts text, numbers, dates, and times. This feature is useful for organizing data that has been pasted or imported from other sources. You can join all or extract part of the contents of cells. Flash Fill analyzes adjacent columns while entering data, detects any patterns, and suggests how the rest of the column should be completed.

For example, in Project 2a, instead of using Text to Columns to split the client names into two columns, you could use Flash Fill. To do this, insert two new columns instead of one. Type the first name *Joseph* in column E, as shown in Figure 3.4. Press Enter and then type *R* to start the second name, *Robert*. Excel recognizes that you are taking the first word of the adjacent column D and suggests doing the same for the remaining cells in column E. Notice that the rest

Quick Steps

Extract Data Using Flash Fill
1. Insert blank column(s) next to source data.
2. Type the first record.
3. Press Enter.
4. Start typing second record.
5. When grayed-out text appears, press Enter.

HINTS provide useful tips on how to use features efficiently and effectively.

QUICK STEPS provide feature summaries for reference and review.

MAGENTA TEXT identifies material to type.

6. Create a third custom view to show only the evening swimming sessions by completing the following steps:
   a. Select rows 4 through 23 and hide the rows by completing a step similar to Step 4a.
   b. Create a custom view named *EveningSessions* by completing steps similar to Steps 4b–4f.
7. Click the Custom Views button and then double-click *DaytimeSessions* in the *Views* list box at the Custom Views dialog box.
8. Show the *EveningSessions* custom view.
9. Show the *AllSessions* custom view.
10. Save and then close **EL2-C7-P2-NWinterSch-CV.xlsx**.

HINT Custom views cannot be created for any worksheet in which a table resides.

If you no longer need a custom view you previously created, delete it by opening the Custom Views dialog box, selecting the custom view name in the *Views* list box, and then clicking the Delete button.

Project 3 Save a Workbook as a Template · 2 Parts

You will modify an existing workbook and save the revised version as a template.

Saving a Workbook as a Template ■■■■■■■■■■■■■■■■

♥ **Quick Steps**

Save a Workbook as a Template
1. Open workbook.
2. Make desired changes.
3. Click FILE tab.
4. Click Save As.
5. Click Browse button.
6. Change *Save as type* option to *Excel Template (*.xltx).*
7. Type desired file name.
8. Click OK.

HINT If macros exist in the template workbook, change the *Save as type* option to *Excel Macro-Enabled Template (*.xltm).*

Templates are workbooks with standard text, formulas, and formatting. Cell entries are created and formatted for all of the data that does not change. Cells that will contain variable information have formatting applied, but are left empty since they will be filled in when the template is used to generate a worksheet. Examples of worksheets that are well suited to templates include invoices, purchase orders, time cards, and expense forms. These types of worksheets are usually filled in with the same kinds of data, but the data itself varies.

Several templates have already been created and are installed on your computer or can be installed after they are downloaded. If you want to use a template to create a worksheet, first check the New backstage area to see if a template already exists that is suited to your purpose. You can also search online for templates using categories such as *Budget, Invoice, Calendars,* and *Expenses.* Once you have selected a topic in Suggested Searches, you can either download one of the templates shown or choose another topic from the Category task pane.

If none of the existing templates meet your needs, you can create your own custom template. To do this, create a workbook that contains all of the standard data, formulas, and formatting. Leave cells empty for any information that is variable; however, format those cells as required. When you are ready to save the workbook as a template, use the Save As dialog box and change the *Save as type* option to *Excel Template (*.xltx).* Before saving it as a template, consider protecting the worksheet by locking all of the cells except those that will hold variable data.

Project 3a Saving a Workbook as a Template · Part 1 of 2

1. Open **EL2-C7-P2-NWinterSch.xlsx**.
2. Redisplay the row and column headers in the worksheet. Refer to Project 2c if you need assistance with this step.
3. Assume that you work at the Noranda Sportsplex, which publishes swimming schedules on a continual basis. The sportsplex manager never changes the days or times the pool operates, but the activities and assigned pools often change. You decide to modify this workbook and then save it as a template to be reused whenever the schedule changes. To begin, make the following changes to the worksheet:
   a. Clear the cell contents for the ranges D5:E23 and D25:E37.
   b. Make cell A2 the active cell and then delete *Winter* in *Winter Swimming Schedule* so that the subtitle reads *Swimming Schedule.*
   c. Insert a new row between rows 2 and 3 and merge and center the cells in the new row to match the subtitle. (This will be used later to enter the timeframe for the new schedule.)

Step 3b

This new row is inserted in Step 3c.

The contents of columns D and E are cleared in Step 3a.

   d. Select and turn off the lock attribute for cell A3 and the ranges D6:E24 and D26:E38. Deselect the range.
   e. Protect the worksheet. Do not assign a password to unprotect.
4. Save the revised workbook as a template by completing the following steps:
   a. Click the FILE tab.
   b. Click *Save As.*
   c. Click the Browse button.
   d. Click *Save as type* and then click *Excel Template (*.xltx)* at the pop-up list.
   e. Select the current text in the *File name* text box and then type SwimSchTemplate-StudentName, substituting your name for *StudentName.*
   f. Click the Save button.

Step 4d   Step 4e   Step 4f

5. Close **SwimSchTemplate-StudentName.xltx**.

CHAPTER REVIEW ACTIVITIES: A Hierarchy of Learning Assessments

Chapter Summary

- A formula that references a cell in another worksheet within the same workbook contains a worksheet reference and cell reference separated by an exclamation point.
- Range names can be used to simplify the references to cells in another worksheet, since the worksheet reference is automatically included in the definition of the range name.
- A disadvantage to using range names to reference other worksheets emerges if several worksheets are to be summarized, since each name has to be defined before the formula can be created.
- A 3-D reference is used to summarize the same cell in a range that extends over two or more worksheets.
- A 3-D reference includes the starting wo[...] name separated by a colon, similar to th[...] cells.
- A formula that references another works[...] a change made in the source cell is auto[...]
- A formula that references a cell in anoth[...] reference in front of the worksheet and [...] enclosed in square brackets.
- When you create a formula that links to [...] the drive and folder name in the path to [...] location of the source workbook or char[...] must edit the linked reference.
- Open the Edit Links dialog box to edit [...]
- The Consolidate feature is another met[...] multiple worksheets or workbooks.
- The Consolidate button is located in the [...]
- At the Consolidate dialog box, choose t[...] for the data that will be consolidated, a[...] you want to summarize, specify the loc[...] indicate whether to create a link to the [...]
- PivotTables are interactive tables that o[...] categories in rows or columns.
- Preview different PivotTable scenarios w[...] button.
- Create a PivotTable using the PivotTable [...] INSERT tab.
- Add fields to the PivotTable using the fi[...] Fields task pane.
- Once created, a PivotTable can be used [...] filtering the row, column, or report head[...]
- Use buttons in the contextual PIVOTT[...] tabs to format the PivotTable and/or edi[...]

- Slicers are used to filter data in a PivotTable without having to open a filter drop-down list.
- A Slicer pane contains all of the items in the designated field, so the report can be filtered with one mouse click.
- Click the Insert Slicer button in the Filter group on the PIVOTTABLE TOOLS ANALYZE tab to add a Slicer pane to a PivotTable.
- Timelines are used to group and filter data in a PivotTable using timeframes such as years, quarters, months, and days.
- Click the Insert Timeline button in the Filter group on the PIVOTTABLE TOOLS ANALYZE tab to add a Timeline pane to a PivotTable.
- A PivotChart displays the data in a PivotTable in a specified chart type.
- Filter a PivotChart using the legend or axis field buttons located on the PivotChart.
- Sparklines are miniature charts inserted into the backgrounds of cells.
- Add Sparklines to a worksheet to show trends or high or low values in a range of source data next to the data.
- To add Sparklines, select an empty range next to the source data, click the INSERT tab, and then click the desired chart type in the Sparklines group. At the Create Sparklines dialog box, type the range containing the values you want to graph or drag to select the range and then click OK.
- Sparklines can be customized using options in the SPARKLINE TOOLS DESIGN tab.

Commands Review

FEATURE	RIBBON TAB, GROUP	BUTTON	KEYBOARD SHORTCUT
Consolidate	DATA, Data Tools		
edit links	DATA, Connections		
manage range names	FORMULAS, Defined Names		Ctrl + F3
PivotChart	INSERT, Charts OR PIVOTTABLES TOOLS ANALYZE, Tools		
PivotTable	INSERT, Tables		
Slicer	INSERT, Filters		

Concepts Check Test Your Knowledge SNAP

Completion: In the space provided at the right, indicate the correct term, command, or number.

1. This symbol separates a worksheet reference from a cell reference.

2. This term describes a formula that references the same cell in a range that spans two or more worksheets.

3. Assume that a workbook contains the following defined range names that reference cells in four worksheets: Qtr1, Qtr2, Qtr3, and Qtr4. Provide the formula to add the data in the four ranges.

4. Create this formula entry for QtrlySales.xlsx to link to an external reference cell C12 in a worksheet named *Summary*.

5. Open this dialog box to change the source of a linked external reference after moving the source workbook to another folder.

6. Click this button to permanently remove a linked external reference and convert the linked cells to their existing values.

7. This default function is active when you open the Consolidate dialog box.

8. Use this button to preview different PivotTable scenarios.

9. Add fields to a PivotTable by clicking the field check box in this task pane.

10. The PivotTable Styles gallery is accessible from this tab.

11. Insert this type of pane to filter a PivotTable with one mouse click.

12. Insert this type of pane to filter a PivotTable by dates.

13. Choose a function other than Sum for a PivotTable numeric field by clicking this button in the Active Group on the PIVOTTABLE TOOLS ANALYZE tab.

14. The buttons to filter a PivotChart are found here.

15. This is the first step in adding Sparklines to a worksheet.

16. Click this tab to customize Sparklines.

CHAPTER SUMMARY captures the purpose and execution of key features.

COMMANDS REVIEW summarizes visually the major features and alternative methods of access.

CONCEPTS CHECK questions assess knowledge recall. Students enrolled in SNAP can complete the Concepts Check online. SNAP automatically scores student work.

Skills Check — Assess Your Performance

Note: If you submit your work in hard copy, check with your instructor before completing these Assessments to see if you need to print two copies of worksheets in which you have created formulas, with one copy showing the cell formulas.

Assessment

1 SUMMARIZE DATA IN MULTIPLE WORKSHEETS USING RANGE NAMES Grade It

1. Open **NADQ1Fees.xlsx**.
2. Save the workbook and name it **EL2-C4-A1-NADQ1Fees**.
3. The workbook contains three worksheets showing dental fees earned in January, February, and March for three dentists at a dental clinic. Create a range name in cell ... each dentist for the ...
   a. Type PopovichTo...
   b. Type VanketTo...
   c. Type JovanovicT...
4. Make FeeSummary ... in cell A6: Quarter...
5. Make cell F6 the a... earned by each den...
6. Apply accounting f... AutoFit.
7. Print the FeeSumm...
8. Save and then close...

Assessment

2 SUMMARIZE DATA USING...

1. Open **PFSalesSum...**
2. Save the workbook ...
3. Open **PFQ1.xlsx, ...**
4. Tile all of the open... *VIEW tab*.
5. Starting in cell B5... populate the cells i... **PFQ1.xlsx.** *Hint: ... use a relative refere... you can copy and p...*
6. Create formulas to... and fourth-quarter...
7. Close the four quar... save changes.
8. Maximize **EL2-C4-...**
9. Make cell B5 the a...
10. Print the workshee...
11. Save and then clos...

SKILLS CHECK exercises ask students to create a variety of documents using multiple features without how-to directions. Versions of the activities marked with a SNAP Grade It icon are available for automatic scoring in SNAP.

Visual Benchmark — Demonstrate Your Proficiency

SUMMARIZING REAL ESTATE SALES AND COMMISSION DATA

1. Open **HROctSales.xlsx**.
2. Save the workbook and name it **EL2-C4-VB-HROctSales**.
3. Create the PivotTable shown in Figure 4.11 in a new worksheet named *PivotTable*. Apply the Pivot Style Medium 11 style and set the column widths to 18 characters.
4. Create the PivotChart shown in Figure 4.12 in a new worksheet named *PivotChart*. Use the 3-D Clustered Column chart type and apply the Style 11 style.
5. Print the PivotTable and PivotChart worksheets.
6. Save and then close **EL2-C4-VB-HROctSales.xlsx**.

Figure 4.11 Visual Benchmark PivotTable

	A	B	C	D	E
		Hillsdale Realtors			
1					
2		October Sales			
3	Sum of Sale Price	Column Labels			
4	Row Labels	Condominium	Single family home	Townhome	Grand Total
5	Chandler	$ 610,900	$ 325,800	$ 952,100	$ 1,888,800
6	Glendale	640,400	881,375		1,521,775
7	Mesa	275,800	846,750	165,800	1,288,380
8	Phoenix	695,000	2,148,100	174,900	3,018,000
9	Grand Total	$ 2,222,100	$ 4,201,725	$ 1,292,800	$ 7,716,625

VISUAL BENCHMARK assessments test students' problem-solving skills and mastery of program features.

Figure 4.12 Visu...

Case Study — Apply Your Skills

Part 1

Yolanda Robertson of NuTrends Market Research is continuing to work on the franchise expansion plan for the owners of Pizza By Mario. Yolanda has received a new workbook from the owners with profit information by store and would like you to summarize the data. Open the workbook named **PBMSales&Profits.xlsx** and review the structure of the data. Yolanda would like to have a PivotTable that provides the average gross sales and average net income by city and state. You determine how to organize the layout of the report. *Hint: You can add more than one numeric field to the Values list box.* Remove the grand totals at the right of the report so that only a grand total row appears at the bottom of the PivotTable. *Hint: Use the Grand Totals button in the Layout group on the PIVOTTABLE TOOLS DESIGN tab.* Apply formatting options to improve the report's appearance and make sure the report prints on one page in landscape orientation. Rename the worksheet containing the report *PivotTable*. Save the revised workbook and name it **EL2-C4-CS-P1-PBMRpt**.

Part 2

Yolanda would like to have a chart that graphs the average net income data for the state of Michigan. Create a PivotChart in a new sheet named *PivotChart* and filter the chart appropriately to meet Yolanda's request. You determine the appropriate chart style and elements to include in the chart. Yolanda will use this chart at an upcoming meeting with the franchise owners and wants the chart to be of professional quality. Print the chart. Save the revised workbook and name it **EL2-C4-CS-P2-PBMRpt** and then close the workbook.

Part 3

Open **EL2-C4-CS-P1-PBMRpt.xlsx**. Use the Help feature to find out how to modify a numeric field setting to show values as ranked numbers, from largest to smallest. For example, instead of displaying the average value next to the city name, you will display the city's ranking as it compares to other cities in the same state. Ranking from largest to smallest means the highest value in the state is ranked as 1. Using the information you have learned in Help, change the display of the average sales to show the values ranked from largest to smallest using *City* as the base field. Remove the *Net Income* field from the PivotTable. Remove the *Grand Total* row at the bottom of the PivotTable. Make any other formatting changes to the report that you think will improve its appearance. Print the PivotTable. Save the revised workbook and name it **EL2-C4-CS-P3-PBMRpt**.

Part 4

Yolanda would like you to do some comparison research with another pizza franchise. Use the Internet to research the sales and net income of a pizza franchise with which you are familiar. Create a new workbook that compares the total annual sales and net income values of the pizza franchise you researched with the Pizza By Mario information in **EL2-C4-CS-P1-PBMRpt.xlsx**. Provide the URL of the website from which you obtained the information about the competitor. Create a chart that presents the comparison data. Save the workbook and name it **EL2-C4-CS-P4-PizzaFranchiseComparison**. Print the comparison data and the chart. Close **EL2-C4-CS-P4-PizzaFranchiseComparison.xlsx**.

CASE STUDY requires analyzing a workplace scenario and then planning and executing multipart projects.

Students search the Web and/or use the program's Help feature to locate additional information required to complete the Case Study.

UNIT PERFORMANCE ASSESSMENT: Cross-Disciplinary, Comprehensive Evaluation

UNIT 2

MICROSOFT EXCEL Performance Assessment

Excel
EL2U2

Note: Before beginning unit assessments, copy to your storage medium the EL2U2 subfolder from the EL2 folder on the CD that accompanies this textbook and then make EL2U2 the active folder.

Assessing Proficiency ■■■■■■■■■■■■

In this unit, you learned to use features in Excel that facilitate performing what-if analysis, identifying relationships between worksheet formulas, collaborating with others by sharing and protecting workbooks, and automating repetitive tasks using macros. You also learned how to customize the Excel environment to suit your preferences and to integrate Excel data by importing from and exporting to external resources. Finally, you learned how to prepare and distribute a workbook to others by removing items that are private or confidential, marking the workbook as final, checking for features incompatible with earlier versions of Excel, and saving and sending a worksheet in various formats.

Assessment 1 Use Goal Seek and Scenario Manager to Calculate Investment Proposals

1. Open **HillsInvtPlan.xlsx**.
2. Save the workbook and name it **EL2-U2-A1-HillsInvtPlan**.
3. Use Goal Seek to find the monthly contribution amount the client must make to increase the projected value of the plan to $65,000 at the end of the term. Accept the solution Goal Seek calculates.
4. Assign the range name *AvgReturn* to cell E8.
5. Create three scenarios for changing cell E8 as follows:

Scenario name	Interest rate
Moderate	5.5%
Conservative	4.0%
Aggressive	12.5%

6. Apply the Aggressive scenario and then print the worksheet.
7. Change the Moderate scenario's interest rate to 8.0% and then apply the scenario.
8. Create and then print a scenario summary report.
9. Save and then close **EL2-U2-A1-HillsInvtPlan.xlsx**.

ASSESSING PROFICIENCY checks mastery of features.

WRITING ACTIVITIES involve applying program skills in a communication context.

Writing Activities ■■■■■■■■■■■■

The following activities give you the opportunity to practice your writing skills while demonstrating an understanding of some of the important Excel features you have mastered in this unit. Use appropriate word choices and correct grammar, capitalization, and punctuation when setting up new worksheets. Labels should clearly describe the data that is presented.

Create a Computer Maintenance Template

The Computing Services department of National Online Marketing Inc. wants to create a computer maintenance template for Help Desk employees to complete electronically and save to a document management server. This system will make it easy for a technician to check the status of any employee's computer from any location within the company. Help Desk employees perform the following computer maintenance tasks at each computer twice annually:

- Delete temporary Internet files
- Delete temporary document files that begin with a tilde (~)
- Update hardware drivers
- Reconfirm all serial numbers and asset records
- Have employee change password
- Check that automatic updates for the operating system are active
- Check that automatic updates for virus protection are active
- Confirm that automatic backup to the computing services server is active

Internet Research ■■■■■■■■■■■■

Apply What-If Analysis to a Planned Move

Following graduation, you plan to move out of the state/province for a few years to live on your own. Create a new workbook to use as you plan this move to develop a budget for expenses in the first year. Research typical rents for apartments in the city in which you want to find your first job. Estimate other living costs in the city including transportation, food, entertainment, clothes, telephone, cable/satellite, cell phone, Internet, and so on. Calculate total living costs for an entire year. Next, research annual starting salaries for your chosen field of study in the same area. Estimate the take-home pay at approximately 70% of the annual salary you decide to use. Using the take-home pay and the total living costs for the year, calculate whether you will have enough money to cover your expenses.

Next, assume you want to save money to go on a vacation at the end of the year. Use Goal Seek to find the take-home pay you need to earn to have $2,000 left over at the end of the year. Accept the solution that Goal Seek provides and then create two scenarios in the worksheet, as follows:

- A scenario named *LowestValues*, in which you adjust each value down to the lowest amount you think is reasonable
- A scenario named *HighestValues*, in which you adjust each value up to the highest amount you think is reasonable

Apply each scenario and watch the impact on the amount left over at the end of the year. Display the worksheet in the *HighestValues* scenario and then create a scenario summary report. Print the worksheet, applying print options as necessary to minimize the pages required. Print the scenario summary report.

INTERNET RESEARCH project reinforces research and spreadsheet development skills.

JOB STUDY at the end of Unit 2 presents a capstone assessment requiring critical thinking and problem solving.

Job Study ■■■■■■■■■■■■■■■■■■■■

Prepare a Wages Budget and Link the Budget to a Word Document

You work at a small, independent, long-term care facility named Gardenview Place Long-Term Care. As assistant to the business manager, you are helping with the preparation of next year's hourly wages budget. Create a worksheet to estimate next year's hourly wage expenses using the average wage costs in Table U2.1 and the following information about hourly paid workers:

- The facility runs three 8-hour shifts, 7 days per week, 52 weeks per year: 6 a.m. to 2 p.m., 2 p.m. to 10 p.m., and 10 p.m. to 6 a.m.
- Each shift requires two registered nurses, four licensed practical nurses, and two health-care aid workers.
- On each shift, one of the registered nurses is designated as the charge nurse and is paid a premium of 15% his or her regular hourly rate.
- The shifts from 6 a.m. to 2 p.m. and 2 p.m. to 10 p.m. require one custodian; the shift from 10 p.m. to 6 a.m. requires two custodians.
- Each shift requires the services of an on-call physician and on-call pharmacist. Budget for the physician and pharmacist at 4 hours per shift.
- Add 14% to each shift's total wage costs to cover the estimated costs of benefits such as vacation pay, holiday pay, and medical care coverage plans for all workers *except* the on-call physician and on-call pharmacist, who do not receive these benefits.

Make use of colors, themes, and table features to make the budget calculations workbook easy to read. Save the workbook and name it EL2-U2-JS-WageBdgt. Prin...

Student Courseware ■■■■■■■■■■■■■■■■■■■■■■■■■■■■

Student Resources CD Each Benchmark Series textbook is packaged with a Student Resources CD containing the data files required for completing the projects and assessments. A CD icon and folder name displayed on the opening page of chapters reminds students to copy a folder of files from the CD to the desired storage medium before beginning the project exercises. Directions for copying folders are printed on the inside back cover.

Internet Resource Center Additional learning tools and reference materials are available at the book-specific website at www.paradigmcollege.net/BenchmarkExcel13. Students can access the same files that are on the Student Resources CD along with study aids, web links, and tips for using computers effectively in academic and workplace settings.

SNAP Training and Assessment Available at snap2013.emcp.com, SNAP is a web-based program offering an interactive venue for learning Microsoft Office 2013, Windows 8, and Internet Explorer 10. Along with a web-based learning management system, SNAP provides multimedia tutorials, performance skill items, Concepts Check matching activities, Grade It Skills Check Assessment activities, comprehensive performance evaluations, a concepts test bank, an online grade book, and a set of course planning tools. A CD of tutorials teaching the basics of Office, Windows, and Internet Explorer is also available if instructors wish to assign additional SNAP tutorial work without using the web-based SNAP program.

eBook For students who prefer studying with an eBook, the texts in the Benchmark Series are available in an electronic form. The web-based, password-protected eBooks feature dynamic navigation tools, including bookmarking, a linked table of contents, and the ability to jump to a specific page. The eBook format also supports helpful study tools, such as highlighting and note taking.

Instructor Resources ■■■■■■■■■■■■■■■■■■■■■■■■■■

Instructor's Guide and Disc Instructor support for the Benchmark Series includes an *Instructor's Guide and Instructor Resources Disc* package. This resource includes planning information, such as Lesson Blueprints, teaching hints, and sample course syllabi; presentation resources, such as PowerPoint slide shows with lecture notes and audio support; and assessment resources, including an overview of available assessment venues, live model answers for chapter activities, and live and PDF model answers for end-of-chapter exercises. Contents of the *Instructor's Guide and Instructor Resources Disc* package are also available on the password-protected section of the Internet Resource Center for this title at www.paradigmcollege.net/BenchmarkExcel13.

Computerized Test Generator Instructors can use the ExamView® Assessment Suite and test banks of multiple-choice items to create customized web-based or print tests.

Blackboard Cartridge This set of files allows instructors to create a personalized Blackboard website for their course and provides course content, tests, and the mechanisms for establishing communication via e-discussions and online group conferences. Available content includes a syllabus, test banks, PowerPoint presentations with audio support, and supplementary course materials. Upon request, the files can be available within 24–48 hours. Hosting the site is the responsibility of the educational institution.

System Requirements ■■■■■■■■■■■■■■■■■■■■■■■■■■■■■

This text is designed for the student to complete projects and assessments on a computer running a standard installation of Microsoft Office Professional Plus 2013 and the Microsoft Windows 8 operating system. To effectively run this suite and operating system, your computer should be outfitted with the following:

- 1 gigahertz (GHz) processor or higher; 1 gigabyte (GB) of RAM (32 bit) or 2 GB of RAM (64 bit)
- 3 GB of available hard-disk space
- .NET version 3.5, 4.0, or 4.5
- DirectX 10 graphics card
- Minimum 1024 × 576 resolution (or 1366 × 768 to use Windows Snap feature)
- Computer mouse, multi-touch device, or other compatible pointing device

Office 2013 will also operate on computers running the Windows 7 operating system.

Screen captures in this book were created using a screen resolution display setting of 1600 × 900. Choose the resolution that best matches your computer; however, be aware that using a resolution other than 1600 × 900 means that your screens may not match the illustrations in this book.

About the Authors ■■■■■■■■■■■■■■■■■■■■■■■■■■■■■■■■■■■

Denise Seguin has served in the Faculty of Business at Fanshawe College of Applied Arts and Technology in London, Ontario, since 1986. She has developed curriculum and taught a variety of office technology, software applications, and accounting courses to students in postsecondary Information Technology diploma programs and in Continuing Education courses. Seguin has served as Program Coordinator for Computer Systems Technician, Computer Systems Technology, Office Administration, and Law Clerk programs and was acting Chair of the School of Information Technology in 2001. In addition to co-authoring the Level 2 *Access 2013* and *Excel 2013* books in the Benchmark Series, she has authored *Computer Concepts and Applications for Microsoft Office 2013* and *Microsoft Outlook 2013, 2010, 2007, 2003, 2002,* and *2000.* She has also co-authored *Our Digital World* first and second editions; *Marquee Series: Microsoft Office 2013, 2010, 2007,* and *2003; Office 2003; Office XP;* and *Using Computers in the Medical Office: Microsoft Word, Excel, and PowerPoint 2010, 2007,* and *2003* for Paradigm Publishing, Inc.

Jan Davidson started her teaching career in 1997 as a corporate trainer and postsecondary instructor. Since 2001, she has been a faculty member of the School of Business and Information Technology at Lambton College of Applied Arts and Technology in Sarnia, Ontario. In this role, she has developed curriculum and taught a variety of office technology, software applications, and office administration courses to domestic and international students in postsecondary Office Administration Executive, General, and Medical; Human Resources; and Fashion Business programs. In addition to co-authoring the Level 2 *Access 2013* and *Excel 2013* books in the Benchmark Series, she has written instructor resources and SNAP content for Paradigm Publishing, Inc. since 2006.

MICROSOFT® EXCEL®

Level 2

Unit 1 ■ Advanced Formatting, Formulas, and Data Management

MICROSOFT® EXCEL®

Advanced Formatting Techniques

PERFORMANCE OBJECTIVES

Upon successful completion of Chapter 1, you will be able to:

- Apply conditional formatting by entering parameters for a rule
- Apply conditional formatting using a predefined rule
- Create and apply a new rule for conditional formatting
- Edit, delete, and clear conditional formatting rules
- Apply conditional formatting using an icon set, data bars, and color scale
- Apply conditional formatting using a formula
- Apply fraction and scientific formatting
- Apply a special format for a number
- Create a custom number format
- Apply wrap text and shrink to fit text control options
- Modify text using the text functions PROPER, UPPER, LOWER, SUBSTITUTE, RIGHT, LEFT, MID and TRIM
- Filter a worksheet using a custom AutoFilter
- Filter and sort a worksheet using conditional formatting or cell attributes

Tutorials

1.1 Applying Conditional Formatting

1.2 Applying Conditional Formatting Using Icon Sets

1.3 Applying Conditional Formatting Using Data Bars and Color Scales

1.4 Applying Conditional Formatting Using a Formula

1.5 Using Fraction, Scientific, and Special Number Formatting

1.6 Creating a Custom Number Format

1.7 Wrapping and Shrinking Text to Fit within a Cell

1.8 Filtering and Sorting Data Using Conditional Formatting and Cell Attributes

1.9 Using Text Functions

1.10 Filtering a Worksheet Using a Custom AutoFilter

Although many worksheets can be formatted using buttons available in the Font, Alignment, and Number groups on the HOME tab of the ribbon, on the Mini toolbar, or with the new Quick Analysis button, some situations require format categories that are not represented with a button. In other worksheets, you may want to make use of Excel's advanced formatting techniques to format based on a condition. In this chapter, you will learn how to create, edit, and apply advanced formatting and filtering techniques. Model answers for this chapter's projects appear on the following pages.

Excel
EL2C1

Note: Before beginning the projects, copy to your storage medium the EL2C1 subfolder from the EL2 folder on the CD that accompanies this textbook and make EL2C1 the active folder. Steps on how to copy a folder are presented on the inside of the back cover of this textbook. Do this every time you start a chapter's projects.

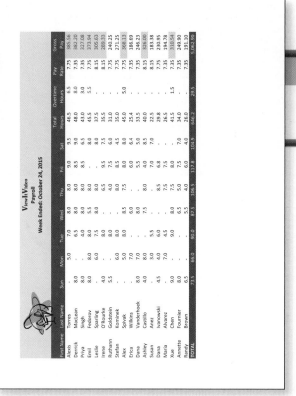

Project 1 Format Cells Based on Values

EL2-C1-P1-VIVPay-Oct24.xlsx

| | | | **AllClaims Insurance Brokers** | | | | | |
| | | | **Policy Information** | | | | | |
Customer ID	Policy ID	No. of Autos	All Perils Deductible	Liability Limit	No. of Drivers	Rating	Claims	Premium
C-025	6512485	2	500	500,000	3	1	0	1,875.00
C-055	6123584	1	250	500,000	2	1	0	995.00
C-072	6583157	2	775	1,000,000	2	2	1	1,575.00
C-085	6124893	3	1,000	500,000	4	2	1	2,250.00
C-094	3481274	1	500	2,000,000	1	5	3	2,150.00
C-114	4956875	2	250	750,000	2	4	2	2,345.00
C-124	3354867	1	250	1,000,000	2	2	1	1,168.00
C-131	6598642	3	775	500,000	4	5	2	3,247.00
C-148	4668457	3	1,000	1,000,000	3	5	2	2,948.00
C-155	8512475	4	500	2,000,000	6	8	4	4,177.00
C-168	6984563	2	250	675,000	2	5	3	2,110.00
C-171	4856972	1	500	500,000	2	6	3	1,845.00
C-184	5124876	1	500	500,000	2	1	0	995.00
C-190	6845962	1	775	900,000	1	3	2	1,550.00
C-199	8457326	1	1,000	2,000,000	1	5	3	2,150.00
C-201	4968532	2	500	500,000	3	2	1	2,025.00
C-212	2698715	2	500	500,000	2	1	0	1,140.00
						Total Policy Premiums:		$ 34,545.00
						Average Number of Claims:	1.6	

Project 2 Apply Conditional Formatting to Insurance Policy Data

EL2-C1-P2-ACInsce-Autos2+.xlsx

EL2-C1-P2-ACInsce.xlsx

Project 3 Use Fraction and Scientific Formatting Options

EL2-C1-P3-JTutor.xlsx, Step 6 and Step 8

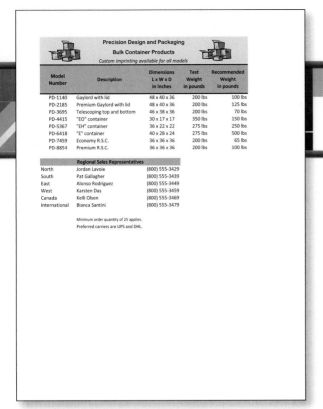

Project 4 Apply Advanced Formatting Options

EL2-C1-P4-Precision.xlsx

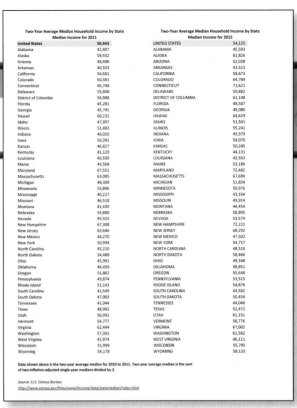

Project 5 Convert Text Using Text Functions

EL2-C1-P5-USIncomeStats.xlsx

ViewItVideo
Proposed Computer Logins 10/24/2015

Imported				Codes		
First Name	Last Name	SSN	SSN	First Name	Last Name	SSN
Terri	Burkowski	000 25 548	000 25 548	T	Burk	25
Beatriz	Santiago	000 46 584	000 46 584	B	Sant	46
Aram	Haji	000 78 859	000 78 859	A	Haji	78
Gerri	Kinnear	000 14 014	000 14 014	G	Kinn	14
Sam	Quinn	000 56 567	000 56 567	S	Quin	56
Andrea	Ruiz	000 99 123	000 99 123	A	Ruiz	99
Martina	Tisdale	000 21 321	000 21 321	M	Tisd	21
Carl	Wisenberg	000 54 457	000 54 457	C	Wise	54
Chen	Zhao	000 33 458	000 33 458	C	Zhao	33

Date: 10/24/2015

EL2-C1-P5b-VIVCodes.xlsx

AllClaims Insurance Brokers								
Policy Information								
Customer ID	Policy ID	No. of Autos	All Perils Deductible	Liability Limit	No. of Drivers	Rating	Claims	Premium
C-114	4956875	2	250	750,000	2	4	2	2,345.00
C-131	6598642	3	775	500,000	4	5	2	3,247.00
C-148	4668457	3	1,000	1,000,000	3	5	2	2,948.00
C-168	6984563	2	250	675,000	2	5	3	2,110.00
C-171	4856972	1	500	500,000	2	6	3	1,845.00
C-190	6845962	1	775	900,000	1	3	2	1,550.00

Project 6 Filter and Sort Data Based on Values, Icon Set, and Font Color

EL2-C1-P6-ACInsce.xlsx

AllClaims Insurance Brokers								
Policy Information								
Customer ID	Policy ID	No. of Autos	All Perils Deductible	Liability Limit	No. of Drivers	Rating	Claims	Premium
C-055	6123584	1	250	500,000	2	1	0	995.00
C-094	3481274	1	500	2,000,000	2	5	3	2,150.00
C-124	3354867	1	250	1,000,000	2	2	1	1,168.00
C-171	4856972	1	500	500,000	2	6	3	1,845.00
C-184	5124876	1	500	500,000	2	1	0	995.00
C-190	6845962	1	775	900,000	1	3	2	1,550.00
C-199	8457326	1	1,000	2,000,000	1	5	3	2,150.00

EL2-C1-P6-ACInsce-1Auto.xlsx

EL2-C1-P6-VIVPay-Oct24-HighOT.xlsx

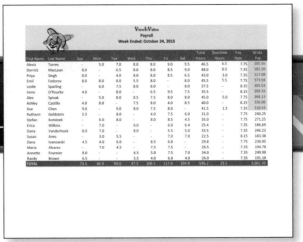

EL2-C1-P6-VIVPay-Oct24-Sorted.xlsx

Project 1   Format Cells Based on Values   2 Parts

Working with a payroll worksheet, you will change the appearance of cells based on criteria related to overtime hours and gross pay.

Applying Conditional Formatting ■■■■■■■■■■■■■■■■

▼ Quick Steps

Apply Conditional Formatting Using a Predefined Rule
1. Select desired range.
2. Click Conditional Formatting button.
3. Point to desired rule category.
4. Click desired rule.
5. If necessary, enter parameter value.
6. If necessary, change format options.
7. Click OK.

Conditional Formatting

Quick Analysis

Conditional formatting applies special formatting to those cells within a specified range that meet a specific condition. The formatting of the cells that do not meet the condition remains unchanged. Changing the appearance of a cell based on a condition allows you to quickly identify values that are high or low and makes it easier to spot trends. Formatting can be applied based on a specific value or a value that falls within a range, or it can be applied by using a comparison operator, such as equals (=), greater than (>), or less than (<). Conditional formats can also be based on dates, text entries, or duplicated values. Consider using conditional formatting to analyze a question, such as *Which store locations earned sales above their target?* Using a different color to identify those stores that exceeded their target sales makes it easy to quickly identify the top performers.

The Quick Analysis button is a new feature in Excel 2013. When you select data, the Quick Analysis button appears near the fill handle at the bottom right corner of the selection and the options shown in Figure 1.1 are made available. You can use these options to quickly apply conditional formatting, create charts, add totals, create tables or add Sparklines. With predefined conditional formatting rules, Excel can quickly analyze and format your data. If you require more options than the Quick Analysis button provides, you can access the rules from the Conditional Formatting button drop-down list, as shown in Figure 1.2, or you can create your own conditional formatting rules.

Figure 1.1 Quick Analysis Button

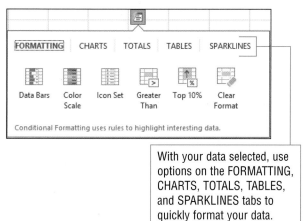

With your data selected, use options on the FORMATTING, CHARTS, TOTALS, TABLES, and SPARKLINES tabs to quickly format your data.

Figure 1.2 Conditional Formatting Button Drop-down List

Project 1a **Using Quick Analysis to Format Cells Based on a Value Comparison**   **Part 1 of 2**

1. Start Excel.
2. Open **VIVPay-Oct24.xlsx**. (This workbook is located in the EL2C1 folder you copied to your storage medium.)
3. Save the workbook and name it **EL2-C1-P1-VIVPay-Oct24**.
4. Apply conditional formatting to highlight overtime hours that exceeded five hours for the week by completing the following steps:
   a. Select K6:K23.
   b. Click the Quick Analysis button located at the bottom right of the selected cells.
   c. Click the Greater Than button on the FORMATTING tab.
   d. At the Greater Than dialog box, with the text already selected in the *Format cells that are GREATER THAN* text box, type 5.
   e. Click the down-pointing arrow next to the option box to the right of *with* (which currently displays *Light Red Fill with Dark Red Text*) and then click *Red Text* at the drop-down list.
   f. Click OK to close the Greater Than dialog box.
   g. Click in any cell to deselect the range.
   h. Review the cells that have been conditionally formatted. Notice that cells with overtime hours greater than five hours are formatted with red text.
5. Save **EL2-C1-P1-VIVPay-Oct24.xlsx**.

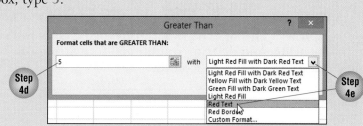

Using the Top/Bottom Rules list, you can elect to highlight cells based on a top 10 or bottom 10 value or percentage, or by above average or below average values.

1. With **EL2-C1-P1-VIVPay-Oct24.xlsx** open, apply conditional formatting to the Gross Pay values to identify employees who earned above average wages for the week by completing the following steps:

   a. Select M6:M23.

   b. Click the Conditional Formatting button in the Styles group on the HOME tab.

   c. Point to *Top/Bottom Rules* and then click *Above Average* at the drop-down list.

   d. At the Above Average dialog box, with *Light Red Fill with Dark Red Text* selected in the *Format cells that are ABOVE AVERAGE* option box, click OK.

   e. Click in any cell to deselect the range.

   f. Review the cells that have been conditionally formatted.

2. Print the worksheet.

3. Save and then close **EL2-C1-P1-VIVPay-Oct24.xlsx**.

Project 2   Apply Conditional Formatting to Insurance Policy Data   4 Parts

You will format cells in an insurance claims worksheet by creating, editing, clearing, and deleting conditional formatting rules and by classifying data into categories using an icon set.

Creating a New Formatting Rule

Cells are conditionally formatted based on a rule. A rule defines the criterion by which cells are selected for formatting and includes the formatting attributes that are applied to cells that meet the criterion. The predefined rules that you used in Project 1a and Project 1b allowed you to use the feature without having to specify each component in a rule's parameters. At the New Formatting Rule dialog box, shown in Figure 1.3, you can create your own custom conditional formatting rule in which you define all parts of the criterion and the formatting. The *Edit the Rule Description* section of the dialog box varies depending on the active option in the *Select a Rule Type* section.

Figure 1.3 New Formatting Rule Dialog Box

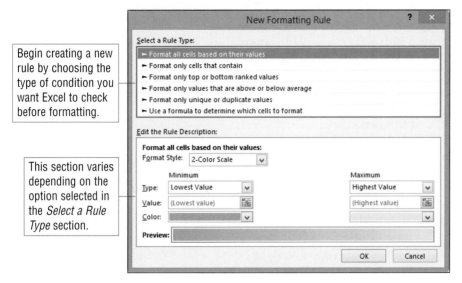

Begin creating a new rule by choosing the type of condition you want Excel to check before formatting.

This section varies depending on the option selected in the *Select a Rule Type* section.

▼ **Quick Steps**

Create and Apply a New Formatting Rule
1. Select desired range.
2. Click Conditional Formatting button.
3. Click *New Rule*.
4. Click desired rule type.
5. Add criteria as required.
6. Click Format button.
7. Select desired formatting attributes.
8. Click OK to close Format Cells dialog box.
9. Click OK to close New Formatting Rule dialog box.

Project 2a **Creating and Applying New Formatting Rules** **Part 1 of 4**

1. Open **ACInsce.xlsx**.
2. Save the workbook and name it **EL2-C1-P2-ACInsce**.
3. The owner of AllClaims Insurance Brokers is considering changing the discount plan for those customers with no claims or with only one claim. The owner would like to see the two claim criteria formatted in color to provide a reference for how many customers this discount would affect. Create a formatting rule that changes the appearance of cells in the *Claims* column that contain *0* by completing the following steps:
   a. Select H4:H20.
   b. Click the Conditional Formatting button in the Styles group on the HOME tab.
   c. Click *New Rule* at the drop-down list.
   d. At the New Formatting Rule dialog box, click *Format only cells that contain* in the *Select a Rule Type* section.
   e. Click the down-pointing arrow at the right of the second option box from the left (which currently displays *between*) in the *Format only cells with* section and then click *equal to* at the drop-down list.

x

bar

x

bar

f. Click in the blank text box next to *equal to* and then type **0**.

g. Click the Format button in the *Preview* section.

h. At the Format Cells dialog box with the Font tab selected, apply the Dark Red color (in the *Standard Colors* section), turn on bold formatting, and then click OK.

i. Click OK at the New Formatting Rule dialog box.

4. Create a second formatting rule that changes the appearance of cells in the *Claims* column that contain *1* by completing the following steps:

a. With H4:H20 still selected, click the Conditional Formatting button and then click *New Rule*.

b. At the New Formatting Rule dialog box, click *Format only cells that contain* in the *Select a Rule Type* section.

c. Click the down-pointing arrow located at the right of the second option box from the left in the *Format only cells with* section (which currently displays *between*) and then click *equal to* at the drop-down list.

d. Click in the blank text box next to *equal to* and then type **1**.

e. Click the Format button.

f. At the Format Cells dialog box with the Font tab selected, apply the Blue color (in the *Standard Colors* section), turn on bold formatting, and then click OK.

g. Click OK at the New Formatting Rule dialog box.

5. Click in any cell to deselect the range and review the conditionally formatted cells in column H.

Rating	Claims
1	0
1	0
2	1
2	1
5	3
4	2
2	1
5	2
5	2
8	4
5	3
6	3
1	0
3	2
5	3
2	1
1	0

Step 4c

Step 4d

Step 4e

Step 5

Bold dark red formatting has been applied to cells containing *0* and bold blue formatting has been applied to cells containing *1*.

This box displays a preview of the text formatting that will be applied to cells that meet the condition.

Step 4g

6. Save **EL2-C1-P2-ACInsce.xlsx**.

▼ **Quick Steps**

Edit a Formatting Rule
1. Select range.
2. Click Conditional Formatting button.
3. Click *Manage Rules*.
4. Click desired rule.
5. Click Edit Rule button.
6. Make desired changes.
7. Click OK twice.

Editing and Deleting Conditional Formatting Rules

To edit the comparison rule criteria and/or formatting options for a conditional formatting rule, open the Conditional Formatting Rules Manager dialog box. Click to select the rule that you want to change and then click the Edit Rule button. At the Edit Formatting Rule dialog box, make the desired changes and then click OK twice. By default, *Show formatting rules for* is set to *Current Selection* when you open the Conditional Formatting Rules Manager dialog box. If necessary, click the down-pointing arrow at the right of the option box and then select *This Worksheet* to show all of the formatting rules in the current sheet.

To remove conditional formatting from a range, select the range, click the Quick Analysis button, and then click the Clear Format button, or click the Conditional Formatting button in the Styles group on the HOME tab, point to *Clear Rules* at the drop-down list, and then click either *Clear Rules from Selected Cells* or *Clear Rules from Entire Sheet*. You can also delete a custom rule at the Conditional Formatting Rules Manager dialog box. Formatting options applied to the cells by the rule that was deleted will be removed.

▼ **Quick Steps**

Remove Conditional Formatting
1. Select range.
2. Click Quick Analysis button.
3. Click Clear Format button.

Project 2b **Creating, Editing, and Deleting a Formatting Rule** Part 2 of 4

1. With **EL2-C1-P2-ACInsce.xlsx** open, create a new formatting rule to add a fill color to the cells in the *No. of Autos* column for those policies that have more than two cars by completing the following steps:
   a. Select C4:C20.
   b. Click the Conditional Formatting button and then click *New Rule* at the drop-down list.
   c. Click *Format only cells that contain* in the *Select a Rule Type* section of the New Formatting Rule dialog box.
   d. In the *Edit the Rule Description* section, change the rule's parameters to format only cells with a value greater than 2. (If necessary, refer to Project 2a, Steps 3e–3f, for assistance.)
   e. Click the Format button and then click the Fill tab at the Format Cells dialog box.
   f. Click the *Yellow* color (fourth from left in bottom row) in the *Background Color* palette and then click OK.
   g. Click OK to close the New Formatting Rule dialog box.
   h. Deselect the range by clicking any cell.
2. After reviewing the formatted cells, you decide that cells should be formatted for all policies with 2 or more cars. Edit the formatting rule by completing the following steps:
   a. Select C4:C20.
   b. Click the Conditional Formatting button and then click *Manage Rules* at the drop-down list.
   c. Click to select *Cell Value > 2* in the Conditional Formatting Rules Manager dialog box and then click the Edit Rule button.

Customer ID	Policy ID	No. of Autos
C-025	6512485	2
C-055	6123584	1
C-072	6583157	2
C-085	6124893	3
C-094	3481274	1
C-114	4956875	2
C-124	3354867	1
C-131	6598642	3
C-148	4668457	3
C-155	8512475	4
C-168	6984563	2
C-171	4856972	1
C-184	5124876	1
C-190	6845962	1
C-199	8457326	1
C-201	4968532	2
C-212	2698715	2

Formatting has been applied to cell values greater than 2.

d. Click the down-pointing arrow next to the second option box from the left (which currently displays *greater than*) and then click *greater than or equal to* at the drop-down list.

e. Click OK.

f. Click OK to close the Conditional Formatting Rules Manager dialog box.

g. Deselect the range by clicking any cell.

3. Save and print the worksheet.

4. After reviewing the printed copy of the formatted worksheet, you decide to experiment with another method of formatting the data that classifies the policies by the number of cars. You will do this in the next project. In preparation, save the revised worksheet under a new name and then delete the formatting rule in the original worksheet by completing the following steps:

a. Save the workbook and name it **EL2-C1-P2-ACInsce-Autos2+**. By saving the workbook under a new name, you will be able to keep a copy of the workbook with the conditional formatting applied in this project.

b. Close **EL2-C1-P2-ACInsce-Autos2+.xlsx**.

c. Open **EL2-C1-P2-ACInsce.xlsx**.

d. Click the Conditional Formatting button and then click *Manage Rules* at the drop-down list.

e. Click the down-pointing arrow next to the *Show formatting rules for* option box and then click *This Worksheet*.

f. Click to select *Cell Value >= 2* and then click the Delete Rule button.

g. Click OK to close the Conditional Formatting Rules Manager dialog box. Notice the formatting has been removed from the cells in column C.

5. Save **EL2-C1-P2-ACInsce.xlsx**.

Applying Conditional Formatting Using an Icon Set

Green Up Arrow

Red Down Arrow

Yellow Sideways Arrow

Format a range of values using an icon set to classify data into three to five categories. Excel places an icon in a cell to visually portray the cell's value relative to the other cell values within the selected range. Using an icon set, you can group similar data to easily identify high points, low points, or other trends. Icons are assigned to cells based on default threshold values for the selected range. For example, if you choose the *3 Arrows (Colored)* icon set, icons are assigned as follows:

- Green up arrow for values greater than or equal to 67%
- Red down arrow for values less than 33%
- Yellow sideways arrow for values between 33% and 67%

The available icon sets, shown in Figure 1.4, are grouped into four sections: *Directional, Shapes, Indicators,* and *Ratings.* Choose the icon set that best represents the number of different categories within the range and desired symbol type, such as

Figure 1.4 Conditional Formatting Icon Sets Gallery

directional colored arrows, traffic light shapes, flag indicators, star ratings, and so on. You can modify the default threshold values or create your own icon set by opening the Manage Rules dialog box and editing an existing rule or creating a new rule.

▼ **Quick Steps**

Apply Conditional Formatting Using an Icon Set
1. Select desired range.
2. Click Conditional Formatting button.
3. Point to *Icon Sets*.
4. Click desired icon set.
5. Deselect range.

Project 2c | **Applying Conditional Formatting Using an Icon Set** | **Part 3 of 4**

1. With **EL2-C1-P2-ACInsce.xlsx** open, select C4:C20.
2. Use an icon set to classify the number of automobiles into categories by completing the following steps:
   a. Click the Conditional Formatting button.
   b. Point to *Icon Sets*.
   c. Click *Red To Black* at the Icon Sets drop-down gallery (third icon set in the left column of the *Shapes* section).
   d. Click in any cell to deselect the range. Notice that Excel assigns an icon to each cell, and that these icons correlate with the cell's value. For example, all cells containing the value *1* have the same icon, all cells containing the value *2* have the same icon, and so on.
3. Save **EL2-C1-P2-ACInsce.xlsx**.

Applying Conditional Formatting Using Data Bars and Color Scales

Excel 2013 also provides the ability to conditionally format cells using two-color scales, three-color scales, and data bars to provide visual guides for identifying distributions or variations within a range.

Use data bars to easily identify the higher and lower values within a range. A data bar appears in the background of a cell, and the length of the bar depends on the value within the cell. A cell with a higher value within the range displays a longer bar than a cell with a lower value within the range. Excel offers six colors for data bars and each color is available in a gradient or solid fill.

Color scales format a range using a two-color or three-color palette. Excel provides 12 color scale color gradients, half of which are two-color combinations and half of which are three-color combinations. The gradation of color applied to a cell illustrates the cell's value relative to the rest of the range. Color scales are useful for reviewing the distribution of data. In a two-color scale, the shade applied to a cell represents either a higher or lower value within the range. In a three-color scale, the shade applied to a cell represents a higher, middle, or lower value within the range.

Be careful not to use too many icon sets, color scales, and/or data bars. Readers can quickly lose focus when too many items compete for attention.

Figure 1.5 displays the payroll worksheet for ViewItVideo with data bar and color scale conditional formatting applied. The Red Data Bar format from the *Gradient Fill* section has been applied to the *Gross Pay* column (column M). Notice that the lengths of the colored bars in the cells reflect various gross pay amounts, with longer bars representing higher gross pay. In column J, *Total Hours*, the Red-White Color Scale color gradient has been applied to show the distribution of total hours. The cell with the highest value is displayed in red and as the values decrease, the cells become increasingly lighter colored. Notice that the cell with the lowest value is displayed in white.

Figure 1.5 Data Bar and Color Scale Conditional Formatting Applied to a Payroll Worksheet

	First Name	Last Name	Sun	Mon	Tue	Wed	Thu	Fri	Sat	Total Hours	Overtime Hours	Pay Rate	Gross Pay
6	Alexis	Torres	-	5.0	7.0	8.0	8.0	9.0	9.5	46.5	6.5	7.75	385.56
7	Derrick	MacLean	8.0	-	6.5	8.0	8.0	8.5	9.0	48.0	8.0	7.35	382.20
8	Priya	Singh	8.0	-	4.0	8.0	8.0	8.5	6.5	43.0	3.0	7.35	327.08
9	Emil	Fedorov	8.0	8.0	8.0	5.5	8.0	-	8.0	45.5	5.5	7.75	373.94
10	Leslie	Sparling	-	6.0	7.5	8.0	8.0	-	8.0	37.5	-	8.15	305.63
11	Irene	O'Rourke	4.0	-	8.0	-	6.5	9.5	7.5	35.5	-	8.15	289.33
12	Ruthann	Goldstein	5.5	-	8.0	-	4.0	7.5	6.0	31.0	-	7.75	240.25
13	Stefan	Kominek	-	6.0	8.0	-	8.0	8.5	4.5	35.0	-	7.75	271.25
14	Alex	Spivak	-	5.0	8.0	8.5	7.5	8.0	8.0	45.0	5.0	7.75	368.13
15	Erica	Wilkins	-	7.0	-	6.0	-	6.0	6.4	25.4	-	7.35	186.69
16	Dana	Vanderhoek	8.0	7.0	-	8.0	-	5.5	5.0	33.5	-	7.35	246.23
17	Ashley	Castillo	4.0	8.0	-	7.5	8.0	4.0	8.5	40.0	-	8.15	326.00
18	Susan	Anez	-	3.0	5.5	-	-	7.0	7.0	22.5	-	8.15	183.38
19	Dana	Ivanowski	4.5	4.0	6.0	-	8.5	6.8	-	29.8	-	7.75	230.95
20	Maria	Alvarez	-	7.0	4.5	-	7.5	7.5	-	26.5	-	7.35	194.78
21	Xue	Chen	9.0	-	9.0	8.0	7.5	8.0	-	41.5	1.5	7.35	310.54
22	Annette	Fournier	8.0	-	-	6.5	5.0	7.5	7.0	34.0	-	7.35	249.90
23	Randy	Brown	6.5	-	-	5.5	4.0	6.0	4.0	26.0	-	7.35	191.10
24	TOTAL		73.5	66.0	90.0	87.5	106.5	117.8	104.9	646.2	29.5		5,062.90

ViewItVideo
Payroll
Week Ended: October 24, 2015

Conditional formatting using the Red Data Bar format has been applied to the data in the *Gross Pay* column.

Conditional formatting using the Red - White Color Scale color gradient has been applied to the data in the *Total Hours* column.

Applying Conditional Formatting Using a Formula

Sometimes you may want to format a cell based on the value in another cell or using some logical test. At the New Formatting Rule dialog box, choose *Use a formula to determine which cells to format* in the *Select a Rule Type* section. You can enter a formula, such as an IF statement, that will be used to determine whether a cell will be formatted.

For example, in Project 2d, you will format the premium values in the insurance worksheet in column I based on the rating value for each policy that is stored in column G. In this project, using an IF statement allows you to conditionally format the premiums if the rating value for the policy is greater than 3. The IF function's logical test returns only a true or false result. The value in the rating cell is either greater than 3 (true) or it is not greater than 3 (false). Excel conditionally formats only those cells in the *Premium* column for which the conditional test returns a true result.

The formula that you will enter into the New Formatting Rule dialog box in Project 2d is *=if(g4:g20>3,true,false)*. Excel treats any formula entered for conditional formatting as an ***array formula***, which means you only need to add one rule for the range G4:G20. In the first cell in the selected range (cell I4), Excel will perform the following test: *Is the value in G4 greater than 3?* In the first row, this test returns a false result, so Excel will not conditionally format the value in cell I4. Excel will apply bold formatting and the Red font color to those cells in column I for which the test returns a true result based on the corresponding cell in column G.

Project 2d **Applying Conditional Formatting Using a Formula**   **Part 4 of 4**

1. With **EL2-C1-P2-ACInsce.xlsx** open, clear the conditional formatting applied in the *Claims* column by completing the following steps:
   a. Select H4:H20.
   b. Click the Conditional Formatting button, point to *Clear Rules*, and then click *Clear Rules from Selected Cells*.
   c. Click in any cell to deselect the range.
2. The owner of AllClaims Insurance Brokers would like the premiums for those clients who have a rating higher than 3 to stand out. You decide to conditionally format the premiums in column I using a formula that checks the ratings in column G by completing the following steps:
   a. Select I4:I20 and then click the Conditional Formatting button.
   b. Click *New Rule* at the drop-down list.

Step 1b

---

c. At the New Formatting Rule dialog box, click *Use a formula to determine which cells to format* in the *Select a Rule Type* section.

d. Click in the *Format values where this formula is true* text box in the *Edit the Rule Description* section of the New Formatting Rule dialog box and then type =if(g4:g20>3,true,false).

e. Click the Format button.

f. At the Format Cells dialog box, click the Font tab and apply the Red font color (in the *Standard Colors* section), apply bold formatting, and then click OK.

g. Click OK to close the New Formatting Rule dialog box and apply the rule to the selected cells.

h. Click in any cell to deselect the range. Notice that the cells in column I that have bold formatting and the Red font color applied are those for which the corresponding rating value in column G is greater than 3.

3. Save, print, and then close **EL2-C1-P2-ACInsce.xlsx**.

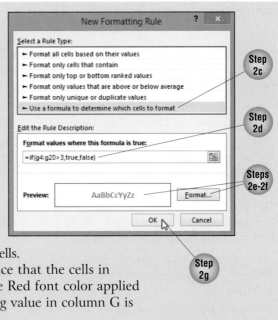

Project **3** Use Fraction and Scientific Formatting Options   1 Part

Using two lesson plan worksheets for a math tutor, you will format cells in a solution column to the appropriate format to display the answers for the tutor.

▼ **Quick Steps**

Apply Fraction Formatting
1. Select desired range.
2. Click Number Format button arrow.
3. Click *More Number Formats*.
4. Click *Fraction* in Category list box.
5. Click desired option in Type list box.
6. Click OK.
7. Deselect range.

Apply Scientific Formatting
1. Select desired range.
2. Click Number Format button arrow.
3. Click *Scientific*.
4. Deselect range.

Applying Fraction and Scientific Formatting ■■■■■■■

While most worksheet values are formatted using the Accounting Number Format, Percent Style, or Comma Style buttons in the Number group on the HOME tab, some worksheets contain values that require other number formats. When clicked, the Number Format button arrow in the Number group on the HOME tab displays a drop-down list with additional format options, including date, time, fraction, scientific, and text options. Click *More Number Formats* at the Number Format drop-down list to open the Format Cells dialog box with the Number tab selected, as shown in Figure 1.6. At this dialog box, you can specify additional parameters for the number format categories. For example, with the *Fraction* category selected, you can choose the type of fraction you want displayed.

Scientific formatting converts a number to exponential notation. Part of the number is replaced with E+n, where E means "exponent" and n represents the power. For example, the number *1,500,000.00* formatted in scientific number format displays as *1.50E+06*. In this example, *+06* means "Add six zeros to the right of the number left of E and then move the decimal point six positions to the right." Scientists, mathematicians, engineers, and statisticians often use exponential notation to write very large numbers and very small numbers in a more manageable way.

Figure 1.6 Format Cells Dialog Box with the Number Tab Selected and *Fraction* Category Active

Project 3 | Applying Fraction and Scientific Formatting | Part 1 of 1

1. Open **JTutor.xlsx**.
2. Save the workbook and name it **EL2-C1-P3-JTutor**.
3. Make Fractions the active worksheet by clicking the Fractions sheet tab located at the bottom of the worksheet area just above the Status bar.
4. Apply fraction formatting to the values in column D to create the solution column for the tutor, Janelle, by completing the following steps:
   a. Select D11:D20.
   b. Click the Number Format button arrow (which currently displays *General*) in the Number group on the HOME tab.
   c. Click *More Number Formats* at the drop-down list.

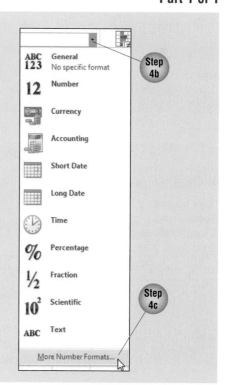

d. At the Format Cells dialog box with the Number tab selected, click *Fraction* in the *Category* list box.

e. Click *Up to two digits (21/25)* in the *Type* list box.

f. Click OK.

g. Click in any cell to deselect the range.

5. Save **EL2-C1-P3-JTutor**.

6. Print the worksheet.

7. Click the Exponents sheet tab.

8. Apply scientific formatting to the values in column D to create the solution column for Janelle by completing the following steps:

a. Select D11:D25.

b. Click the Number Format button arrow (which currently displays *Custom*) in the Number group on the HOME tab and then click *Scientific* at the drop-down list.

c. Click in any cell to deselect the range.

8. Print the worksheet.

9. Save and then close **EL2-C1-P3-JTutor.xlsx**.

	Format Cells					
Number	Alignment	Font	Border	Fill	Protection	

Category:
General
Number
Currency
Accounting
Date
Time
Percentage
Fraction
Scientific
Text
Special
Custom

Sample

Type:
Up to one digit (1/4)
Up to two digits (21/25)
Up to three digits (312/943)
As halves (1/2)
As quarters (2/4)
As eighths (4/8)
As sixteenths (8/16)

Step 4e

Step 4d

10	Examples		Converted to Scientific Notation	
11	1,000,000,000		1.00E+09	
12	100,000,000		1.00E+08	
13	10,000,000		1.00E+07	
14	1,000,000		1.00E+06	
15	100,000		1.00E+05	
16	10,000		1.00E+04	
17	1,000		1.00E+03	
18	100		1.00E+02	
19	10		1.00E+01	
20	1		1.00E+00	
21	0.1		1.00E-01	
22	0.01		1.00E-02	
23	0.001		1.00E-03	
24	0.0001		1.00E-04	
25	0.00001		1.00E-05	

Scientific formatting is applied to the range D11:D25 in Steps 7a–7c.

Project 4 — Apply Advanced Formatting Options   3 Parts

You will update a product worksheet by formatting telephone numbers, creating a custom number format to add descriptive characters before and after a value, and applying text alignment options for long labels.

Applying Special Number Formats ■■■■■■■■■■■■■■■■■■

▼ **Quick Steps**

Apply a Special Number Format
1. Select desired range.
2. Click Number group dialog box launcher.
3. Click *Special* in *Category* list box.
4. Click desired option in *Type* list box.
5. Click OK.
6. Deselect range.

At the Format Cells dialog box with the Number tab active, Excel provides special number formats that are specific to a country and language. As shown in Figure 1.7, when *Special* is selected in the *Category* list box and *English (United States)* is selected in the *Locale (location)* option box, the *Type* list box includes *Zip Code, Zip Code + 4, Phone Number,* and *Social Security Number*. When the *English (Canadian)* option is selected in the *Locale (location)* option box, the *Type* list box includes *Phone Number* and *Social Insurance Number*.

Applying special number formatting can save you time and keystrokes, as well as help to ensure consistent formatting. For example, if you apply special social security number formatting to a range, you can type the social security numbers into the range without hyphens and Excel will add the hyphens for you. Typing 000223456 will enter 000-22-3456 in the cell with special formatting applied.

Figure 1.7 Format Cells Dialog Box with the Number Tab Selected and the *Special* Category Active

These special number format types are available for the active locale.

Project 4a | **Applying Special Formatting** | Part 1 of 3

1. Open **Precision.xlsx**.
2. Save the workbook and name it **EL2-C1-P4-Precision**.
3. Format the range that will contain telephone numbers to include brackets around the area code and a hyphen between the first three and last four digits of the number by completing the following steps:
   a. Select C15:C20.
   b. Click the Number group dialog box launcher located at the bottom right of the Number group on the HOME tab.
   c. At the Format Cells dialog box with the Number tab selected, click *Special* in the *Category* list box.
   d. Click *Phone Number* in the *Type* list box and make sure the *Locale (location)* option box is set to *English (United States)*.
   e. Click OK.
   f. Click in cell C15 to deselect the range and make the first cell to contain a telephone number the active cell.
4. Type the telephone numbers for the sales representatives as follows:
   C15: 8005553429
   C16: 8005553439
   C17: 8005553449
   C18: 8005553459
   C19: 8005553469
   C20: 8005553479
5. Save **EL2-C1-P4-Precision.xlsx**.

Step 3d

Step 3c

14	Regional Sales Representatives		
15	North	Jordan Lavoie	(800) 555-3429
16	South	Pat Gallagher	(800) 555-3439
17	East	Alonso Rodriguez	(800) 555-3449
18	West	Karsten Das	(800) 555-3459
19	Canada	Kelli Olsen	(800) 555-3469
20	International	Bianca Santini	(800) 555-3479

Step 4

Creating Custom Number Formats ■■■■■■■■■■■■■■

Create a Custom Number Format
1. Select desired range.
2. Click Number group dialog box launcher.
3. Click *Custom* in *Category* list box.
4. Select *General* in *Type* text box.
5. Press Delete.
6. Type desired custom format codes.
7. Click OK.
8. Deselect range.

You can create a custom number format for a worksheet into which you want to enter values that do not conform to predefined number formats or for values for which you want to add punctuation, text, or formatting, such as color. For example, in Project 4b, you will create a custom number format to automatically add a product category letter preceding each model number.

Formatting codes are used in custom formats to specify the type of formatting to apply. You can type a custom number format code from scratch or select from a list of custom formats and modify the codes as necessary. Table 1.1 displays commonly used format codes along with examples of their usage.

Once you have created a custom format, you can apply it elsewhere within the workbook. To do this, open the Format Cells dialog box with the Number tab selected, select the *Custom* category, scroll down to the bottom of the *Type* list box, click to select the custom format code, and then click OK.

Custom number formats are stored in the workbook in which they are created.

Text, numbers, and punctuation added as part of a custom number format are not saved as part of the cell value. In Project 4b, you create a custom number format that displays *PD-* in front of each model number. The value in cell A5 displays as *PD-1140*, but *1140* is the actual value that is stored. This is important to remember when you search for or filter data.

Table 1.1 Custom Number Format Code Examples

Format Code	Description	Custom Number Format Example	Display Result
#	Represents a digit; type one for each number. Excel rounds numbers if necessary to fit the number of places after the decimal point.	####.###	Typing *145.0068* displays *145.007*.
0	Also represents a digit. Excel rounds numbers to fit the number of places after the decimal point but also fills in leading zeros.	000.00	Typing *50.45* displays *050.45*.
?	Rounds numbers to fit the number of places after the decimal point but also aligns numbers vertically on the decimal point by adding spaces.	???.???	Typing *123.5*, *.8*, and *55.356* one below the other in a column aligns the numbers vertically on the decimal point.
"text"	Adds the characters between the quotation marks to the entry.	"Model No." ##	Typing *58* displays *Model No. 58*.
[color]	Applies the font color specified in square brackets to the cell entry.	[Blue]##.##	Typing *55.346* displays *55.35*.
;	Separates the positive value format from the negative value format.	[Blue];[Red]	Typing *25* displays as *25* and typing *-25* displays as *25*.

1. With **EL2-C1-P4-Precision.xlsx** open, select A5:A12.
2. Create a custom number format to insert *PD-* in front of each model number by completing the following steps:
   a. Click the Number group dialog box launcher located at the bottom right of the Number group on the HOME tab.
   b. Click *Custom* in the *Category* list box in the Format Cells dialog box with the Number tab selected.
   c. Scroll down the list of custom formats in the *Type* list box, noticing the various combinations of format codes for numbers, dates, and times.
   d. Select *General* in the *Type* text box, press Delete, and then type "PD-"####.
   e. Click OK.
   f. With A5:A12 still selected, click the Center button in the Alignment group on the HOME tab.
   g. Deselect the range.

3. Create a custom number format to insert *lbs* after the weights in columns D and E by completing the following steps:
   a. Select D5:E12.
   b. Click the Number group dialog box launcher.
   c. Click *Custom* in the *Category* list box.
   d. Select *General* in the *Type* text box, press Delete, and then type ### "lbs". Make sure to include one space after ###.
   e. Click OK.
   f. Deselect the range.

4. Save **EL2-C1-P4-Precision.xlsx**.

To delete a custom number format, open the workbook in which you created the custom format code, open the Format Cells dialog box with the Number tab selected, click *Custom* in the *Category* list box, scroll down the list of custom formats in the *Type* list box to the bottom of the list, click the custom format code that you created, and then click the Delete button. Deleting the formatting code also removes the custom formatting from any cells to which it was applied.

▼ **Quick Steps**

Wrap Text in a Cell
1. Select desired cell(s).
2. Click Wrap Text button.
3. Deselect cell(s).

Shrink Text to Fit within a Cell
1. Select desired cell(s).
2. Click Alignment group dialog box launcher.
3. Click *Shrink to fit* in *Text control* section.
4. Click OK.
5. Deselect cell(s).

Wrap Text

Wrapping Text and Shrinking Text to Fit within Cells ■ ■ ■ ■

You have several options for formatting long labels that do not fit within the column width. You can expand column width, reduce the font to a smaller size, merge a group of cells, or allow the text to spill over into adjacent unused columns. Additional options available in the *Text Control* section of the Format Cells dialog box with the Alignment tab selected include *Wrap text* and *Shrink to fit*. Text wrapping within a cell causes the row height to automatically increase to accommodate the number of lines needed. Alternatively, shrinking the text to fit within the cell causes the font size to automatically scale down to the size required to fit all of the text on one line. Consider widening the column before wrapping text or shrinking text to fit.

Project 4c | **Applying Wrap Text and Shrink to Fit Text Control Options** | **Part 3 of 3**

1. With **EL2-C1-P4-Precision.xlsx** open, wrap text within cells by completing the following steps:
   a. Select B22:B23.
   b. Click the Wrap Text button in the Alignment group on the HOME tab.
2. You decide to try the *Shrink to Fit* option on the same cells to see if a better result is produced. Press Ctrl + Z or click the Undo button on the Quick Access toolbar to restore the cells back to their original state.
3. Shrink the text to fit within the cells by completing the following steps:
   a. With B22:B23 still selected, click the Alignment group dialog box launcher located in the bottom right corner of the Alignment group on the HOME tab.
   b. At the Format Cells dialog box with the Alignment tab selected, click the *Shrink to fit* check box in the *Text control* section to insert a check mark.
   c. Click OK.
   d. Deselect the range.
4. Save, print, and then close **EL2-C1-P4-Precision.xlsx**.

19	Canada	Kelli Olsen	(800) 555-3469
20	International	Bianca Santini	(800) 555-3479
21			
22		Minimum order quantity of 25 applies.	
23		Preferred carriers are UPS and DHL.	

The *Shrink to fit* option is applied to B22:B23 in Steps 3b–3c.

Project 5 Convert Text Using Text Functions 2 Parts

You will use text functions to modify a heading, convert state names to uppercase, and extract data.

Using Text Functions ■■■■■■■■■■■■■■■■■■■■■■■■■

Text can be formatted or modified using text functions. You can insert a text function by typing it or by clicking the Text button in the Functions group on the FORMULAS tab and then selecting a function from the drop-down list. For example, you can use the LOWER and UPPER functions to covert text from uppercase to lowercase and vice versa. Text that has incorrect capitalization can be changed to initial case using the PROPER function. New text can be substituted for existing text using the SUBSTITUTE function.

When you want to copy some of the characters in a cell, you can use text functions to extract the data. Text can be extracted from the rightmost, leftmost, or middle of a string of characters using the RIGHT, LEFT, or MID functions. These three functions, along with the TRIM function that removes extra spaces between characters, also can be used on data that has been imported or copied from another source. Table 1.2 provides more information about each text function.

Table 1.2 Text Function Examples

Text Function	Description	Example
=PROPER(text)	Capitalizes the first letter of each word.	=PROPER("annual budget") returns *Annual Budget* in formula cell OR A3 holds the text *annual budget*; =PROPER(A3) entered in C3 causes C3 to display *Annual Budget*
=UPPER(text)	Converts text to uppercase.	=UPPER("annual budget") returns *ANNUAL BUDGET* in formula cell OR A3 holds the text *annual budget*; =UPPER(A3) entered in C3 causes C3 to display *ANNUAL BUDGET*
=LOWER(text)	Converts text to lowercase.	=LOWER("ANNUAL BUDGET") returns *annual budget* in formula cell OR A3 holds the text *ANNUAL BUDGET*; =LOWER(A3) entered in C3 causes C3 to display *annual budget*
=SUBSTITUTE(text)	Inserts new text in place of old text.	A3 holds the text *Annual Budget*; =SUBSTITUTE(A3,"Annual","2015") entered in C3 causes C3 to display *2015 Budget*

▼ **Quick Steps**

Use the SUBSTITUTE Function
1. Make desired cell active.
2. Type =substitute(.
3. Type source text cell address.
4. Type ,.
5. Type text to be changed within quotation marks.
6. Type ,.
7. Type replacement text within quotation marks.
8. Type).
9. Press Enter.

Use the UPPER Function
1. Make desired cell active.
2. Type =upper(.
3. Type source cell address.
   OR
   Type text to convert within quotation marks.
4. Type).
5. Press Enter.

Text

continues

Table 1.2 Text Function Examples—*Continued*

Text Function	Description	Example
=RIGHT(text,num_chars)	Extracts the requested number of characters, starting at the rightmost character.	=RIGHT("2015 Annual Budget",13) returns *Annual Budget* in formula cell OR A3 holds the text *2015 Annual Budget*; =RIGHT(C3,13) entered in C3 causes C3 to display *Annual Budget*
=LEFT(text,num_chars)	Extracts the requested number of characters, starting at the leftmost character.	=LEFT("2015 Annual Budget",4) returns *2015* in formula cell OR A3 holds the text *2015 Annual Budget*; =LEFT(C3,4) entered in C3 causes C3 to display *2015*
=MID(text,start-num, num-chars)	Extracts the requested number of characters, starting at a given position.	=MID("2015 Annual Budget",6,13) returns *Annual Budget* in formula cell OR A3 holds the text *2015 Annual Budget*; =MID(C3,6,13) entered in C3 causes C3 to display *Annual Budget*
=TRIM(text)	Removes extra spaces between words.	=TRIM("2015 Annual Budget") returns 2015 *Annual Budget* in formula cell OR A3 holds the text *2015 Annual Budget*; =TRIM(C3) entered in C3 causes C3 to display *2015 Annual Budget*

1. Open **USIncomeStats.xlsx**.
2. Save the workbook and name it **EL2-C1-P5-USIncomeStats**.
3. The worksheet contains 2011 median income data downloaded from the US Census Bureau. You want to estimate 2015 median income using a formula based on 2011 statistics. To begin, copy and substitute text at the top of the worksheet to create the layout for 2015 data by completing the following steps:
   a. Copy cell A1 and then click cell F1. Click the Paste Options button and then click the Keep Source Column Widths button in the *Paste* section of the drop-down gallery.

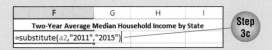

   b. Press Esc to remove the scrolling marquee from cell A1.
   c. Make cell F2 active, type **=substitute(a2,"2011","2015")**, and then press Enter.

F	G	H	I
Two-Year Average Median Household Income by State			Step 3c
=substitute(a2,"2011","2015")			

   d. Merge and center cell F2 across F2:I2 and apply bold formatting.
4. Copy cell A3 and the state names below cell A3 from column A to column F and convert the text to uppercase by completing the following steps:
   a. Make cell F3 active.
   b. Type **=lower(a3)** and then press Enter. Excel returns the text *united states* in cell F3. Press Ctrl + Z or click the Undo button the Quick Access toolbar to reverse this action.
   c. Type **=upper(a3)** and then press Enter. Excel returns the text *UNITED STATES*.

F	G	H	I
Two-Year Average Median Household Income by State			Step 4c
Median Income for 2015			
=upper(a3)			

   d. Make cell F3 active and then drag the fill handle down to cell F54.
5. Enter the formula to estimate 2015 median income based on 2011 data plus 7.3% by completing the following steps:
   a. Make cell H3 active, type **=c3+(c3*7.3%)**, and then press Enter.
   b. Select cell H3 and apply comma formatting with no places after the decimal point.
   c. Drag the fill handle in cell H3 down to cell H54.
   d. Deselect the range.
6. Select F3:H3, apply bold formatting, and then apply the Orange, Accent 6, Lighter 80% fill color (last option in second row of *Theme Colors* section). Deselect the range.
7. Save, print, and then close **EL2-C1-P5-USIncomeStats.xlsx**.

1. Open **VIVCodes.xlsx**.
2. Save the workbook as **EL2-C1-P5-VivCodes**.
3. The IT director wants to create new computer user names by extracting different parts of the employees' personal information. A workbook has been created from various sources with the employees' first names, last names, and social security numbers (SSN). The director notices that the SSNs include extra spaces. Use the TRIM function to remove the extra spaces between the characters by completing the following steps:
   a. Make cell D6 active, type =trim(c6), and then press Enter.

   b. Drag the fill handle in cell D6 down to cell D14.
   c. Deselect the range.
4. Use the LEFT function to extract the first letter of the first name by completing the following steps:
   a. Make cell E6 active, type =left(a6,1), and then press Enter.

   b. Drag the fill handle in cell E6 down to cell E14.
   c. Deselect the range.
5. Use the LEFT function to extract the first four letters of the last name by completing the following steps:
   a. Make cell F6 active, type =left(b6,4), and then press Enter.
   b. Drag the fill handle in cell F6 down to cell F14.
   c. Deselect the range.
6. Extract the middle two digits of the SSN using the MID function by completing the following steps:
   a. Make cell G6 active, type =mid(d6,5,2), and then press Enter.

   b. Drag the fill handle in cell G6 down to cell G14.
   c. Deselect the range.
7. Use the RIGHT function to extract the date from the end of the text string in cell A2 by completing the following steps.
   a. Make cell B16 active, type =right(a2,10), and then press Enter.
   b. Deselect the range.
8. Save, print, and then close **EL2-C1-P5-VivCodes.xlsx**.

You will filter an insurance policy worksheet to show policies based on a range of liability limits and by number of claims, filter policies based on the number of automobiles, and filter and sort a payroll worksheet by font and cell colors.

Filtering a Worksheet Using a Custom AutoFilter ■■■■■

The Custom AutoFilter feature is used to display only the rows that meet specific criteria defined using the filter arrow at the top of each column. Rows that do not meet the criteria are temporarily hidden from view. At the top of each column in the selected range or table, you can click a filter arrow to display a drop-down list containing each unique field value that exists within the column. Display the Custom AutoFilter dialog box, shown in Figure 1.8, in a worksheet where you want to filter values by more than one criterion using a comparison operator. You can use the ? and * wildcard characters in a custom filter. For example, you can filter a list of products by a product number beginning with P by using *P** as the criteria.

To display the Custom AutoFilter dialog box, select the range to filter and then click the Sort & Filter button in the Editing group. Click *Filter* at the drop-down list and then deselect the range. Click the filter arrow in the column that contains the criteria. Point to *Number Filters* or *Text Filters* and then choose one of the options at the drop-down list. The type of filter and options available depend on the type of data in the column—for example, text or numbers.

▼ **Quick Steps**

Filter Using a Custom AutoFilter
1. Select range.
2. Click Sort & Filter button.
3. Click *Filter*.
4. Deselect range.
5. Click filter arrow at top of desired column.
6. Point to *Number Filters*.
7. Click desired filter category.
8. Enter criteria at Custom AutoFilter dialog box.
9. Click OK.

Sort & Filter

Figure 1.8 Custom AutoFilter Dialog Box

Use the Custom AutoFilter dialog box to specify two criteria by which to filter using either an *And* or *Or* statement.

1. Open **ACInsce.xlsx**.
2. Save the workbook and name it **EL2-C1-P6-ACInsce**.
3. The owner of AllClaims Insurance Brokers wants to review policies with liability limits from $500,000 to $1,000,000 that have more than one claim to determine if customers should increase their coverage. Filter the policy information to produce the list of policies that meet the owner's request by completing the following steps:
   a. Select A3:I20.
   b. Click the Sort & Filter button in the Editing group on the HOME tab.
   c. Click *Filter* at the drop-down list. A filter arrow displays at the top of each column.
   d. Deselect the range.
   e. Click the filter arrow next to *Liability Limit* in cell E3.
   f. Point to *Number Filters* and then click *Between* at the drop-down list.
   g. At the Custom AutoFilter dialog box with the insertion point positioned in the blank text box next to *is greater than or equal to*, type 500000.
   h. Notice that *And* is the option selected between the criteria. This is correct, since the owner wants a list of policies with a liability limit greater than or equal to $500,000 *and* less than or equal to $1,000,000.
   i. Click in the blank text box next to *is less than or equal to* and type 1000000.
   j. Click OK to close the Custom AutoFilter dialog box. The range is filtered to display the rows with liability limits from $500,000 to $1,000,000.
   k. Click the filter arrow next to *Claims* in cell H3.
   l. Point to *Number Filters* and then click *Greater Than* at the drop-down list.
   m. At the Custom AutoFilter dialog box with the insertion point positioned in the blank text box next to *is greater than*, type 1 and then click OK.
4. Print the filtered worksheet.
5. Save and then close **EL2-C1-P6-ACInsce.xlsx**.

Step 3b

Step 3c

Step 3e

Step 3f

Step 3g

Step 3i

Step 3j

Step 3m

Filtering and Sorting Data Using Conditional Formatting or Cell Attributes ■■■■■■■■■■■■■■■■■

A worksheet with cells that have been formatted manually or by conditional formatting to change the cell or font color can be filtered by color. In addition, a worksheet conditionally formatted using an icon set can be filtered using an icon.

To do this, select the range, click the Sort & Filter button, click *Filter*, and then deselect the range. Click the filter arrow in the column by which you want to filter and then point to *Filter by Color* at the drop-down list. Depending on the formatting that has been applied, the list contains cell colors, font colors, or icon sets. Click the desired color or icon option to filter the column.

The filter drop-down list also contains a *Sort by Color* option that you can use to sort rows within a range or table by a specified cell color, font color, or cell icon. Follow similar steps to sort by color as you would to filter by color. For example, to sort a column by font color, point to *Sort by Color* from the column's filter drop-down list and then click the desired font color. Excel sorts the column by placing cells with the specified font color at the top.

You can also sort or filter using the shortcut menu. To do this, right-click a cell that contains the color or icon by which you want to filter, point to *Filter*, and then click *Filter by Selected Cell's Color*, *Filter by Selected Cell's Font Color*, or *Filter by Selected Cell's Icon*.

▼ **Quick Steps**

Filter or Sort by Color or Icon Set
1. Select range.
2. Click Sort & Filter button.
3. Click *Filter*.
4. Deselect range.
5. Click filter arrow at top of desired column.
6. Point to *Filter by Color* or *Sort by Color*.
7. Click desired color or icon.

OR
1. Right-click cell with desired color or icon.
2. Point to *Filter* or *Sort*.
3. Click desired filter or sort option.

Project 6b　**Filtering by Icon Set**　　　　　　　　　　　　　　　**Part 2 of 4**

1. Open **EL2-C1-P2-ACInsce.xlsx**.
2. Save the workbook and name it **EL2-C1-P6-ACInsce-1Auto**.
3. Filter the worksheet to display the policies that have coverage for only one automobile by completing the following steps:
   a. Select A3:I20.
   b. Click the Sort & Filter button in the Editing group on the HOME tab.
   c. Click *Filter* at the drop-down list. A filter arrow displays at the top of each column.
   d. Deselect the range.
   e. In Project 2c, you applied the Red to Black icon set to the data in column C. Note that the black circle icon represents the *1* data set. Click the filter arrow next to *No. of Autos* in cell C3.
   f. Point to *Filter by Color* at the drop-down list.
   g. Click the black circle icon in the *Filter by Cell Icon* list.
4. Print the filtered worksheet and then close **EL2-C1-P6-ACInsce-1Auto.xlsx**.

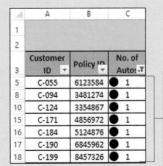

The worksheet has been filtered by the black circle icon representing the policies with one auto.

1. Open **EL2-C1-P1-VIVPay-Oct24.xlsx**.
2. Save the workbook and name it **EL2-C1-P6-VIVPay-Oct24-HighOT**.
3. The store manager wants a list of employees who worked more than five overtime hours during the pay period. You recall conditionally formatting the overtime hours by applying a red font color to cells with values greater than 5. Filter the worksheet by the conditional formatting by completing the following steps:

   a. Right-click cell K6 (or any other cell in column K with a red font color).
   b. Point to *Filter* and then click *Filter by Selected Cell's Font Color* at the shortcut menu.
4. Print the filtered worksheet.
5. Save and then close **EL2-C1-P6-VIVPay-Oct24-HighOT.xlsx**.

1. Open **EL2-C1-P1-VIVPay-Oct24.xlsx**.
2. Save the workbook and name it **EL2-C1-P6-VIVPay-Oct24-Sorted**.
3. Sort the payroll worksheet in descending order by cell color by completing the following steps:

   a. Select A5:M23, click the Sort & Filter button in the Editing group on the HOME tab, and then click *Filter* at the drop-down list.
   b. Deselect the range.
   c. Click the filter arrow next to *Gross Pay* in cell M5.
   d. Point to *Sort by Color* and then click the pink fill color box in the *Sort by Cell Color* section.
4. Print the sorted worksheet.
5. Save and then close **EL2-C1-P6-VIVPay-Oct24-Sorted.xlsx**.

In a worksheet with more than one cell or font color applied to a column, you have to define a custom sort. Click the Sort & Filter button in the Editing group on the HOME tab and then click *Custom Sort* at the drop-down list. At the Sort dialog box shown in Figure 1.9, define the color by which to sort first and

Figure 1.9 Sort Dialog Box with Four-Color Sort Defined

Cells will be sorted first by the black icon, then by the gray icon, then by the pink icon, and lastly by the red icon.

then add a level for each other color in the order in which you want the sorting to occur. The *Sort On* drop-down list at the Sort dialog box allows you to select *Values*, *Cell Color*, *Font Color*, or *Cell Icon*. Figure 1.9 contains a sort definition for a column in which four cell icons have been used.

Chapter Summary

- Conditional formatting applies format changes to cells based on a condition; cells that meet the condition have the formatting applied, and cells that do not meet the condition remain unformatted.
- Conditional formats can be based on values, dates, text entries, or duplicated values.
- Use the Quick Analysis button to quickly apply predefined conditional formats.
- Use the *Highlight Cells Rules* option at the Conditional Formatting button drop-down list to conditionally format based on a value comparison.
- Use the *Top/Bottom Rules* option at the Conditional Formatting button drop-down list to conditionally format based on the top 10 or bottom 10 percentage or average values.
- Conditional formats are based on rules that specify the criterion by which the cells are tested and the formatting attributes to apply to cells that meet the condition.
- Create your own conditional formatting rules by selecting *New Rule* at the Conditional Formatting button drop-down list.
- Edit or delete a rule at the Conditional Formatting Rules Manager dialog box.
- Conditionally format using data bars, color scales, or icon sets to add small bar charts, gradations of color, or icons to cells to make it easier to identify certain data.
- Conditionally format using a formula to apply desired formatting to the selected range of cells based on values in other cells. Excel treats any formula entered for conditional formatting as an array formula, which means you only need to add one rule for a selected range.
- An IF statement can be used to conditionally format those cells that calculate to a true result for the logical test.

- Fraction formatting converts decimal values to fractions.
- To choose the type of fraction you want to convert, open the Format Cells dialog box with the Number tab selected.
- Scientific formatting displays numbers in exponential notation, in which part of the number that is formatted is replaced with E+n, where E stands for "exponent" and n represents the power.
- Excel provides special number formats specific to countries and languages to format entries such as telephone numbers and social security numbers.
- Custom number formats use formatting codes to create the format definition.
- A custom number format can be used to add text or punctuation to a value entered into a cell.
- Long labels can be formatted to fit within a cell by wrapping the text within the cell or shrinking the font size to fit the cell.
- Convert the case of text from lowercase to uppercase or uppercase to lowercase using the UPPER and LOWER text functions.
- Replace existing text with new text using the SUBSTITUTE text function.
- Display the Custom AutoFilter dialog box to filter values by more than one criterion using a comparison operator such as greater than or equal to.
- A worksheet that has been formatted manually or by conditional formatting can be filtered by colors or icons.
- Define a custom sort if the worksheet contains more than one cell color, font color, or cell icon and you want to specify the order of the colors to sort.

Commands Review

FEATURE	RIBBON TAB, GROUP	BUTTON	KEYBOARD SHORTCUT
conditional formatting	HOME, Styles		
custom AutoFilter	HOME, Editing		Ctrl + Shift + L
custom number format	HOME, Number		Ctrl + 1
fraction formatting	HOME, Number		Ctrl + 1
scientific formatting	HOME, Number		Ctrl + 1
shrink text to fit	HOME, Alignment		
special number formatting	HOME, Number		Ctrl + 1
text functions	FORMULAS, Function Library		
wrap text	HOME, Alignment		Alt + Enter

Concepts Check   Test Your Knowledge

Completion: In the space provided at the right, indicate the correct term, command, or number.

1. Point to this option at the Conditional Formatting button drop-down list to format cells based on a comparison operator such as *greater than*.

2. To conditionally format a range using the *Above Average* condition, click this option at the Conditional Formatting button drop-down list.

3. Open this dialog box to create, edit, or delete a conditional formatting rule.

4. Excel uses threshold values to classify data into three to five categories when applying conditional formatting using this option.

5. Click this option in the *Select a Rule Type* section of the New Formatting Rule dialog box to create a rule that conditionally formats cells based on the value(s) in another cell.

6. Open this dialog box with this tab active to format a selected range as fractions and select the type of fraction to display.

7. Scientific formatting is used by scientists and others who need to write very large numbers using this notation.

8. The special number format options displayed in the *Type* list box are dependent on the setting in this option box.

9. If you type *156.3568* in a cell with the custom number format code ###.## applied, this result will display.

10. Use either of these two text control options to format a long label within the existing column width.

11. Use this text function to change existing text in the source cell to new text in the formula cell.

12. Open this dialog box to filter by more than one criterion using a comparison operator.

13. A worksheet can be filtered by a cell color that has been applied manually or by this feature.

14. Open this dialog box to organize cells in a worksheet by more than one color.

Skills Check   Assess Your Performance

Assessment

1 USE CONDITIONAL AND FRACTION FORMATTING

1. Open **RSRServRpt.xlsx**.
2. Save the workbook and name it **EL2-C1-A1-RSRServRpt**.
3. Apply the following formatting changes to the Sep worksheet:
   a. Format the values in C6:C23 as fractions using the *As quarters (2/4)* type.
   b. Format the rate codes in D6:D22 with the 3 Traffic Lights (Rimmed) icon set. (This is the first option in the right column of the *Shapes* section.)
   c. Format the parts values in F6:F22 with Light Red Fill color (sixth column, second row) for those cells with values that are equal to 0.
   d. Format the total invoice values in G6:G22 using the *Red Data Bar* option in the *Gradient Fill* section of the Data Bars side menu.
4. Save, print, and then close **EL2-C1-A1-RSRServRpt.xlsx**.

Assessment

2 APPLY CUSTOM NUMBER FORMATTING

1. Open **EL2-C1-A1-RSRServRpt.xlsx**.
2. Save the workbook and name it **EL2-C1-A2-RSRServRpt**.
3. Create and apply the following custom number formats to the Sep worksheet:
   a. Create a custom number format that displays *hrs* one space after each value in C6:C23. **Hint: After selecting Custom in the Category list box, click after the existing format codes in the Type text box and then add the required entry. (Do not delete what is already in the Type text box.)**
   b. Create a custom number format that displays *RSR-* in front of each work order number in B6:B22.
4. Save, print, and then close **EL2-C1-A2-RSRServRpt.xlsx**.

Assessment

3 USE CUSTOM AUTOFILTER; FILTER AND SORT BY COLOR

1. Open **EL2-C1-A2-RSRServRpt.xlsx**.
2. Save the workbook and name it **EL2-C1-A3-RSRServRpt**.
3. Make the following changes to the Sep worksheet:
   a. Select A5:G22 and turn on the Filter feature.
   b. Using the filter arrow at the top of the *Hours Billed* column, display those invoices for which the hours billed are between 1.75 and 3.75. **Hint: Type in the values 1.75 and 3.75. Do not select 1 3/4 hrs and 3 3/4 hrs from the drop-down lists in the Custom AutoFilter dialog box.**
4. Make the following changes to the Oct worksheet:
   a. Select A5:G22 and then turn on the Filter feature.
   b. Filter the *Parts* column by color to show only those invoices for which no parts were billed.
5. Make the following changes to the Nov worksheet:
   a. Clear the filter from the *Date* column.
   b. Filter the worksheet by the icon associated with rate code 3.

6. Make the following changes to the Dec worksheet:
   a. Remove the filter arrows from the worksheet.
   b. Make active any cell within the invoice list.
   c. Open the Sort dialog box.
   d. Define three sort levels as follows:

Sort by	*Sort On*	*Order*
rate code	cell icon	Red Traffic Light (On Top)
rate code	cell icon	Yellow Traffic Light (On Top)
rate code	cell icon	Green Traffic Light (On Top)

7. Print the workbook.
8. Save and then close **EL2-C1-A3-RSRServRpt.xlsx**.

Assessment

 4 **CREATE, EDIT, AND DELETE FORMATTING RULES**

1. Open **VIVPay-Oct31.xlsx**.
2. Save the workbook and name it **EL2-C1-A4-VIVPay-Oct31**.
3. Create and apply two conditional formatting rules for the values in the *Pay Rate* column as follows:
   a. Apply the Light Blue fill color (fifth column, third row) to values from 7.50 to 8.00.
   b. Apply a light green fill color (seventh column, third row) to values greater than 8.00.
4. Create a conditional formatting rule for the *Gross Pay* column that will format the values in the Dark Red font color (first option in the *Standard Colors* section) if the employee has worked overtime hours.
5. Use the Quick Analysis button to find the top 10% for the *Gross Pay* column.
6. Edit the formatting rule for *Cell Value <7.5* by applying the Light Orange fill color (tenth column, third row).
7. Use the Quick Analysis button to delete the formatting rule for *Overtime Hours*.
8. Save, print, and then close **EL2-C1-A4-VIVPay-Oct31.xlsx**.

Visual Benchmark Demonstrate Your Proficiency

FORMAT A BILLING SUMMARY

1. Open **BillingsOct5to9.xlsx**.
2. Save the workbook and name it **EL2-C1-VB-BillingsOct5to9**.
3. Format the worksheet to match the one shown in Figure 1.10 using the following information:
   - The data in the *Billing Code* column has been custom formatted to add the text *Amicus#-* in the Blue font color in front of the code number.
   - Icon sets have been used in the *Attorney Code* column and the same icon set should be applied in the *Attorney Code Table* section of the worksheet.
   - The data bars added to the values in the *Legal Fees* column have been formatted with the Turquoise, Accent 3 gradient fill. **Hint: Select More Rules in the Data Bars side menu**.
   - Values below 1500.00 in the *Total Due* column have been conditionally formatted and the worksheet has been sorted by the font color used for the conditional format.
4. Save, print, and then close **EL2-C1-VB-BillingsOct5to9.xlsx**.

Figure 1.10 Visual Benchmark

	A	B	C	D	E	F	G	H	I	J
1					O'DONOVAN & SULLIVAN LAW ASSOCIATES					
2					BILLING SUMMARY					
3					OCTOBER 5 TO 9, 2015					
4	File	Client	Date	Billing Code	Attorney Code	Legal Fees	Disbursements	Total Due		Billing Code Table
5	EP-652	10106	10/5/2015	Amicus#-3	● 1	1,028.50	23.75	1,052.25	Code	Area of Practice
6	EL-632	10225	10/6/2015	Amicus#-5	○ 3	1,211.00	37.85	1,248.85	1	Corporate
7	CL-501	10341	10/7/2015	Amicus#-1	◔ 2	1,143.75	55.24	1,198.99	2	Divorce & Separation
8	IN-745	10210	10/8/2015	Amicus#-6	○ 3	1,450.00	24.25	1,474.25	3	Wills & Estates
9	CL-412	10125	10/9/2015	Amicus#-1	◔ 2	1,143.75	38.12	1,181.87	4	Real Estate
10	IN-801	10346	10/9/2015	Amicus#-6	○ 3	1,425.00	62.18	1,487.18	5	Employment Litigation
11	RE-501	10384	10/9/2015	Amicus#-4	◕ 4	1,237.50	34.28	1,271.78	6	Insurance Personal Injury
12	FL-325	10104	10/5/2015	Amicus#-2	● 1	2,273.75	95.10	2,368.85	7	Other
13	CL-412	10125	10/5/2015	Amicus#-1	◔ 2	2,493.75	55.40	2,549.15		
14	IN-745	10210	10/6/2015	Amicus#-6	○ 3	2,425.00	65.20	2,490.20		Attorney Code Table
15	RE-475	10285	10/6/2015	Amicus#-4	◕ 4	3,807.00	48.96	3,855.96	Code	Attorney
16	CL-521	10334	10/7/2015	Amicus#-1	◔ 2	1,518.75	27.85	1,546.60	● 1	Marty O'Donovan
17	PL-348	10420	10/7/2015	Amicus#-7	○ 3	2,500.00	34.95	2,534.95	◔ 2	Toni Sullivan
18	RE-492	10425	10/7/2015	Amicus#-4	◕ 4	2,043.00	38.75	2,081.75	○ 3	Rosa Martinez
19	EL-632	10225	10/8/2015	Amicus#-5	○ 3	2,300.00	42.15	2,342.15	◕ 4	Kyle Williams
20	PL-512	10290	10/8/2015	Amicus#-7	○ 3	1,620.00	65.15	1,685.15		
21	FL-385	10278	10/8/2015	Amicus#-2	● 1	2,040.00	85.47	2,125.47		
22	CL-450	10358	10/9/2015	Amicus#-1	◔ 2	1,762.50	55.24	1,817.74		
23	EP-685	10495	10/9/2015	Amicus#-3	○ 3	2,375.00	94.55	2,469.55		

Case Study   Apply Your Skills

You work as a market research assistant at NuTrends Market Research. Yolanda Robertson has provided you with a workbook named **USIncomeStats.xlsx**. This workbook contains data she obtained from the US Census Bureau with the two-year average median household income by state for 2011. Open the workbook and name it **EL2-C1-CS-P1-USIncomeStats**. Yolanda wants you to format the data using colors to differentiate income levels. She has proposed the following categories for which she would like you to apply color formatting:

Average Median Income Range

Less than $45,000

Between $45,000 and $55,000

Greater than $55,000

Apply color formatting using conditional formatting for this request, since Yolanda may change these salary ranges after she reviews the data and you want to be able to edit the formatting rule if that happens. Choose colors that will be easy to distinguish from one another. Create a reference table starting in cell E3 that provides Yolanda with a legend to read the colors. For example, in cell E3, type Less than 45,000 and in cell H3 type a sample value (such as 35,000) and then format each cell to the color that represents the formatting you applied to the rule category. Save and then print the worksheet. *Note: If you submit your work in hard copy and do not have access to a color printer, write on the printout the color format you applied to each category*.

Yolanda has reviewed the worksheet from Part 1 and has requested some further work. Before you begin modifying the file, you decide to keep a copy of the original file intact in case that data can be used for another purpose. Save the workbook and name it **EL2-C1-CS-P2-USIncomeStats**. You will use this workbook to make the modifications. Yolanda would like the worksheet sorted in descending order from the highest income level to the lowest. Do not include the entries in row 3 for the US average in the sort operation. After sorting the worksheet, filter the median incomes to display the top 20 states. *Hint: You can customize the value in the Top 10 AutoFilter*. Yolanda wants to add a contact telephone list next to the top 20 state data. Create the list using the following telephone numbers and place them in a suitable location:

Yolanda (cell)	800 555 3117
Yolanda (office)	800 555 4629
Yolanda (home)	800 555 2169
Yolanda (fax)	800 555 6744

Apply the special number format for phone numbers to ensure the data is displayed consistently. Save and then print the worksheet.

Part 3

Continuing with the worksheet formatted in Part 2 of this Case Study, you decide to experiment with the filtered census data worksheet to see if formatting using color scales will highlight the spread between the highest and lowest median incomes more distinctly. Apply conditional formatting using a two-color or three-color scale to the filtered cells in column C. (Exclude the US median income at the top of the column.) Save the workbook and name it **EL2-C1-CS-P3-USIncomeStats**. Print the worksheet. *Note: If you submit your work in hard copy and do not have access to a color printer, write on the printout the two- or three-color scale conditional formatting you applied to the filtered values in column C.*

Part 4

Yolanda is preparing a seminar for new market researchers hired at NuTrends Market Research. For background material for the training section on US Census Bureau statistics, Yolanda has asked you to research the history of the bureau. Using the Internet, go to www.census.gov/ and find the page that describes the history of the US Census Bureau. **Hint: Explore the tabbed pages at the <u>History</u> link under ABOUT US at the bottom of the home page**. In a new sheet in the same file as the median income data, type in column A five to seven interesting facts you learned about the bureau from the website. Adjust the width of column A and apply wrap text or shrink to fit formatting to improve the appearance of the sheet. Save the revised workbook and name it **EL2-C1-CS-P4-USIncomeStats**. Print the worksheet and then close the workbook.

EXCEL

Advanced Functions and Formulas

PERFORMANCE OBJECTIVES

Upon successful completion of Chapter 2, you will be able to:

- Create and use named ranges in formulas
- Use the functions COUNTA, COUNTIF, and COUNTIFS
- Use the functions AVERAGEIF and AVERAGEIFS
- Use the functions SUMIF and SUMIFS
- Edit a named range
- Rename and delete a named range
- Look up data using the lookup functions VLOOKUP and HLOOKUP
- Analyze loan payments using PPMT
- Use the conditional logic functions IF, AND, and OR

Tutorials

2.1 Creating and Managing Range Names

2.2 Using Statistical Functions: COUNT, COUNTA, COUNTIF, and COUNTIFS

2.3 Using Statistical Functions: AVERAGEIF and AVERAGEIFS

2.4 Using Math and Trigonometry Functions: SUMIF and SUMIFS

2.5 Using Lookup Functions

2.6 Using the PPMT Function

2.7 Using Logical Functions

Excel includes numerous built-in functions grouped by function category. Thirteen categories contain preprogrammed formulas to facilitate complex calculations for worksheets containing statistical, financial, scientific, database, and other data. The Insert function dialog box assists with locating and building function formulas. The structure of a function formula begins with an equals sign (=), followed by the name of the function, and then the function argument. *Argument* is the term given to the values to be included in the calculation. The structure of the argument is dependent on the type of function being used and can include a single cell, a range, multiple ranges, or any combination of these. Model answers for this chapter's projects appear on the following pages.

Excel
EL2C2

Note: Before beginning the projects, copy to your storage medium the EL2C2 subfolder from the EL2 folder on the CD that accompanies this textbook and then make EL2C2 the active folder.

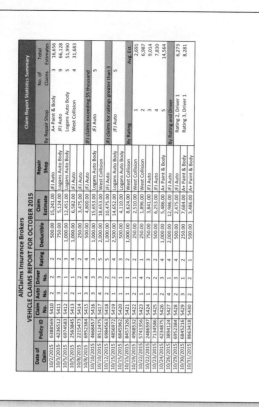

Project 1 Calculate Statistics and Sums Using Conditional Formulas

EL2-C2-P1-ACOct15VehRpt.xlsx

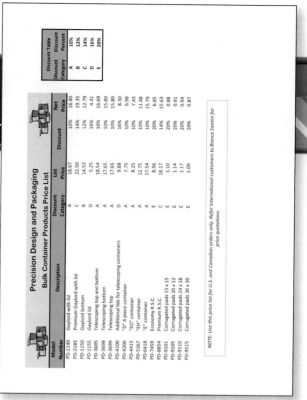

Project 2 Populate Cells by Looking Up Data

EL2-C2-P2-PrecisionPrices.xlsx

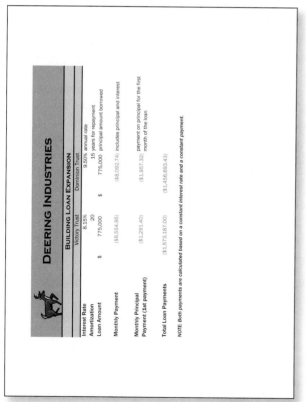

Project 3 Analyze an Expansion Project Loan

EL2-C2-P3-DExpansion.xlsx

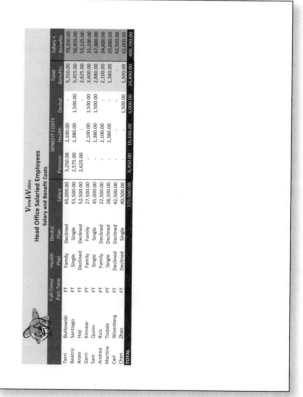

Project 4 Calculate Benefit Costs Using Conditional Logic

EL2-C2-P4-VIVSalCost.xlsx

Project 1   Calculate Statistics and Sums Using Conditional Formulas

7 Parts

You will create and manage range names in an insurance claims worksheet and use the range names in statistical formulas that count, find averages, and sum based on single and multiple criteria.

Creating Name Ranges ■■■■■■■■■■■■■■■■■■■■■■■■■

Assigning a name to a cell or range of cells allows you to reference the source using a descriptive label, rather than the cell address or range address, when creating formulas, printing, or navigating a worksheet. Creating range names makes the task of managing complex formulas easier and helps others who may work in or edit the worksheet to understand a formula's purpose more quickly.

To demonstrate the use of range names for clarity, read the formula examples in Table 2.1. Each row provides two formulas that reference the same source cells; however, the formula on the right is easier to understand than the formula on the left. The formulas in the left column might require you to locate the source cells in the worksheet to figure out the calculation steps, whereas you will understand the formulas in the right column almost immediately.

By default, the range to which a range name applies is referenced using absolute references. Later in this chapter, when you create a lookup formula, you will take advantage of the absolute referencing of a range name when you include a group of cells in the formula that stay fixed when the formula is copied.

Create a range name by selecting a single cell or range, clicking in the Name box located to the left of the Formula bar, typing the name, and then pressing Enter. The Name box displays the active cell address or cell name when one has been defined. When creating a name for a cell or a range of cells, follow these naming rules:

- Names can be a combination of letters, numbers, underscore characters, and periods up to 255 characters.
- The first character must be a letter, underscore, or backslash (\).
- Spaces are not valid. Use underscore characters or periods to separate words.
- A valid cell address cannot become a range name.
- Range names are not case sensitive.

▼ Quick Steps

Create a Range Name
1. Select cell(s).
2. Click in Name box.
3. Type desired range name.
4. Press Enter.

The FORMULAS tab contains a Create from Selection button in the Defined Names group that can be used to automatically create range names for a list or table. Select the list or table and click the button. Excel uses the names in the top row or left-most column as the range names.

Table 2.1 Standard Formulas and Formulas with Named Ranges

Standard Formula	Same Formula Using Named Ranges
=D3-D13	=Sales-Expenses
=J5*K5	=Hours*PayRate
=G10/J10	=ThisYear/LastYear
=IF(E4-B2>0,E4*D2,0)	=IF(Sales-Target>0,Sales*Bonus,0)

1. Open **ACOct15VehRpt.xlsx**.
2. Save the workbook and name it **EL2-C2-P1-ACOct15VehRpt**.
3. Assign names to ranges by completing the following steps:
   a. Select D4:D24.
   b. Click in the Name box located to the left of the Formula bar, type *AutoNo*, and then press Enter.
   c. Select E4:E24, click in the Name box, type *DriverNo*, and then press Enter.
   d. Select F4:F24, click in the Name box, type *Rating*, and then press Enter.
   e. Select H4:H24, click in the Name box, type *ClaimEst*, and then press Enter.
   f. Select I4:I24, click in the Name box, type *RepShop*, and then press Enter.
4. View the range names by clicking the down-pointing arrow at the right of the Name box.
5. Click *AutoNo* at the drop-down list to move the selected range to column D. One reason for creating range names is to make it easier to navigate quickly in a large worksheet.
6. Deselect the range by clicking anywhere in the worksheet.
7. Save **EL2-C2-P1-ACOct15VehRpt.xlsx**.

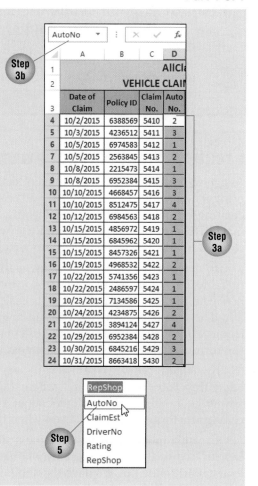

Using Statistical Functions ■■■■■■■■■■■■■■■■■■■■■■

Commonly used statistical functions include AVERAGE, MAX, and MIN, where AVERAGE returns the arithmetic mean, MAX returns the largest value, and MIN returns the smallest value in the range. Another function used often is COUNT, which returns the number of cells that contain numbers or dates. Empty cells, text labels, or error values in the range are ignored. Excel provides additional AVERAGE and COUNT functions that are used to count text entries and find averages for a range based on a criterion.

Using the COUNTA Function

In a worksheet that requires cells containing text or a combination of text and numbers (such as *Model-2146*) to be counted, Excel provides the COUNTA function. COUNTA returns the number of cells that are not empty; therefore, this formula can be used to count a range of cells other than values. As shown in the worksheet in Figure 2.1, when the regular COUNT function is used in cell E8 to count parts in the range A2:A6, Excel returns a value of 0. However, in cell E9, when the same range is counted using COUNTA, Excel returns a value of 5.

Figure 2.1 COUNTA Example

The formula =COUNT(A2:A6) returns 0.

The formula =COUNTA(A2:A6) returns the correct result.

▼ **Quick Steps**

Create a COUNTIF Formula
1. Make desired cell active.
2. Click Insert Function button.
3. Change category to *Statistical*.
4. Select *COUNTIF*.
5. Click OK.
6. Enter range address or range name to select by in *Range* text box.
7. Enter condition expression or text in *Criteria* text box.
8. Click OK.

Create a COUNTIFS Formula
1. Make desired cell active.
2. Click Insert Function button.
3. Change category to *Statistical*.
4. Select *COUNTIFS*.
5. Click OK.
6. Enter range address or range name to select by in *Criteria_range1* text box.
7. Enter condition expression or text in *Criteria1* text box.
8. Enter range address or range name to select by in *Criteria_range2* text box.
9. Enter condition expression or text in *Criteria2* text box.
10. Continue adding criteria range expressions and criteria as needed.
11. Click OK.

Using the COUNTIF and COUNTIFS Functions

Use the COUNTIF function to count cells within a range that meet a single criterion. For example, in a grades worksheet, you might use a COUNTIF function to count the number of students who achieved greater than 75%. This function uses conditional logic, in which the criterion defines a conditional test so that only those cells that meet the test are selected for action. The structure of a COUNTIF function is *=COUNTIF(range,criteria)*. For the grades worksheet example, the function to count the cells of students who achieved greater than 75% is *=COUNTIF(grades,">75")*, assuming the range name *grades* has been defined. Notice that the syntax of the argument requires the criterion to be enclosed in quotation marks. If you use the Insert Function dialog box to create a formula, Excel adds the required syntax automatically. A cell reference may also be used as the criterion. A cell reference is not enclosed in quotation marks and should only contain the exact criterion.

The COUNTIFS function is used to count cells that meet multiple criteria. The formula uses the same structure as COUNTIF with additional ranges and criteria within the argument. The structure of a COUNTIFS function is *=COUNTIFS(range1,criteria1,range2,criteria2. . .)*. Figure 2.2 illustrates a nursing education worksheet with a single criterion COUNTIF to count the number of

Figure 2.2 COUNTIF and COUNTIFS Formulas

	A	B	C	D	E	F	G	H	I	J	K
1					Department of Human Resources						
2					Full-Time Nursing Education Worksheet						
3	Employee Number	Employee Last Name	Employee First Name	Title	Unit	Extension	Years Experience	PD Current?		Nursing Educational Statistical Summary	
4	FT02001	Santos	Susan	RN	Med/Surg	36415	30	Yes		Number of RNs	16
5	FT02002	Daniels	Jasmine	RN	Med/Surg	36415	27	No		Number of LPNs	12
6	FT02003	Walden	Virgina	RN	ICU	34211	22	No			
7	FT02004	Jaffe	Paul	LPN	CSRU	36418	24	Yes		RNs who are current with PD	9
8	FT02005	Salvatore	Terry	LPN	ICU	34211	22	Yes		LPNs who are current with PD	7
9	FT02006	Mander	Kaitlynn	RN	ICU	34211	24	Yes			
10	FT02007	Friesen	Jessica	LPN	ICU	34211	20	Yes			
11	FT02008	Lavigne	Gisele	RN	CSRU	36418	20	No			
12	FT02009	Gauthier	Jacqueline	RN	PreOp	32881	19	No			
13	FT02010	Williamson	Forman	RN	CSRU	36418	19	Yes			
14	FT02011	Orlowski	William	RN	Ortho	31198	22	No			
15	FT02012	Kadri	Ahmed	LPN	Ortho	31198	21	No			
16	FT02013	El-Hamid	Lianna	LPN	Med/Surg	36415	20	No			
17	FT02014	Vezina	Ursula	LPN	Ortho	31198	20	No			
18	FT02015	Adams	Sheila	LPN	Med/Surg	36415	25				
19	FT02016	Jorgensen	Macy	RN	Med/Surg	36415	10	No			
20	FT02017	Pieterson	Eric	RN	ICU	34211	8	Yes			
21	FT02018	Keller	Douglas	RN	ICU	34211	10	No			
22	FT02019	Costa	Michael	RN	Ortho	31198	10	No			
23	FT02020	Li-Kee	Su-Lynn	LPN	PreOp	32881	8	No			
24	FT02021	Besterd	Mary	RN	PreOp	32881	7	Yes			

Formula =COUNTIF(Title,"RN")

Formula =COUNTIFS(Title,"RN",PDCurrent,"Yes")

Insert Function

nurses (RNs) and a multiple criteria COUNTIFS to count the number of RNs who are current with their professional development (PD) activities. The formulas shown in Figure 2.2 include range names for which *Title* references the entries in column D and *PDCurrent* references the entries in column H.

Project 1b   **Creating COUNTIF Functions**   **Part 2 of 7**

1. With **EL2-C2-P1-ACOct15VehRpt.xlsx** open, make cell L4 active.
2. Create a COUNTIF function to count the number of claims for which A+ Paint & Body is the repair shop by completing the following steps:

   a. Click the Insert Function button in the Formula bar.

   b. At the Insert Function dialog box, click the down-pointing arrow at the right of the *Or select a category* option box and then click *Statistical* at the drop-down list. ***Note: Skip this step if Statistical is already selected as the category.***

   c. Scroll down the *Select a function* list box and then click *COUNTIF*.

   d. Read the formula description below the function list box and then click OK.

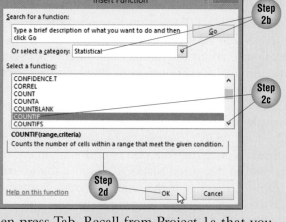

   e. At the Function Arguments dialog box with the insertion point positioned in the *Range* text box, type RepShop and then press Tab. Recall from Project 1a that you defined a range name for the entries in column I. ***Note: If the dialog box is obscuring your view of the worksheet, drag the Function Arguments dialog box title bar left or right.***

   f. With the insertion point positioned in the *Criteria* text box, type A+ Paint & Body and then press Tab. When you press Tab, Excel adds quotation marks to the criteria text.

   g. Click OK. Excel returns the value *3* in cell L4.

   h. Look at the formula in the Formula bar created by the Function Arguments dialog box: =COUNTIF(RepShop,"A+ Paint & Body").

3. Make cell L5 active. The repair shop names are located in K4:K7. Use cell K5 as the cell reference for JFJ Auto by typing the formula =countif(repshop,k5) and then press Enter. (When entering formulas, type cell references and named ranges in lowercase letters. Excel will automatically display uppercase letters once the formula has been entered.)

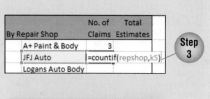

4. Use the fill handle to copy the formula in cell L5 to cells L6 through L7. When completed, the COUNTIF formulas will be as follows:

       L6: =COUNTIF(RepShop,K6)
       L7: =COUNTIF(RepShop,K7)

5. Save **EL2-C2-P1-ACOct15VehRpt.xlsx**.

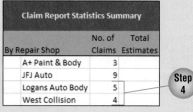

1. With **EL2-C2-P1-ACOct15VehRpt.xlsx** open, make cell L10 active.
2. Create a COUNTIFS function to count the number of claims for which the repair shop is JFJ Auto and the claims estimate is greater than $5,000 by completing the following steps:
   a. Click the Insert Function button in the Formula bar.
   b. With *Statistical* selected in the *Or select a category* option box, scroll down the *Select a function* list box and then click *COUNTIFS*.
   c. Read the formula description below the function list box and then click OK.

   d. At the Function Arguments dialog box with the insertion point positioned in the *Criteria_range1* text box, type **repshop** and then press Tab. After you press Tab, a *Criteria_range2* text box is added to the dialog box.
   e. With the insertion point positioned in the *Criteria1* text box, type **k10** as the cell reference for JFJ Auto and then press Tab. After you press Tab, a *Criteria2* text box is added to the dialog box.
   f. With the insertion point positioned in the *Criteria_range2* text box, type **claimest** and then press Tab. After you press Tab, a *Criteria_range3* text box is added to the dialog box.
   g. With the insertion point positioned in the *Criteria2* text box, type **>5000** and then press Tab. When you press Tab, Excel adds quotation marks to the criteria text.
   h. Click OK. Excel returns the value *5* in cell L10.

3. Look at the formula in the Formula bar created by the Function Arguments dialog box: =COUNTIFS(RepShop,K10,ClaimEst,">5000").
4. Enter the following COUNTIFS formula in cell L13 by using the Insert Function dialog box or by typing the formula directly into the cell:
   =countifs(repshop,k13,rating,">3")
5. Save **EL2-C2-P1-ACOct15VehRpt.xlsx**.

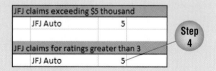

Create an
AVERAGEIF Formula
1. Make desired cell active.
2. Click Insert Function button.
3. Change category to *Statistical*.
4. Select *AVERAGEIF*.
5. Click OK.
6. Enter range address or range name to select by in *Range* text box.
7. Enter condition expression or text in *Criteria* text box.
8. Enter range address or range name to average in *Average_ range* text box.
9. Click OK.

Create an
AVERAGEIFS
Formula
1. Make desired cell active.
2. Click Insert Function button.
3. Change category to *Statistical*.
4. Select *AVERAGEIFS*.
5. Click OK.
6. Enter range address or range name to average in *Average_ range* text box.
7. Enter range address or range name to select by in *Criteria_ range1* text box.
8. Enter condition expression or text in *Criteria1* text box.
9. Enter range address or range name to select by in *Criteria_ range2* text box.
10. Enter condition expression or text in *Criteria2* text box.
11. Continue adding criteria range expressions and criteria as needed.
12. Click OK.

Using the AVERAGEIF and AVERAGEIFS Functions

The AVERAGEIF function is used to find the arithmetic mean of the cells within a specified range that meet a single criterion. The structure of an AVERAGEIF function is *=AVERAGEIF(range,criteria,average_range)*, where *range* is the cells to be tested for the criterion, *criteria* is the conditional statement used to select cells, and *average_range* is the range containing the values you want to average. The AVERAGEIFS function is used to average cells that meet multiple criteria using the formula *=AVERAGEIFS(average_range,criteria_range1,criteria1,criteria_ range2,criteria2. . .)*.

Figure 2.3 illustrates an executive management salary report for a hospital. Below the salary data, average salary statistics are shown. In the first two rows of salary statistics, the average total salary is calculated for each of two hospital campuses. In the second two rows of salary statistics, the average total salary is calculated for each campus for those executives hired before 2013. The formulas shown in Figure 2.3 include range names for which *Year* references the values in column E, *Campus* references the entries in column F, and *Total* references the values in column I.

Figure 2.3 AVERAGEIF and AVERAGEIFS Formulas

	A	B	C	D	E	F	G	H	I
1				**Columbia River General Hospital**					
2				Executive Management Salary Report					
3				For the fiscal year 2014-2015					
4				Job Title	Year Hired	Campus	Salary	Benefits	Total
5	Ms.	Michelle	Tan	Chief Executive Officer	2001	Sunnyside	$ 155,000	$ 18,400	$ 173,400
6	Mr.	Douglas	Brown	Legal Counsel	2011	Sunnyside	90,500	17,500	108,000
7	Mrs.	Lauren	Quandt	Chief Financial Officer	2014	Portland	110,750	18,400	129,150
8	Dr.	Dana	Pembroke	Medical Director	2005	Portland	101,500	14,650	116,150
9	Mrs.	Gina	Wright	Director of Nursing	2010	Portland	95,475	14,650	110,125
10	Mr.	Fernando	Ortiega	Director of Patient Care Services	2011	Sunnyside	87,750	12,675	100,425
11	Mr.	Joshua	Vitello	Director of Facilities	2008	Sunnyside	85,000	9,275	94,275
12	Miss	Carin	Ledicke	Director of Human Resources	2006	Portland	85,000	9,275	94,275
13	Mr.	William	Formet	Director of Planning	2004	Portland	85,000	9,275	94,275
14	Mr.	Paul	Unraue	Director, Community Relations	1998	Sunnyside	72,500	8,975	81,475
15									
16							$ 968,475	$133,075	$1,101,550
17									
18				Salary Statistics					
19				Average executive total salary at Portland campus			$ 108,795		
20				Average executive total salary at Sunnyside campus			$ 111,515		
21									
22				Average executive total salary at Portland campus hired before 2013			$ 103,706		
23				Average executive total salary at Sunnyside campus hired before 2013			$ 111,515		

Formula
=AVERAGEIFS(Total,Campus,"Sunnyside",Year,"<2013")

Formula
=AVERAGEIF(Campus,"Portland",Total)

1. With **EL2-C2-P1-ACOct15VehRpt.xlsx** open, make cell M16 active.
2. Create an AVERAGEIF function to calculate the average claim estimate for those claims with a rating of 1 by completing the following steps:
   a. Click the Insert Function button in the Formula bar.
   b. With *Statistical* selected in the *Or select a category* option box, click *AVERAGEIF* in the *Select a function* list box.
   c. Read the formula description below the function list box and then click OK.
   d. At the Function Arguments dialog box with the insertion point positioned in the *Range* text box, type rating and then press Tab.
   e. With the insertion point positioned in the *Criteria* text box, type 1 and then press Tab.
   f. With the insertion point positioned in the *Average_range* text box, type claimest.
   g. Click OK. Excel returns the value *2691* in cell M16.

   h. Look at the formula in the Formula bar created by the Function Arguments dialog box:
      =AVERAGEIF(Rating,1,ClaimEst).
3. Apply comma formatting with no places after the decimal point to cell M16.
4. Make cell M17 active, type the formula =averageif(rating,2,claimest), and then press Enter.
5. Apply comma formatting with no places after the decimal point to cell M17.
6. Make cell M17 active and then drag the fill handle down to M18:M20.
7. Edit the formulas in cells M18, M19, and M20 by changing the rating criterion values from *2* to *3*, *4*, and *5*, respectively. When completed, the AVERAGEIF formulas will be as follows:
      M18: =AVERAGEIF(Rating,3,ClaimEst)
      M19: =AVERAGEIF(Rating,4,ClaimEst)
      M20: =AVERAGEIF(Rating,5,ClaimEst)
8. Save **EL2-C2-P1-ACOct15VehRpt.xlsx**.

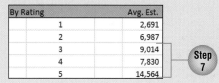

By Rating	Avg. Est.
1	2,691
2	6,987
3	9,014
4	7,830
5	14,564

1. With **EL2-C2-P1-ACOct15VehRpt.xlsx** open, make cell M22 active.
2. Create an AVERAGEIFS function to calculate the average claim estimate for those claims with a rating of 2 and a driver number of 1 by completing the following steps:
   a. Click the Insert Function button in the Formula bar.
   b. With *Statistical* selected in the *Or select a category* option box, click *AVERAGEIFS* in the *Select a function* list box.
   c. Read the formula description and then click OK.

   d. At the Function Arguments dialog box with the insertion point positioned in the *Average_range* text box, type **claimest** and then press Tab.
   e. Type **rating** in the *Criteria_range1* text box and then press Tab.
   f. Type **2** in the *Criteria1* text box and then press Tab.
   g. Type **driverno** in the *Criteria_range2* text box and then press Tab.
   h. Type **1** in the *Criteria2* text box and then click OK. Excel returns the value *6272.667* in the cell.

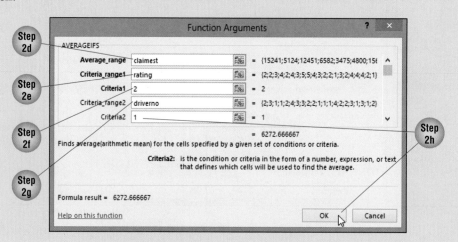

   i. Apply comma formatting with no places after the decimal point to cell M22.
3. Copy the AVERAGEIFS formula in cell M22 and paste it into cell M23.
4. Edit the formula in cell M23 to change the rating criterion from *2* to *3*. When completed, the AVERAGEIFS formula will be *=AVERAGEIFS(ClaimEst,Rating,3,DriverNo,1)*.
5. If necessary, apply comma formatting with no places after the decimal point to cell M23.
6. Save **EL2-C2-P1-ACOct15VehRpt.xlsx**.

Using Math and Trigonometry Functions:
SUMIF and SUMIFS ■■■■■■■■■■■■■■■■■■■■■■■■

Excel provides several math and trigonometry functions, such as ABS to return the absolute value of a number, SQRT to find the square root of a number, and RAND to return a random number between 0 and 1, to name a few. At the Insert Function dialog box, change the *Or select a category* option to *Math & Trig* and scroll down the list of available functions in the category.

Within the category of math and trigonometry functions, Excel includes SUMIF to add the cells within a range that meet a single criterion and SUMIFS to add the cells within a range that meet multiple criteria. The structure of the SUMIF formula is *=SUMIF(range,criteria,sum_range)*, where *range* is the cells to be tested for the criterion, *criteria* is the conditional statement used to select cells, and *sum_range* is the range containing the values to add. The SUMIFS function is used to add cells that meet multiple criteria using the formula *=SUMIFS(sum_range,criteria_range1,criteria1,criteria_range2,criteria2. . .)*.

Figure 2.4 provides an example of how the SUMIF and SUMIFS formulas are used in a medical clinic's standard cost worksheet for examination room supplies. At the right of the clinic supplies inventory, a SUMIF formula sums the cost for items by supplier number. A SUMIFS formula sums the cost by supplier number for items that require a minimum stock quantity of more than four. The formulas shown in Figure 2.4 include the range names *Supplier*, which references the entries in column C; *MinQty*, which references the values in column E; and *StdCost*, which references the values in column F.

▼ **Quick Steps**

Create a SUMIF Formula
1. Make desired cell active.
2. Click FORMULAS tab.
3. Click Math & Trig button.
4. Scroll down and click *SUMIF*.
5. Enter range address or range name to select by in *Range* text box.
6. Enter condition expression or text in *Criteria* text box.
7. Enter range address or range name to add in *Sum_range* text box.
8. Click OK.

Math & Trig

Figure 2.4 SUMIF and SUMIFS Formulas

Formula
=SUMIF(Supplier,"101",StdCost)

	A	B	C	D	E	F	G	H	I
1	North Shore Medical Clinic								
2	Clinic Supplies Inventory Units and Price								
3	Item	Unit	Supplier Number	Price	Minimum Stock Qty	Standard Cost		Exam Room Cost Analysis	
4	Sterile powder-free synthetic gloves, size Small	per 100	101	35.95	4	143.80		Cost by Supplier	
5	Sterile powder-free synthetic gloves, size Mediu	per 100	101	35.95	8	287.60		Supplier Number 101	1,401.40
6	Sterile powder-free synthetic gloves, size Large	per 100	101	35.95	10	359.50		Supplier Number 155	364.33
7	Sterile powder-free latex gloves, size Small	per 100	101	16.25	4	65.00		Supplier Number 201	1,918.00
8	Sterile powder-free latex gloves, size Medium	per 100	101	16.25	8	130.00		Supplier Number 350	790.80
9	Sterile powder-free latex gloves, size Large	per 100	101	16.25	10	162.50			
10	Sterile powder-free vinyl gloves, size Small	per 100	101	11.50	4	46.00			
11	Sterile powder-free vinyl gloves, size Medium	per 100	101	11.50	8	92.00		Cost by Supplier with	
12	Sterile powder-free vinyl gloves, size Large	per 100	101	11.50	10	115.00		Minimum Qty over 4	
13	Disposable earloop mask	per 50	155	5.61	8	44.88		Supplier Number 101	1,146.60
14	Disposable patient gown	per dozen	155	7.90	16	126.40		Supplier Number 155	310.80
15	Disposable patient slippers	per dozen	155	4.27	16	68.32		Supplier Number 201	1,330.00
16	Cotton patient gown	per dozen	201	133.00	10	1,330.00		Supplier Number 350	659.00
17	Cotton patient robe	per dozen	201	147.00	4	588.00			
18	Disposable examination table paper	per roll	155	8.90	8	71.20			
19	Lab coat, size Small	each	350	32.95	4	131.80			
20	Lab coat, size Medium	each	350	32.95	8	263.60			
21	Lab coat, size Large	each	350	32.95	12	395.40			
22	Disposable shoe cover	per 300	155	37.75	1	37.75			
23	Disposable bouffant cap	per 100	155	7.89	2	15.78			
24	TOTAL STANDARD EXAM ROOM SUPPLIES COST:					4,474.53			

Formula
=SUMIFS(StdCost,Supplier,"350",MinQty,">4")

Note: In Step 4, you are directed to save and print the worksheet. Check with your instructor before printing to see if you need to print two copies of the worksheets for the projects in this chapter: one as displayed and another displaying the cell formulas. Save the worksheet before displaying formulas (Ctrl + `) so that you can adjust column widths as necessary and then close without saving the changes.

1. With **EL2-C2-P1-ACOct15VehRpt.xlsx** open, make cell M4 active.
2. Create a SUMIF function to sum the claim estimates for those claims being repaired at A+ Paint & Body by completing the following steps:
   a. Click the FORMULAS tab.
   b. Click the Math & Trig button in the Function Library group.
   c. Scroll down the drop-down list and then click *SUMIF*.
   d. At the Function Arguments dialog box with the insertion point positioned in the *Range* text box, type **repshop** and then press Tab.
   e. Designate cell K4 as the cell reference for JFJ Auto by typing **k4** in the *Criteria* text box. Press Tab.
   f. Type **claimest** in the *Sum_range* text box and then click OK. Excel returns the value *16656* in cell M4.

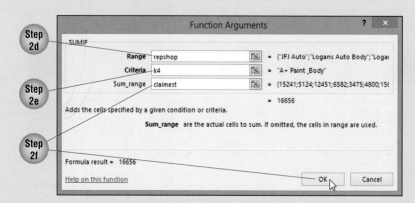

   g. Apply comma formatting with no places after the decimal point to cell M4.
3. Use the fill handle to copy the formula in cell M4 to cells M5 through M7. When completed, the SUMIF formulas will be as follows:
   - M5: =SUMIF(RepShop,K5,ClaimEst)
   - M6: =SUMIF(RepShop,K6,ClaimEst)
   - M7: =SUMIF(RepShop,K7,ClaimEst)
4. Save and then print **EL2-C2-P1-ACOct15VehRpt.xlsx**.

Claim Report Statistics Summary		
By Repair Shop	No. of Claims	Total Estimates
A+ Paint & Body	3	16,656
JFJ Auto	9	66,128
Logans Auto Body	5	51,990
West Collision	4	31,683

Managing Range Names ■■■■■■■■■■■■■■■■■■■■■■

The Name Manager dialog box, which you can open by clicking the Name Manager button in the Defined Names group on the FORMULAS tab, can be used to create, edit, and delete range names. A range name can be edited by changing the name or modifying the range address associated with the name. A range name can also be deleted, but you should use extra caution when doing so. If you delete a range name used in a formula, cells that used that formula will display the error text *#NAME?* You can also use the Name Manager dialog box to add new range names to a worksheet. The Name Manager dialog box is shown in Figure 2.5.

▼ Quick Steps

Delete a Range Name
1. Click FORMULAS tab.
2. Click Name Manager button.
3. Click desired range name.
4. Click Delete button.
5. Click OK.
6. Click Close.

Edit a Range Name
1. Click FORMULAS tab.
2. Click Name Manager button.
3. Click desired range name.
4. Click Edit button.
5. Type new range name in *Name* text box.
6. Click OK.
7. Click Close.

Name Manager

Figure 2.5 Name Manager Dialog Box

| **Project 1g** | **Editing and Deleting a Range Name** | **Part 7 of 7** |

1. With **EL2-C2-P1-ACOct15VehRpt.xlsx** open, click the FORMULAS tab if it is not currently active.
2. Delete the range name *AutoNo* by completing the following steps:
   a. Click the Name Manager button in the Defined Names group.
   b. At the Name Manager dialog box, with *AutoNo* already selected in the *Name* column, click the Delete button.
   c. At the Microsoft Excel message box asking you to confirm the deletion of the name *AutoNo*, click OK.

3. Edit the range name for the range named *ClaimEst* by completing the following steps:
   a. Click *ClaimEst* in the *Name* column at the Name Manager dialog box and then click the Edit button.
   b. At the Edit Name dialog box with *ClaimEst* selected in the *Name* text box, type ClaimEstimate and then click OK. Notice the new range name is now displayed in the *Name* column.
   c. Click the Close button located at the bottom right of the Name Manager dialog box.
4. Click in cell M4 and look at the formula in the Formula bar. Notice that Excel automatically changed the range name in the formula from *ClaimEst* to *ClaimEstimate*.
5. Save and then close **EL2-C2-P1-ACOct15VehRpt.xlsx**.

Project 2 Populate Cells by Looking Up Data 1 Part

You will use a lookup formula to automatically enter discounts for containers and then calculate net prices.

Lookup & Reference

▼ **Quick Steps**

Create a VLOOKUP Formula
1. Make desired cell active.
2. Click FORMULAS tab.
3. Click Lookup & Reference button.
4. Click *VLOOKUP*.
5. Enter cell address, range name, or value in *Lookup_value* text box.
6. Enter range or range name in *Table_array* text box.
7. Type column number to return values from in *Col_index_num* text box.
8. Type false or leave blank for TRUE in *Range_lookup* text box.
9. Click OK.

Using Lookup Functions ■■■■■■■■■■■■■■■■■■■■■■

The Lookup & Reference functions provide formulas that can be used to look up values in a range. For example, in a grades worksheet, the final numerical score for a student can be looked up in a range of cells that contain the letter grades with a corresponding numerical score for each grade. The letter grade can be returned in the formula cell by looking up the student's score. Being able to look up a value automates data entry in large worksheets and, when used properly, can prevent inaccuracies caused by data entry errors.

Excel provides the VLOOKUP and HLOOKUP functions, which refer to vertical and horizontal lookups, respectively. The layout of the lookup range (referred to as a *lookup table*) determines whether to use VLOOKUP or HLOOKUP. VLOOKUP is more commonly used, since most lookup tables are arranged with comparison data in columns (which means Excel searches for the lookup value in a vertical order). HLOOKUP is used when the lookup range contains comparison data in rows (which means Excel searches for the lookup value in a horizontal pattern).

Using the VLOOKUP Function

The structure of a VLOOKUP formula is *=VLOOKUP(lookup_value,table_array,col_index_num,range_lookup)*. Table 2.2 explains each section of the VLOOKUP argument.

Table 2.2 VLOOKUP Argument Parameters

Argument Parameter	Description
lookup_value	This is the value that you want Excel to search for in the lookup table. You can enter a value or cell reference to a value.
table_array	This is the range address or range name for the lookup table that you want Excel to search.
col_index_num	This is the column number from the lookup table that contains the data you want placed in the formula cell.
range_lookup	Enter TRUE to instruct Excel to find an exact or approximate match for the lookup value. If this parameter is left out of the formula, Excel assumes TRUE, which means if an exact match is not found, Excel returns the value for the next largest number that is less than the lookup value. For the formula to work properly, the first column of the lookup table must be sorted in ascending order. Enter FALSE to instruct Excel to return only exact matches to the lookup value.

The VLOOKUP function is easier to understand when explained using an example. In the worksheet shown in Figure 2.6, VLOOKUP is used to return the starting salary for new hires at a medical center. Each new hire is assigned a salary grid number depending on education and years of work experience. This salary grid number determines his or her starting salary. The lookup table contains the grid numbers with the corresponding starting salaries. In column E, VLOOKUP formulas automatically insert the starting salary for each new employee based on his or her grid number in column D. In the formula shown in Figure 2.6, range names have been included, where *Rating* references the values in column D and *grid* represents the lookup table in G4:H8.

Figure 2.6 VLOOKUP Example

The formula in E4 is =VLOOKUP(Rating,grid,2).

The lookup table is named *grid*.

The VLOOKUP formula populates E4:E13 by matching the salary grid rating number in column D with the corresponding salary grid rating number in the lookup table named *grid*.

1. Open **PrecisionPrices.xlsx**.
2. Save the workbook and name it **EL2-C2-P2-PrecisionPrices**.
3. Create a VLOOKUP formula to find the correct discount values for each product by completing the following steps:
   a. Select H4:I8 and name the range *DiscTable*.
   b. Make cell E4 active and then click the FORMULAS tab.
   c. Click the Lookup & Reference button in the Function Library group.
   d. Click *VLOOKUP* at the drop-down list.
   e. If necessary, drag the Function Arguments dialog box out of the way so that you can see the first few rows of the product price list and the discount table data.
   f. With the insertion point positioned in the *Lookup_value* text box, type **c4** and then press Tab. Product discounts are categorized by letter codes. To find the correct discount, you need Excel to look for the matching category letter code for the product within the first column of the discount table. Notice that the letter codes in the discount table are listed in ascending order.
   g. Type **disctable** in the *Table_array* text box and then press Tab. Using a range name for a reference table is a good idea, since the formula will be copied and absolute references are needed for the cells in the lookup table.
   h. Type **2** in the *Col_index_num* text box and then press Tab. You want the discount percentage in column 2 of DiscTable placed in cell E4.
   i. Type **false** in the *Range_lookup* text box and then click OK. By entering *false*, you are instructing Excel to return a value for exact matches only. Should a discount category be typed into a cell in column C for which no entry exists in the discount table, Excel will return *#N/A* in the formula cell, which will alert you that an error has occurred in the data entry.
4. Look at the formula in the Formula bar: *=VLOOKUP(C4,DiscTable,2,FALSE)*.

5. Apply percent formatting to cell E4.
6. Make cell F4 active, type the formula **=d4-(d4*e4)**, and then press Enter.

7. Select E4:F4 and then drag the fill handle down to row 21.
8. Deselect the range.
9. Print the worksheet.
10. Save and then close **EL2-C2-P2-PrecisionPrices.xlsx**.

C	D	E	F	G	H	I
and Packaging						
ducts Price List					**Discount Table**	
Discount Category	**List Price**	**Discount**	**Net Price**		**Discount Category**	**Discount Percent**
A	18.67		10% =d4-(d4*e4)		A	10%
C	22.50				B	12%
B	14.53				C	14%
D	5.25				D	16%
A	18.54				E	20%

Step 6

Using the HLOOKUP Function

The HLOOKUP function uses the same argument parameters as the VLOOKUP function. Use HLOOKUP when the table in which you want to search for a comparison value is arranged horizontally, like the one shown in J3:O4 in Figure 2.7. Excel searches across the table in the first row for a matching value and then returns to the formula cell the value from the same column.

The structure of an HLOOKUP formula is *=HLOOKUP(lookup_value,table_array,row_index_num,range_lookup)*. The argument parameters are similar to the VLOOKUP parameters described in Table 2.2 on page 53. Excel searches the first row of the table for the lookup value. When a match is found, Excel returns the value from the same column in the row number specified in the *row_index_num* argument.

Figure 2.7 HLOOKUP Example

The formula in cell G4 is =HLOOKUP(F4,GradeTable,2).

	A	B	C	D	E	F	G	H	I	J	K	L	M	N	O
1	**Math by Janelle Tutoring Service**														
2	Student Progress Report														
3	**Student Name**	**Test 1**	**Test 2**	**Test 3**	**Test 4**	**Total**	**Grade**		**Score**	0	50	60	70	80	90
4	Dana Rosenthal	51	48	55	50	51.0	D		Grade	F	D	C	B	A	A+
5	Kelsey Williams	75	82	66	72	73.8	B								
6	Hilary Orbet	81	88	79	83	82.8	A								
7	Jose Alvarez	67	72	65	78	70.5	B								
8	Linden Porter	42	51	40	55	47.0	F		The lookup table is						
9	Carl Quenneville	65	44	72	61	60.5	C		named *GradeTable*.						
10	Andrewa Desmond	55	48	60	50	53.3	D								
11	Kylie Winters	78	82	67	71	74.5	B								
12	Lindsay Cortez	82	78	85	88	83.3	A								

The HLOOKUP formula populates G4:G12 by looking up the total value in column F in the first row in the lookup table (GradeTable). The formula stops at the largest value in the table that is less than or equal to the lookup value. For example, looking for *62.3* would cause Excel to stop at *60*.

You will use a financial function to calculate the principal portion of an expansion loan payment for two lenders.

Using Financial Functions: PPMT and IPMT ■■■■■■■■

▼ Quick Steps

Create a PPMT Formula

1. Make desired cell active.
2. Click FORMULAS tab.
3. Click Financial button.
4. Click *PPMT*.
5. Enter value, cell address, or range name for interest rate in *Rate* text box.
6. Enter number representing payment to find principal for in *Per* text box.
7. Enter value, cell address, or range name for total number of payments in *Nper* text box.
8. Enter value, cell address, or range name for amount borrowed in *Pv* text box.
9. Click OK.

Financial functions can be used to perform a variety of financial analyses, including loan amortizations, annuity payments, investment planning, depreciation, and so on. The PMT function is used to calculate a payment for a loan based on a constant interest rate and constant payments for a set period of time. Excel provides two related financial functions: PPMT, to calculate the principal portion of the loan payment; and IPMT, to calculate the interest portion.

Knowing the principal portion of a loan payment is useful in determining the amount of the payment that is being used to reduce the principal balance owed. The difference between the loan payment and PPMT value represents the interest cost. The function returns the principal portion of a specific payment for a loan. For example, you can calculate the principal on the first payment, last payment, or any payment in between. The structure of a PPMT function is $=PPMT(rate,per,nper,pv,fv,type)$, where

- *rate* is the interest rate per period,
- *per* is the period for which you want to find the principal portion of the payment,
- *nper* is the number of payment periods,
- *pv* is the amount of money borrowed,
- *fv* is the balance at the end of the loan (if left blank, 0 is assumed), and
- *type* is either 0 (payment at end of period) or 1 (payment at beginning of period).

Make sure to be consistent with the units for the interest rate and payment periods. If you divide the interest rate by 12 for a monthly rate, make sure the payment period is also expressed monthly. For example, multiply the term by 12 if the amortization is entered in the worksheet in years.

Financial

Project 3 | Calculating Principal Portions of Loan Payments

Part 1 of 1

1. Open **DExpansion.xlsx**.
2. Save the workbook and name it **EL2-C2-P3-DExpansion.xlsx**.
3. Calculate the principal portions of loan payments for two loan proposals to fund a building expansion project by completing the following steps:
   a. Make cell C10 active.
   b. If necessary, click the FORMULAS tab.

c. Click the Financial button in the Function Library group.

d. Scroll down the drop-down list and then click *PPMT*.

e. If necessary, move the Function Arguments dialog box to the right side of the screen so that you can see all of the values in column C.

f. With the insertion point positioned in the *Rate* text box, type c4/12 and then press Tab. Since the interest rate is stated per annum, dividing the rate by 12 calculates the monthly rate.

g. Type 1 in the *Per* text box to calculate principal for the first loan payment and then press Tab.

h. Type c5*12 in the *Nper* text box and then press Tab. Since a loan payment is made each month, the number of payments is 12 times the amortization period.

i. Type c6 in the *Pv* text box and then click OK. *Pv* refers to present value and, in this example, means the loan amount for which the payments are being calculated. It is positive because it represents cash received by the company. Excel returns the value *-1,291.40* in cell C10. Payments are shown as negative numbers because they represent cash that is paid out. In this worksheet, negative numbers have been formatted to display in red and enclosed in parentheses.

4. Copy and paste the formula from cell C10 to cell E10 and then press Esc to remove the scrolling marquee from cell C10.

5. Make cell C12 active, type =c8*12*c5, and then press Enter.

6. Copy and paste the formula from cell C12 to cell E12. Press Esc to remove the scrolling marquee from cell C12 and then AutoFit the width of column E. Notice that the loan from Dominion Trust is a better choice for Deering Industries, assuming the company can afford the higher monthly payments. Although the interest rate is higher than that for the Victory Trust loan, the shorter term means the loan will be repaid faster and at a lesser total cost.

7. Print the worksheet.

8. Save and then close **EL2-C2-P3-DExpansion.xlsx**.

		Victory Trust
4	Interest Rate	8.15%
5	Amortization	20
6	Loan Amount	$ 775,000
7		
8	Monthly Payment	($6,554.95)
9		
10	Monthly Principal Payment (1st payment)	($1,291.40)
11		
12	Total Loan Payments	=c8*12*c5

Step 5

Project 4 — Calculate Benefit Costs Using Conditional Logic   2 Parts

You will create formulas to calculate the employee benefit costs for ViewItVideo using logical functions to test multiple conditions.

Using Logical Functions ■■■■■■■■■■■■■■■■■■■■■■■■■

▼ Quick Steps

Create an IF Formula
1. Make desired cell active.
2. Click FORMULAS tab.
3. Click Logical button.
4. Click IF.
5. Type conditional test argument in *Logical_test* text box.
6. Press Tab.
7. Type argument in *Value_if_true* text box.
8. Press Tab.
9. Type argument in *Value_if_false* text box.
10. Click OK.

Logical

If you type a nested IF function directly into a cell, Excel color-codes the parentheses for each IF function so you can keep track of each IF function separately.

The number of right parentheses needed to end a nested IF statement equals the number of times IF appears in the formula.

Using conditional logic in a formula requires Excel to perform a calculation based on the outcome of a logical or conditional test. One calculation is performed if the test proves true and another calculation is performed if the test proves false. For example, the following is an IF formula using named ranges that could be used to calculate a salesperson's bonus if his or her sales exceed a target: *=IF(Sales>Target,Bonus,0)*. Excel first tests the value in the cell named *Sales* to see if the value is greater than the value in the cell named *Target*. If the condition proves true, Excel returns the value of the bonus in the cell named *Bonus;* if the sales are not greater than the target, the condition proves false and Excel places a *0* in the cell. The structure of the IF statement is *=IF(logical_test,value_if_true,value_if_false)*.

Creating Nested Functions

If you need Excel to perform more than two actions, create a nested IF function. A nested IF function is one IF function inside of another. The structure of a nested IF statement is *=IF(logical_test,value_if_true,IF(logical_test,value_if_true,value_if_false))*. Excel evaluates the first *logical_test*. If the answer is true, then depending on what is entered for the *value_if_true*, a calculation is performed, text or numbers are entered, or if the *value_if_true* is omitted, a 0 is entered. If the first *logical_test* is not true, then the next *logical_test* is evaluated and if the answer is true, the *value_if_true* is placed in the cell. Excel stops evaluating the formula once the *logical_test* has been answered as true. If the answer is never true, then depending on what is entered as the *value_if_false,* a calculation is performed, text or numbers are entered, or if the *value_if_false* is omitted, a 0 is entered.

For example, assume that a company has three sales commission rates based on the level of sales achieved by the salesperson. If sales are less than $40,000, the salesperson earns a 5% commission; if sales are greater than or equal to $40,000 but less than $80,000, the salesperson earns a 7% commission; and if sales are greater than or equal to $80,000, the salesperson earns a 9% commission. Since there are three possible sales commission rates, a single IF function will not work. To correctly calculate the sales commission rate, two conditional tests must be done. The last level (or in this case, the third commission rate of 9%) is used for the *value_if_false*.

Consider the following formula: *=IF(Sales<40000,Sales*5%,IF(Sales< 80000,Sales*7%,Sales*9%))*. This formula includes two IF functions. In the first IF function, the conditional test is to determine if the sales value is less than $40,000 (*Sales<40000*). If the test proves true (for example, sales are $25,000), then Excel calculates the sales times 5% and returns the result in the active cell. If the test is not true, then Excel reads the next section of the argument, which is the next IF function that includes the conditional test to determine if sales are less than $80,000 (*Sales<80000*). If this second conditional test proves true, then Excel calculates the sales times 7%. If the test proves false, Excel calculates the sales times 9%. Since these are the only three possible actions, the formula ends. While up to 64 IF functions can be nested, doing that would be a very complex formula. Consider using a VLOOKUP or HLOOKUP to test different conditions.

You can nest any function inside another function. For example, in the PPMT formula you learned in the previous section, Excel returns a negative value for the principal portion of the payment. You can nest the PPMT formula inside the ABS formula to have the principal payment displayed without a negative symbol. ABS is the function used to return the absolute value of a number (that is, the number without its sign). For example, *=ABS(PPMT(C4/12,1,C5*12,C6))* displays the payment calculated in Project 3 as $1,291.40 instead of -$1,291.40.

Using the AND and OR Functions

Other logical functions offered in Excel include AND and OR. These functions use Boolean logic to construct a conditional test in a formula. Table 2.3 describes how each function works to test a statement and also provides an example of each function.

Table 2.3 AND and OR Logical Functions

Logical Function	Description	Example
AND	Excel returns *True* if all of the conditions test true. Excel returns *False* if any one of the conditions tests false.	*=AND(Sales>Target,NewClients>5)* Returns *True* if both test true. Returns *False* if Sales is greater than Target but NewClients is less than 5. Returns *False* if Sales is less than Target but NewClients is greater than 5.
OR	Excel returns *True* if any of the conditions test true. Excel returns *False* if all of the conditions test false.	*=OR(Sales>Target,NewClients>5)* Returns *True* if Sales is greater than Target or NewClients is greater than 5. Returns *False* only if Sales is not greater than Target and NewClients is not greater than 5.

Project 4a   Calculating Pension Costs Using Nested IF and AND Functions   Part 1 of 2

1. Open **VIVSalCost.xlsx**.
2. Save the workbook and name it **EL2-C2-P4-VIVSalCost**.
3. ViewItVideo contributes 5% of an employee's salary into a privately managed company retirement account if the employee works full time and earns more than $45,000 a year in salary. Calculate the pension benefit costs for eligible employees by completing the following steps:
   a. Make cell H6 the active cell.
   b. Click the FORMULAS tab.

c. Click the Logical button in the Function Library group and then click *IF* at the drop-down list.

d. If necessary, drag the Function Arguments dialog box down until you can see all of row 6 in the worksheet.

e. With the insertion point positioned in the *Logical_test* text box, type `and(c6="FT",g6>45000)` and then press Tab. An AND function is required, since both conditions must be true for the company to contribute to the pension plan. ***Note: Excel requires quotation marks around text when it is used in a conditional test formula.***

f. Type `g6*5%` in the *Value_if_true* text box and then press Tab.

g. Type `0` in the *Value_if_false* text box and then click OK.

h. Look at the formula *=IF(AND(C6="FT",G6>45000),G6*5%,0)* in the Formula bar. Notice the AND function is nested within the IF function. Since both conditions for the first employee tested true, the pension cost is calculated.

i. Copy the formula in cell H6 to H7:H14. Notice that only the first three employees have pension benefit values. This is because they are the only employees who both work full time and earn over $45,000 a year in salary.

4. Save **EL2-C2-P4-VIVSalCost.xlsx**.

BENEFIT COSTS	
Pension	Health
3,250.00	
2,575.00	
2,625.00	
-	
-	
-	
-	
-	
8,450.00	-

Step 3i

Project 4b   **Calculating Health and Dental Costs Using Nested IF and OR Functions**   **Part 2 of 2**

1. With **EL2-C2-P4-VIVSalCost.xlsx** open, make cell I6 the active cell.

2. ViewItVideo offers to pay the annual health premiums for employees not covered by any other medical plan. The company pays $2,100 per year per employee for family coverage, $1,380 per year per employee for single coverage, and $0 per year if the employee declines coverage. Calculate the cost for each employee who opted into the health plan by completing the following steps:

a. This formula requires a nested IF statement, since the result will be *$2,180, $1,380,* or *0* depending on the contents of cell D6. (An OR statement will not work for this formula, since two different health premiums are used.) Type the formula shown below in cell I6 and then press Enter. ***Note: Recall that Excel requires the use of quotation marks around text entries within an IF function.*** `=if(d6="Family",2100,if(d6="Single",1380,0))`

BENEFIT COSTS			Total	Salary +
Pension	Health	Dental	Benefits	Benefits
3,250.00	=if(d6="Family",2100,if(d6="Single",1380,0))			
2,575.00			2,575.00	54,075.00

Step 2a

b. Copy the formula in cell I6 to I7:I14. Notice the cells in column I for which no value is entered. In column D in the corresponding row, the text *Declined* displays. Excel returned a value of 0 in column I since conditions *D6="Family"* and *D6="Single"* both proved false.

3. ViewItVideo negotiated a flat fee with its dental benefit service provider. The company pays $1,500 per year for each employee, regardless of the type of coverage. The service provider requires ViewItVideo to report each person's coverage as *Family* or *Single* for audit purposes. The dental plan is optional and some employees have declined the coverage. Calculate the cost of the dental plan by completing the following steps:

a. Make cell J6 the active cell.

b. If necessary, click the FORMULAS tab.

c. Click the Logical button and then click *IF* at the drop-down list.

d. If necessary, drag the Function Arguments dialog box down until you can see all of row 6 in the worksheet.

e. With the insertion point positioned in the *Logical_test* text box, type or(e6="Family",e6="Single") and then press Tab. An OR function is suited to this benefit, since either condition can be true for the company to contribute to the dental plan.

f. Type 1500 in the *Value_if_true* text box and then press Tab.

g. Type 0 in the *Value_if_false* text box and then click OK.

h. Look at the formula *=IF(OR(E6="Family", E6="Single"),1500,0)* in the Formula bar. Notice that the OR function is nested within the IF function. Since cell E6 contains neither *Family* nor *Single*, the OR statement tests false and *0* is returned in cell J6.

i. Copy the formula in cell J6 to J7:J14.

4. Save **EL2-C2-P4-VIVSalCost.xlsx**.

5. Print and then close **EL2-C2-P4-VIVSalCost.xlsx**.

BENEFIT COSTS			Total	Salary +
Pension	Health	Dental	Benefits	Benefits
3,250.00	2,100.00	-	5,350.00	70,350.00
2,575.00	1,380.00	1,500.00	5,455.00	56,955.00
2,625.00	-	-	2,625.00	55,125.00
-	2,100.00	1,500.00	3,600.00	31,100.00
-	1,380.00	1,500.00	2,880.00	47,880.00
-	2,100.00	-	2,100.00	24,600.00
-	1,380.00	-	1,380.00	29,880.00
-	-	-	-	42,500.00
-	-	1,500.00	1,500.00	42,000.00
8,450.00	10,440.00	6,000.00	24,890.00	400,390.00

In this chapter, you learned how to use a small sampling of functions from the statistical, math and trigonometry, lookup, financial, and logical categories. Excel provides more than 300 functions in 13 categories. When you need to enter a complex formula and are not sure if Excel includes a preprogrammed function, open the Insert Function dialog box, type a description of the function in the *Search for a function* text box, and then click the Go button.

Chapter Summary

- Assign names to cells or ranges to reference in formulas or navigation.

- Using range names in formulas makes it easier to understand the formulas.

- Create a range name by selecting the source range and then typing a name in the Name box.

- The COUNTA statistical function counts cells that are not blank.. Use the function to count cells containing text and a combination of text and numbers.

- The COUNTIF statistical function counts cells within a range based on a single criterion.

- The COUNTIFS statistical function counts cells within a range based on multiple criteria.

- Find the arithmetic mean of a range of cells based on a single criterion using the statistical AVERAGEIF function.

- The AVERAGEIFS statistical function finds the arithmetic mean for a range based on multiple criteria.

- The math function SUMIF adds cells within a range based on a single criterion.

- To add cells within a range based on multiple criteria, use the SUMIFS math function.

- Open the Name Manager dialog box to create, edit, or delete a range name or edit the cells that a range name references.

- The Lookup & Reference functions VLOOKUP and HLOOKUP look up data in a reference table and return in the formula cell a value from a column or row in the lookup table.

- The PPMT financial function returns the principal portion of a specified loan payment within the term based on an interest rate, total number of payments, and loan amount.

- Conditional logic in a formula performs a calculation based on the outcome of a conditional test, in which one action is performed if the test proves true and another action is performed if the test proves false.

- A nested function is one function inside another function.

- Use the AND logical function to test multiple conditions. Excel returns *TRUE* if all of the conditions test true and *FALSE* if any of the conditions test false.

- The OR logical function also tests multiple conditions. The function returns *TRUE* if any of the conditions tests true and *FALSE* if all of the conditions test false.

Commands Review

FEATURE	RIBBON TAB, GROUP	BUTTON	KEYBOARD SHORTCUT
financial functions	FORMULAS, Function Library		
Insert Function dialog box	FORMULAS, Function Library	fx	Shift + F3
logical functions	FORMULAS, Function Library		
lookup and reference functions	FORMULAS, Function Library		
math and trigonometry functions	FORMULAS, Function Library		
Name Manager dialog box	FORMULAS, Defined Names		Ctrl + F3
statistical functions accessed from More Functions button	FORMULAS, Function Library		

Concepts Check   Test Your Knowledge

Completion: In the space provided at the right, indicate the correct term, command, or number.

1. Assign a name to a selected range by typing the desired name in this box.

2. A range name can be a combination of letters, numbers, underscore characters, and this punctuation character.

3. Use this function to count cells that contain text or a combination of text and numbers.

4. Write the COUNTIF function that will count the number of cells in a range named *Sales* in which the values are greater than $50,000.

5. Use this statistical function to find the mean of a range based on two criteria.

6. SUMIF is found in this category of functions.

7. Open this dialog box to delete a range name.

8. Use this lookup function to locate a value in a reference table in which the comparison data is arranged in rows.

9. This financial function returns the principal portion of a specified loan payment. _____

10. Access the IF function from this button in the Function Library group on the FORMULAS tab. _____

11. This term refers to a formula in which one function is created inside another function. _____

12. Excel's AND and OR functions use this type of logic to construct conditional tests. _____

Skills Check   Assess Your Performance

Assessment

1   CREATE RANGE NAMES AND USE THE LOOKUP FUNCTION

Note: If you submit your work in hard copy, check with your instructor before printing assessments to see if you need to print two copies: one with numbers displayed and another with cell formulas displayed.

1. Open **RSROctLabor.xlsx**.
2. Save the workbook and name it **EL2-C2-A1-RSROctLabor**.
3. Create the following range names:

F7:F22	*LaborCost*
I3:J5	*RateChart*

4. Change the range name for the range named *Hr* to *Hours*.
5. In cell E7, create a VLOOKUP formula to return the correct hourly rate based on the technician code in cell D7. Use the range name *RateChart* within the formula to reference the hourly rate chart. Make sure Excel will return values for exact matches only.
6. Create or copy the following formulas:
   a. Copy the VLOOKUP formula in cell E7 and paste it into E8:E22.
   b. In cell F7, multiply the named range *Hours* by the hourly rate in cell E7.
   c. Copy the formula in cell F7 and paste it into F8:F22.
   d. Create the formula in cell F23 to sum the column.
7. Preview and then print the worksheet.
8. Save and then close **EL2-C2-A1-RSROctLabor.xlsx**.

Assessment

2   USE CONDITIONAL STATISTICAL AND MATH FUNCTIONS

Note: For all functions in Assessment 2 with the exception of Step 3, use range names in the formulas to reference sources.

1. Open **EL2-C2-A1-RSROctLabor.xlsx**.
2. Save the workbook and name it **EL2-C2-A2-RSROctLabor**.

3. In cell I23, create a COUNTA formula to count the number of calls made in October using the dates in column A as the source range.
4. Using the range named *TechCode*, create COUNTIF formulas in the cells indicated below:
     I9:   Count the number of calls made by technician 1.
     I10:   Count the number of calls made by technician 2.
     I11:   Count the number of calls made by technician 3.
5. Using range names where possible, in cell I14, create a COUNTIFS formula to count the number of calls made by technician 3 for which the hours logged were greater than three.
6. Using the ranges named *TechCode* and *LaborCost*, create SUMIF formulas in the cells indicated below:
     J9:   Add the labor cost for calls made by technician 1.
     J10:   Add the labor cost for calls made by technician 2.
     J11:   Add the labor cost for calls made by technician 3.
7. Using the ranges named *TechCode*, *LaborCost*, and *Hours*, create a SUMIFS formula in cell J14 to add the labor cost for calls made by technician 3 (criteria 1) in which the hours logged were greater than three (criteria 2).
8. Using the named ranges *TechCode* and *LaborCost*, create AVERAGEIF formulas in the cells indicated below:
     J18:   Average the labor cost for calls made by technician 1.
     J19:   Average the labor cost for calls made by technician 2.
     J20:   Average the labor cost for calls made by technician 3.
9. Apply comma formatting to the following cells:
     J9:J11
     J14
     J18:J20
10. Save, print, and then close **EL2-C2-A2-RSROctLabor.xlsx**.

Assessment

3 USE THE FINANCIAL FUNCTIONS PMT AND PPMT

1. Open **PrecisionWarehouse.xlsx**.
2. Save the workbook and name it **EL2-C2-A3-PrecisionWarehouse.xlsx**.
3. Using cell references, create a PMT formula in cell D8 to calculate the monthly loan payment for a proposed loan from NewVentures Capital Inc. *Note: The PMT payment uses the same arguments as PPMT with the exception that there is no **Per** criterion. Remember to divide the rate by 12 and multiply the nper by 12 to use monthly units.*
4. Using cell references, find the principal portion of the loan payment for the first loan payment in cell D10 and the last loan payment in cell D11 using PPMT formulas.
5. In cell D13, create a formula to calculate the total cost of the loan by multiplying the monthly loan payment times the amortization period in years times 12.
6. Print the worksheet.
7. Save and then close **EL2-C2-A3-PrecisionWarehouse.xlsx**.

Assessment

4 USE LOGICAL FUNCTIONS

1. Open **ACPremiumReview.xlsx**.
2. Save the workbook and name it **EL2-C2-A4-ACPremiumReview.xlsx**.
3. Create the following range names:

B4:B23	*Claims*
C4:C23	*AtFault*
D4:D23	*Rating*
E4:E23	*Deductible*

4. Using the named ranges created in Step 3, create a formula in cell G4 to display the text *Yes* if the number of at-fault claims is greater than one and the current rating is greater than two. Both conditions must test true to display *Yes*; otherwise, display *No* in the cell. ***Hint: Use a nested IF and AND formula.***
5. Using the named ranges created in Step 3, create a formula in cell H4 to display the text *Yes* in the cell if either the number of claims is greater than two or the current deductible is less than $1,000.00; otherwise, display *No* in the cell. ***Hint: Use a nested IF and OR formula.***
6. Center the results in cells G4 and H4 and then copy the formulas to G5:G23 and H5:H23, respectively. Deselect the range after copying.
7. Save, print, and then close **EL2-C2-A4-ACPremiumReview.xlsx**.

Assessment

5 USE THE HLOOKUP FUNCTION

1. Open **JTutorProgressRpt.xlsx**.
2. Save the workbook and name it **EL2-C2-A5-JTutorProgressRpt**.
3. Make ProgressComments the active worksheet and review the layout of the lookup table. Notice that the data is organized in rows, with the scores in row 1 and the grade comments in row 2.
4. Select A1:G2 and type GradeTable as the range name.
5. Deselect the range and then make StudentProgress the active worksheet.
6. Create a formula in cell G4 that will look up the student's total score in the range named *GradeTable* and return the appropriate progress comment.
7. Copy the formula in cell G4 and paste it to G5:G12. Deselect the range.
8. Save, print, and then close **EL2-C2-A5-JTutorProgressRpt.xlsx**.

Visual Benchmark   Demonstrate Your Proficiency

1 USE LOOKUP, STATISTICAL, AND MATH FUNCTIONS IN A BILLING SUMMARY

1. Open **BillHrsOct5to9.xlsx**.
2. Save the workbook and name it **EL2-C2-VB1-BillHrsOct5to9**.
3. Review the worksheet shown in Figure 2.8. The gray shaded cells require formulas to complete the worksheet. Use the following information to create the required formulas. Create range names to use in all of the formulas so that the reader can easily interpret the formula:

   * In column F, create a formula to look up the attorney's hourly rate from the table located at the bottom right of the worksheet.

   * In column G, calculate the legal fees billed by multiplying the billable hours times the hourly rate.

   * In J6:J9, calculate the total legal fees billed by attorney.

   * In J13:J16, calculate the average hours billed by attorney.

4. Save, print, and then close **EL2-C2-VB1-BillHrsOct5to9.xlsx**.

Figure 2.8   Visual Benchmark 1

	A	B	C	D	E	F	G	H	I	J
1					**O'DONOVAN & SULLIVAN LAW ASSOCIATES**					
2					**BILLING SUMMARY**					
3					OCTOBER 5 TO 9, 2015					
4	**File**	**Client**	**Date**	**Attorney Code**	**Billable Hours**	**Hourly Rate**	**Legal Fees**		**Billing Statistics**	
5	FL-325	10104	10/5/2015	1	26.75	85.00	2,273.75	**Total Legal Fees Billed by Attorney**		
6	EP-652	10106	10/5/2015	1	12.10	85.00	1,028.50	1	Marty O'Donovan	$ 5,342.25
7	CL-412	10125	10/5/2015	2	33.25	75.00	2,493.75	2	Toni Sullivan	$ 8,062.50
8	IN-745	10210	10/6/2015	3	24.25	100.00	2,425.00	3	Rosa Martinez	$ 15,306.00
9	EL-632	10225	10/6/2015	3	12.11	100.00	1,211.00	4	Kyle Williams	$ 7,087.50
10	RE-475	10285	10/6/2015	4	42.30	90.00	3,807.00		**TOTAL**	$ 35,798.25
11	CL-501	10341	10/7/2015	2	15.25	75.00	1,143.75			
12	CL-521	10334	10/7/2015	2	20.25	75.00	1,518.75	**Average Billable Hours by Attorney**		
13	PL-348	10420	10/7/2015	3	25.00	100.00	2,500.00	1	Marty O'Donovan	$ 1,780.75
14	RE-492	10425	10/7/2015	4	22.70	90.00	2,043.00	2	Toni Sullivan	$ 1,612.50
15	EL-632	10225	10/8/2015	3	23.00	100.00	2,300.00	3	Rosa Martinez	$ 1,913.25
16	PL-512	10290	10/8/2015	3	16.20	100.00	1,620.00	4	Kyle Williams	$ 2,362.50
17	IN-745	10210	10/8/2015	3	14.50	100.00	1,450.00			
18	FL-385	10278	10/8/2015	1	24.00	85.00	2,040.00		**Attorney Code Table**	
19	CL-412	10125	10/9/2015	2	15.25	75.00	1,143.75	**Code**	**Attorney**	**Hourly Rate**
20	CL-450	10358	10/9/2015	2	23.50	75.00	1,762.50	1	Marty O'Donovan	85.00
21	IN-801	10346	10/9/2015	3	14.25	100.00	1,425.00	2	Toni Sullivan	75.00
22	EP-685	10495	10/9/2015	3	23.75	100.00	2,375.00	3	Rosa Martinez	100.00
23	RE-501	10384	10/9/2015	4	13.75	90.00	1,237.50	4	Kyle Williams	90.00

USE LOOKUP AND LOGICAL FUNCTIONS TO CALCULATE CARDIOLOGY COSTS

1. Open **WPMCCardioCosts.xlsx**.
2. Save the workbook and name it **EL2-C2-VB2-WPMCCardioCosts**.
3. Range names for this worksheet have already been created for you. Spend a few moments reviewing the range names and the cells each name references to become familiar with the worksheet.
4. Review the worksheet shown in Figure 2.9 and complete the worksheet to match the one shown by creating formulas using the following information:
   - In column G, create a formula to look up the surgery fee in the table located at the bottom of the worksheet. Specify in the formula to return results for exact matches only.
   - In column H, insert the aortic or mitral valve cost if the cardiac surgery required a replacement valve; otherwise, place a 0 in the cell. *Hint: The surgery codes for surgeries that include a replacement valve are ART and MRT*.
   - In column I, calculate the postoperative hospital cost by multiplying the number of days the patient was in hospital by the postoperative cost per day.
   - In column J, calculate the total cost as the sum of the surgery fee, valve cost, and postoperative hospital cost.
   - Calculate the total cost for each column in row 22.
5. Format the numbers as shown in Figure 2.9.
6. Save, print, and then close **EL2-C2-VB2-WPMCCardioCosts.xlsx**.

Figure 2.9 Visual Benchmark 2

	A	B	C	D	E	F	G	H	I	J
1					Wellington Park Medical Center					
2					Division of Cardiology					
3					Adult Cardiac Surgery Costs					
4	Month:	October		Surgeon:	Novak					
5	Patient Number	Patient Last Name	Patient First Name	Surgery Code	Days in Hospital		Surgery Fee	Valve Cost	Postoperative Hospital Cost	Total Cost
6	60334124	Wagner	Sara	MRP	7		$ 5,325.00	$ -	$ 6,317.50	$ 11,642.50
7	60334567	Gonzalez	Hector	ARP	10		4,876.00	-	9,025.00	13,901.00
8	60398754	Vezina	Paula	ABP	5		4,820.00	-	4,512.50	9,332.50
9	60347821	Dowling	Jager	MRT	11		6,240.00	775.00	9,927.50	16,942.50
10	60328192	Ashman	Carl	ARP	4		4,876.00	-	3,610.00	8,486.00
11	60321349	Kaiser	Lana	ART	12		6,190.00	775.00	10,830.00	17,795.00
12	60398545	Van Bomm	Emile	ABP	7		4,820.00	-	6,317.50	11,137.50
13	60342548	Youngblood	Frank	ABP	6		4,820.00	-	5,415.00	10,235.00
14	60331569	Lorimar	Hannah	MRT	8		6,240.00	775.00	7,220.00	14,235.00
15	60247859	Peterson	Mark	ART	9		6,190.00	775.00	8,122.50	15,087.50
16	60158642	O'Connor	Terry	ABP	7		4,820.00	-	6,317.50	11,137.50
17	60458962	Jenkins	Esther	MRP	9		5,325.00	-	8,122.50	13,447.50
18	68521245	Norfolk	Leslie	ABP	8		4,820.00	-	7,220.00	12,040.00
19	63552158	Adams-Wiley	Susan	MRT	6		6,240.00	775.00	5,415.00	12,430.00
20	68451278	Estevez	Stefan	ARP	6		4,876.00	-	5,415.00	10,291.00
21										
22	Postoperative hospital cost per day:		$ 902.50		Total Cost:		$ 80,478.00	$ 3,875.00	$ 103,787.50	$ 188,140.50
23	Aortic or mitral valve cost:		$ 775.00							
24										
25		Surgery Code	Surgery Fee	Surgery Procedure						
26		ABP	4,820	Artery Bypass						
27		ARP	4,876	Aortic Valve Repair						
28		ART	6,190	Aortic Valve Replacement						
29		MRP	5,325	Mitral Valve Repair						
30		MRT	6,240	Mitral Valve Replacement						

Case Study   Apply Your Skills

Part 1

Yolanda Robertson of NuTrends Market Research was pleased with your previous work and has requested that you be assigned to assist her with a new client. Yolanda is preparing a marketing plan for a franchise expansion for the owners of Pizza By Mario. The franchise was started in Michigan and has stores in Ohio, Wisconsin, and Iowa. The owners plan to double the number of locations within the next two years by expanding into neighboring states. The owners have provided a confidential franchise sales report to Yolanda in an Excel file named **PBMSales.xlsx**. Yolanda needs your help with Excel to extract some statistics and calculate franchise royalty payments. With this information, Yolanda will develop a franchise communication package for prospective franchisees. Open the workbook and save it as **EL2-C2-CS-P1-PBMSales**. Yolanda has asked for the following statistics:

- A count of the number of stores with sales greater than $500,000
- A count of the number of stores located in Michigan with sales greater than $500,000
- Average sales for the stores in Detroit, Michigan
- Average sales for the Michigan stores established prior to 2004
- Total sales for stores established prior to 2010
- Total sales for the Michigan stores established prior to 2010

Create the above formulas for Yolanda in rows 3 to 16 of columns H and I. Create range names for the data so Yolanda will be able to easily understand the formula when she reviews the worksheet. You determine the layout, labels, and other formats for the statistics section. The royalty rate and fee will be completed in Part 2. Save and print the worksheet.

Part 2

In the marketing package for new prospects, Yolanda plans to include sample sales figures and related franchise royalty payments. Pizza By Mario charges each store a royalty percentage based on its annual sales. As sales increase, the royalty percentage increases. For example, a store that sells $430,000 pays a royalty of 2% of sales, while a store that sells $765,000 pays a royalty of 5% of sales. A royalty rate table is included in the worksheet. Create a range name for the table and then create a lookup formula to insert the correct royalty percentage for each store in column F. Next, create a formula to calculate the dollar amount of the royalty payment based on the store's sales multiplied by the percentage value in column F. Format the royalty percentage and royalty fee columns appropriately. Save the revised workbook and name it **EL2-C2-CS-P2-PBMSales**. Print the worksheet.

Part 3

Use the Help feature to learn about the MEDIAN and STDEV functions. Yolanda would like to calculate further statistics in a separate worksheet. Copy A2:E29 to Sheet2, keeping the source column widths. Using the sales data in column E, calculate the following statistics. (You determine the layout, labels, and other formats.)

- Average sales
- Maximum store sales
- Minimum store sales
- Median store sales
- Standard deviation of the sales data

Create a text box below the statistics and write an explanation in each box to explain what the median and standard deviation numbers mean based on what you learned by researching in Help. Print the worksheet, making sure all of the data fits on one page. Save the revised workbook and name it **EL2-C2-CS-P3-PBMSales**.

Part 4

Choose two states near Michigan, Ohio, Wisconsin, and/or Iowa and find statistics on the Internet that Yolanda can use to prepare a marketing plan for expanding Pizza By Mario into these states. Within each new state, find population and income statistics for two cities. In a new worksheet within the Pizza By Mario franchise workbook, prepare a summary of your research findings. Include the URLs of the sites from which you obtained your data in the worksheet, in case Yolanda wants to explore the links for further details. Print the worksheet, making sure all of the data fits on one page. Save the revised workbook and name it **EL2-C2-CS-P4-PBMSales**. Close the workbook.

MICROSOFT EXCEL

CHAPTER 3

Working with Tables and Data Features

PERFORMANCE OBJECTIVES

Upon successful completion of Chapter 3, you will be able to:

- Create a table in a worksheet
- Expand a table to include new rows and columns
- Add a calculated column in a table
- Format a table by applying table styles and table style options
- Add a *Total* row to a table and formulas to total cells
- Sort and filter a table
- Split contents of a cell into separate columns
- Use Flash Fill
- Remove duplicate records
- Restrict data entry by creating validation criteria
- Convert a table to a normal range
- Create subtotals in groups of related data
- Group and ungroup data

A *table* is a range that can be managed separately from other rows and columns in a worksheet. Data in a table can be sorted, filtered, and totaled as a separate unit. A worksheet can contain more than one table, which allows multiple groups of data to be managed separately within the same workbook. In this chapter, you will learn how to use the table feature to manage a range. You will use tools such as data validation, searching for and removing duplicate records, and converting text to a table. You will also convert a table back to a normal range and use data tools such as grouping related records and calculating subtotals. Model answers for this chapter's projects appear on the following pages.

Excel
EL2C3

Note: Before beginning the projects, copy to your storage medium the EL2C3 subfolder from the EL2 folder on the CD that accompanies this textbook and then make EL2C3 the active folder.

Model Answers

Project 1 Create and Modify a Table

Project 1c, EL2-C3-P1-BillSumOctWk1.xlsx

Project 1d, Step 1d, EL2-C3-P1-BillSumOctWk1.xlsx

Project 1d, Step 4, EL2-C3-P1-BillSumOctWk1.xlsx

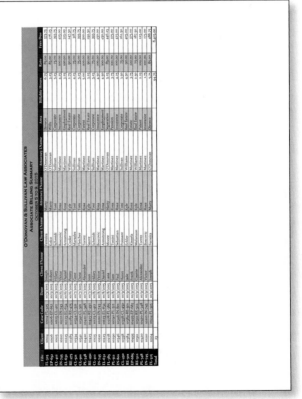

Project 2 Use Data Tools to Split Data and Ensure Data Integrity

Project 2f, EL2-C3-P2-BillSumOctWk1.xlsx

Project 3 Group and Subtotal Related Records

Project 3a, Step 6, EL2-C3-P3-BillSumOctWk1.xlsx

Project 3b, EL2-C3-P3-BillSumOctWk1-Prj3b.xlsx

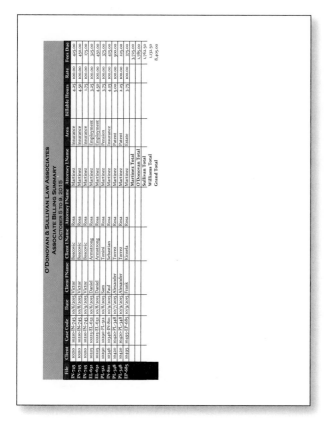

Project 3c, EL2-C3-P3-BillSumOctWk1-Prj3c.xlsx

Project 1 Create and Modify a Table

4 Parts

You will convert data in a billing summary worksheet to a table and then modify the table by applying Table Style options and sorting and filtering the data.

Creating Tables ■■■■■■■■■■■■■■■■■■■■■■■■■

A table in Excel is similar in structure to a database. Columns are called *fields*. Each field is used to store a single unit of information about a person, place, or object. The first row of the table contains column headings and is called the *field names row* or *header row*. Each column heading in the table should be unique. Below the field names, data is entered in rows called *records*. A record contains all of the field values related to one person, place, or object that is the topic of the table. No blank rows exist within the table, as shown in Figure 3.1.

To create a table in Excel, enter the data in the worksheet and then define the range as a table using the Table button in the Tables group on the INSERT tab, the Format as Table button in the Styles group on the HOME tab, or the Table button on the TABLES tab in the Quick Analysis button located at the bottom right of the selected range. Before converting a range to a table, delete any blank rows between the column headings and the data or within the data range.

Figure 3.1 Worksheet with the Range Formatted as a Table

The first row of a table contains field names and is called the *header row*.

Stock No.	Title	Year	Genre	Stock Date	Director	Copies	VHS	DVD	Blu-ray	Category	Cost Price
				ViewItVideo							
				Classic Video Collection							
CV-1001	Abbott & Costello Go to Mars	1953	Comedy	9/4/2010	Charles Lamont	2	Yes	No	No	7-day rental	5.87
CV-1002	Miracle on 34th Street	1947	Family	9/14/2010	George Seaton	8	Yes	No	Yes	2-day rental	7.55
CV-1003	Moby Dick	1956	Action	10/3/2010	John Huston	3	No	Yes	No	7-day rental	8.10
CV-1004	Dial M for Murder	1954	Thriller	10/11/2010	Alfred Hitchcock	5	No	Yes	No	7-day rental	6.54
CV-1005	Breakfast at Tiffany's	1961	Comedy	10/31/2010	Blake Edwards	1	Yes	No	Yes	7-day rental	4.88
CV-1006	Gone with the Wind	1939	Drama	11/28/2010	Victor Fleming	4	Yes	No	Yes	7-day rental	8.22
CV-1007	Doctor Zhivago	1965	Drama	12/7/2010	David Lean	4	Yes	No	Yes	7-day rental	5.63
CV-1008	The Great Escape	1963	War	1/14/2011	John Sturges	3	Yes	No	No	2-day rental	6.15
CV-1009	The Odd Couple	1968	Comedy	2/14/2011	Gene Saks	4	Yes	Yes	No	2-day rental	4.95
CV-1010	The Sound of Music	1965	Musical	3/8/2011	Robert Wise	5	Yes	Yes	Yes	2-day rental	5.12
CV-1011	A Christmas Carol	1951	Family	7/17/2011	Brian Hurst	4	Yes	Yes	Yes	2-day rental	5.88
CV-1012	The Bridge on the River Kwai	1957	War	8/14/2011	David Lean	2	Yes	No	No	2-day rental	6.32
CV-1013	Cool Hand Luke	1967	Drama	10/22/2011	Stuart Rosenberg	5	Yes	Yes	Yes	2-day rental	5.42
CV-1014	Patton	1970	War	12/17/2011	Franklin Schaffner	3	Yes	Yes	Yes	7-day rental	6.84
CV-1015	Blue Hawaii	1961	Musical	1/24/2012	Norman Taurog	1	Yes	No	No	7-day rental	4.52
CV-1016	Psycho	1960	Horror	1/30/2012	Alfred Hitchcock	2	Yes	No	Yes	2-day rental	7.54
CV-1017	The Longest Day	1962	War	2/4/2012	Ken Annakin	5	Yes	Yes	No	7-day rental	6.51
CV-1018	To Kill a Mockingbird	1962	Drama	2/11/2012	Robert Mulligan	2	Yes	No	Yes	2-day rental	8.40
CV-1019	Bonnie and Clyde	1967	Drama	3/14/2013	Arthur Penn	3	Yes	Yes	Yes	2-day rental	8.95
CV-1020	The Maltese Falcon	1941	Drama	11/9/2013	John Huston	1	No	No	Yes	2-day rental	12.15
CV-1007	Doctor Zhivago	1965	Drama	12/7/2010	David Lean	4	Yes	No	Yes	7-day rental	5.63
CV-1022	The Wizard of Oz	1939	Musical	5/2/2014	Victor Fleming	5	Yes	Yes	Yes	7-day rental	9.56
CV-1023	Rear Window	1954	Thriller	8/14/2014	Alfred Hitchcock	3	Yes	Yes	Yes	7-day rental	8.55
CV-1004	Dial M for Murder	1954	Thriller	10/11/2010	Alfred Hitchcock	5	No	Yes	No	7-day rental	6.54
CV-1024	Citizen Kane	1941	Drama	6/9/2015	Orson Welles	2	No	Yes	Yes	2-day rental	9.85
CV-1025	Ben-Hur	1959	History	10/14/2015	William Wyler	1	No	No	Yes	7-day rental	9.85

A row in a table is called a *record*.

A column in a table contains a single unit of information for each record and is called a *field*.

1. Open **BillSumOctWk1.xlsx**.
2. Save the workbook and name it **EL2-C3-P1-BillSumOctWk1**.
3. Convert the billing summary data to a table by completing the following steps:
   a. Select A4:I24.
   b. Click the INSERT tab.
   c. Click the Table button in the Tables group.
   d. At the Create Table dialog box with *=$A$4:$I$24* selected in the *Where is the data for your table?* text box and the *My table has headers* check box selected, click OK.
   e. Deselect the range.
4. Select columns A through I and AutoFit the column widths.
5. Save **EL2-C3-P1-BillSumOctWk1.xlsx**.

Step 3b

Step 3c

Step 3d

Modifying a Table

Once a table has been defined, typing new data in the row immediately below the last row of the table or in the column immediately right of the last column causes the table to automatically expand to include the new entries. Excel displays the AutoCorrect Options button when the table is expanded. Click the button to display a drop-down list with the options *Undo Table AutoExpansion* and *Stop Automatically Expanding Tables*. If you want to add data near a table without having the table expand, leave a blank column or row between the table and the new data.

Typing a formula in the first record of a new table column automatically creates a calculated column. In a calculated column, Excel copies the formula from the first cell to the remaining cells in the column as soon as you enter the formula. The AutoCorrect Options button appears when Excel converts a column to a calculated column. Click the button to display the options *Undo Calculated Column*, *Stop Automatically Creating Calculated Columns*, and *Control AutoCorrect Options*.

▼ **Quick Steps**

Add Rows or Columns to a Table
Type data in first row below table or first column to right of table.

Add a Calculated Column
1. Type formula in first record in column.
2. Press Enter.

1. With **EL2-C3-P1-BillSumOctWk1.xlsx** open, add a new record to the table by completing the following steps:
   a. Make cell A25 active, type RE-522, and then press Enter. Excel automatically expands the table to include the new row and displays the AutoCorrect Options button.
   b. Make cell B25 active and then type the remainder of the record as follows. Press Tab to move from column to column in the table.

Client	10512
Date	10/9/2015
Client Name	Connie Melanson
Attorney FName	Kyle
Attorney LName	Williams

Step 1a

AutoCorrect Options button

	Area	Real Estate
	Billable Hours	2.5

Rate ▼	Fees Due ▼
85.00	573.75
85.00	276.25
75.00	393.75
100.00	425.00
100.00	325.00
90.00	247.50
75.00	393.75
75.00	318.75
100.00	500.00
90.00	292.50
100.00	450.00
100.00	375.00
100.00	450.00
85.00	446.25
75.00	393.75
75.00	393.75
75.00	262.50
100.00	425.00
100.00	375.00
90.00	405.00
75.00	187.50

Step 2a

Step 2b

   c. With cell I25 active, type 75 and then press Enter. (If you press Tab, a new table row will be created.)

2. Add a calculated column to multiply billable hours times rate by completing the following steps:

   a. Make cell J4 active, type **Fees Due**, and then press Enter. Excel automatically expands the table to include the new column.

   b. With cell J5 active, type =h5*i5 and then press Enter. Excel creates a calculated column and copies the formula to the rest of the rows in the table.

   c. Double-click the column J boundary to AutoFit the column.

3. Adjust the centering and fill color of the titles across the top of the table by completing the following steps:

   a. Select A1:J1 and then click the Merge & Center button in the Alignment group on the HOME tab twice.

   b. Select A2:J2 and press F4 to repeat the command to merge and center row 2 across columns A through J.

   c. Select A3:J3 and press F4 to repeat the command to merge and center row 3 across columns A through J.

4. Save **EL2-C3-P1-BillSumOctWk1.xlsx**.

Applying Table Styles and Table Style Options

Quick Steps

Change the Table Style
1. Make table cell active.
2. If necessary, click TABLE TOOLS DESIGN tab.
3. Click desired style in Table Styles gallery.
OR
1. Click More button in Table Styles gallery.
2. Click desired style at drop-down gallery.

Add a *Total* Row
1. Make table cell active.
2. If necessary, click TABLE TOOLS DESIGN tab.
3. Click *Total Row* check box.
4. Click in desired cell in *Total* row.
5. Click down-pointing arrow.
6. Click desired function.

The contextual TABLE TOOLS DESIGN tab, shown in Figure 3.2, contains options for formatting the table. Apply a different visual style to the table using the Table Styles gallery. Excel provides several table styles categorized by Light, Medium, and Dark color themes. By default, Excel bands the rows within the table, which means that even-numbered rows are formatted differently from odd-numbered rows. ***Banding*** rows or columns makes it easier to read data across a row or down a column in a large table. You can remove the banding from the rows and/or add banding to the columns. Use the *First Column* and *Last Column* check boxes in the Table Style Options group to add emphasis to the first or last column in the table by formatting them differently than the rest of the table. The *Header Row* check box is used to show or hide the column headings row in the table. New to Excel 2013, the *Filter Button* check box removes the filter arrows from the header row.

Adding a *Total* row to the table causes Excel to add the word *Total* in the leftmost cell of a new row at the bottom of the table. A Sum function is added automatically to the last numeric column in the table. Click in a cell in the *Total* row to display a down-pointing arrow that you can click to display a pop-up list from which you can select a function formula.

Figure 3.2 TABLE TOOLS DESIGN Tab

Click this check box to add a *Total* row to the table. Once you add the *Total* row, you can choose the function to apply to numeric columns.

Click this check box to show or hide the column headings in the table.

Add emphasis to the first or last column with these check boxes. The formatting depends on the table style in effect.

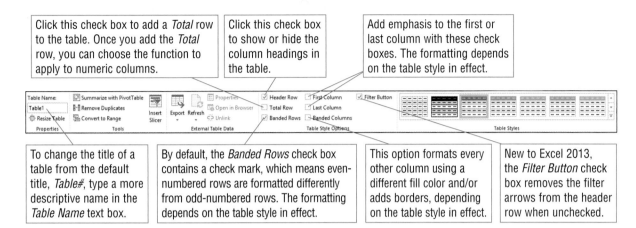

To change the title of a table from the default title, *Table#*, type a more descriptive name in the *Table Name* text box.

By default, the *Banded Rows* check box contains a check mark, which means even-numbered rows are formatted differently from odd-numbered rows. The formatting depends on the table style in effect.

This option formats every other column using a different fill color and/or adds borders, depending on the table style in effect.

New to Excel 2013, the *Filter Button* check box removes the filter arrows from the header row when unchecked.

Project 1c Formatting a Table and Adding a *Total* Row   Part 3 of 4

1. With **EL2-C3-P1-BillSumOctWk1.xlsx** open, change the table style by completing the following steps:

   a. Click any cell within the table to activate the table and the contextual TABLE TOOLS DESIGN tab.

   b. Click the TABLE TOOLS DESIGN tab.

   c. Click the More button in the Table Styles gallery.

   d. Click *Table Style Medium 15* at the drop-down gallery (first column, third row in *Medium* section).

Step 1d

Table Style Medium 15

2. Change the table style options to remove the row banding, insert column banding, and emphasize the first column in the table by completing the following steps:

   a. Click the *Banded Rows* check box in the Table Style Options group on the TABLE TOOLS DESIGN tab to remove the check mark. All of the rows in the table are now formatted the same.

   b. Click the *Banded Columns* check box in the Table Style Options group to insert a check mark. Every other column in the table is now formatted differently.

   c. Click the *First Column* check box in the Table Style Options group to insert a check mark. Notice that the first column has a darker fill color and reverse font color applied.

Step 2c

Step 2a   Step 2b

   d. Click the *Header Row* check box in the Table Style Options group to uncheck the box. Notice that the first row of the table (the row containing the column headings) disappears and is replaced with empty cells. The row is also removed from the table range definition.

e. Click the *Header Row* check box to insert a check mark and redisplay the column headings.

f. Click the *Filter Button* check box to remove the check mark. Notice that the filter arrows disappear from the header row.

g. Click the *Filter Button* check box to insert a check mark and redisplay the filter arrows.

h. Click in the *Table Name* text box, type OctWk1, and then press Enter to define the table title.

3. Add a *Total* row and add function formulas to numeric columns by completing the following steps:

a. Click the *Total Row* check box in the Table Style Options group to add a *Total* row to the bottom of the table. Excel formats row 26 as a *Total* row, adds the label *Total* in cell A26, and automatically creates a Sum function in cell J26.

b. In the *Billable Hours* column, make cell H26 active, click the down-pointing arrow that appears just at the right of the cell, and then click *Sum* at the pop-up list.

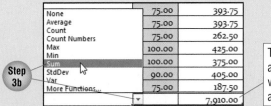

None	75.00	393.75
Average	75.00	393.75
Count		
Count Numbers	75.00	262.50
Max	100.00	425.00
Min		
Sum	100.00	375.00
StdDev	90.00	405.00
Var		
More Functions...	75.00	187.50
		7,910.00

Step 3b

The *Fees Due* column is automatically summed when a *Total* row is added in Step 3a.

c. Make cell B26 active, click the down-pointing arrow that appears, and then click *Count* at the pop-up list.

19	CL-412	None	/8/2015	Hilary Schmidt	Toni	Sullivan	Corporate		5.25	75.00	393.75
20	CL-412	Average	/8/2015	Hilary Schmidt	Toni	Sullivan	Corporate		5.25	75.00	393.75
21	CL-450	Count	/9/2015	Henri Poissant	Toni	Sullivan	Corporate		3.50	75.00	262.50
22	IN-801	Count Numbers / Max	/9/2015	Paul Sebastian	Rosa	Martinez	Insurance		4.25	100.00	425.00
23	EP-685	Min / Sum	/9/2015	Frank Kinsela	Rosa	Martinez	Estate		3.75	100.00	375.00
24	RE-501	StdDev	/9/2015	Jade Eckler	Kyle	Williams	Real Estate		4.50	90.00	405.00
25	RE-522	Var / More Functions...	/9/2015	Connie Melanson	Kyle	Williams	Real Estate		2.50	75.00	187.50
26	Total								90.25		7,910.00

Step 3c

4. Click the PAGE LAYOUT tab and change *Width* to *1 page* in the Scale to Fit group.

5. Preview and then print the worksheet.

6. Save **EL2-C3-P1-BillSumOctWk1.xlsx**.

▼ **Quick Steps**

Sort or Filter a Table
1. Click desired filter arrow.
2. Click desired sort or filter options.
3. Click OK.

Custom Sort a Table
1. Click Sort & Filter button.
2. Click *Custom Sort.*
3. Define sort levels.
4. Click OK.

Sorting and Filtering Tables ▪▪▪▪▪▪▪▪▪▪▪▪▪▪▪▪▪▪▪

By default, Excel displays a filter arrow next to each label in the table header row. Click the filter arrow to display a drop-down list with the same sort and filter options you used in Chapter 1.

1. With **EL2-C3-P1-BillSumOctWk1.xlsx** open, filter
   the table by the attorney's last name to print a list
   of billable hours for O'Donovan by completing the
   following steps:
   a. Click the filter arrow located next to *Attorney LName*
      in cell F4.
   b. Click the *(Select All)* check box to remove the check
      mark.
   c. Click the *O'Donovan* check box to insert a check mark
      and then click OK. The table is filtered to display only
      those records with *O'Donovan* in the *Attorney LName*
      field. The Sum functions in columns H and J reflect
      the totals for the filtered records only.
   d. Print the filtered worksheet.

2. Redisplay all of the records by clicking the *Attorney
   LName* filter arrow and then clicking *Clear Filter From
   "Attorney LName"* at the drop-down list.
3. Use the Sort dialog box to sort the table first by the attorney's last name, then by the area
   of law, and then by the client name by completing the following steps:
   a. With the active cell positioned anywhere within the
      table, click the HOME tab.
   b. Click the Sort & Filter button in the Editing group
      and then click *Custom Sort* at the drop-down list.
   c. At the Sort dialog box, click the down-pointing
      arrow next to the *Sort by* option box in the *Column*
      section and then click *Attorney LName* at the drop-
      down list. The default options for *Sort On* and *Order*
      are correct, since you want to sort by the column
      values in ascending order.

   d. Click the Add Level
      button.
   e. Click the down-pointing
      arrow next to the *Then
      by* option box and then
      click *Area* at the drop-
      down list.
   f. Click the Add Level
      button.
   g. Click the down-pointing
      arrow next to the second
      Then by option box and
      then click *Client Name* at
      the drop-down list.
   h. Click OK.

4. Print the sorted table.
5. Save and then close **EL2-C3-P1-BillSumOctWk1.xlsx**.

Project 2 | Use Data Tools to Split Data and Ensure Data Integrity
6 Parts

You will use Excel's data tools to split the client's first and last names into two separate columns, combine two columns, remove duplicate records, and restrict the type of data that can be entered into a field.

▼ **Quick Steps**

Split Text into Multiple Columns
1. Insert blank column(s) next to source data.
2. Select data to be split.
3. Click DATA tab.
4. Click Text to Columns button.
5. Click Next at first dialog box.
6. Select delimiter check box for character that separates data.
7. Click Next.
8. Click Finish.
9. Deselect range.

Working with Data Tools ■■■■■■■■■■■■■■■■■■■■■■■

The Data Tools group on the DATA tab, shown in Figure 3.3, includes useful features for working with data in tables. A worksheet in which more than one field has been entered into the same column can be separated into multiple columns using the Text to Columns feature. For example, a column that has first and last names in the same cell can be split so that the first name appears in one column and the last name appears in a separate column. Breaking up the data into separate columns better facilitates sorting and other data management tasks.

Before using the Text to Columns feature, insert the number of blank columns you will need to separate the data immediately to the right of the column to be split. Next, select the column to be split and then click the Text to Columns button to start the Convert Text to Columns Wizard. The wizard contains three dialog boxes to guide you through the steps of separating the data.

Figure 3.3 Data Tools Group on the DATA Tab

Text to Columns

Project 2a | Separating Client Names into Two Columns
Part 1 of 6

1. Open **EL2-C3-P1-BillSumOctWk1.xlsx**.
2. Save the workbook and name it **EL2-C3-P2-BillSumOctWk1**.
3. Position the active cell anywhere within the table, click the Sort & Filter button in the Editing group on the HOME tab, and then click *Clear* at the drop-down list to clear the existing sort criteria.
4. Create a custom sort to sort the table first by date (oldest to newest) and then by client (smallest to largest). Refer to Project 1d, Step 3, if you need assistance with this step.
5. Split the client first and last names in column D into two columns by completing the following steps:
   a. Right-click column letter E at the top of the worksheet area and then click *Insert* at the shortcut menu to insert a blank column between the *Client Name* and *Attorney FName* columns in the table.
   b. Select D5:D25.
   c. Click the DATA tab.
   d. Click the Text to Columns button in the Data Tools group.

e. At the Convert Text to Columns Wizard - Step 1 of 3 dialog box, with *Delimited* selected in the *Choose the file type that best describes your data* section, click Next.

f. In the *Delimiters* section of the Convert Text to Columns Wizard - Step 2 of 3 dialog box, click the *Space* check box to insert a check mark and then click Next. The *Data preview* section of the dialog box updates after you click the *Space* check box to show the names split into two columns.

Step 5e

Step 5f

Step 6

Step 7

Client FName	Client LName
Joseph	Ferreira
Robert	Kolcz
Hilary	Schmidt
Victor	Boscovic
Daniel	Armstrong
Penny	Cooke
Gene	Marsales
Dana	Fletcher
Alexander	Torrez
Jean	Sauve
Hilary	Schmidt
Hilary	Schmidt
Victor	Boscovic
Daniel	Armstrong
Lana	Moore
Sam	Tonini
Paul	Sebastian
Henri	Poissant
Jade	Eckler
Frank	Kinsela
Coonie	Melanson

Client first and last names are split into two columns in Steps 5a–5g.

g. Click Finish at the last Convert Text to Columns Wizard dialog box to accept the default General data format for both columns.

h. Deselect the range.

6. Make cell D4 active, change the label to *Client FName*, and then AutoFit the column width.

7. Make cell E4 active, change the label to *Client LName*, and then AutoFit the column width.

8. Save **EL2-C3-P2-BillSumOctWk1.xlsx**.

Populating Data Using Flash Fill

Flash Fill is a new feature added to Excel 2013 that extracts, joins, and inserts text, numbers, dates, and times. This feature is useful for organizing data that has been pasted or imported from other sources. You can join all or extract part of the contents of cells. Flash Fill analyzes adjacent columns while entering data, detects any patterns, and suggests how the rest of the column should be completed.

For example, in Project 2a, instead of using Text to Columns to split the client names into two columns, you could use Flash Fill. To do this, insert two new columns instead of one. Type the first name *Joseph* in column E, as shown in Figure 3.4. Press Enter and then type *R* to start the second name, *Robert*. Excel recognizes that you are taking the first word of the adjacent column D and suggests doing the same for the remaining cells in column E. Notice that the rest

Quick Steps

Extract Data Using Flash Fill
1. Insert blank column(s) next to source data.
2. Type the first record.
3. Press Enter.
4. Start typing second record.
5. When grayed-out text appears, press Enter.

Figure 3.4 Flash Fill for Project 2a

Start typing a cell entry. Once Excel recognizes the pattern, press Enter.

of names are grayed out. Press Enter to accept the suggestion or continue typing to reject the suggestion. Repeat the process for the last name.

In Project 2b, the file and client numbers are joined to create the case code number. A few rows of data may need to be entered before Excel recognizes the pattern. Once the pattern is established, click the Fill button in the Editing Group on the HOME tab and then choose *Flash Fill* from the drop-down menu. You can also click the Flash Fill button in the Data Tools group on the DATA Tab, press Ctrl + E, or press Enter if the grayed-out text appears.

Flash Fill

Another method to join together the content of two or more cells is to use the CONCATENATE function. You can join text, numbers, or cell references. The formula used in Project 2b, =*CONCATENATE(A5,"-",B5)*, joins the case code and the client number together with a dash. In the formula, cell references are separated by commas and any spaces or characters (text, numbers, or symbols) added directly into the formula are enclosed in quotation marks.

Removing Duplicate Records

▼ **Quick Steps**

Remove Duplicate Rows
1. Select range or make cell active in table.
2. Click DATA tab.
3. Click Remove Duplicates button.
4. Select columns to compare.
5. Click OK.
6. Click OK.

Remove Duplicates

Excel can compare records within a worksheet and automatically delete duplicate rows based on the columns you select that might contain duplicate values. When you open the Remove Duplicates dialog box, shown in Figure 3.5, all columns are selected by default. If you do not want Excel to check for duplicates in every column, click the Unselect All button to remove the check marks from all of the columns, click the individual columns you want to compare, and then click OK. When you click OK, Excel automatically deletes rows containing duplicate values and, when the operation is completed, displays a message informing you of the number of rows that were removed from the worksheet or table and the number of unique values that remain.

Consider conditionally formatting duplicate values first to view the records that will be deleted. To do this, use the *Duplicate Values* option, which can be accessed by pointing to *Highlight Cells Rules* at the Conditional Formatting drop-down list. (Display the Conditional Formatting drop-down list by clicking the Conditional Formatting button in the Styles group on the HOME tab.)

Figure 3.5 Remove Duplicates Dialog Box

Choose the columns in which you want Excel to compare data and flag duplicate entries for removal.

Excel includes the Remove Duplicates button in the Data Tools group on the DATA tab and in the Tools group on the TABLE TOOLS DESIGN tab. Click Undo to restore any duplicate rows you remove by mistake.

Project 2b | **Combining Client and File Numbers to Create Case Codes** | **Part 2 of 6**

1. With **EL2-C3-P2-BillSumOctWk1.xlsx** open, combine the information in the *File* and *Client* columns to create the data in the *Case Code* column by completing the following steps:
    a. Insert a column between the *Client* and *Date* columns in the table. Refer to Project 2a, Step 5a, if you need assistance with this step.
    b. Change the column width to 13 characters.
    c. In cell C4, type **Case Code** and then press Enter.
    d. In cell C5, type =concatenate(a5,"-",b5) and then press Enter. (The case code is the file number followed by a dash and then the client number.)
2. After reviewing the data, you decide that the client number should come before the file number in the case code. Delete the column from the table by right-clicking the column letter C at the top of the worksheet area and then clicking *Delete* at the shortcut menu.
3. Combine the client and file information by completing the following steps:
    a. Insert a column between the *Client* and *Date* columns in the table, change the column width to 13 characters, and then type **Case Code** in cell C4. In cell C5, type **10104-FL-325** and then press Enter. (You typed the client number, a dash, and then the file number.)
    b. In cell C6, type 1. Flash Fill recognizes the sequence and suggests how to fill the rest of the column.
    c. Press Enter to accept the suggestions. If Excel does not recognize the pattern right away, continue to type the client number, a dash, and then the file number, or click the Flash Fill button in the Data Tools group on the DATA tab.
4. Save **EL2-C3-P2-BillSumOctWk1.xlsx**.

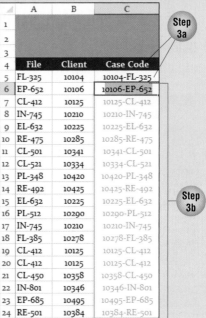

1. With **EL2-C3-P2-BillSumOctWk1.xlsx** open, remove duplicate rows in the billing summary table by completing the following steps:
   a. With the active cell positioned anywhere in the table, click the Remove Duplicates button in the Data Tools group on the DATA tab.
   b. At the Remove Duplicates dialog box with all of the columns selected in the *Columns* list box, click the Unselect All button.
   c. The billing summary table should have only one record per case code per date, since attorneys record once per day the total hours spent on each case. A record is a duplicate if the same values exist in the two columns that store the case code number and date. Click the *Case Code* check box to insert a check mark.
   d. Click the *Date* check box to insert a check mark and then click OK.
   e. Click OK at the Microsoft Excel message box that says a duplicate value was found and removed and 20 unique values remain.
2. Scroll down the worksheet to view the total in cell L25. Compare the total with your printout from Project 1d, Step 4. Notice the total of the fees due is now *7,516.25* compared to *7,910.00* in the printout.
3. Save **EL2-C3-P2-BillSumOctWk1.xlsx**.

Validating and Restricting Data Entry

Data
Validation

▼ **Quick Steps**

Create a Data Validation Rule
1. Select desired range.
2. Click DATA tab.
3. Click Data Validation button.
4. Specify validation criteria in Settings tab.
5. Click Input Message tab.
6. Type input message title and text.
7. Click Error Alert tab.
8. Select error style.
9. Type error alert title and message text.
10. Click OK.

Excel's data validation feature allows you to control the type of data that is accepted for entry in a cell. You can specify the type of data that is allowed, as well as parameters that validate whether the entry is within a certain range of acceptable values, dates, times, or text lengths. You can also set up a list of values that display in a drop-down list when the cell is made active.

To do this, click the Data Validation button in the Data Tools group on the DATA tab. At the Data Validation dialog box, shown in Figure 3.6, begin by choosing the type of data you want to validate in the *Allow* option box on the Settings tab. Additional list or text boxes appear in the dialog box depending on the option chosen in the *Allow* drop-down list.

If a custom number format adds punctuation or text to the appearance of a cell, ignore the added characters when validating or restricting data entry. For example, a cell that contains the number *1234*, has the custom number format *"PD-"####*, and displays as *PD-1234* has a text length equal to 4 characters.

In addition to defining acceptable data entry parameters, you have the option to add an input message and an error alert message to the range. You define the text that appears in these messages.

Figure 3.6 Data Validation Dialog Box with Settings Tab Selected

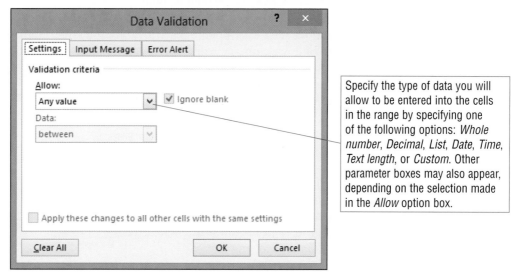

Specify the type of data you will allow to be entered into the cells in the range by specifying one of the following options: *Whole number, Decimal, List, Date, Time, Text length,* or *Custom.* Other parameter boxes may also appear, depending on the selection made in the *Allow* option box.

An input message displays when a cell is made active for which data validation rules apply. This kind of message is informational in nature. An error alert is a message that appears when incorrect data is entered in a cell. Three styles of error alerts are available, and a description and example of each type of alert is provided in Table 3.1. If an error alert message has not been defined, Excel displays the Stop error alert with the default error message *The value you entered is not valid. A user has restricted values that can be entered into this cell.*

Table 3.1 Data Validation Error Alert Message Styles

Error Alert Icon	Error Alert Style	Description	
⊗	Stop	Prevents the data from being entered into the cell. The error alert message box provides three buttons to ensure new data is entered.	Date is outside accepted range — Please enter a date from October 5 to October 9, 2015. [Retry] [Cancel] [Help]
⚠	Warning	Does not prevent the data from being entered into the cell. The error alert message box provides four buttons displayed below the prompt *Continue?*	Check number of hours — The hours you have entered are greater than 8. Continue? [Yes] [No] [Cancel] [Help]
ⓘ	Information	Does not prevent the data from being entered into the cell. The error alert message box provides three buttons displayed below the error message.	Verify hours entered — The hours you have entered are outside the normal range. [OK] [Cancel] [Help] Was this information helpful?

1. With **EL2-C3-P2-BillSumOctWk1.xlsx** open, create a validation rule, input message, and error alert for dates in the billing summary worksheet by completing the following steps:

   a. Select D5:D24.

   b. Click the Data Validation button in the Data Tools group on the DATA tab.

   c. With Settings the active tab in the Data Validation dialog box, click the down-pointing arrow next to the *Allow* option box (currently displays *Any value*) and then click *Date* at the drop-down list. Validation options are dependent on the *Allow* setting. When you choose *Date*, Excel adds *Start date* and *End date* text boxes to the *Validation criteria* section.

   d. With *between* selected in the *Data* option box, click in the *Start date* text box and then type 10/5/2015.

   e. Click in the *End date* text box and then type 10/9/2015. (Since the billing summary worksheet is for the week of October 5 to 9, 2015, entering this validation criteria will ensure that only dates between the start date and end date are accepted.)

   f. Click the Input Message tab.

   g. Click in the *Title* text box and then type Billing Date.

   h. Click in the *Input message* text box and then type This worksheet is for the week of October 5 to October 9 only.

   i. Click the Error Alert tab.

   j. With *Stop* selected in the *Style* option box, click in the *Title* text box and then type Date is outside accepted range.

   k. Click in the *Error message* text box and then type Please enter a date from October 5 to October 9, 2015.

   l. Click OK. Since the range is active for which the data validation rules apply, the input message box appears.

   m. Deselect the range.

2. Add a new record to the table to test the date validation rule by completing the following steps:

   a. Right-click row number 25 and then click *Insert* at the shortcut menu to insert a new row into the table.

   b. Make cell A25 active, type PL-348, and then press Tab.

   c. Type 10420 in the *Client* column and then press Tab.

   d. Type 10420-PL-348 and then press Tab. The input message title and text appear when the *Date* column is made active.

   e. Type 10/10/2015 and then press Tab. Since the date entered is invalid, the error alert message box appears.

f. Click the Retry button.

g. Type 10/9/2015 and then press Tab.

h. Enter the data in the remaining fields as follows (pressing Tab to move from column to column in the table and pressing Enter after the Fees Due calculation is done):

Client FName	Alexander
Client LName	Torrez
Attorney FName	Rosa
Attorney LName	Martinez
Area	Patent
Billable Hours	2.25
Rate	100.00

3. Save **EL2-C3-P2-BillSumOctWk1.xlsx**.

Project 2e | **Restricting Data Entry to Values Within a List** | **Part 5 of 6**

1. With **EL2-C3-P2-BillSumOctWk1.xlsx** open, create a list of values that are allowed in a cell by completing the following steps:

a. Select K5:K25.

b. Click the Data Validation button in the Data Tools group.

c. If necessary, click the Settings tab.

d. Click the down-pointing arrow next to the *Allow* option box and then click *List* at the drop-down list.

e. Click in the *Source* text box and then type 75.00,85.00,90.00,100.00.

f. Click OK.

g. Deselect the range.

2. Add a new record to the table to test the rate validation list by completing the following steps:

a. Right-click row number 26 and then click *Insert* at the shortcut menu to insert a new row in the table.

b. Make cell A26 active and then type data in the fields as follows (pressing Tab to move from column to column in the table):

File	IN-745
Client	10210
Case Code	10210-IN-745
Date	10/9/2015
Client FName	Victor
Client LName	Boscovic
Attorney FName	Rosa
Attorney LName	Martinez
Area	Insurance
Billable Hours	1.75

c. At the *Rate* field, the validation list
becomes active and a down-pointing
arrow appears to the right of the cell.
Type 125.00 and then press Tab to
test the validation rule. Since no error
alert message was entered, the default
message appears.

Step 2d

d. Click the Cancel button. The value
is cleared from the field.

e. Make cell K26 the active cell, click the down-pointing
arrow at the right side of the cell, click *100.00* at the
drop-down list, and then press Tab.

Step 2e

3. Save **EL2-C3-P2-BillSumOctWk1.xlsx**.

Project 2f **Ensuring Data Entered Is a Specified Text Length**   **Part 6 of 6**

1. With **EL2-C3-P2-BillSumOctWk1.xlsx** open, create a validation rule to ensure that all
   client identification numbers are 5 characters in length (to be compatible with the firm's
   accounting system) by completing the following steps:
   a. Select B5:B26 and then click the
      Data Validation button in the Data
      Tools group on the DATA tab.
   b. With the Settings tab active, click
      the down-pointing arrow next to the
      Allow option box and then click *Text
      length* at the drop-down list.
   c. Click the down-pointing arrow next
      to the *Data* option box and then
      click *equal to* at the drop-down list.
   d. Click in the *Length* text box, type 5,
      and then click OK.
   e. Deselect the range.

Step 1b

Step 1c

Step 1d

2. Add a new record to the table to test
   the client identification validation rule
   by completing the following steps:
   a. Right-click row number 27 and then click *Insert* at the shortcut menu.
   b. Make cell A27 active, type FL-325, and then press Tab.
   c. Type 1010411 in cell B27 and then press Tab. Since this value is greater than the
      specified number of characters allowed in the cell, the default error message appears.
   d. Click the Retry button.
   e. Delete the selected text, type 1010, and then press Tab. Since this value is less than
      the specified text length, the default error message appears again. (Using a Text Length
      validation rule ensures that all entries in the range have the same number of characters.
      This rule is useful to validate customer numbers, employee numbers, inventory
      numbers, or any other data that requires a consistent number of characters.)
   f. Click the Cancel button, type 10104, and then press Tab. Since this entry is 5
      characters in length, Excel moves to the next field.

g. Enter the remaining fields as follows:

Case Code	10104-FL-325
Date	10/9/2015
Client FName	Joseph
Client LName	Ferreira
Attorney FName	Marty
Attorney LName	O'Donovan
Area	Divorce
Billable Hours	5.75
Rate	85.00

3. Save, print, and then close **EL2-C3-P2-BillSumOctWk1.xlsx**.

Project ③ Group and Subtotal Related Records   3 Parts

You will convert the billing summary table to a normal range, sort the rows by the attorney names, and then add subtotals to display total fees due, a count of fees, and the average billable hours and fees due for each attorney.

Converting a Table to a Normal Range ■■■■■■■■■■■■■■■

A table can be converted to a normal range using the Convert to Range button in the Tools group on the TABLE TOOLS DESIGN tab. Convert a table to a range to use the Subtotal feature or if you no longer need to treat the table data as a range independent of data in the rest of the worksheet. You may want to remove some or all of the table styles before you convert the table to a range. Use the Clear button in the Table Styles gallery or click the individual options in the Table Style Options group to remove any unwanted formatting.

Subtotaling Related Data ■■■■■■■■■■■■■■■■■■■■■■■■

A range of data with a column that has multiple rows with the same field value can be grouped and subtotals can be created for each group automatically. For example, a worksheet with multiple records with the same department name in a field can be grouped by department name and a subtotal of a numeric field can be calculated for each department. You can choose from a list of functions for the subtotal, such as Average and Sum, and you can also create multiple subtotal values for each group. Before creating subtotals, sort the data by the fields in which you want the records grouped. Make sure no blank rows exist within the range that is to be grouped and subtotaled.

Excel displays a new row with a summary total when the field value for the specified subtotal column changes content. A grand total is also automatically included at the bottom of the range. Excel displays the subtotals with buttons along the left side of the worksheet area used to show or hide the details for each group using the Outline feature. Excel can create an outline with up to eight levels.

Figure 3.7 illustrates the data you will group and subtotal in Project 3a displayed with the worksheet at level 2 of the outline. In Figure 3.8, the same worksheet is shown with two attorney groups expanded to show the detail records.

▼ Quick Steps

Convert a Table to a Range
1. Make table cell active.
2. Click TABLE TOOLS DESIGN tab.
3. Click Convert to Range button.
4. Click Yes.

Create a Subtotal
1. Select range.
2. Click DATA tab.
3. Click Subtotals button.
4. Select field to group by in *At each change in* option box.
5. Select desired function in *Use function* option box.
6. Select field(s) to subtotal in *Add subtotal to* list box.
7. Click OK.
8. Deselect range.

Convert to Range

Figure 3.7 Worksheet with Subtotals by Attorney Last Name Displaying Level 2 of the Outline

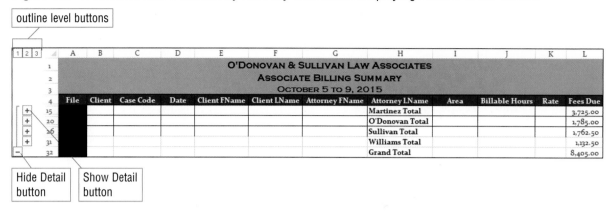

Figure 3.8 Worksheet with Subtotals by Attorney Last Name with Martinez and Sullivan Groups Expanded

	File	Client	Case Code	Date	Client FName	Client LName	Attorney FName	Attorney LName	Area	Billable Hours	Rate	Fees Due
1					O'DONOVAN & SULLIVAN LAW ASSOCIATES							
2					ASSOCIATE BILLING SUMMARY							
3					OCTOBER 5 TO 9, 2015							
4	File	Client	Case Code	Date	Client FName	Client LName	Attorney FName	Attorney LName	Area	Billable Hours	Rate	Fees Due
5	IN-745	10210	10210-IN-745	10/6/2015	Victor	Boscovic	Rosa	Martinez	Insurance	4.25	100.00	425.00
6	IN-745	10210	10210-IN-745	10/8/2015	Victor	Boscovic	Rosa	Martinez	Insurance	4.50	100.00	450.00
7	IN-745	10210	10210-IN-745	10/9/2015	Victor	Boscovic	Rosa	Martinez	Insurance	1.75	100.00	175.00
8	EL-632	10225	10225-EL-632	10/6/2015	Daniel	Armstrong	Rosa	Martinez	Employment	3.25	100.00	325.00
9	EL-632	10225	10225-EL-632	10/8/2015	Daniel	Armstrong	Rosa	Martinez	Employment	4.50	100.00	450.00
10	PL-512	10290	10290-PL-512	10/8/2015	Sam	Tonini	Rosa	Martinez	Pension	3.75	100.00	375.00
11	IN-801	10346	10346-IN-801	10/9/2015	Paul	Sebastian	Rosa	Martinez	Insurance	4.25	100.00	425.00
12	PL-348	10420	10420-PL-348	10/7/2015	Alexander	Torrez	Rosa	Martinez	Patent	5.00	100.00	500.00
13	PL-348	10420	10420-PL-348	10/9/2015	Alexander	Torrez	Rosa	Martinez	Patent	2.25	100.00	225.00
14	EP-685	10495	10495-EP-685	10/9/2015	Frank	Kinsela	Rosa	Martinez	Estate	3.75	100.00	375.00
15								Martinez Total				3,725.00
20								O'Donovan Total				1,785.00
21	CL-412	10125	10125-CL-412	10/5/2015	Hilary	Schmidt	Toni	Sullivan	Corporate	5.25	75.00	393.75
22	CL-412	10125	10125-CL-412	10/8/2015	Hilary	Schmidt	Toni	Sullivan	Corporate	5.25	75.00	393.75
23	CL-521	10334	10334-CL-521	10/7/2015	Gene	Marsales	Toni	Sullivan	Corporate	4.25	75.00	318.75
24	CL-501	10341	10341-CL-501	10/7/2015	Dana	Fletcher	Toni	Sullivan	Corporate	5.25	75.00	393.75
25	CL-450	10358	10358-CL-450	10/9/2015	Henri	Poissant	Toni	Sullivan	Corporate	3.50	75.00	262.50
26								Sullivan Total				1,762.50
31								Williams Total				1,132.50
32								Grand Total				8,405.00

Project 3a Converting a Table to a Range and Creating Subtotals Part 1 of 3

1. Open **EL2-C3-P2-BillSumOctWk1.xlsx**.
2. Save the workbook and name it **EL2-C3-P3-BillSumOctWk1.xlsx**.
3. Remove style options and convert the table to a normal range to group and subtotal the records by completing the following steps:
   a. Position the active cell anywhere within the table and click the TABLE TOOLS DESIGN tab.
   b. Click the *Total Row* check box in the Table Style Options group to remove the *Total* row from the table. The Subtotal feature includes a grand total automatically, so the *Total* row is no longer needed.
   c. Click the *Banded Columns* check box in the Table Style Options group to remove the banded formatting.
   d. Click the Convert to Range button in the Tools group.

e. Click Yes at the Microsoft Excel message box asking if you want to convert the table to a normal range.

f. Select columns A through L and AutoFit the column widths.

g. Deselect the columns.

4. Sort the data by the fields you want to subtotal and group by completing the following steps:

a. Select A4:L27.

b. Click the Sort & Filter button in the Editing group on the HOME tab and then click *Custom Sort* at the drop-down list.

c. At the Sort dialog box, define three levels to group and sort the records as follows:

Column	*Sort On*	*Order*
Attorney LName	Values	A to Z
Client	Values	Smallest to Largest
Date	Values	Oldest to Newest

d. Click OK.

5. Create subtotals at each change in attorney last name by completing the following steps:

a. With A4:L27 still selected, click the DATA tab.

b. Click the Subtotal button in the Outline group.

c. At the Subtotal dialog box, click the down-pointing arrow to the right of the *At each change in* option box (which currently displays *File*), scroll down the list, and then click *Attorney LName*.

d. With *Use function* set to *Sum* and *Fees Due* selected in the *Add subtotal to* list box, click OK.
e. Deselect the range.
6. Print the worksheet.
7. Show and hide levels in the outlined worksheet by completing the following steps:
a. Click the level 1 button located at the top left of the worksheet area below the Name text box. Excel collapses the worksheet to display only the grand total of the *Fees Due* column.

Step 7a

Step 5d

b. Click the level 2 button to display the subtotals by attorney last name. Notice that a button with a plus symbol displays next to each subtotal in the Outline section at the left side of the worksheet area. The button with the plus symbol is the Show Detail button and the button with the minus symbol is the Hide Detail button. Compare your worksheet with the one shown in Figure 3.7 on page 90.

Step 7b

Step 7c

c. Click the Show Detail button (which displays as a plus symbol) next to the row with the Martinez subtotal. The detail rows for the group of records for Martinez are displayed.
d. Click the Show Detail button next to the row with the Sullivan subtotal.
e. Compare your worksheet with the one shown in Figure 3.8 on page 90.
f. Click the level 3 button to display all of the detail rows.
8. Save **EL2-C3-P3-BillSumOctWk1.xlsx**.

Project 3b **Modifying Subtotals** **Part 2 of 3**

1. With **EL2-C3-P3-BillSumOctWk1.xlsx** open, add a subtotal to count the number of billable records for each attorney for the week by completing the following steps:
a. Select A4:L32 and then click the Subtotal button in the Outline group on the DATA tab. The Subtotal dialog box opens with the settings used for the subtotals created in Project 3a.
b. Click the *Replace current subtotals* check box to remove the check mark. By clearing the check box, you are instructing Excel to add another subtotal row to each group.
c. Click the down-pointing arrow next to the *Use function* option box and then click *Count* at the drop-down list.
d. With *Fees Due* still selected in the *Add subtotal to* list box, click OK. Excel adds a new subtotal row to each group with the count of records displayed.

Step 1c

Step 1b

Step 1d

2. Add a subtotal to calculate the average billable hours and average fees due for each attorney by completing the following steps:

a. With the data range still selected, click the Subtotal button.

b. Click the down-pointing arrow next to the *Use function* option box and then click *Average* at the drop-down list.

c. Click the *Billable Hours* check box in the *Add subtotal to* list box and then click OK. Excel adds a new subtotal row to each group with the average billable hours and average fees due for each attorney.

Attorney LName	Area	Billable Hours	Rate	Fees Due
Martinez	Insurance	4.25	100.00	425.00
Martinez	Insurance	4.50	100.00	450.00
Martinez	Insurance	1.75	100.00	175.00
Martinez	Employment	3.25	100.00	325.00
Martinez	Employment	4.50	100.00	450.00
Martinez	Pension	3.75	100.00	375.00
Martinez	Insurance	4.25	100.00	425.00
Martinez	Patent	5.00	100.00	500.00
Martinez	Patent	2.25	100.00	225.00
Martinez	Estate	3.75	100.00	375.00
Martinez Average		3.73		372.50
Martinez Count				10
Martinez Total				3,725.00

The averages of the *Billable Hours* and *Fees Due* columns are added to the subtotals for all attorneys in Steps 2a–2c. The data for the Martinez group is shown.

d. Deselect the range.

3. Save the revised workbook and name it **EL2-C3-P3-BillSumOctWk1-Prj3b**.

4. Click the PAGE LAYOUT tab and scale the height of the worksheet to 1 page.

5. Print the worksheet.

6. Save and then close **EL2-C3-P3-BillSumOctWk1-Prj3b.xlsx**.

Grouping and Ungrouping Data ■■■■■■■■■■■■■■■

When a worksheet is outlined, use the Group and Ungroup buttons in the Outline group on the DATA tab to individually manage collapsing and expanding groups of records at the various levels. For example, in an outlined worksheet with detailed rows displayed, selecting a group of records and clicking the Ungroup button opens the Ungroup dialog box, shown in Figure 3.9. Clicking OK with *Rows* selected removes the group feature applied to the selection and removes the Hide Detail button so the records remain displayed at the outline level. Selecting records that have been ungrouped and clicking the Group button reattaches the group feature to the selection and redisplays the Hide Detail button.

Figure 3.9 Ungroup Dialog Box

▼ **Quick Steps**

Group Data by Rows
1. Select range to be grouped within outlined worksheet.
2. Click DATA tab.
3. Click Group button.
4. Click OK.

Ungroup Data by Rows
1. Select grouped range within outlined worksheet.
2. Click DATA tab.
3. Click Ungroup button.
4. Click OK.

Group Ungroup

Columns can also be grouped and ungrouped. The outline section with the level numbers and Show and Hide Detail buttons displays across the top of the worksheet area. For example, in a worksheet in which two columns are used to arrive at a formula, the source columns can be grouped and the details hidden so that only the formula column with the calculated results is displayed in an outlined worksheet.

Project 3c   Grouping and Ungrouping Data   Part 3 of 3

1. Open **EL2-C3-P3-BillSumOctWk1.xlsx**. Group client data within the Martinez attorney group by completing the following steps:

   a. Select A5:L7. These three rows contain billing information for client 10210.

   b. Click the Group button in the Outline group on the DATA tab. (Make sure to click the button and not the button arrow.)

   c. At the Group dialog box with *Rows* selected, click OK. Excel adds a fourth outline level to the worksheet and a Hide Detail button is added below the last row of the grouped records in the Outline section.

   d. Select A12:L13, click the Group button, and then click OK at the Group dialog box.

These records are grouped in Step 1d.

   e. Deselect the range.

2. Experiment with the Hide Detail buttons in the Martinez group by hiding the detail for client 10210 and then hiding the detail for client 10420.

3. Redisplay the detail rows by clicking the Show Detail button for each client.

4. Select A5:L7, click the Ungroup button (make sure to click the button and not the button arrow), and then click OK at the Ungroup dialog box.

5. Select A12:L13, click the Ungroup button, and then click OK at the Ungroup dialog box.

6. Select A5:L14, click the Ungroup button, and then click OK at the Ungroup dialog box. Notice that the Hide Detail button is removed for the entire Martinez group.

7. Deselect the range and then click the level 2 button at the top of the outline section. Notice that the Martinez records do not collapse like the others, since they are no longer grouped.

8. Save the revised workbook and name it **EL2-C3-P3-BillSumOctWk1-Prj3c**.

9. Print and then close **EL2-C3-P3-BillSumOctWk1-Prj3c.xlsx**.

Chapter Summary

- A table in Excel is a range of cells similar in structure to a database in which no blank rows exist and the first row of the range contains column headings.

- Define a range as a table using the Table button in the Tables group on the INSERT tab.

- Columns in a table are called *fields* and rows are called *records*.

- The first row of a table contains column headings and is called the *field names row* or *header row*.

- A table automatically expands to include data typed in a row or column immediately adjacent to a range that has been defined as a table.

- Typing a formula in the first record of a new column causes Excel to define the column as a calculated column and automatically copy the formula to the remaining rows in the table.

- The contextual TABLE TOOLS DESIGN tab contains options for formatting tables.

- The Table Styles gallery contains several options that you can use to change the visual appearance of a table.

- Banding rows or columns formats every other row or column differently to make reading a large table easier.

- You can add emphasis to the first column or last column in a table. Excel generally formats the column with a darker fill color and reverse font or bold font and borders, depending on the Table Style in effect.

- The row containing field names in a table can be shown or hidden using the *Header Row* option in the Table Style Options group.

- Adding a *Total* row to a table causes Excel to add the word *Total* in the left-most column and create a Sum function in the last numeric column in the table. You can add additional functions by clicking in the desired column in the *Total* row and selecting a function from the pop-up list.

- Excel automatically includes a filter arrow at the top of each column in a table. Use these arrows to filter and sort the table.

- A column containing text that you want to split can be separated into multiple columns using the Text to Columns button in the Data Tools group on the DATA tab. The Convert Text to Columns Wizard contains three dialog boxes to define how to split the data.

- Use Flash Fill to extract, join, and insert text, numbers, dates, and times.

- Using the Remove Duplicates dialog box, you can instruct Excel to compare records within a worksheet and automatically delete rows that are duplicated.

- Data can be validated as it is being entered into a worksheet, and invalid data can be prevented from being stored or a warning can be issued to state that data has been entered that does not conform to the restrictions.

- At the Settings tab in the Data Validation dialog box, you define the validation criteria for the cell entry. You can allow data based on values, dates, times, and text lengths or restrict the entries to values within a drop-down list.

- At the Input Message tab in the Data Validation dialog box, you can define a message that pops up when a cell for which data is restricted becomes active.
- At the Error Alert tab in the Data Validation dialog box, you can define the type of error alert to display and the content of the error message.
- Convert a table to a normal range when you want to use the Subtotal feature or no longer need to treat a range of cells independently from the rest of the worksheet.
- Sort a worksheet by the column(s) for which you want to group data for subtotals before opening the Subtotals dialog box.
- The Subtotals button is located in the Outline group on the DATA tab.
- Excel adds a subtotal automatically at each change in content for the column you specify as the subtotal field. A grand total is also automatically added to the bottom of the range.
- You can display more than one subtotal row for a group to calculate multiple functions, such as Sum and Average.
- A subtotaled range is outlined and record details can be collapsed or expanded using the level number, Hide Detail, and Show Detail buttons.
- When a worksheet is outlined, use the Group and Ungroup buttons in the Outline group on the DATA tab to manage the display of individual groups.

Commands Review

FEATURE	RIBBON TAB, GROUP	BUTTON	KEYBOARD SHORTCUT
convert table to range	TABLE TOOLS DESIGN, Tools		
convert text to table	DATA, Data Tools		
create table	INSERT, Tables		Ctrl + T
Flash Fill	HOME, Editing OR DATA, Data Tools		Ctrl + E
group data	DATA, Outline		Shift + Alt + Right Arrow key
remove duplicates	DATA, Data Tools OR TABLE TOOLS DESIGN, Tools		
sort and filter table	HOME, Editing		
subtotals	DATA, Outline		
table styles	TABLE TOOLS DESIGN, Table Styles		
Total row	TABLE TOOLS DESIGN, Table Style Options		Ctrl + Shift + T
ungroup	DATA, Outline		Shift + Alt + Left Arrow key
validate data	DATA, Data Tools		

Concepts Check   Test Your Knowledge

Completion: In the space provided at the right, indicate the correct term, command, or number.

1. The first row of a table that contains the column headings is called the field names row or this row.

_____

2. Typing a formula in the first record of a column in a table causes Excel to define the field as this type of column.

_____

3. Change the visual appearance of a table using this gallery in the TABLE TOOLS DESIGN tab.

_____

4. This term describes the formatting feature in a table in which even-numbered rows are formatted differently from odd-numbered rows.

_____

5. Clicking this button causes the Convert Text to Columns Wizard to appear.

_____

6. Open this dialog box to instruct Excel to compare the entries in the columns you specify and automatically delete rows that contain repeated data.

_____

7. Open this dialog box to restrict entries in a cell to those that you set up in a drop-down list.

_____

8. This option in the *Allow* option box is used to require that data entered into a cell be a specific number of characters.

_____

9. This is the default error alert style that prevents invalid data from being entered into a cell.

_____

10. The Convert to Range button is found on this tab.

_____

11. Prior to creating subtotals using the Subtotal button in the Outline group on the DATA tab, arrange the data in this order.

_____

12. In a worksheet with subtotal rows only displayed, click this button next to a subtotal row to view the grouped rows.

_____

13. Click this button in an outlined worksheet to collapse the rows for a group.

_____

14. In an outlined worksheet, use this button to collapse all records and display only the row with the grand total.

_____

15. Clicking this button in an outlined worksheet will cause the Hide Detail button for the selected rows to be removed.

_____

Skills Check   Assess Your Performance

Assessment

1   CREATE AND FORMAT A TABLE

1. Open **VIVClassics.xlsx**.
2. Save the workbook and name it **EL2-C3-A1-VIVClassics**.
3. Select A4:L30 and create a table using the Table Style Medium 12 table style (fifth column, second row in *Medium* section). The table has headers.
4. Add a calculated column to the table in column M by completing the following:
   a. Type Total Cost as the column heading in cell M4.
   b. Create a formula in the first record that multiplies the number of copies in column G times the cost price in column L. The formula will copy to the rest of the rows in the table.
5. Adjust the three rows above the table to merge and center across columns A through M and adjust all column widths to AutoFit.
6. Add banding to the columns, remove banding from the rows, and emphasize the last column in the table.
7. Add a *Total* row to the table. Add Average functions that calculate the average number of copies and the average cost price of a video. Format the average value in the *Copies* column of the *Total* row to no places after the decimal point and M5:M31 to two places after the decimal point.
8. The video *Blue Hawaii* cannot be located and the manager would like you to remove the record from the table. Delete the row in the table for the record with stock number CV-1015.
9. Save, print, and then close **EL2-C3-A1-VIVClassics.xlsx**.

Assessment

2   USE DATA TOOLS

1. Open **EL2-C3-A1-VIVClassics.xlsx**.
2. Save the workbook and name it **EL2-C3-A2-VIVClassics**.
3. Make the following changes:
   a. Insert a new blank column to the right of the column containing the director names and change the column headings to *Director FName* and *Director LName*.
   b. Split the director names into two columns (first and last names).
4. Use the Remove Duplicates feature to find and remove any duplicate rows using *Title* as the comparison column.
5. Create the following validation rules:
   a. A custom format of "CV-"#### has been applied to the stock numbers. Create a validation rule for the *Stock No.* column that ensures all new entries are 4 characters in length. (With custom number formats, you do not include the characters between the quotation marks in the text length.)
   b. Add an input message to the column that reads Enter the last four digits of the stock number. Use the default error alert options.

c. The manager would like to ensure that in the future, five copies is the maximum inventory of any individual classic video in the collection. Create a validation rule that restricts entries in the *Copies* column to a number less than six. Do not add an input message and use the default Stop error alert.

d. Create a drop-down list for the *Genre* column with the entries provided. Do not enter an input message and use the default error alert settings.

6. Add the record below to the table to test the data validation rules. (Initially enter incorrect values in the *Stock No.*, *Genre*, and *Copies* columns to make sure the rule and the messages work correctly.)

Stock No.	CV-1026
Title	The Philadelphia Story
Year	1940
Genre	Comedy
Stock Date	12/12/2015
Director FName	George
Director LName	Cukor
Copies	3
VHS	No
DVD	Yes
Blu-ray	Yes
Category	7-day rental
Cost Price	10.15

7. Save, print, and then close **EL2-C3-A2-VIVClassics.xlsx**.

Assessment

3 SUBTOTAL RECORDS

1. Open **EL2-C3-A2-VIVClassics.xlsx**.
2. Save the workbook and name it **EL2-C3-A3-VIVClassics**.
3. Remove the *Total* row and remove the emphasis from the last column in the table.
4. Convert the table to a normal range.
5. Adjust all column widths to AutoFit.
6. Sort the list first by the genre, then by the director's last name, and then by the title of the video. Use the default sort values and sort order for each level.
7. Using the Subtotal button in the Outline group on the DATA tab, add subtotals to the *Total Cost* column to calculate the sum and average total costs of videos by genre.
8. Display the worksheet at level 2 of the outline.
9. Show the details for the Comedy, Drama, and Family genres.
10. Print the worksheet.
11. Save and then close **EL2-C3-A3-VIVClassics.xlsx**.

Visual Benchmark   Demonstrate Your Proficiency

1 USING TABLE AND DATA TOOLS IN A CALL LIST

1. Open **WPMCallList.xlsx**.
2. Save the workbook and name it **EL2-C3-VB1-WPMCallList**.
3. Format and apply data tools as required to duplicate the worksheet in Figure 3.10 using the following information:
   - The worksheet has *Table Style Medium 5* applied to the table range.
   - Look closely at the sorted order. The table is sorted by three levels using the fields *Designation*, *Hourly Rate*, and *Hire Date*.
   - Shift cost equals the hourly rate times 8 hours.
   - Use Flash Fill to split the names into two columns.
   - Include the *Total* row and apply the appropriate banded options.
4. Save, print, and then close **EL2-C3-VB1-WPMCallList.xlsx**.

2 USING SUBTOTALS IN A CALL LIST

1. Open **EL2-C3-VB1-WPMCallList.xlsx**.
2. Save the workbook and name it **EL2-C3-VB2-WPMCallList**.
3. Create subtotals and view the revised worksheet at the appropriate level to display as shown in Figure 3.11 on the next page.
4. Save, print, and then close **EL2-C3-VB2-WPMCallList.xlsx**.

Figure 3.10 Visual Benchmark 1

Wellington Park Medical Center
Nursing Division Casual Relief Call List

Payroll No.	First Name	Last Name	Designation	Hire Date	Telephone	OR Exp?	Day Shift Only?	Night Shift Only?	Either Shift?	Hourly Rate	Shift Cost
19658	Paula	Sanderson	RN	4/28/2000	555-3485	No	No	No	Yes	38.50	308.00
38642	Tania	Ravi	RN	6/22/2002	555-6969	Yes	Yes	No	Weekends only	38.50	308.00
78452	Terry	Mason	RN	10/8/2015	555-1279	Yes	No	Yes	No	38.50	308.00
96523	Lynn	Pietre	RN	10/22/1998	555-2548	Yes	Yes	No	Weekends only	35.00	280.00
45968	David	Featherstone	RN	9/9/2001	555-5961	No	No	No	Yes	35.00	280.00
46956	Orlando	Zambian	RN	11/10/2001	555-1186	No	Yes	No	No	35.00	280.00
56983	Amanda	Sanchez	RN	4/27/1999	555-4896	Yes	No	Yes	No	33.00	264.00
68429	Rene	Quenneville	RN	8/15/2003	555-4663	Yes	Yes	No	Weekends only	22.50	180.00
69417	Denis	LaPierre	RN	8/23/2003	555-8643	No	No	Yes	No	22.50	180.00
37944	Fernando	Este	RN	7/18/2005	555-4545	No	No	No	Yes	22.50	180.00
78647	Jay	Bjorg	RN	5/14/2007	555-6598	No	No	No	Yes	22.50	180.00
95558	Sam	Vargas	RN	3/2/2009	555-4571	No	No	No	Yes	22.50	180.00
98731	Zail	Singh	RN	5/6/2011	555-3561	Yes	Yes	No	No	22.50	180.00
58612	Savana	Ruiz	RN	4/15/2012	555-8457	Yes	No	Yes	Weekends only	22.50	180.00
96721	Noreen	Kalir	RN	4/3/2009	555-1876	Yes	Yes	No	No	21.50	172.00
89367	Xiu	Zheng	LPN	4/23/2006	555-7383	Yes	Yes	No	No	18.75	150.00
14586	Alma	Fernandez	LPN	8/3/1997	555-7412	Yes	No	No	Yes	16.75	134.00
48652	Dana	Casselman	LPN	10/15/1997	555-6325	Yes	No	No	Yes	16.75	134.00
85412	Kelly	Lund	LPN	11/19/1998	555-3684	No	Yes	No	Weekends only	15.75	126.00
98364	Lana	Bourne	LPN	7/15/2008	555-9012	Yes	Yes	No	No	15.50	124.00
90467	Nadir	Abouzeen	LPN	8/12/2008	555-9023	No	No	No	Yes	14.50	116.00
68475	Kelly	O'Brien	LPN	1/20/2012	555-6344	No	Yes	No	Weekends only	13.75	110.00
									Average Hourly Rate and Shift Cost:	24.74	197.91

Figure 3.11 Visual Benchmark 2

	A	B	C	D	E	F	G	H	I	J	K	L
1						Wellington Park Medical Center						
2						Nursing Division Casual Relief Call List						
3	Payroll No.	First Name	Last Name	Designation	Hire Date	Telephone	OR Exp?	Day Shift Only?	Night Shift Only?	Either Shift?	Hourly Rate	Shift Cost
19				RN Average							28.83	230.67
27				LPN Average							15.96	127.71
28				Grand Average							24.74	197.91

Case Study   Apply Your Skills

Part 1

Rajiv Patel, Vice-President of NuTrends Market Research, has sent you a file named **NuTrendsMktPlans.xlsx**. The workbook contains client information for the company's first-quarter marketing plans for three marketing consultants. Rajiv would like you to improve the reporting in the file by completing the following tasks:

- Set up the data as a table sorted first by the consultant's last name and then by the marketing campaign's start date, both in ascending order. Rajiv would prefer that consultant names be split into two columns.

- Improve the formatting of the dollar values.

- Add a *Total* row to sum the columns containing dollar amounts.

- Add formatting to the titles above the table that are suited to the colors in the table style you selected.

- Make any other formatting changes you think will improve the worksheet's appearance.

Save the revised workbook and name it **EL2-C3-CS-P1-NuTrendsMktPlans**. Print the worksheet in landscape orientation with the width scaled to one page.

Part 2

Rajiv would like statistics for each consultant added to the workbook. Specifically, he would like to see the following information:

- The total marketing plan budget values being managed by each consultant, as well as the total planned expenditures by month

- The average marketing plan budget being managed by each consultant, as well as the average planned expenditures by month

Rajiv would like a printout that displays only the total and average values for each consultant, as well as the grand average and grand total. Save the revised workbook and name it **EL2-C3-CS-P2-NuTrendsMktPlans**. Print and then close the worksheet.

Part

3

In addition, Rajiv has asked that you provide another report from the file named **NuTrendsMktPlans.xlsx**. Specifically, he would like a printout of the worksheet that shows the original data at the top of the worksheet and a few blank rows below the worksheet. Rajiv would like to see the marketing plan details for Yolanda Robertson's clients that have campaigns starting after January 31, 2015.

Research in Help how to filter a range of cells using the Advanced Filter button in the Sort & Filter group on the DATA tab. Make sure you read how to copy rows that meet your filter criteria to another area of the worksheet. Using the information you have learned, open **NuTrendsMktPlans.xlsx**, insert three new rows above the worksheet, and use these rows to create the criteria range. Filter the list according to Rajiv's specifications. Rows that meet the criteria should be copied below the worksheet starting in cell A21. Add an appropriate title to describe the copied data in cell A20. Make any formatting changes you think will improve the appearance of the worksheet. Save the revised workbook and name it **EL2-C3-CS-P3-NuTrendsMktPlans**. Print the worksheet and then close the workbook.

Part

4

Rajiv is looking for information on current salary ranges for a market researcher in the United States. Use the Internet to find this information. If possible, find salary information that is specific to your state for a minimum of three cities. Find a low salary and high salary for a market researcher in each city.

Create a workbook that summarizes the results of your research. Include in the workbook the website addresses as hyperlinked cells next to items about salary range. Organize the data in the workbook as a table. Apply table formatting options so the data is attractively presented and easy to read. Add a *Total* row to the table and include an Average function to find the average salary from the three cities. Find a minimum of three and a maximum of five resources. Save the workbook and name it **EL2-C3-CS-P4-NuTrendsSalaryAnalysis**. Print the worksheet and then close the workbook.

MICROSOFT EXCEL

Summarizing and Consolidating Data

PERFORMANCE OBJECTIVES

Upon successful completion of Chapter 4, you will be able to:

- Summarize data by creating formulas with range names that reference other worksheets
- Modify the range assigned to a range name
- Summarize data by creating 3-D references
- Create formulas that link to cells in other worksheets or workbooks
- Edit a link to a source workbook
- Break a link to an external reference
- Use the Consolidate feature to summarize data in multiple worksheets
- Create, edit, and format a PivotTable
- Filter a PivotTable using Slicers
- Filter a PivotTable using Timelines
- Create and format a PivotChart
- Create and format Sparklines

Tutorials

4.1 Summarizing Data in Multiple Worksheets Using Range Names and 3-D References

4.2 Summarizing Data by Linking Ranges in Other Worksheets or Workbooks

4.3 Summarizing Data Using the Consolidate Feature

4.4 Creating a PivotTable

4.5 Filtering a PivotTable Using Slicers

4.6 Filtering a PivotTable Using a Timeline

4.7 Creating a PivotChart

4.8 Summarizing Data with Sparklines

You can summarize data by creating formulas that reference cells in other areas of the active worksheet or other worksheets within the same workbook or by linking to cells in other worksheets or workbooks. The Consolidate feature can also be used to summarize data from other worksheets or other workbooks into a master worksheet. Once the data has been summarized, consider presenting or analyzing the data by creating and formatting a PivotTable or PivotChart. Sparklines are miniature charts that are inserted into cells and allow you to see at a glance a trend or other pattern in the data. Timelines allow you to filter a PivotTable or PivotChart using a specified timeframe. In this chapter, you will learn how to summarize and filter data using a variety of methods and present visually summarized data for analysis. Model answers for this chapter's projects appear on the following pages.

Excel
EL2C4

Note: Before beginning the projects, copy to your storage medium the EL2C4 subfolder from the EL2 folder on the CD that accompanies this textbook and then make EL2C4 the active folder.

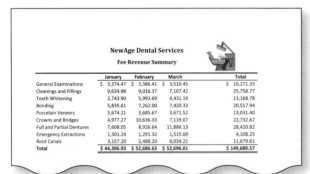

National Park Service
U.S. Department of the Interior
May 2015
Attendance Summary
Southwest Region, Zone C

Private Vehicle and Individual Entrances Only	10,460
Commercial Tour Vehicles Only	15,069
Total Attendance	25,529

National Park Service
U.S. Department of the Interior
May 2015
Attendance Summary
Southwest Region, Zone C

Private Vehicle and Individual Entrances Only	10,460
Commercial Tour Vehicles Only	15,434
Total Attendance	25,894

Project 1 Calculate Park Attendance Totals

Project 1c, EL2-C4-P1-MayEntries.xlsx

Project 1d, EL2-C4-P1-MayEntries.xlsx

NewAge Dental Services
Fee Revenue Summary

	January	February	March	Total
General Examinations	$ 3,374.47	$ 3,386.41	$ 3,510.45	$ 10,271.33
Cleanings and Fillings	9,634.98	9,016.37	7,107.42	25,758.77
Teeth Whitening	2,743.90	5,993.69	4,431.19	13,168.78
Bonding	5,835.61	7,262.00	7,420.33	20,517.94
Porcelain Veneers	5,674.21	3,685.67	3,671.52	13,031.40
Crowns and Bridges	4,977.27	10,636.33	7,119.07	22,732.67
Full and Partial Dentures	7,608.05	8,926.64	11,886.13	28,420.82
Emergency Extractions	1,301.24	1,291.32	1,515.69	4,108.25
Root Canals	3,157.20	2,488.20	6,034.21	11,679.61
Total	$ 44,306.93	$ 52,686.63	$ 52,696.01	$ 149,689.57

Project 2 Calculate Total Fees Billed by Three Dentists

EL2-C4-P2-NADQ1Fees.xlsx

Project 3 Analyze Fitness Equipment Sales Data in a PivotTable and PivotChart

Project 3c, EL2-C4-P3-PF1stQSales.xlsx

Model (Multiple Items)

Sum of Sale Price	Column Labels			
Row Labels	Clarke	Fernandez	Kazmarek	Grand Total
Central	4,470		5,224	9,694
North	1,150		8,099	9,249
South	2,499	1,150		3,649
West			1,575	1,575
Grand Total	**8,119**	**1,150**	**14,898**	**24,167**

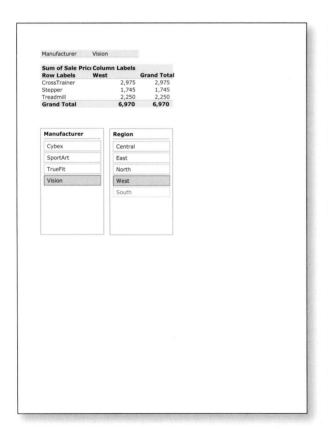

Manufacturer   Vision

Sum of Sale Price	Column Labels	
Row Labels	West	Grand Total
CrossTrainer	2,975	2,975
Stepper	1,745	1,745
Treadmill	2,250	2,250
Grand Total	**6,970**	**6,970**

Manufacturer	Region
Cybex	Central
SportArt	East
TrueFit	North
Vision	West
	South

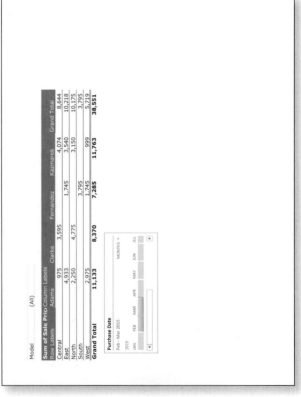

Project 3d, EL2-C4-P3-PF1stQSales.xlsx

Project 3e, EL2-C4-P3-PF1stQSales.xlsx

Model Answers

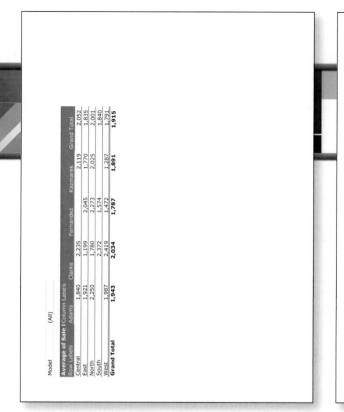

Model	(All)				
Average of Sale Price	**Column Labels**				
Row Labels	Adams	Clarke	Fernandez	Kazmarek	Grand Total
Central	1,840	2,235	2,045	2,119	2,052
East	1,921	1,199	1,770	1,770	1,835
North	2,250	1,780	2,273	2,025	2,001
South		2,372	1,574	1,287	1,840
West	1,987	2,419	1,472		1,791
Grand Total	**1,943**	**2,034**	**1,787**	**1,891**	**1,915**

Project 3f, EL2-C4-P3-PFAvg1stQSales.xlsx

Project 3g, EL2-C4-P3-PF1stQSales.xlsx

Sum of Sale Price	Column Labels					
Row Labels	Central	East	North	South	West	Grand Total
Cybex	9694		9249	3649	1575	24167
SportArt	1295	8877	1295	2245	2588	16300
TrueFit		5889	4845	5145	3197	19076
Vision	7475	1745	6625		6970	22815
Grand Total	**18464**	**16511**	**22014**	**11039**	**14330**	**82358**

Project 3h, EL2-C4-P3-PFChart.xlsx

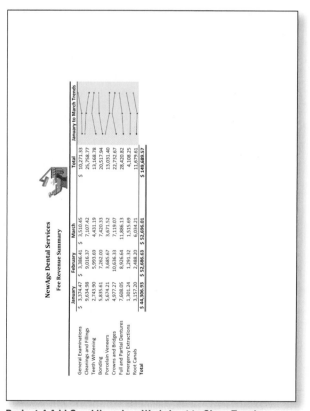

NewAge Dental Services
Fee Revenue Summary

	January	February	March	Total	January to March Trends
General Examinations	$ 3,374.47	$ 3,386.41	$ 3,510.45	$ 10,271.33	
Cleanings and Fillings	9,634.98	9,016.37	7,107.42	25,758.77	
Teeth Whitening	2,743.90	5,993.69	4,431.19	13,168.78	
Bonding	5,835.61	7,262.00	7,420.33	20,517.94	
Porcelain Veneers	5,674.21	3,685.67	3,671.52	13,031.40	
Crowns and Bridges	4,977.27	10,636.33	7,119.07	22,732.67	
Full and Partial Dentures	7,608.05	8,926.64	11,886.13	28,420.82	
Emergency Extractions	1,301.24	1,291.32	1,515.69	4,108.25	
Root Canals	3,157.20	2,488.20	6,034.21	11,679.61	
Total	**$ 44,306.93**	**$ 52,686.63**	**$ 52,696.01**	**$ 149,689.57**	

Project 4 Add Sparklines in a Worksheet to Show Trends
EL2-C4-P4-NADQ1Fees.xlsx

> You will create and modify range names and calculate total park attendance at three national parks by using data stored in separate worksheets and linking to a cell in another workbook. You will also edit a linked workbook and update the link in the destination file.

Summarizing Data in Multiple Worksheets Using Range Names and 3-D References ■■■■■■■■■■■■■■■■

A workbook that has been organized with data in separate worksheets can be summarized by creating formulas that reference cells in other worksheets. When you create a formula that references a cell in the same worksheet, you do not need to include the sheet name in the reference. For example, the formula =A3+A4 causes Excel to add the value in cell A3 in the active worksheet to the value in cell A4 in the active worksheet. However, when you create a formula that references a cell in a different worksheet, you must include the sheet name in the formula.

Assume that you want Excel to add the value in cell A3 that resides in Sheet2 to the value in cell A3 that resides in Sheet3 in the workbook. To do this, you need to include the worksheet name in the formula by typing =Sheet2!A3+Sheet3!A3 into the formula cell. This formula contains both worksheet references and cell references. The worksheet reference precedes the cell reference and is separated from the cell reference with an exclamation point. Without a worksheet reference, Excel assumes cells are in the active worksheet. A formula that references the same cell in a range that extends over two or more worksheets is often called a **3-D reference**. For a formula that includes a 3-D reference, the 3-D reference can be typed directly in a cell or entered using a point-and-click approach. Formulas that include a 3-D reference are sometimes referred to as *3-D formulas*.

As an alternative, consider using range names to simplify formulas that summarize data in multiple worksheets. A range name includes the worksheet reference by default; therefore, typing the range name in the formula automatically references the correct worksheet. For example, assume cell A3 in Sheet2 has been named *ProductA* and cell A3 in Sheet3 has been named *ProductB*. To add the two values, you type the formula =*ProductA*+*ProductB* in the formula cell. Notice that you do not need to include worksheet references. Another advantage to using range names is that the name can describe the worksheet with the source data. By using range names, you also do not have to make both worksheets identical in organizational structure. Recall from your work with range names in Chapter 2 that cell references in range names are absolute references. To view, edit, or delete existing range names, use the Name Manager button in the Defined Names group on the FORMULAS tab.

Project 1a | **Modifying a Named Range and Summarizing Data in Multiple Worksheets** | **Part 1 of 5**

1. Open **MayEntries.xlsx**.
2. Save the workbook and name it **EL2-C4-P1-MayEntries**.
3. Click each sheet tab and review the data. Each park has attendance data entered as a separate worksheet. In the workbook, range names have already been created. Check each range name to make sure the cell references are correct before creating the summary formula by completing the following steps:

   Step 3a

   a. Click the down-pointing arrow next to the Name box and then click *Bryce* at the drop-down list. Notice that the BryceCanyon sheet is active and the ranges B7:B22 and E7:E21 are selected.
   b. Click the down-pointing arrow next to the Name box and then click *Grand* at the drop-down list. Notice that the GrandCanyon sheet is active and the range B7:B22 is selected. This range is missing the entries for days 17 through 31. You will correct this range in Step 4.
   c. Click the down-pointing arrow next to the Name box and then click *Mesa* at the drop-down list. Notice that the MesaVerde sheet is active and the ranges B7:B22 and E7:E21 are selected.

   These ranges are automatically selected when you select *Bryce* from the Name box.

4. Modify the references in a named range by adding the data in column E of the GrandCanyon worksheet to the range named *Grand* by completing the following steps:
   a. Click in any cell to deselect the Mesa range.
   b. Click the FORMULAS tab.
   c. Click the Name Manager button in the Defined Names group.
   d. Click *Grand* in the *Name* list at the Name Manager dialog box.
   e. Click the Edit button.
   f. At the Edit Name dialog box, click the Collapse Dialog button located at the right of the *Refers to* text box (which currently displays =*GrandCanyon!$B$7:$B$22*).

   Step 4e

   Step 4d

   Step 4f

g. With GrandCanyon the active worksheet and the range B7:B22 selected, hold down the Ctrl key and then select E7:E21.

h. Click the Expand Dialog button to restore the Edit Name dialog box. Notice that a comma separates the nonadjacent ranges in the range name and that the cell addresses are absolute references.

This range is automatically selected when you collapse the Edit Name dialog box.

i. Click OK to close the Edit Name dialog box.

j. Click Close to close the Name Manager dialog box.

k. Click the down-pointing arrow next to the Name box and then click *Grand* at the drop-down list to make sure the revised range name is referencing B7:B22 and E7:E21 in the GrandCanyon worksheet.

5. Create a formula to add the total attendance for May at all three parks by completing the following steps:

a. Click the AttendanceSummary tab to activate the worksheet.

b. If necessary, make cell F7 active, type **=sum(bryce,grand,mesa)**, and then press Enter. Notice that in a Sum formula, multiple range names are separated with commas. Excel returns the result *10460* in cell F7 of the AttendanceSummary worksheet.

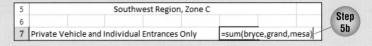

c. Apply comma formatting with no places after the decimal point to cell F7.

6. Save and then close **EL2-C4-P1-MayEntries.xlsx**.

A disadvantage to using range names emerges when several worksheets need to be summarized, since the range name reference must be created in each individual worksheet. If several worksheets need to be summed, a more efficient method is to use a 3-D reference. Generally, when using a 3-D reference, it is a good idea to set up the data in each worksheet in identical cells. In Project 1b, you will calculate the same attendance total for the three parks using a 3-D reference instead of range names.

1. Open **MayEntries.xlsx**.
2. Save the workbook and name it **EL2-C4-P1-3D-MayEntries**.
3. Calculate the attendance total for the three parks using a point-and-click approach to creating a 3-D reference by completing the following steps:

a. In the AttendanceSummary worksheet, make cell F7 active and then type =sum(.

b. Click the BryceCanyon sheet tab.

c. Hold down the Shift key and then click the MesaVerde sheet tab. (Using the Shift key while clicking a sheet tab selects all worksheets from the first sheet tab to the last sheet tab clicked.) Notice in the Formula bar that the formula reads =sum('BryceCanyon:MesaVerde'!

d. With BryceCanyon the active worksheet, select B7:B22, hold down the Ctrl key, and then select E7:E21.

e. Type) and then press Enter. Excel returns the value *10460* in cell F7 in the AttendanceSummary worksheet.

f. Apply comma formatting with no places after the decimal point to cell F7.

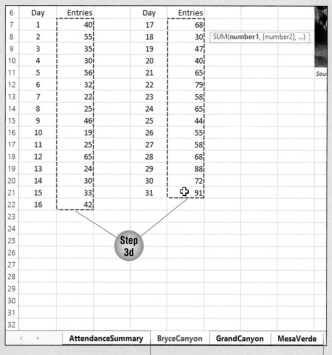

The three worksheets are grouped into the 3-D reference in Steps 3b and 3c.

4. With cell F7 the active cell, compare your formula with the one shown in Figure 4.1.
5. Save and then close **EL2-C4-P1-3D-MayEntries.xlsx**.

Figure 4.1 3-D Formula Created in Project 1b

This 3-D formula is created in Project 1b, Step 3, using a point-and-click approach.

F7   fx   =SUM(BryceCanyon:MesaVerde!B7:B22,BryceCanyon:MesaVerde!E7:E21)

	A	B	C	D	E	F	G	H	I	J	K
1				National Park Service							
2				U.S. Department of the Interior							
3				May 2015							
4				Attendance Summary							
5				Southwest Region, Zone C							
6											
7	Private Vehicle and Individual Entrances Only					10,460					

Summarizing Data by Linking to Ranges in
Other Worksheets or Workbooks ■■■■■■■■■■■■■■■

⬇ Quick Steps

Create a Link to an External Reference
1. Open source workbook.
2. Open destination workbook.
3. Arrange windows as desired.
4. Make formula cell active in destination workbook.
5. Type =.
6. Click to activate source workbook.
7. Click source cell.
8. Press Enter.

Using a method similar to that used in Project 1a or Project 1b, you can summarize data in one workbook by linking to a cell, range, or range name in another worksheet or workbook. When data is linked, a change made in the source cell (the cell in which the original data is stored) is updated in any other cell to which the source cell has been linked. A link is established by creating a formula that references the source data. For example, entering the formula =*Sheet1!B10* into a cell in Sheet2 creates a link. The cell in Sheet2 displays the value in the source cell. If the data in cell B10 in Sheet1 is changed, the value in the linked cell in Sheet2 is also changed.

As an alternative to creating a formula yourself, copy the source cell to the Clipboard task pane. Make the destination cell active, click the Paste button arrow in the Clipboard group, and then click the Paste Link button in the *Other Paste Options* section of the drop-down gallery. Excel creates the link formula for you using an absolute reference to the source cell.

Linking to a cell in another workbook incorporates external references and requires that a workbook name reference be added to a formula. For example, linking to cell A3 in a sheet named *ProductA* in a workbook named *Sales* requires that you enter =*[Sales.xlsx]ProductA!A3* in the cell. Notice that the workbook reference is entered first in square brackets. The workbook in which the external reference is added becomes the **destination workbook**. The workbook containing the data that is linked to the destination workbook is called the **source workbook**. In Project 1c, you will create a link to an external cell containing the attendance total for the tour group entrances for the three parks.

The point-and-click approach to creating a linked external reference creates an absolute reference to the source cell. Delete the dollar symbols in the cell reference if you plan to copy the formula and need the source cell to be relative. Note that workbook and worksheet references remain absolute regardless.

Project 1c   **Summarizing Data by Linking to Another Workbook**   **Part 3 of 5**

1. Open **EL2-C4-P1-MayEntries.xlsx**.
2. Open **MayGroupSales.xlsx**. This workbook contains tour group attendance data for the three national parks. Tour groups are charged a flat rate entrance fee, so their attendance values represent bus capacity rather than not the actual number of patrons on each bus.
3. Click the VIEW tab, click the Arrange All button in the Window group, click *Vertical* in the *Arrange* section of the Arrange Windows dialog box, and then click OK.
4. In the worksheet you created in Project 1a, create a linked external reference to the total attendance in the worksheet with the commercial tour vehicle attendance data by completing the following steps:
   a. Click in **EL2-C4-P1-MayEntries.xlsx** to make the workbook active. Make sure the active worksheet is AttendanceSummary.
   b. Make cell A9 active, type Commercial Tour Vehicles Only, and then press Enter.
   c. Make cell F9 active and then type =.

d. Click the **MayGroupSales.xlsx** title bar to activate the workbook and then click cell F7. Notice that the formula being entered into the formula cell contains a workbook reference and a worksheet reference in front of the cell reference.

e. Press Enter.

f. Apply comma formatting with no places after the decimal point to cell F9.

g. With cell F9 active, compare your worksheet with the one shown below at the right.

This formula contains the linked external reference created in Step 4.

This source cell is linked to cell F9 in the other open workbook.

This destination cell is linked to cell F7 in the other open workbook.

5. Click the Maximize button in the **EL2-C4-P1-MayEntries.xlsx** title bar.

6. Make cell A11 active, type **Total Attendance**, and then press Enter.

7. Make cell F11 active and then create a formula to add the values in cells F7 and F9.

8. Print the AttendanceSummary worksheet in **EL2-C4-P1-MayEntries.xlsx**. *Note: If you submit your work in hard copy, check with your instructor to see if you need to print two copies of the worksheet, with one copy displaying cell formulas.*

9. Save and then close **EL2-C4-P1-MayEntries.xlsx**.

10. Close **MayGroupSales.xlsx**. Click Don't Save when prompted to save changes.

Maintaining External References ■■■■■■■■■■■■■■■■

When you link to an external reference, Excel includes the drive and folder names in the path to the source workbook. If you move the source workbook or change the workbook name, the link will no longer work. By default, when you open a workbook with a linked external reference, automatic updates is disabled and Excel displays a security warning message in the Message bar area located above the workbook. From the message bar, you can enable the content so that links can be updated.

Links can be edited or broken at the Edit Links dialog box, shown in Figure 4.2. If more than one link is present in the workbook, begin by clicking the link to be changed in the Source list. Click the Change Source button to open the Change Source dialog box, in which you can navigate to the drive and/or folder in which the source workbook was moved or renamed. Click the Break Link button to permanently remove the linked reference and convert the linked cells to their existing values. The Undo feature does not operate to restore a link. If you break a link that you later decide you want to restore, you will have to recreate the linked formula.

▼ **Quick Steps**

Edit a Link to an External Reference
1. Open destination workbook.
2. Click DATA tab.
3. Click Edit Links button.
4. Click link.
5. Click Change Source button.
6. Navigate to drive and/or folder.
7. Double-click source workbook file name.
8. Click Close button.
9. Save and close destination workbook.

Edit Links

Figure 4.2 Edit Links Dialog Box

▼ **Quick Steps**

Break a Link to an External Reference
1. Open destination workbook.
2. Click DATA tab.
3. Click Edit Links button.
4. Click link.
5. Click Break Link button.
6. Click Break Links button.
7. Click Close button.
8. Save and close destination workbook.

Project 1d   Editing Source Data and Updating an External Link   Part 4 of 5

1. Open **MayGroupSales.xlsx** and maximize the screen.
2. Save the workbook and name it **EL2-C4-P1-Source**.
3. Edit the attendance data value at each park by completing the following steps:
   a. Click the BryceCanyon sheet tab.
   b. Make cell B8 active and then change the value from *55* to *361*.
   c. Click the GrandCanyon sheet tab.
   d. Make cell B20 active and then change the value from *275* to *240*.
   e. Click the MesaVerde sheet tab.
   f. Make cell E21 active and then change the value from *312* to *406*.
4. Click the AttendanceSummary tab. Note that the updated value in cell F7 is *15,434*.
5. Save and then close **EL2-C4-P1-Source.xlsx**.
6. Open **EL2-C4-P1-MayEntries.xlsx**. Notice the security warning that appears in the Message bar above the worksheet area with the message that automatic update of links has been disabled. Instruct Excel to allow automatic updates for this workbook, since you are sure the content is from a trusted source, by clicking the Enable Content button next to the message. *Note: If a Security Warning dialog box appears asking if you want to make the file a trusted document, click No.*

7. Edit the link to retrieve the data from the workbook you revised in Steps 2–5 by completing the following steps:
   a. Click the DATA tab.
   b. Click the Edit Links button in the Connections group.

c. At the Edit Links dialog box, click the Change Source button.

d. At the Change Source: MayGroupSales.xlsx dialog box, double-click *EL2-C4-P1-Source.xlsx* in the file list box. Excel returns to the Edit Links dialog box and updates the source workbook file name and path.

e. Click the Close button.

8. Click cell F9 in the AttendanceSummary worksheet to view the updated linked formula. Notice that the workbook reference in the formula is *[EL2-C4-P1-Source.xlsx]* and the drive and path are included in the formula. (Your drive and/or path may vary from the one shown.)

9. Print the AttendanceSummary worksheet.

10. Save and then close **EL2-C4-P1-MayEntries.xlsx**.

Project 1e Removing a Linked External Reference   Part 5 of 5

1. Open **EL2-C4-P1-MayEntries.xlsx**.

2. At the Microsoft Excel message box that appears stating that the workbook contains links to other sources, read the message text and then click the Update button to update the links. *Note: Depending on the system settings on the computer you are using, this message may not appear. Proceed to Step 3.*

3. Remove the linked external reference to attendance values for commercial tour vehicles by completing the following steps:
   a. With the DATA tab active, click the Edit Links button in the Connections group.
   b. Click the Break Link button at the Edit Links dialog box.
   c. Click the Break Links button at the Microsoft Excel message box warning you that breaking links permanently converts formulas and external references to their existing values and asking you if you are sure you want to break the links.

   d. Click the Close button at the Edit Links dialog box with no links displayed.
4. In the AttendanceSummary worksheet with cell F9 active, look in the Formula bar. Notice that the linked formula has been replaced with the latest cell value, *15434*.
5. Save and then close **EL2-C4-P1-MayEntries.xlsx**.
6. Reopen **EL2-C4-P1-MayEntries.xlsx**. Notice that since the workbook no longer contains a link to an external reference, the security warning no longer appears in the Message bar.
7. Close **EL2-C4-P1-MayEntries.xlsx**. Click Don't Save if prompted to save changes.

Project 2 Calculate Total Fees Billed by Three Dentists   1 Part

You will use the Consolidate feature to summarize the total dental fees billed by treatment category for three dentists.

Summarizing Data Using the Consolidate Feature ▪▪▪▪▪

Consolidate

The Consolidate feature is another tool that can be used to summarize data from multiple worksheets into a master worksheet. The worksheets can be located in the same workbook as the master worksheet or in a separate workbook. Open the Consolidate dialog box, shown in Figure 4.3, by clicking the Consolidate button in the Data Tools group on the DATA tab.

Figure 4.3 Consolidate Dialog Box

When the Consolidate dialog box opens, the Sum function is selected by default. Change to a different function, such as Count or Average, using the *Function* drop-down list. In the *Reference* text box, type the range name or use the Collapse Dialog button to navigate to the cells to be consolidated. If the cells are located in another workbook, use the Browse button to navigate to the drive and/or folder and locate the file name. Once the correct reference is inserted in the *Reference* text box, click the Add button. Continue adding references for all of the units of data to be summarized.

In the *Use labels in* section, click to insert a check mark in the *Top row* or *Left column* check boxes to indicate where the labels are located in the source ranges. Insert a check mark in the *Create links to source data* check box to instruct Excel to update the data automatically when the source ranges change. Make sure enough empty cells are available to the right of and below the active cell when you open the Consolidate dialog box, since Excel populates the rows and columns based on the size of the source data.

▼ **Quick Steps**

Consolidate Data
1. Make starting cell active.
2. Click DATA tab.
3. Click Consolidate button.
4. If necessary, change function.
5. Enter first range in *Reference* text box.
6. Click Add button.
7. Enter next range in *Reference* text box.
8. Click Add button.
9. Repeat Steps 7–8 until all ranges have been added.
10. If necessary, click *Top row* and/or *Left column* check boxes.
11. If necessary, click *Create links to source data* check box.
12. Click OK.

Project 2 **Summarizing Data Using the Consolidate Feature** Part 1 of 1

1. Open **NADQ1Fees.xlsx**.
2. Save the workbook and name it **EL2-C4-P2-NADQ1Fees**.
3. The workbook is organized with the first quarter's fees for each of three dentists entered in separate worksheets. Range names have been defined for each dentist's first-quarter earnings. Review the workbook structure by completing the following steps:
   a. Click the down-pointing arrow in the Name box and then click *Popovich* at the drop-down list. Excel makes the Popovich worksheet active and selects the range A2:F13.
   b. Deselect the range.
   c. Display the defined range for the range name *Vanket* and then deselect the range.
   d. Display the defined range for the range name *Jovanovic* and then deselect the range.
4. Use the Consolidate feature to total the fees billed by treatment category for each month by completing the following steps:
   a. Make FeeSummary the active worksheet.
   b. With cell A5 active, click the DATA tab.
   c. Click the Consolidate button in the Data Tools group.

d. With *Sum* selected in the *Function* option box at the Consolidate dialog box and with the insertion point positioned in the *Reference* text box, type Popovich and then click the Add button.

e. With the text *Popovich* selected in the *Reference* text box, type Vanket and then click the Add button.

f. With the text *Vanket* selected in the *Reference* text box, type Jovanovic and then click the Add button.

g. Click the *Top row* and *Left column* check boxes in the *Use labels in* section to insert a check mark in each check box.

h. Click OK.

5. Deselect the consolidated range in the FeeSummary worksheet.

6. Adjust the width of each column in the FeeSummary worksheet to AutoFit.

7. Move the data in E5:E15 to F5:F15 and then AutoFit the column width.

8. Use Format Painter to apply the formatting options for the column headings and the total row from any of the three dentist worksheets to the FeeSummary worksheet.

9. Print page one of the FeeSummary worksheet.

10. Save and then close **EL2-C4-P2-NADQ1Fees.xlsx**.

Project 3 · Analyze Fitness Equipment Sales Data in a PivotTable and PivotChart · 8 Parts

You will create and edit a PivotTable and PivotChart to analyze fitness equipment sales by region, product, manufacturer, and salesperson.

▼ Quick Steps

Create a PivotTable
1. Select source range.
2. Click INSERT tab.
3. Click PivotTable button.
4. Click OK.
5. Add fields as needed using PivotTable Fields task pane.
6. Modify and/or format as desired.

PivotTable

Creating PivotTables ■■■■■■■■■■■■■■■■■■■■

A *PivotTable* is an interactive table that organizes and summarizes data based on fields (column headings) and records (rows). A numeric column that you select is then grouped by the rows and columns category and the data is summarized using a function such as Sum, Average, or Count. PivotTables are useful management tools, since they allow you to analyze data in a variety of scenarios by filtering a row or column category and instantly seeing the change in results. The interactivity of a PivotTable allows you to examine a variety of scenarios with just a few mouse clicks. Create a PivotTable using the PivotTable button in the Tables group on the INSERT tab.

Before creating a PivotTable, examine the source data and determine the following elements:

- Which rows and columns will define how to format and group the data?
- Which numeric field contains the values that should be grouped?
- Which summary function will be applied to the values? For example, do you want to sum, average, or count?
- Do you want to be able to filter the report as a whole, as well as by columns or rows?
- Do you want the PivotTable to be beside the source data or in a new sheet?
- How many reports do you want to extract from the PivotTable by filtering fields?

Make sure that the source data contains no blank rows or columns and is structured in such a way that repeated data in columns or rows can be grouped.

Excel 2013 has a new feature called ***Recommended PivotTables***. This feature analyzes the data and creates different PivotTable previews for you to choose from. The PivotTable can then be edited and formatted further if required. (You will learn how to format a PivotTable in Project 3c.)

To have Excel analyze your data and create a PivotTable using a recommended view, select the source range, click the INSERT tab, change the source data if required, and then click the Recommended PivotTables button in the Tables group. Click a PivotTable in the left panel of the Recommended PivotTables dialog box to preview it. Click OK to insert the selected PivotTable.

Recommended PivotTables

To build a PivotTable using the PivotTable button in the Tables group on the INSERT tab, select the source range or make sure the active cell is positioned within the list range, click the INSERT tab, and then click the PivotTable button in the Tables group. At the Create PivotTable dialog box, confirm the source range

Figure 4.4 PivotTable and PivotTable Fields Task Pane Used to Define Report Layout is correct and select whether to place the PivotTable in the existing worksheet or a new worksheet. Figure 4.4 presents the initial PivotTable and PivotTable Fields task pane, in which you define the report layout. Each column or row heading in the source range becomes a field in the PivotTable Fields task pane list. You can also create the initial PivotTable using the PivotTable button in the TABLES tab of the Quick Analysis button.

Build a PivotTable by selecting fields in the PivotTable Fields task pane. Click the check box next to a field to add it to the PivotTable. By default, non-numeric fields are added to the *Rows* box and numeric fields are added to the *Values* box in the layout section of the pane. Once a field has been added, you can move it to a different box by dragging the field header or clicking the field to display a shortcut menu. As you add each field, the PivotTable updates to show the results. If you do not like the results, uncheck the check box for the field to remove it from the report. Figure 4.5 displays the PivotTable you will build in Project 3b.

Project 3a   Creating a PivotTable Using Recommended PivotTables   Part 1 of 8

1. Open **PF1stQSales.xlsx**.
2. Save the workbook and name it **EL2-C4-P3-PF1stQSales**.
3. Create a PivotTable to summarize the sale price by product by completing the following steps:
   a. A range has been defined to select the list data. Click the down-pointing arrow in the Name box and then click *FirstQ* at the drop-down list.
   b. Click the INSERT tab.
   c. Click the Recommended PivotTables button in the Tables group.
   d. Click the <u>Change Source Data</u> hyperlink at the bottom of the Recommended PivotTables dialog box to expand the range.

   e. At the Choose Data Source dialog box, with *FirstQuarterSales!$A$4:$G$47* entered in the *Table/Range* text box, click OK.

f. Click the second PivotTable scenario in the left column to select the *Sum of Sale Price by Product* PivotTable.

g. Click OK to insert the PivotTable in a new worksheet.

4. Apply comma formatting with no places after the decimal point to B4:B9.

5. Rename the worksheet *PriceByProduct*.

6. Save **EL2-C4-P3-PF1stQSales.xlsx**.

Figure 4.5 PivotTable for Project 3b

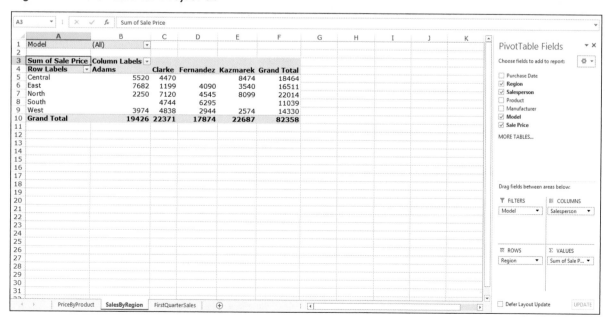

1. With **EL2-C4-P3-PF1stQSales.xlsx** open, make the FirstQuarterSales worksheet active. The FirstQ range should still be selected.
2. Create a PivotTable to summarize the fitness equipment sales by region and salesperson, as shown in Figure 4.5, by completing the following steps:
   a. Click the INSERT tab.
   b. Click the PivotTable button in the Tables group.
   c. At the Create PivotTable dialog box, with *FirstQuarterSales!$A$4:$G$47* entered in the *Table/Range* text box and *New Worksheet* selected for *Choose where you want the PivotTable report to be placed*, click OK.

   d. Click the *Region* check box in the PivotTable Fields task pane. *Region* is added to the *ROWS* list box in the layout section of the task pane and the report updates to show one row per region with a filter arrow at the top of the column and a *Grand Total* row automatically added to the bottom of the table. Since *Region* is a non-numeric field, Excel automatically places it in the *ROWS* list box.

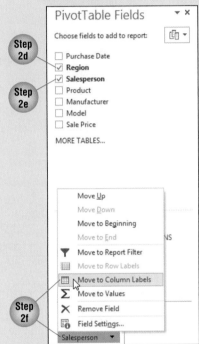

   e. Click the *Salesperson* check box in the PivotTable Fields task pane. Excel automatically adds *Salesperson* to the *ROWS* list box in the layout section. (In the next step, you will correct the placement of the field to move it to the *COLUMNS* list box.)
   f. Click the *Salesperson* field header in the *ROWS* list box in the layout section and then click *Move to Column Labels* at the pop-up list. Notice that the layout of the report now displays one row per region and one column per salesperson. (In the next step, you will drag a field from the PivotTable Fields list to the desired list box in the layout section.)
   g. Position the mouse pointer over *Model* in the PivotTable Fields task pane, hold down the left mouse button, drag the field to the *FILTERS* list box in the layout section, and then release the mouse button. Notice that *Model* is added as a filter at the top left of the PivotTable in A1:B1.

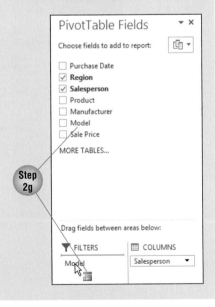

   h. Click the *Sale Price* check box in the PivotTable Fields task pane. Since the field is a numeric field, Excel adds it automatically to the *VALUES* list box in the layout section and the report updates to show the Sum function applied to the grouped values in the PivotTable. Compare your results with the PivotTable shown in Figure 4.5 on the previous page.
3. Rename the worksheet *SalesByRegion*.
4. Save **EL2-C4-P3-PF1stQSales.xlsx**.

When the active cell is positioned inside a PivotTable, the contextual PIVOTTABLE TOOLS ANALYZE and PIVOTTABLE TOOLS DESIGN tabs become available. Features on the PIVOTTABLE TOOLS DESIGN tab, shown in Figure 4.6, are similar to those on the TABLE TOOLS DESIGN tab, which you learned about in Chapter 3.

Figure 4.6 PIVOTTABLE TOOLS DESIGN Tab

| Project 3c | Formatting and Filtering a PivotTable | Part 3 of 8 |

1. With **EL2-C4-P3-PF1stQSales.xlsx** open and the SalesByRegion worksheet active, apply formatting options to the PivotTable to improve the report's appearance by completing the following steps:
   a. With the active cell positioned in the PivotTable, click the PIVOTTABLE TOOLS DESIGN tab.
   b. Click the More button in the PivotTable Styles gallery.
   c. Click *Pivot Style Medium 2* at the drop-down gallery (first row, second column of the *Medium* section).
   d. Click the *Banded Rows* check box in the PivotTable Style Options group to insert a check mark. Excel adds border lines between rows in the PivotTable. Recall from Chapter 3 that banding rows or columns adds a fill color or border style, depending on the style that has been applied to the PivotTable.
   e. Apply comma formatting with no places after the decimal point to B5:F10.
   f. Change the column width of columns B through F to 12 characters.

1	Model	(All)				
2						
3	**Sum of Sale Price**	Column Labels				
4	Row Labels	Adams	Clarke	Fernandez	Kazmarek	Grand Total
5	Central	5,520	4,470		8,474	18,464
6	East	7,682	1,199	4,090	3,540	16,511
7	North	2,250	7,120	4,545	8,099	22,014
8	South		4,744	6,295		11,039
9	West	3,974	4,838	2,944	2,574	14,330
10	**Grand Total**	**19,426**	**22,371**	**17,874**	**22,687**	**82,358**

Formatting options are applied to the PivotTable in Steps 1a-1f.

   g. To stop Excel from using AutoFit to adjust the column widths after you update cell content, right-click in the PivotTable and then click *PivotTable Options* at the shortcut menu. The PivotTable Options dialog box opens.

h. On the Layout & Format tab of the PivotTable Options dialog box, click the *Autofit column widths on update* check box to remove the check mark.

i. Click OK.

2. Filter the PivotTable to view sales for a group of model numbers by completing the following steps:

a. Click the filter arrow next to *(All)* in cell B1.

b. Click the *Select Multiple Items* check box to insert a check mark and turn on the display of check boxes next to all of the model numbers in the drop-down list.

c. Click the *(All)* check box to remove the check marks next to all of the model numbers.

d. Click the check boxes for those model numbers that begin with *CX* to insert check marks. This selects all six models from Cybex.

e. Click OK.

f. Print the filtered PivotTable.

g. Click the filter arrow next to *(Multiple Items)* in cell B1, click the *(All)* check box to select all of the model numbers in the drop-down list, and then click OK.

h. Experiment with the Column Labels and Row Labels filter arrows to filter the PivotTable by region or salesperson.

i. Make sure all of the filters are cleared.

3. Save **EL2-C4-P3-PF1stQSales.xlsx**.

Quick Steps

Add a Slicer to a PivotTable
1. Make any cell within PivotTable active.
2. Click PIVOTTABLE TOOLS ANALYZE tab.
3. Click Insert Slicer button.
4. Click check box for desired field.
5. Click OK.

Insert Slicer

Filtering a PivotTable Using Slicers

Slicers allow you to filter a PivotTable or PivotChart without opening the FILTERS list box. When Slicers are added to a PivotTable or PivotChart, a Slicer pane containing all of the unique values for the specified field is added to the window. Click the desired option in the Slicer pane to immediately filter the PivotTable or PivotChart. You can add several Slicer panes to a PivotTable or PivotChart to filter by more than one field as needed.

To insert a Slicer pane, make any cell within the PivotTable active, click the PIVOTTABLE TOOLS ANALYZE tab, and then click the Insert Slicer button in the Filter group. Excel opens the Insert Slicers dialog box, which contains a list of the fields in the PivotTable with a check box next to each field. Click to insert a check mark in the check box for each field for which you want to add a Slicer pane and then click OK.

1. With **EL2-C4-P3-PF1stQSales.xlsx** open, make PriceByProduct the active worksheet and then display a Slicer pane for the manufacturer by completing the following steps:

    a. Make any cell active within the PivotTable.

    b. Add *Manufacturer* to the *FILTERS* list box and *Region* to the *COLUMNS* list box. (If necessary, refer to Project 3b, Steps 2e–2g for assistance.)

    c. Click the PIVOTTABLE TOOLS ANALYZE tab.

    d. Click the Insert Slicer button in the Filter group.

    e. At the Insert Slicers dialog box, click the *Manufacturer* check box to insert a check mark and then click OK. Excel inserts a Slicer pane in the worksheet with all of the manufacturer numbers.

2. If necessary, position the mouse pointer at the top of the Manufacturer Slicer pane until the pointer changes to a four-headed arrow and then drag the pane to an empty location below the PivotTable.

3. Click *Vision* in the Manufacturer Slicer pane to filter the PivotTable. Excel filters the PivotTable by the Vision manufacturer. Notice that the *Manufacturer* filter arrow in cell B1 displays *Vision*.

4. Click the Clear Filter button at the top right of the Manufacturer Slicer pane to redisplay all of the data.

5. Add a second Slicer pane and filter by two fields by completing the following steps:

    a. If necessary, make any cell active within the PivotTable.

    b. Click the PIVOTTABLE TOOLS ANALYZE tab and then click the Insert Slicer button.

    c. At the Insert Slicers dialog box, click the *Region* check box to insert a check mark and then click OK.

    d. Drag the Region Slicer pane so that it is positioned below the PivotTable next to the Manufacturer Slicer pane.

e. Click *West* in the Region Slicer pane to filter the PivotTable.

f. Click *Vision* in the Manufacturer Slicer pane to filter the West region sales by the Vision manufacturer.

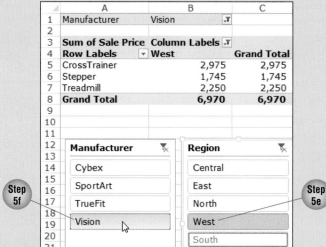

6. Print the filtered PivotTable.
7. Redisplay all of the data and remove the two Slicer panes by completing the following steps:
    a. Click the Clear Filter button at the top right of the Region Slicer pane.
    b. Click the Clear Filter button at the top right of the Manufacturer Slicer pane.
    c. Right-click the top of the Manufacturer Slicer pane and then click *Remove "Manufacturer"* at the shortcut menu.
    d. Right-click the top of the Region Slicer pane and then click *Remove "Region"* at the shortcut menu.

8. Save **EL2-C4-P3-PF1stQSales.xlsx**.

▼ **Quick Steps**

Add a Timeline to a PivotTable
1. Make any cell within PivotTable active.
2. Click PIVOTTABLE TOOLS ANALYZE tab.
3. Click Insert Timeline button.
4. Click check box for desired field.
5. Click OK.
6. Select desired timeframe.

Insert Timeline

A Slicer pane can be customized with buttons on the SLICER TOOLS OPTIONS tab. Click a Slicer pane to activate the SLICER TOOLS OPTIONS tab. Click the tab to display customization options such as Slicer Styles. You can also change the height and width of the buttons in the Slicer pane and/or the height and width of the pane.

Filtering a PivotTable Using Timelines

Timelines is a new feature added to Excel 2013 that allows you to group and filter a PivotTable or PivotChart based on specific timeframes. A date field you select adds a Timeline pane containing a timeline slicer that you can extend or shorten to instantly filter the data by the selected date range.

To insert a timeline, make any cell within the PivotTable active, click the PIVOTTABLE TOOLS ANALYZE tab, and then click the Insert Timeline button in the Filter group. Excel opens the Insert Timelines dialog box and displays any field that contains data that has been formatted as a date, with a check box next to each field. Click to insert a check mark in the check box of any date field for which you want to add a Timeline pane and then click OK. Even though you can have more than one Timeline pane, you only filter the data using one Timeline at a time. The PivotTable will display the data for the time period you select. Use the Time Level indicator located near the upper right of the pane to change the grouping to years, quarters, months, or days.

Project 3e   **Using a Timeline to Filter a PivotTable**   Part 5 of 8

1. With **EL2-C4-P3-PF1stQSales.xlsx** open, make the SalesByRegion worksheet active. Display one Timeline for January and then another for February and March combined by completing the following steps:
    a. Make any cell active within the PivotTable.
    b. Click the PIVOTTABLE TOOLS ANALYZE tab.
    c. Click the Insert Timeline button in the Filter group. Excel displays an Insert Timelines dialog box with all of the fields that have been formatted as dates.
    d. Click the check box next to *Purchase Date* in the Insert Timelines dialog box to insert a check mark.
    e. Click OK. Excel inserts a Timeline pane in the worksheet. The selection label displays *All Periods* to indicate that PivotTable displays all periods.
2. If necessary, position the mouse pointer at the top of the Timeline pane until the pointer changes to a four-headed arrow and then drag the pane to an empty location below the PivotTable.
3. Using the scroll bar at the bottom of the Timeline pane, scroll to the left and then click *JAN*. Excel filters the PivotTable by January. Notice that the selection label displays *Jan 2015*.
4. Click immediately to the right of the orange box on the timeline to filter the PivotTable to include only the sales for February 2015. The selection label displays *Feb 2015*.

5. Click and drag the orange box to the right so that the February timeframe is extended to include March. The selection label displays *Feb - Mar 2015* to indicate that the PivotTable has been filtered to include data for February and March.

6. Change the page orientation to landscape and print the filtered PivotTable.
7. Redisplay all of the data and remove the Timeline pane by completing the following steps:
   a. Click the Clear Filter button at the top right of the Timeline pane.
   b. Right-click the top of the Timeline pane and then click *Remove Timeline* at the shortcut menu.
8. Save **EL2-C4-P3-PF1stQSales.xlsx**.

▼ **Quick Steps**

Change the PivotTable Summary Function
1. Make any PivotTable cell active.
2. Click PIVOTTABLE TOOLS ANALYZE tab.
3. Click Field Settings button.
4. Click desired function.
5. Click OK.

Field Settings

You can customize the Timeline pane with buttons on the TIMELINE TOOLS OPTIONS tab. Click a Timeline pane to activate the TIMELINE TOOLS OPTIONS tab. Click the tab to display customization options such as Timeline styles. You can also change the height and width of the buttons in the Timeline pane and/or the height and width of the pane.

Changing the Summary Function

By default, Excel uses the Sum function to summarize the numeric value added to a PivotTable. To change Sum to another function, click any numeric value within the PivotTable or click the cell containing *Sum of [Fieldname]* at the top left of the PivotTable. Click the PIVOTTABLE TOOLS ANALYZE tab and then click the Field Settings button in the Active Field group. This opens the Value Field Settings dialog box, in which you can choose a function other than Sum. Alternatively, you can right-click any numeric value within the PivotTable, point to *Summarize Values By* at the shortcut menu, and then click the desired function name.

Project 3f **Changing the Values Function in a PivotTable** Part 6 of 8

1. With **EL2-C4-P3-PF1stQSales.xlsx** open, save the workbook and name it **EL2-C4-P3-PFAvg1stQSales**.
2. With the SalesByRegion worksheet active, change the function for the *SalePrice* field from Sum to Average by completing the following steps:
   a. Make cell A3 the active cell in the PivotTable. This cell contains the label *Sum of Sale Price*.
   b. Click the PIVOTTABLE TOOLS ANALYZE tab.
   c. Click the Field Settings button in the Active Field group.
   d. At the Value Field Settings dialog box with the Summarize Values By tab active, click *Average* in the *Summarize value field by* list box and then click OK.
3. Print the revised PivotTable.
4. Save and then close **EL2-C4-P3-PFAvg1stQSales.xlsx**.

Creating PivotCharts ■■■■■■■■■■■■■■■■■■■■■■■■■

A *PivotChart* visually displays data in chart form. As with a PivotTable, you can filter the data in a PivotChart to examine various scenarios between categories. As you make changes to the PivotChart, the PivotTable associated with the PivotChart is also updated. Figure 4.7 displays the PivotChart you will create in Project 3g.

In a worksheet that already contains a PivotTable, position the active cell anywhere within the PivotTable, click the PIVOTTABLE TOOLS ANALYZE tab, and then click the PivotChart button in the Tools group to create a chart from the existing summary data. Excel displays the Insert Chart dialog box, in which you choose the type of chart to create. Once the PivotChart has been generated, the PivotTable and PivotChart become connected. Changes made to the data by filtering in one object cause the other object to update with the same filter. For example, filtering the PivotChart by an individual salesperson name causes the PivotTable to also filter by the same salesperson name.

If you open a worksheet that does not contain a pre-existing PivotTable and create a PivotChart, Excel displays a blank chart, a PivotTable placeholder, and the PivotChart Fields task pane. Build the chart using the same techniques you used to build a PivotTable. As you build a PivotChart, Excel also builds a PivotTable that is connected to the PivotChart.

Before you begin creating a PivotChart from scratch, examine the source data and determine the following:

- Which fields do you want to display along the *x* (horizontal) axis? In other words, how do you want to compare data when viewing the chart: by time period (such as months or years), by salesperson names, by department names, or by some other category?

- Which fields do you want to display in the legend? In other words, how many data series (bars in a column chart) do you want to view in the chart: one for each region, product, salesperson, department, or some other category?

- Which numeric field contains the values you want to graph in the chart?

▼ **Quick Steps**

Create a PivotChart from a PivotTable
1. Make cell active within PivotTable.
2. Click PIVOTTABLE TOOLS ANALYZE tab.
3. Click PivotChart button.
4. Select desired chart type.
5. Click OK.

Create a PivotChart without an Existing PivotTable
1. Select range containing data for chart.
2. Click INSERT tab.
3. Click PivotChart button arrow.
4. Click *PivotChart*.
5. Click OK.
6. Add fields as needed in PivotTable Fields task pane to build chart.
7. Modify and/or format as required.

PivotChart

Figure 4.7 PivotChart for Project 3g

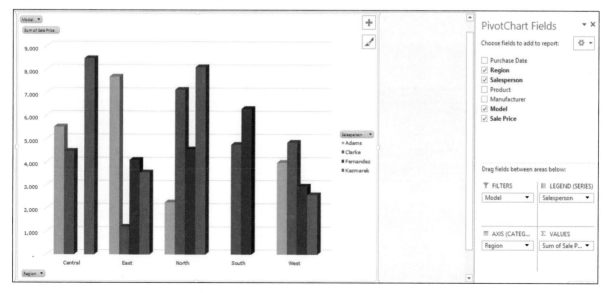

Use the Chart Elements button and the Chart Styles button located in the top right corner of the PivotChart to add or remove titles, labels, or other chart elements and apply a style or color scheme to your PivotChart. To move the chart to a new sheet, use the Move Chart button in the Actions group on the PIVOTCHART TOOLS ANALYZE tab.

Move Chart

Project 3g **Creating a PivotChart**   **Part 7 of 8**

1. Open **EL2-C4-P3-PF1stQSales.xlsx** and, if necessary, make the SalesByRegion sheet active.
2. Create a PivotChart to visually present the data in the PivotTable by completing the following steps:
   a. If necessary, click any cell within the PivotTable to activate the PivotTable contextual tabs.
   b. Click the PIVOTTABLE TOOLS ANALYZE tab.
   c. Click the PivotChart button in the Tools group.
   d. At the Insert Chart dialog box with *Column* selected in the left pane, click *3-D Clustered Column* (fourth option above preview) and then click OK.

3. Filter the PivotChart to display sales for only one salesperson by completing the following steps:
   a. Click the Salesperson field button in the PivotChart. (This is the button above the salesperson names in the PivotChart legend.)
   b. Click the *(Select All)* check box to clear all of the check boxes.
   c. Click the *Kazmarek* check box to insert a check mark and then click OK.
   d. Notice the PivotTable behind the chart is also filtered to reflect the chart's display. ***Note: If the chart is obscuring your view of the PivotTable, drag the PivotChart border to move the chart out of the way.***
   e. Click the Salesperson field button in the PivotChart and then click *Clear Filter From "Salesperson"*.

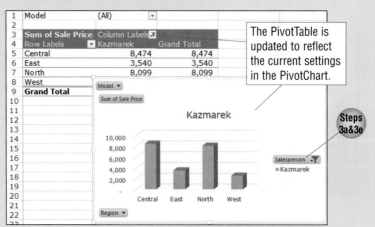

The PivotTable is updated to reflect the current settings in the PivotChart.

4. Move the PivotChart to a separate worksheet by completing the following steps:

a. Click the Move Chart button in the Actions group on the PIVOTCHART TOOLS ANALYZE tab.

Step 4a

b. At the Move Chart dialog box, click the *New sheet* option, type PivotChart in the *New sheet* text box, and then click OK. Excel moves the PivotChart to a separate worksheet. Compare your PivotChart with the one shown in Figure 4.7 on page 127.

Move Chart

Choose where you want the chart to be placed:

New sheet: PivotChart

Object in: SalesByRegion

OK   Cancel

Step 4b

5. Print the PivotChart.

6. Save and then close **EL2-C4-P3-PF1stQSales.xlsx**.

Project 3h   **Creating a PivotChart from Scratch**   **Part 8 of 8**

1. Open **PF1stQSales**.
2. Save the workbook and name it **EL2-C4-P3-PFChart**.
3. Create a PivotChart to display the sales by manufacturer by region by completing the following steps:

a. Select the *FirstQ* named range and then click the INSERT tab.

b. Click the PivotChart button arrow in the Charts group and then click *PivotChart* at the drop-down list.

Step 3b

PivotChart

PivotChart & PivotTable

c. At the Create PivotChart dialog box, with *FirstQuarterSales!$A$4:$G$47* entered in the *Table/Range* text box and *New Worksheet* selected in the *Choose where you want the PivotChart to be placed* section, click OK.

d. Excel displays a blank sheet with the PivotChart Fields task pane at the right side of the window. A PivotTable placeholder and chart placeholder appear in the worksheet area. As you build the PivotChart, notice that a PivotTable is created automatically.

e. Click the *Manufacturer* check box in the PivotChart Fields task pane. Excel adds the field to the *AXIS (CATEGORIES)* list box in the layout section.

f. Click the *Region* check box in the PivotChart Fields task pane. Excel adds the field below *Manufacturer* in the *AXIS (CATEGORIES)* list box in the layout section.

g. Click the *Region* field header in the *AXIS (CATEGORIES)* list box and then click *Move to Legend Fields (Series)* at the pop-up list. Excel moves the field and updates the chart and PivotTable.

Move Up
Move Down
Move to Beginning
Move to End
Move to Report Filter
Move to Axis Fields (Categories)
Move to Legend Fields (Series)
Move to Values
Hide Axis Field Buttons on Chart
Hide All Field Buttons on Chart
Remove Field
Field Settings...
Region

Step 3g

h. Click the *Sale Price* check box in the PivotTable Fields task pane. Excel graphs the sum of the sale price values in the PivotChart and updates the PivotTable.

4. Point to the border of the PivotChart and then drag the PivotChart below the PivotTable.
5. Resize the chart to the approximate height and width of the chart shown below.
6. Experiment with the Chart Elements and Chart Styles buttons located in the upper right corner of the chart. (See Level 1, Chapter 7 for more information on these buttons.)

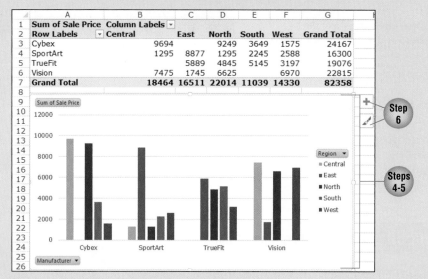

7. Rename the sheet containing the PivotTable and PivotChart as *SummaryData*.
8. Print the PivotTable and PivotChart worksheet.
9. Save and then close **EL2-C4-P3-PFChart.xlsx**.

Project 4 — Add Sparklines in a Worksheet to Show Trends

2 Parts

You will add and format Sparklines to identify trends in fees for dental services over the first quarter.

Summarizing Data with Sparklines ▪▪▪▪▪▪▪▪▪▪▪▪▪▪

Quick Steps

Create Sparklines
1. Select empty range in which to insert Sparklines.
2. Click INSERT tab.
3. Click Line, Column, or Win/Loss in Sparklines group.
4. Type data range address or drag to select data range in *Data Range* text box.
5. Click OK.

Sparklines are miniature charts that are embedded into the background of cells. An entire chart exists in a single cell. Since Sparklines can be placed directly next to the data set that is being represented, viewing them allows you to quickly determine if a trend or pattern exists within the data. Consider using Sparklines to show high and low values within a range, as well as trends and other patterns. Figure 4.8 illustrates the three buttons in the Sparklines group used to create Sparkline charts: Line, Column, and Win/Loss.

Creating a Sparkline

To create a Sparkline, select the empty cell range in which to insert the miniature charts, click the INSERT tab, and then click the desired Sparkline type in the Sparklines group, as shown in Figure 4.9. At the Create Sparklines dialog box, type or click the range for the cells that contain the data you wish to graph in the *Data Range* text box and then click OK.

Figure 4.8 Line, Column, and Win/Loss Sparklines Added to a Worksheet

	Q1 Fees	Q2 Fees	Q3 Fees	Q4 Fees	Fees Summary
NewAge Dental Services					
Fee Revenue Summary					
Popovich	72,148.09	90,435.25	95,123.45	104,356.82	
Vanket	35,070.13	33,188.97	31,876.45	37,908.22	
Jovanovic	42,471.35	47,845.21	32,158.42	38,452.12	
Total	$ 149,689.57	$ 171,469.43	$ 159,158.32	$ 180,717.16	Q4 set new record!
Increase or Decrease in Fees Compared to Last year					
Popovich	-3.0%	2.5%	4.5%	6.0%	
Vanket	5.5%	-8.0%	-10.0%	3.8%	
Jovanovic	4.5%	6.4%	-12.0%	1.2%	

Use the Line or Column buttons to create Sparklines to show trends or patterns over a time period.

Since Sparklines are part of the cell's background, you can add text to the Sparklines cell.

Use the Win/Loss button to create Sparklines to show positive and negative values using bars. Notice that the bars are all the same height but that those quarters in which fees are lower than last year (negative percentages) show as red bars below the baseline.

Figure 4.9 Sparklines Group on the INSERT Tab

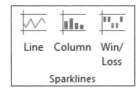

Line   Column   Win/Loss

Sparklines

Project 4a   **Creating Sparklines**   **Part 1 of 2**

1. Open **EL2-C4-P2-NADQ1Fees.xlsx**.
2. Save the workbook and name it **EL2-C4-P4-NADQ1Fees**.
3. Create a Sparkline to illustrate the trends in categories of dental service fees during the first quarter by completing the following steps:
   a. With the FeeSummary worksheet active, select G6:G14.
   b. Click the INSERT tab.
   c. Click the Line button in the Sparklines group.

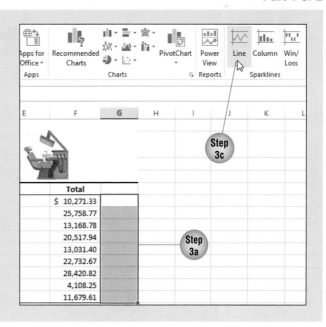

d. At the Create Sparklines dialog box with the insertion point positioned in the *Data Range* text box, type **b6:d14** and then click OK. Excel inserts miniature line charts within the cells.

4. Spend a few moments reviewing the Sparklines to determine what the charts indicate. Notice that the lines in cell G7 (Cleanings and Fillings) and cell G10 (Porcelain Veneers) slope downward and that the lines in cell G8 (Teeth Whitening) and cell G11 (Crowns and Bridges) have a similar shape. This shows that these dental services peaked in February and are on a decline.
5. Save **EL2-C4-P4-NADQ1Fees.xlsx**.

Customizing Sparklines

▼ Quick Steps

Customize Sparklines
1. Click in any Sparklines cell.
2. Click SPARKLINE TOOLS DESIGN tab.
3. Change chart type, show/hide points or markers, and change chart style, color, or marker color.

Activate any Sparkline cell and the SPARKLINE TOOLS DESIGN tab, shown in Figure 4.10, becomes visible. Click the Edit Data button to edit a range used to generate the Sparklines or instruct Excel how to graph hidden or empty cells in the data range. Use buttons in the Type group to change the chart type from line to column or win/loss. Click the check boxes in the Show group to show or hide data points in the chart or show markers. With options in the Style group, you can change the line and/or marker appearance. Click the Axis button in the last group to customize the horizontal or vertical axis in the charts. Sparklines can be grouped, ungrouped, or cleared with the last three buttons in the tab.

Figure 4.10 SPARKLINE TOOLS DESIGN Tab

1. With **EL2-C4-P4-NADQ1Fees.xlsx** open, customize the Sparklines by completing the following steps:

   a. If necessary, click any Sparkline cell to activate the SPARKLINE TOOLS DESIGN tab.

   b. Click the SPARKLINE TOOLS DESIGN tab.

   c. Click the Sparkline Color button in the Style group and then click *Dark Red* (first option in the *Standard Colors* section) at the drop-down color palette.

   d. Click the *High Point* check box in the Show group to insert a check mark. Excel adds a marker at the highest point on each line graph.

   e. Click the *Markers* check box in the Show group to insert a check mark. Excel adds markers to all of the other data points on each line.

   f. Click the Marker Color button in the Style group, point to *Markers*, and then click *Black, Text 1* (first row, second column in the *Theme Colors* section) at the drop-down color palette.

2. Improve the appearance of the Sparklines by widening the column and adding fill color by completing the following steps:

   a. Change the width of column G to 22 characters.

   b. Select G6:G14, click the HOME tab, and then apply the Blue, Accent 1, Lighter 80% fill color (second row, fifth column in the *Theme Colors* section) to the selected cells.

   c. Click in any cell to deselect the range.

3. Make cell G5 active, type January to March Trends, and then format the cell so that it has the same formatting as the other titles in row 5.

4. Change the page orientation to landscape and then print the FeeSummary worksheet.

5. Save and then close **EL2-C4-P4-NADQ1Fees.xlsx**.

Chapter Summary

- A formula that references a cell in another worksheet within the same workbook contains a worksheet reference and cell reference separated by an exclamation point.

- Range names can be used to simplify the references to cells in another worksheet, since the worksheet reference is automatically included in the definition of the range name.

- A disadvantage to using range names to reference other worksheets emerges if several worksheets are to be summarized, since each name has to be defined before the formula can be created.

- A 3-D reference is used to summarize the same cell in a range that extends over two or more worksheets.

- A 3-D reference includes the starting worksheet name and ending worksheet name separated by a colon, similar to the method used to define a range of cells.

- A formula that references another worksheet is linked to that worksheet, so that a change made in the source cell is automatically made in the other worksheet.

- A formula that references a cell in another workbook must include a workbook reference in front of the worksheet and cell references. Workbook references are enclosed in square brackets.

- When you create a formula that links to an external reference, Excel includes the drive and folder name in the path to the source workbook. If you move the location of the source workbook or change the source workbook file name, you must edit the linked reference.

- Open the Edit Links dialog box to edit or remove a linked external reference.

- The Consolidate feature is another method you can use to summarize data in multiple worksheets or workbooks.

- The Consolidate button is located in the Data Tools group on the DATA tab.

- At the Consolidate dialog box, choose the summary function you want to use for the data that will be consolidated, add the references containing the data you want to summarize, specify the location of the labels to duplicate, and indicate whether to create a link to the source data.

- PivotTables are interactive tables that organize and summarize data based on categories in rows or columns.

- Preview different PivotTable scenarios with the Recommended PivotTables button.

- Create a PivotTable using the PivotTable button in the Tables group on the INSERT tab.

- Add fields to the PivotTable using the field name check boxes in the PivotTable Fields task pane.

- Once created, a PivotTable can be used to view a variety of scenarios by filtering the row, column, or report headings.

- Use buttons in the contextual PIVOTTABLE TOOLS ANALYZE and DESIGN tabs to format the PivotTable and/or edit the features used in the table.

- Slicers are used to filter data in a PivotTable without having to open a filter drop-down list.
- A Slicer pane contains all of the items in the designated field, so the report can be filtered with one mouse click.
- Click the Insert Slicer button in the Filter group on the PIVOTTABLE TOOLS ANALYZE tab to add a Slicer pane to a PivotTable.
- Timelines are used to group and filter data in a PivotTable using timeframes such as years, quarters, months, and days.
- Click the Insert Timeline button in the Filter group on the PIVOTTABLE TOOLS ANALYZE tab to add a Timeline pane to a PivotTable.
- A PivotChart displays the data in a PivotTable in a specified chart type.
- Filter a PivotChart using the legend or axis field buttons located on the PivotChart.
- Sparklines are miniature charts inserted into the backgrounds of cells.
- Add Sparklines to a worksheet to show trends or high or low values in a range of source data next to the data.
- To add Sparklines, select an empty range next to the source data, click the INSERT tab, and then click the desired chart type in the Sparklines group. At the Create Sparklines dialog box, type the range containing the values you want to graph or drag to select the range and then click OK.
- Sparklines can be customized using options in the SPARKLINE TOOLS DESIGN tab.

Commands Review

FEATURE	RIBBON TAB, GROUP	BUTTON	KEYBOARD SHORTCUT
Consolidate	DATA, Data Tools		
edit links	DATA, Connections		
manage range names	FORMULAS, Defined Names		Ctrl + F3
PivotChart	INSERT, Charts OR PIVOTTABLES TOOLS ANALYZE, Tools		
PivotTable	INSERT, Tables		
Slicer	INSERT, Filters		
Sparklines	INSERT, Sparklines		
Timelines	INSERT, Filters		

Completion: In the space provided at the right, indicate the correct term, command, or number.

1. This symbol separates a worksheet reference from a cell reference.

   _____

2. This term describes a formula that references the same cell in a range that spans two or more worksheets.

   _____

3. Assume that a workbook contains the following defined range names that reference cells in four worksheets: Qtr1, Qtr2, Qtr3, and Qtr4. Provide the formula to add the data in the four ranges.

   _____

4. Create this formula entry for QtrlySales.xlsx to link to an external reference cell C12 in a worksheet named *Summary*.

   _____

5. Open this dialog box to change the source of a linked external reference after moving the source workbook to another folder.

   _____

6. Click this button to permanently remove a linked external reference and convert the linked cells to their existing values.

   _____

7. This default function is active when you open the Consolidate dialog box.

   _____

8. Use this button to preview different PivotTable scenarios.

   _____

9. Add fields to a PivotTable by clicking the field check box in this task pane.

   _____

10. The PivotTable Styles gallery is accessible from this tab.

    _____

11. Insert this type of pane to filter a PivotTable with one mouse click.

    _____

12. Insert this type of pane to filter a PivotTable by dates.

    _____

13. Choose a function other than Sum for a PivotTable numeric field by clicking this button in the Active Group on the PIVOTTABLE TOOLS ANALYZE tab.

    _____

14. The buttons to filter a PivotChart are found here.

    _____

15. This is the first step in adding Sparklines to a worksheet.

    _____

16. Click this tab to customize Sparklines.

    _____

Skills Check Assess Your Performance

Note: If you submit your work in hard copy, check with your instructor before completing these Assessments to see if you need to print two copies of worksheets in which you have created formulas, with one copy showing the cell formulas.

Assessment

1 SUMMARIZE DATA IN MULTIPLE WORKSHEETS USING RANGE NAMES Grade It

1. Open **NADQ1Fees.xlsx**.
2. Save the workbook and name it **EL2-C4-A1-NADQ1Fees**.
3. The workbook contains three worksheets showing dental fees earned in January, February, and March for three dentists at a dental clinic. Create a range name in cell F13 of each worksheet to reference the total fees earned by each dentist for the quarter as follows:
   a. Type PopovichTotal as the name for cell F13 in the Popovich worksheet.
   b. Type VanketTotal as the name for cell F13 in the Vanket worksheet.
   c. Type JovanovicTotal as the name for cell F13 in the Jovanovic worksheet.
4. Make FeeSummary the active worksheet and then type the following label in cell A6: Quarter 1 fees for Popovich, Vanket, and Jovanovic.
5. Make cell F6 the active cell and create a Sum formula to add the total fees earned by each dentist using the range names created in Step 3.
6. Apply accounting formatting to cell F6 and then adjust the column width to AutoFit.
7. Print the FeeSummary worksheet.
8. Save and then close **EL2-C4-A1-NADQ1Fees.xlsx**.

Assessment

2 SUMMARIZE DATA USING LINKED EXTERNAL REFERENCES

1. Open **PFSalesSum.xlsx**.
2. Save the workbook and name it **EL2-C4-A2-PFSalesSum**.
3. Open **PFQ1.xlsx**, **PFQ2.xlsx**, **PFQ3.xlsx**, and **PFQ4.xlsx**.
4. Tile all of the open workbooks. *Hint: Use the Arrange All button on the VIEW tab.*
5. Starting in cell B5 in **EL2-C4-A2-PFSalesSum.xlsx**, create formulas to populate the cells in column B by linking to the appropriate source cells in **PFQ1.xlsx**. *Hint: After creating the first formula, edit the entry in cell B5 to use a relative reference to the source cell (instead of an absolute reference) so you can copy and paste the formula in cell B5 to B6:B9.*
6. Create formulas to link to the appropriate source cells for the second-, third-, and fourth-quarter sales.
7. Close the four quarterly sales workbooks. Click Don't Save when prompted to save changes.
8. Maximize **EL2-C4-A2-PFSalesSum.xlsx**.
9. Make cell B5 the active cell and break the link to **PFQ1.xlsx**.
10. Print the worksheet.
11. Save and then close **EL2-C4-A2-PFSalesSum.xlsx**.

3 SUMMARIZE DATA USING 3-D REFERENCES

1. Open **JuneEntries.xlsx**.
2. Save the workbook and name it **EL2-C4-A3-JuneEntries**.
3. With AttendanceSummary the active worksheet, summarize the data in the three park worksheets using 3-D references as follows:
   a. Make cell B7 the active cell and then create a 3-D formula to sum the attendance values in the three park worksheets for day 1. Copy and paste the formula into the remaining cells in column B to complete the summary to day 16.
   b. Make cell E7 the active cell and then create a 3-D formula to sum the attendance values in the three park worksheets for day 17. Copy and paste the formula into the remaining cells in column E to complete the summary to day 30.
4. Type the label Total Vehicle and Individual Entrances in cell A24 and create a Sum formula in cell E24 to compute the grand total. Apply comma formatting with no places after the decimal point.
5. Print the AttendanceSummary worksheet.
6. Save and then close **EL2-C4-A3-JuneEntries.xlsx**.

4 SUMMARIZE DATA IN A PIVOTTABLE AND PIVOTCHART

1. Open **BillingSummary3Q.xlsx**.
2. Save the workbook and name it **EL2-C4-A4-BillingSummary3Q**.
3. Create a PivotTable in a new worksheet as follows:
   a. Display the range named *ThirdQ* and then insert a PivotTable in a new worksheet.
   b. Add the *Attorney LName* field as rows.
   c. Add the *Area* field as columns.
   d. Sum the *Fees Due* field.
4. Apply the Pivot Style Medium 2 style to the PivotTable (second column first row in the *Medium* section).
5. Apply comma formatting with no places after the decimal point to the values. Also change the column widths of B through H to 13 characters and right-align the *Martinez, O'Donovan, Sullivan, Williams,* and *Grand Total* labels in column A.
6. Name the worksheet *PivotTable* and then do the following:
   a. In cell A1, type Associate Billing Summary. Change the font to 14-point Copperplate Gothic Bold. Merge and center the text across the PivotTable.
   b. In cell A2, type October - December 2015. Change the font to 14-point Copperplate Gothic Bold. Merge and center the text across the PivotTable.
   c. Change the orientation to landscape and print the PivotTable.
7. Create a PivotChart from the PivotTable using the 3-D Stacked Column chart type and move the chart to its own sheet named *PivotChart*.
8. Apply Style 7 to the PivotChart (seventh style in the Chart Styles gallery).
9. Filter the PivotChart by the attorney named *Martinez*.
10. Print the PivotChart.
11. Save and then close **EL2-C4-A4-BillingSummary3Q.xlsx**.

Assessment

5 FILTERING A PIVOTTABLE USING A SLICER AND TIMELINE

1. Open **EL2-C4-A4-BillingSummary3Q.xlsx**.
2. Save the workbook and name it **EL2-C4-A5-BillingSummary3Q.xlsx**.
3. Click the PivotTable sheet to view the PivotTable.
4. Remove the filter to display all of the attorney names.
5. Insert a Slicer pane for the *Area* field and move the Slicer pane below the PivotTable.
6. Using the Slicer pane, filter the PivotTable by *Corporate*. Hold down the Shift key and then click the button for *Divorce*. (Use the Shift key to filter by multiple fields in a Slicer pane when the two fields are adjacent in the pane.)
7. Insert a Timeline pane for the *Date* field and move the Timeline pane to the right of the Slicer pane.
8. Using the Timeline pane, filter the PivotTable for Oct to Nov 2015.
9. Print the PivotTable.
10. Save and then close **EL2-C4-A5-BillingSummary3Q.xlsx**.

Assessment

6 CREATING AND CUSTOMIZING SPARKLINES

1. Open **EL2-C4-A2-PFSalesSum.xlsx** and enable the content.
2. Save the workbook and name it **EL2-C4-A6-PFSalesSum**.
3. Select H5:H9 and insert line-type Sparklines referencing the data range B5:E9.
4. Show the high point using markers on each line.
5. Change the Sparkline color to *Dark Blue* (in *Standard Colors* section).
6. Change the width of column H to 21 characters and type the label Region Sales by Quarter in cell H4.
7. Change the page orientation to landscape and then print the worksheet.
8. Save and then close **EL2-C4-A6-PFSalesSum.xlsx**.

SUMMARIZING REAL ESTATE SALES AND COMMISSION DATA

1. Open **HROctSales.xlsx**.
2. Save the workbook and name it **EL2-C4-VB-HROctSales**.
3. Create the PivotTable shown in Figure 4.11 in a new worksheet named *PivotTable*. Apply the Pivot Style Medium 11 style and set the column widths to 18 characters.
4. Create the PivotChart shown in Figure 4.12 in a new worksheet named *PivotChart*. Use the 3-D Clustered Column chart type and apply the Style 11 style.
5. Print the PivotTable and PivotChart worksheets.
6. Save and then close **EL2-C4-VB-HROctSales.xlsx**.

Figure 4.11 Visual Benchmark PivotTable

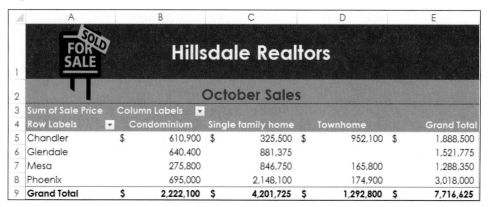

Figure 4.12 Visual Benchmark PivotChart

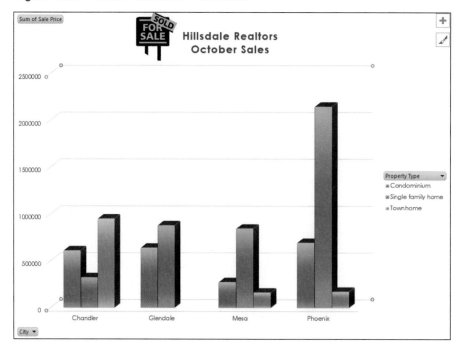

Case Study   Apply Your Skills

Part 1

Yolanda Robertson of NuTrends Market Research is continuing to work on the franchise expansion plan for the owners of Pizza By Mario. Yolanda has received a new workbook from the owners with profit information by store and would like you to summarize the data. Open the workbook named **PBMSales&Profits.xlsx** and review the structure of the data. Yolanda would like to have a PivotTable that provides the average gross sales and average net income by city and state. You determine how to organize the layout of the report. *Hint: You can add more than one numeric field to the* **Values list box**. Remove the grand totals at the right of the report so that only a grand total row appears at the bottom of the PivotTable. *Hint: Use the Grand Totals button in the Layout group on the PIVOTTABLE TOOLS DESIGN tab*. Apply formatting options to improve the report's appearance and make sure the report prints on one page in landscape orientation. Rename the worksheet containing the report *PivotTable*. Save the revised workbook and name it **EL2-C4-CS-P1-PBMRpt**.

Part 2

Yolanda would like to have a chart that graphs the average net income data for the state of Michigan. Create a PivotChart in a new sheet named *PivotChart* and filter the chart appropriately to meet Yolanda's request. You determine the appropriate chart style and elements to include in the chart. Yolanda will use this chart at an upcoming meeting with the franchise owners and wants the chart to be of professional quality. Print the chart. Save the revised workbook and name it **EL2-C4-CS-P2-PBMRpt** and then close the workbook.

Part 3

Open **EL2-C4-CS-P1-PBMRpt.xlsx**. Use the Help feature to find out how to modify a numeric field setting to show values as ranked numbers, from largest to smallest. For example, instead of displaying the average value next to the city name, you will display the city's ranking as it compares to other cities in the same state. Ranking from largest to smallest means the highest value in the state is ranked as 1. Using the information you have learned in Help, change the display of the average sales to show the values ranked from largest to smallest using *City* as the base field. Remove the *Net Income* field from the PivotTable. Remove the *Grand Total* row at the bottom of the PivotTable. Make any other formatting changes to the report that you think will improve its appearance. Print the PivotTable. Save the revised workbook and name it **EL2-C4-CS-P3-PBMRpt**.

Part 4

Yolanda would like you to do some comparison research with another pizza franchise. Use the Internet to research the sales and net income of a pizza franchise with which you are familiar. Create a new workbook that compares the total annual sales and net income values of the pizza franchise you researched with the Pizza By Mario information in **EL2-C4-CS-P1-PBMRpt.xlsx**. Provide the URL of the website from which you obtained the information about the competitor. Create a chart that presents the comparison data. Save the workbook and name it **EL2-C4-CS-P4-PizzaFranchiseComparison**. Print the comparison data and the chart. Close **EL2-C4-CS-P4-PizzaFranchiseComparison.xlsx**.

MICROSOFT® EXCEL® Performance Assessment

Access
EL2U1

Note: Before beginning assessments, copy to your storage medium the EL2U1 subfolder from the EL2 folder on the CD that accompanies this textbook and then make EL2U1 the active folder.

Assessing Proficiency ■■■■■■■■■■■■■

In this unit, you have learned to apply advanced formatting options, such as conditional formatting and custom number formats; perform advanced sort and filtering techniques; create functions that incorporate conditional logic, look up data, convert text, and calculate financial results; define a table and apply data management features to a table or list range; consolidate and summarize data; and present summary information in PivotTables, PivotCharts, and Sparklines.

Assessment 1 Conditionally Format and Filter a Help Desk Worksheet

1. Open **RSRHelpDesk.xlsx**.
2. Save the workbook using the name **EL2-U1-A1-RSRHelpDesk**.
3. Use the icon set from the Quick Analysis button to apply conditional formatting to the values in the *Priority* column.
4. Create a custom format for the values in the *Time Spent* column. The format should display a leading zero, two places after the decimal point, and the text *hrs* after each entry, separated by one space from the number (e.g. 2.20 hrs, 0.25 hrs, etc.).
5. Create two conditional formatting rules for the values in the *Time Spent* column as follows:
   a. For all entries in which the time spent is less than one hour, apply bold formatting and the Olive Green, Accent 3, Lighter 80% fill color (seventh column, second row).
   b. For all entries in which the time spent is more than two hours, apply the Yellow fill color (fourth column, last row).
6. Filter the worksheet by the Yellow fill color applied in the *Time Spent* column.
7. Print the filtered worksheet.
8. Clear the filter and filter arrow(s) and then print the worksheet.
9. Save and then close **EL2-U1-A1-RSRHelpDesk.xlsx**.

Assessment 2 Use Conditional Logic Formulas in a Help Desk Worksheet

1. Open **EL2-U1-A1-RSRHelpDesk.xlsx**.
2. Save the workbook using the name **EL2-U1-A2-RSRHelpDesk.xlsx**.
3. Create range names of your choosing for each of the following ranges:
   - A4:E6, which will be used in a lookup formula
   - E8:E30 in the *Operator ID* column
   - I8:I30 in the *Time Spent* column
   - J8:J30 in the *Status* column
4. In cell I4, create a COUNTA formula to count the number of help desk calls in March, using column A as the source range.
5. In cells I5 and I6, create COUNTIF formulas to count the number of active calls (I5) and number of closed calls (I6). Use range names in the formulas.
6. Create COUNTIF formulas in cells K3 through K6 to count the calls assigned to operator IDs 1, 2, 3, and 4, respectively. Use range names in the formulas.
7. Create SUMIF formulas in cells L3 through L6 to calculate the total time spent on calls assigned to operator IDs 1, 2, 3, and 4, respectively. Use range names in the formulas. Format the results to display two places after the decimal point.
8. Create AVERAGEIF formulas in cells M3 through M6 to find the average time spent on calls assigned to operator IDs 1, 2, 3, and 4, respectively. Use range names in the formulas. Format the results to display two places after the decimal point.
9. Create the HLOOKUP formula with an exact match in cell G8 to return the last name of the operator assigned to the call. Use the range name for the lookup table in the formula.
10. Create the HLOOKUP formula with an exact match in cell H8 to return the first name of the operator assigned to the call. Use the range name for the lookup table in the formula.
11. Copy the HLOOKUP formulas in G8:H8 and paste them to the remaining rows in the list.
12. Save, print, and then close **EL2-U1-A2-RSRHelpDesk.xlsx**.

Assessment 3 Use Table and Data Management Features in a Help Desk Worksheet

1. Open **EL2-U1-A2-RSRHelpDesk.xlsx**.
2. Save the workbook using the name **EL2-U1-A3-RSRHelpDesk.xlsx**.
3. Create the file number in column F using the ticket number in column B followed by a dash, the priority in column C followed by a dash, and the operator ID. *Hint: It may take Flash Fill a few rows before it recognizes the correct sequence.*
4. Format A7:J30 as a table using the Table Style Medium 20 table style.
5. Add a calculated column to the table in column K that multiplies the time spent times 15. Use the column heading *Cost* in cell K7. Apply comma formatting with two places after the decimal point to the results.
6. Add a *Total* row to the table. Display totals for columns I and K.
7. Add emphasis to the last column in the table and band the columns instead of the rows.
8. Create a drop-down list for the *Operator ID* column that displays entries 1, 2, 3, and 4.

9. The help desk policy states that help desk operators cannot spend more than three hours on a call. Any call that requires more than three hours must be routed to the help desk manager and assigned to another group. Create a validation rule in the *Time Spent* column that prevents any value greater than 3 from being entered. Create appropriate input and error messages. ***Note: Ignore the green triangle indicator in cell I17 that specifies that the hours should be less than or equal to 3.***

10. Type the following two records in the table above the total in row 31:

Date	3/31/2015	*Date*	3/31/2015
Ticket No.	14424	*Ticket No.*	14425
Priority	2	*Priority*	2
Type of Call	Email	*Type of Call*	Password
Operator ID	3	*Operator ID*	4
File No.	14424-2-3	*File No.*	14425-2-4
Time Spent	.75	*Time Spent*	.25
Status	Active	*Status*	Closed

11. Filter the table to display only those calls with a *Closed* status.
12. Print the filtered list.
13. Filter the worksheet to display only those calls with a *Closed* status and for which the type of call was *Password*.
14. Print the filtered list.
15. Clear both filters.
16. Save, print, and then close **EL2-U1-A3-RSRHelpDesk.xlsx**.

Assessment 4 Add Subtotals and Outline a Help Desk Worksheet

1. Open **EL2-U1-A3-RSRHelpDesk.xlsx**.
2. Save the workbook using the name **EL2-U1-A4-RSRHelpDesk**.
3. Remove the *Total* row from the table.
4. Convert the table to a normal range.
5. Sort the list first by the operator's last name, then by the operator's first name, then by the call priority, and finally by the type of call—all in ascending order.
6. Add a subtotal to the list at each change in operator last name to calculate the total cost of calls by each operator.
7. Display the outlined worksheet at level 2 and then print the worksheet.
8. Display the outlined worksheet at level 3 and then print the worksheet.
9. Save and then close **EL2-U1-A4-RSRHelpDesk.xlsx**.

Assessment 5 Use Financial and Text Functions to Analyze Data for a Project

1. Open **ACLoan.xlsx**.
2. Save the workbook using the name **EL2-U1-A5-ACLoan**.
3. Create formulas to analyze the cost of the loan from Newfunds Trust and Delta Capital as follows:
   a. In cells C10 and E10, calculate the monthly loan payment from each lender.
   b. In cells C12 and E12, calculate the principal portion of each payment for the first loan payment.
   c. In cells C14 and E14, calculate the total loan payment that will be made over the life of the loan from each lender.
4. In cell E20, use the text function =PROPER to return the loan company name for the loan that represents the lowest total cost to AllClaims Insurance Brokers. ***Hint: The argument for the function will reference either cell C4 or cell E4.***

5. In cell E21, use the text function =LOWER to return the loan application number for the loan company name displayed in cell E20.

6. Save, print, and then close **EL2-U1-A5-ACLoan.xlsx**.

Assessment 6 Analyze Sales Using a PivotTable, PivotChart, and Sparklines

1. Open **PreBulkSales.xlsx**.
2. Save the workbook using the name **EL2-U1-A6-PreBulkSales**.
3. Select A4:I22 and create a PivotTable in a new worksheet as follows:
   a. Add the *Category* field as the report filter field.
   b. Add the *Distributor* field as the rows.
   c. Sum the North, South, East, and West sales values.
   d. Name the worksheet PivotTable.
4. Apply formatting options to the PivotTable to make the data easier to read and interpret.
5. Insert a Slicer for the Model and show the data for *PD-1140, PD-1150,* and *PD-1155*.
6. Move the Slicer pane under the PivotTable and print the PivotTable and Slicer pane on one sheet.
7. Create a PivotChart and move it to a separate sheet named PivotChart that graphs the data from the PivotTable in a 3-D Clustered Column chart.
8. Move the legend to the bottom of the chart.
9. Apply the Style 3 format to the chart.
10. Print the chart.
11. Make Sheet1 the active sheet and then create Sparklines in J5:J22 that show the North, South, East, and West sales in a line chart. Set the width of column J to 18 characters. Customize the Sparklines by changing the Sparkline color and adding data points. (You determine which data point to show and what color to make the points.) Type an appropriate label in cell J4 and add other formatting that will improve the appearance of the worksheet.
12. Save, print, and then close **EL2-U1-A6-PreBulkSales.xlsx**.

Assessment 7 Link to an External Data Source and Calculate Distributor Payments

1. Open **PreDistPymnt.xlsx**.
2. Save the workbook using the name **EL2-U1-A7-PreDistPymnt**.
3. Open **EL2-U1-A6-PreBulkSales.xlsx**.
4. Save the workbook using the name **EL2-U1-A7-PreSource**.
5. Make the PivotTable worksheet active, remove any filters, delete the Slicer pane, and then edit the PivotTable Fields so that *Sum of Total* is the only numeric field displayed in the table.
6. Save **EL2-U1-A7-PreSource.xlsx**.
7. Arrange the display of the two workbooks vertically.
8. Create linked external references starting in cell D6 in **EL2-U1-A7-PreDistPymnt.xlsx** to the appropriate source cells in the PivotTable in **EL2-U1-A7-PreSource.xlsx** so that the distributor payment worksheet displays the total sales for each distributor. *Note: Since you are linking to a PivotTable, Excel automatically generates a GETPIVOTDATA function formula in each linked cell.*
9. Close **EL2-U1-A7-PreSource.xlsx**.
10. Maximize **EL2-U1-A7-PreDistPymnt.xlsx**.
11. Apply comma formatting with no places after the decimal point to D6:D8.

12. Precision Design and Packaging pays each distributor a percentage of sales depending on the total sales achieved. The percentage for each category of sales is shown in the following chart:

Sales	Percentage
Less than $600,000	1%
Greater than or equal to $600,000 but less than $1,000,000	2%
$1,000,000 and above	4%

Calculate the payment owed for the distributors in H6:H8. Perform the calculation using one of the following two methods. (Choose the method that you find easiest to understand.)

- Create a nested IF statement.
- Create a lookup table in the worksheet that contains the sale ranges and three percentage values. Next, add a column next to each distributor with a lookup formula to return the correct percentage and then calculate the payment using total sales times the percentage value.

13. Apply comma formatting with two places after the decimal point to H6:H8.
14. Type TOTALS in cell B10 and then create formulas in cells D10 and H10 to calculate the total sales and total payments, respectively. Format the totals and adjust column widths as necessary.
15. Print the worksheet. Write the GETPIVOTDATA formula for cell D6 at the bottom of the printout.
16. Break the link to the external references and convert the formulas to their existing values.
17. Save, print, and then close **EL2-U1-A7-PreDistPymnt.xlsx**.

Writing Activities ■■■■■■■■■■■■■■■■■■

The following activities give you the opportunity to practice your writing skills along with demonstrating an understanding of some of the important Excel features you have mastered in this unit. Use appropriate word choices and correct grammar, capitalization, and punctuation when setting up new worksheets. Also make sure that labels clearly describe the data that are presented.

Activity 1 Create a Worksheet to Track Movie Rental Memberships

ViewItVideo is offering a new membership program for its frequent customers. Customers will pay an annual membership fee that entitles them to a discount on movie rentals based on their membership levels. Figure U1.1 shows the three membership levels and discounts. The manager of ViewItVideo has asked you to create a worksheet that will be used to provide a master list that includes the

Figure U1.1 Activity 1

Membership Category	Annual Fee	Discount on Movie Rentals
Gold	$45.00	15%
Silver	$30.00	12%
Classic	$20.00	10%

name of each customer participating in the membership program, the membership level for which the customer has paid, and the discount on movie rentals the customer is entitled to receive. The worksheet should provide in list format the following information:

- Date annual membership needs to be renewed
- Customer name
- Customer telephone number
- Membership level
- Annual membership fee
- Discount on movie rentals

Create a worksheet for the membership list. Use a lookup table to populate the cells containing the membership fee and discount level. Create a drop-down list for the cell containing the membership level that restricts the data entered to the three membership categories. Use a special number format for the telephone number column so that all telephone numbers include an area code and are displayed in a consistent format. Enter a minimum of five sample records to test the worksheet with your settings. The manager anticipates that approximately 35 customers will subscribe to the membership program. Format enough rows with the data features to include at least 35 memberships. Save the completed worksheet and name it **EL2-U1-Act01-VIVMemberships**. Print and then close the worksheet.

Activity 2 Create a Worksheet to Log Hours Walked in a Company Fitness Contest

Your company is sponsoring a contest this year to encourage employees to participate in a walking fitness program during the lunch hour. Participating employees in the department that logs the most miles or kilometers during the year will be awarded an expense-paid spa weekend at an exclusive luxury resort. You work in Human Resources and are in charge of keeping track of each department's walking record. Create a worksheet you can use to enter each department's total by month and summarize the data to show the total distance walked by all participating employees at the end of the year as follows:

- Four departments have signed up for the contest: Accounting, Human Resources, Purchasing, and Marketing. Create a separate worksheet for each department.

- Each department will send you a paper copy of its employees' walking log each month. You will use this source document to enter the miles or kilometers walked by day. At the end of each month, you want to calculate statistics by department to show the total distance walked, average distance walked, and number of days that employees walked during the lunch hour. When calculating the average and number of days, include only those days of which employees logged a distance. In other words, exclude from the statistics those days for which employees did not log any distance. *Hint: Consider adding a column that contains* Yes *or* No *to record whether or not employees participated in the walking program each day to use as the criteria range.*

- Create a summary worksheet that calculates the total miles or kilometers walked by participating employees in all four departments.

Test your settings by entering at least five days of sample data in each worksheet. Save the completed workbook and name it **EL2-U1-Act02-FitProgram**. Print the entire workbook and then close the workbook.

Optional: Using the Internet or other sources, find information on the health benefits of walking. Prepare a summary of the information and include it in a memo to employees that announces the contest. The memo is to be sent from Human Resources to all departments. Save the memo and name it **EL2-U2-Act02-FitMemo**. Print the memo and then close the file.

Internet Research ■■■■■■■■■■■■■■■■■■■

Create a Worksheet to Compare Online Auction Listing Fees

You are assisting a friend who is interested in selling a few items on an auction website on the Internet. Research a minimum of two Internet auction sites to identify all of the selling and payment fees associated with selling online. For example, be sure to find out costs for the following activities involved in an auction sale:

- Listing fees (sometimes called *insertion fees*)
- Optional features that can be attached to an ad, such as reserve bid fees, picture fees, listing upgrades, and so on
- Fees paid when the item is sold based on the sale value
- Fees paid to a third party to accept credit card payments (such as PayPal)

Create a worksheet that compares the fees for each auction website you researched. Include for each site two sample transactions and calculate the total fees that would be paid:

> Sample transaction 1: Item sold for $24.99
> Sample transaction 2: Item sold for $49.99

- Add optional features to the listing, such as a picture and reserve bid
- Assume in both sample transactions that the buyer pays by credit card using a third-party service

Based on your analysis, decide which auction site is the best choice from a cost perspective. Apply formatting options to make the worksheet easy to read and explain your recommendation for the lower-cost auction site. Save the completed worksheet and name it **EL2-U1-Act03-AuctionAnalysis**. Print and then close the worksheet.

MICROSOFT EXCEL

Level 2

Unit 2 ■ Managing and Integrating Data and the Excel Environment

MICROSOFT EXCEL

CHAPTER 5

Using Data Analysis Features

PERFORMANCE OBJECTIVES

Upon successful completion of Chapter 5, you will be able to:

- Switch data arranged in columns to rows and vice versa
- Perform a mathematical operation during a paste routine
- Populate a cell using Goal Seek
- Save and display various worksheet models using Scenario Manager
- Create a scenario summary report
- Create a one-variable data table to analyze various outcomes
- Create a two-variable data table to analyze various outcomes
- View relationships between cells in formulas
- Identify Excel error codes and troubleshoot a formula using formula auditing tools
- Circle invalid data
- Use the Watch Window to track a value

Tutorials

5.1 Pasting Data Using Paste Special Options

5.2 Using Goal Seek to Populate a Cell

5.3 Using Scenario Manager

5.4 Performing What-If Analysis Using Data Tables

5.5 Using Auditing Tools

5.6 Circling Invalid Data and Watching Formulas

Excel's Paste Special dialog box includes several options for pasting copied data. You can choose to paste attributes of a copied cell or alter the paste routine to perform a more complex operation. A variety of *what-if* analysis tools allow you to manage data to assist with decision-making and management tasks. Formula-auditing tools can be used to troubleshoot a formula or view dependencies between cells. By working through the projects in this chapter, you will learn about these tools and features available in Excel to assist with accurate data analysis. Model answers for this chapter's projects appear on the following pages.

Note: Before beginning the projects, copy to your storage medium the EL2C5 subfolder from the EL2 folder on the CD that accompanies this textbook and then make EL2C5 the active folder.

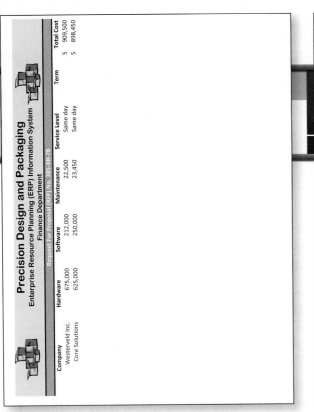

Precision Design and Packaging
Enterprise Resource Planning (ERP) Information System
Finance Department

Company	Hardware	Software	Maintenance	Service Level	Term	Total Cost
		Request For Proposal (RFP) No. 385-XR-78				
Westerveld Inc.	675,000	212,000	22,500	Same day	5	909,500
Core Solutions	625,000	250,000	23,450	Same day	5	898,450

Project 1 Analyze Data from a Request for Proposal

Project 1a, EL2-C5-P1-PreERP.xlsx

Precision Design and Packaging
Enterprise Resource Planning (ERP) Information System
Finance Department

Company	Hardware	Software	Maintenance	Service Level	Term	Total Cost
		Request For Proposal (RFP) No. 385-XR-78				
Westerveld Inc.	675,000	212,000	112,500	Same day	5	999,500
Kampson Ltd.	595,000	281,000	86,700	24 hours	4	962,700
Jensen Systems	615,000	267,000	103,750	24 hours	5	985,750
Core Solutions	625,000	250,000	117,250	Same day	5	992,250
NuTech Partners	596,000	292,000	105,728	Same day	4	993,728

Project 1b, EL2-C5-P1-PreERP.xlsx

Math by Janelle Tutoring Service		
Student Assessment Report		
Whitney Orlowicz		
Assessments	**100**	**Session**
Objective test	64.5	1
Performance test	72.0	6
Problem-solving test	83.5	10
Comprehensive test	78.5	15
Final test	81.5	20
Average grade	76.0	

Project 2 Calculate a Target Test Score

EL2-C5-P2-JTutorOrlowiczRpt.xlsx

Scenario Summary				
	Current Values	LowInflation	HighInflation	OriginalForecast
Changing Cells:				
WageInc	13,016	12,010	15,224	13,016
SuppliesInc	2,255	2,150	2,765	2,255
TrainingInc	6,385	5,276	7,236	6,385
AdminIncrease	2,479	1,998	3,195	2,479
Result Cells:				
TotalNewCosts	659,786	657,085	664,071	659,786

Notes: Current Values column represents values of changing cells at time Scenario Summary Report was created. Changing cells for each scenario are highlighted in gray.

Project 3 Forecast a Budget Based on Various Inflation Rates

EL2-C5-P3-NationalBdgt.xlsx

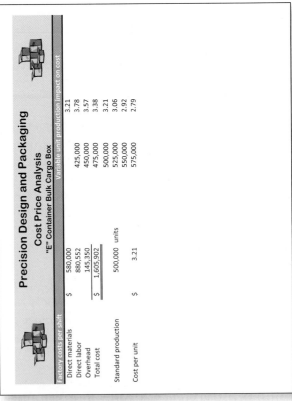

Precision Design and Packaging
Cost Price Analysis
"E" Container Bulk Cargo Box

Factory costs per shift		Variable unit production impact on cost	
Direct materials	$ 580,000		3.21
Direct labor	880,552	425,000	3.78
Overhead	145,350	450,000	3.57
Total cost	$ 1,605,902	475,000	3.38
		500,000	3.21
Standard production	500,000 units	525,000	3.06
		550,000	2.92
Cost per unit	$ 3.21	575,000	2.79

Project 4 Compare the Impacts of Various Inputs Related to Cost and Sales Pricing   Project 4a, EL2-C5-P4-PreEBoxCost.xlsx

Project 4b, EL2-C5-P4-PreEBoxSell.xlsx

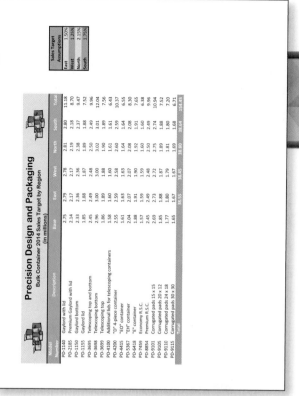

Project 5 Audit a Worksheet to View and Troubleshoot Formulas
Project 5c, EL2-C5-P5-PreSalesTrgt.xlsx

Project **1** **Analyze Data from a Request for Proposal** **2 Parts**

You will manipulate a worksheet containing vendor quotations for an enterprise resource-planning information system by copying and pasting using Paste Special options.

Pasting Data Using Paste Special Options ■■■■■■■■

Clicking the Paste button arrow opens the Paste drop-down gallery. This gallery contains many options for pasting copied data and is grouped into three sections: *Paste, Paste Values,* and *Other Paste Options.* The Paste gallery includes a live preview of how the data will be pasted to assist you in choosing the correct paste option. Click *Paste Special* at the bottom of the Paste gallery to open the Paste Special dialog box, shown in Figure 5.1. Use options in this dialog box to paste specific attributes of the source data, perform a mathematical operation in the destination range based on values in the source range, or carry out a more complex paste sequence.

Paste

Several options in the Paste Special dialog box are also available by clicking a button at the Paste drop-down gallery. For example, if you copy a range of cells that has border formatting applied and want to paste the range without the borders, click the Paste button arrow and then click the No Borders button (first column, second row in the *Paste* section) at the drop-down gallery. This produces the same result as clicking the Paste button arrow, clicking *Paste Special* at the drop-down gallery, clicking *All except borders* in the *Paste* section of the Paste Special dialog box, and then clicking OK.

Figure 5.1 Paste Special Dialog Box

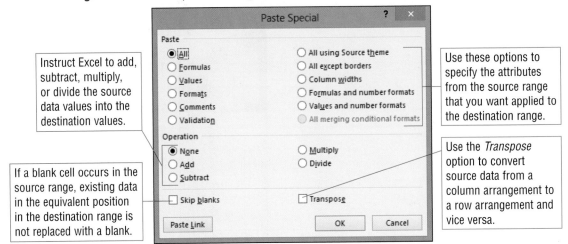

Instruct Excel to add, subtract, multiply, or divide the source data values into the destination values.

Use these options to specify the attributes from the source range that you want applied to the destination range.

Use the *Transpose* option to convert source data from a column arrangement to a row arrangement and vice versa.

If a blank cell occurs in the source range, existing data in the equivalent position in the destination range is not replaced with a blank.

Transposing Data

▼ **Quick Steps**

Transpose a Range
1. Select source range.
2. Click Copy button.
3. Click starting cell in destination range.
4. Click Paste button arrow.
5. Click Transpose button.

A worksheet may have data arranged in a way that is not suitable for the analysis you want to perform. For example, examine the worksheet shown in Figure 5.2. This is the worksheet you will be working with in Project 1. Notice that each company that submitted a proposal appears in a separate column, with the criteria for analysis (such as the cost of the hardware) arranged in rows. At first glance, this layout may seem appropriate, but consider how you will analyze this data if you want to examine only those vendors that offer a five-year contract. To use the filter feature on this data, you would need the contract term to display in a columnar format. Rearranging the data in this worksheet manually would be time consuming and risky due to the possibility of making errors during the conversion process. To avoid this, convert the columns to rows and rows to columns using the Transpose button in the Paste drop-down gallery or Paste Special dialog box.

Figure 5.2 Project 1 Worksheet

	A	B	C	D	E	F
1		**Precision Design and Packaging**				
2		Enterprise Resource Planning (ERP) Information System				
3		Finance Department				
4		Request For Proposal (RFP) No. 385-XR-78				
5	Company	Westerveld Inc.	Kampson Ltd.	Jensen Systems	Core Solutions	NuTech Partners
6	Hardware	675,000	595,000	615,000	625,000	596,000
7	Software	212,000	281,000	267,000	250,000	292,000
8	Maintenance	22,500	21,675	20,750	23,450	26,432
9	Service Level	Same day	24 hours	24 hours	Same day	Same day
10	Term	5	4	5	5	4
11	Total Cost	909,500	897,675	902,750	898,450	914,432

1. Open **PreERP.xlsx**.
2. Save the workbook and name it **EL2-C5-P1-PreERP**.
3. Convert the worksheet to arrange the company names in rows and criteria data in columns by completing the following steps:
   a. Select A5:F11.
   b. Click the Copy button.
   c. Click in cell A13.
   d. Click the Paste button arrow and then position the mouse over the Transpose button (second row, third column in the *Paste* section) at the drop-down gallery. A live preview shows how the copied data will be pasted. Click the Transpose button.

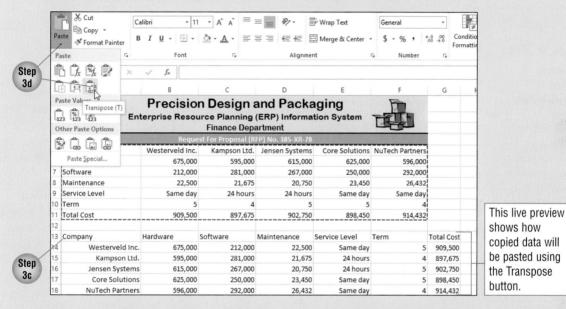

This live preview shows how copied data will be pasted using the Transpose button.

   e. Press the Esc key to remove the scrolling marquee from the source range and then click in any cell to deselect the range.
4. Delete rows 5 through 12.
5. Correct the merge and centering in rows 1 through 4 to extend the titles across columns A through G. If necessary, move or otherwise adjust the position of the clip art at the right side of the worksheet after merging and centering to column G.
6. Add a thick bottom border to cells A3 and A4.
7. Apply bold formatting and center-align the labels in A5:G5.
8. Select A5:G10, turn on the Filter feature, and then click in any cell to deselect the range.
9. Click the filter arrow in cell F5 and then filter the worksheet to display only those vendors offering a five-year contract.

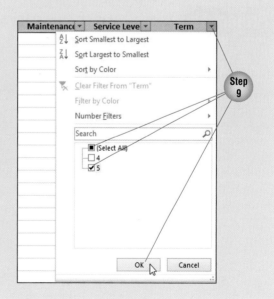

10. Click the filter arrow in cell E5 and then filter the remaining rows to display only those vendors offering same-day service.

Request For Proposal (RFP) No. 385-XR-78						
Company	Hardware	Software	Maintenance	Service Level	Term	Total C(
Westerveld Inc.	675,000	212,000	22,500	Same day	5	909,500
Core Solutions	625,000	250,000	23,450	Same day	5	898,450

Step 10

11. Print the filtered worksheet.
12. Turn off the Filter feature and then save **EL2-C5-P1-PreERP.xlsx**.

Performing a Mathematical Operation While Pasting

Quick Steps

Perform a Mathematical Operation While Pasting
1. Select source range values.
2. Click Copy button.
3. Click starting cell in destination range.
4. Click Paste button arrow.
5. Click *Paste Special*.
6. Click desired mathematical operation.
7. Click OK.

A range of cells in a copied source range can be added to, subtracted from, multiplied by, or divided by the cells in the destination range. To do this, open the Paste Special dialog box and then select the mathematical operation you want to perform. For example, in the worksheet for Project 1a, the values in the *Maintenance* column relate to annual maintenance fees charged by each vendor. To compare the total costs across all of the vendors, you want to see the maintenance value for the life cycle of the contract.

In Project 1b, you will copy and paste using a multiply operation to perform this calculation for you. Using this method means you will not have to add a new column to the worksheet to show the maintenance fees for the entire term of the contract.

Project 1b **Multiplying the Source Cells by the Destination Cells** Part 2 of 2

1. With **EL2-C5-P1-PreERP.xlsx** open, select F6:F10. These are the cells that contain the terms for the individual companies' contracts.
2. Click the Copy button.
3. Paste the source range and instruct Excel to multiply the values when pasting by completing the following steps:
   a. Click in cell D6.
   b. Click the Paste button arrow and then click *Paste Special* at the drop-down gallery.

Step 3b

c. Click *Multiply* in the *Operation* section of the Paste Special dialog box and then click OK.

d. Press the *Esc* key to remove the scrolling marquee from the source range and then click in any cell to deselect the range.

4. Print the worksheet.

5. Save and then close **EL2-C5-P1-PreERP.xlsx**.

Step 3c

Selecting Other Paste Special Options

You can select from a variety of different options at the Paste Special dialog box. Click *Formulas* or *Values* to paste only the source formulas or displayed values, click *Formats* to paste only the formatting options from the source, and click *Validation* to paste a validation rule. Click *All using Source theme* to apply the theme from the source, click *All except borders* to paste everything but the borders from the source, and click *Column widths* to adjust the destination cells to the same column width as the source. To paste formulas or values including the number formats from the source, click the *Formulas and number formats* option or the *Values and number formats* option.

Project 2 Calculate a Target Test Score   1 Part

Using a grades worksheet for a student, you will determine the score the student needs to earn on a final test to achieve a specified final average grade.

Using Goal Seek to Populate Cells ■■■■■■■■■■■■■■■■

Goal Seek calculates a value using a target that you want to achieve in another cell that is dependent on the cell you want Goal Seek to populate. For example, the worksheet shown in Figure 5.3 shows Whitney's grades on the first four tutoring assessments. The value in cell B11 (average grade) is the average of the five values in B5:B9. Note that the final test shows a grade of 0 even though the test has not yet occurred. Once the final test grade is entered, the value in cell B11 will update to reflect the average of all five scores. Suppose Whitney wants to achieve a final average grade of 76% in her tutoring assessments. Using Goal Seek, you can determine the score she needs to earn on the final test to achieve the 76% average. In Project 2, you return a value in cell B9 that the Goal Seek feature will calculate based on the target value you will set in cell B11.

Goal Seek causes Excel to calculate in reverse: you specify the ending value and Excel figures out the input numbers that will achieve the result you want. Note that the cell in which you want Excel to calculate the target value must be referenced by a formula in the *Set cell* text box. Goal Seek is useful for any situation in which you know the result you want to achieve but are not sure what value will get you there.

▼ Quick Steps

Use Goal Seek to Return a Value
1. Make desired cell active.
2. Click DATA tab.
3. Click What-If Analysis button.
4. Click *Goal Seek*.
5. Enter desired cell address in *Set cell* text box.
6. Enter desired target value in *To value* text box.
7. Enter dependent cell address in *By changing cell* text box.
8. Click OK.
9. Click OK or Cancel.

What-If Analysis

Figure 5.3 Project 2 Worksheet

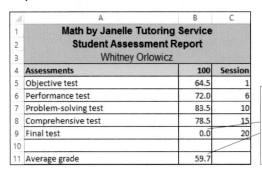

	A	B	C
1	**Math by Janelle Tutoring Service**		
2	**Student Assessment Report**		
3	Whitney Orlowicz		
4	**Assessments**	**100**	**Session**
5	Objective test	64.5	1
6	Performance test	72.0	6
7	Problem-solving test	83.5	10
8	Comprehensive test	78.5	15
9	Final test	0.0	20
10			
11	Average grade	59.7	

Use Goal Seek to determine the value that needs to be entered for the final test to achieve the desired average grade in cell B11.

Project 2 **Using Goal Seek to Return a Target Value** Part 1 of 1

1. Open **JTutorOrlowiczRpt.xlsx**.
2. Save the workbook and name it **EL2-C5-P2-JTutorOrlowiczRpt**.
3. Use Goal Seek to find the score Whitney needs to earn on the final test to achieve a 76% average grade by completing the following steps:
   a. Make cell B11 active.
   b. Click the DATA tab.
   c. Click the What-If Analysis button in the Data Tools group and then click *Goal Seek* at the drop-down list.
   d. If necessary, drag the Goal Seek dialog box to the right of the worksheet so you can see all of the values in column B.
   e. With *B11* already entered in the *Set cell* text box, click in the *To value* text box and then type 76.
   f. Press Tab and then type b9 in the *By changing cell* text box.
   g. Click OK.
   h. Click OK at the Goal Seek Status dialog box that shows Excel found a solution.

Step 3c

Step 3e

Step 3f

Step 3g

Step 3h

4. Notice that Excel entered the value *81.5* in cell B9. This is the score Whitney must earn to achieve a final average grade of 76%.
5. Assume that Whitney wants to achieve a final average grade of 80%. Use Goal Seek to find the score she will need to earn on the final test to accomplish the new target by completing the following steps:
   a. Click the What-If Analysis button in the Data Tools group and then click *Goal Seek* at the drop-down list.
   b. Click in the *To value* text box, type 80, and then press Tab.
   c. Type b9 in the *By changing cell* text box.
   d. Click OK.

e. Notice that the value entered in cell B9 is *101.5*. This is the score that Excel has calculated Whitney needs on the final test to earn an 80% average grade.

Step 5e

Step 5f

f. The final test is worth only 100, so Whitney will not be able to score 101.5. Restore the previous values in the report by clicking the Cancel button at the Goal Seek Status dialog box.

6. Save, print, and then close **EL2-C5-P2-JTutorOrlowiczRpt.xlsx**.

Project 3 Forecast a Budget Based on Various Inflation Rates
3 Parts

You will determine how various rates of inflation impact a department's budget to determine the funding request to present to management to maintain service.

Creating Assumptions for What-If Analysis
Using the Scenario Manager ■■■■■■■■■■■ ■■■■■■■■■

The ***Scenario Manager*** allows you to store multiple sets of assumptions about data and then view how each set of assumptions affects your worksheet. You can switch the display between scenarios to test the various inputs on your worksheet model. You can also save each scenario using a descriptive name, such as *BestCase* or *WorstCase*, to indicate the type of data assumptions you have stored in it.

Examine the worksheet shown in Figure 5.4. In this worksheet, the Computing Services department budget for the next year has been calculated based on projected percentage increases for various expense items. Assume that the department manager has more than one estimate of the percentages based on different inflation rates or

▼ **Quick Steps**

Add a Scenario
1. Click DATA tab.
2. Click What-If Analysis button.
3. Click *Scenario Manager*.
4. Click Add button.
5. Type name in *Scenario name* text box.
6. Type or select variable cells in *Changing cells* text box.
7. Click OK.
8. Enter value for each changing cell.
9. Click OK.
10. Click Close button.

Figure 5.4 Project 3 Worksheet

	A	B	C	D
1	**National Online Marketing Inc.**			
2	**Computing Services Department**			
3		Current budget	Projected increase	New budget
4	Wages and benefits	371,875	13,016	384,891
5	Computer supplies	150,350	2,255	152,605
6	Training and development	63,850	6,385	70,235
7	Other administrative costs	49,576	2,479	52,055
8	Total costs:	635,651		659,786

Create a range name for each changing cell. This allows you to see a descriptive reference next to the input text box, rather than a cell address, when adding a scenario.

vendor rate increases for next year. The manager can create and save various scenarios to view the impact on total costs that results from a combination of different forecasts.

Using the Scenario Manager dialog box, shown in Figure 5.5, you can create as many models as you want to save to test various what-if conditions. For example, two scenarios have been saved in the example shown in Figure 5.5: *LowInflation* and *HighInflation*. When you add a scenario, you define which cells will change and then enter the data to be stored under the scenario name.

Figure 5.5 Scenario Manager Dialog Box and Scenario Values Dialog Box

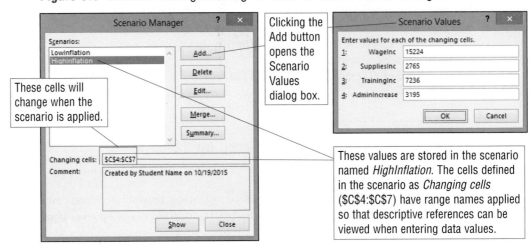

| **Project 3a** | **Adding Scenarios to a Worksheet Model** | **Part 1 of 3** |

1. Open **NationalBdgt.xlsx**.
2. Save the workbook and name it **EL2-C5-P3-NationalBdgt**.
3. View the range names already created in the worksheet by clicking the down-pointing arrow at the right of the Name box and then clicking *WageInc* at the drop-down list. Cell C4 becomes active. A range name has been created for each data cell in column C so that a descriptive label displays when you add scenarios in Steps 4 and 5.
4. Add a scenario with values assuming a low inflation rate for next year by completing the following steps:
   a. Click the DATA tab.
   b. Click the What-If Analysis button in the Data Tools group and then click *Scenario Manager* at the drop-down list.
   c. Click the Add button at the Scenario Manager dialog box.
   d. At the Add Scenario dialog box with the insertion point positioned in the *Scenario name* text box, type LowInflation and then press Tab.
   e. Type c4:c7 in the *Changing cells* text box and then press Enter or click OK. (As an alternative, you can move the dialog box out of the way and select the cells that will change in the worksheet.)

f. With the insertion point positioned in the *1: WageInc* text box, type 12010 and then press Tab.

g. Type 2150 and then press Tab.

h. Type 5276 and then press Tab.

i. Type 1998 and then press Enter or click OK.

5. Add another scenario that assumes a high inflation rate to the worksheet by completing the following steps:

a. Click the Add button at the Scenario Manager dialog box.

b. Type HighInflation in the *Scenario name* text box and then click OK. Notice that the *Changing cells* text box already contains the range C4:C7.

c. At the Scenario Values dialog box, type the following values into the text boxes indicated:

1: WageInc	15224
2: SuppliesInc	2765
3: TrainingInc	7236
4: AdminIncrease	3195

d. Click OK.

6. Add a third scenario, named *OriginalForecast*, that contains the original worksheet values by completing the following steps:

a. Click the Add button at the Scenario Manager dialog box.

b. Type OriginalForecast in the *Scenario name* text box and then click OK.

c. At the Scenario Values dialog box, notice that the original values are already entered in each text box. Click OK.

7. Click the Close button to close the Scenario Manager dialog box.

8. Save **EL2-C5-P3-NationalBdgt.xlsx**.

Applying a Scenario

After you have created the various scenarios you want to save with the worksheet, you can apply the values stored in each scenario to the variable cells to view the effects on your worksheet model. To do this, open the Scenario Manager dialog box, click the name of the scenario that contains the values you want to apply to the worksheet, and then click the Show button. Generally, the first scenario you create should contain the original values in the worksheet, since Excel replaces the content of each changing cell when you show a scenario.

Editing a Scenario

You can change the values associated with a scenario by opening the Scenario Manager dialog box, clicking the name of the scenario that contains the values you want to change, and then clicking the Edit button. At the Edit Scenario dialog box, make any desired changes to the scenario name and/or changing cells and then click OK to open the Scenario Values dialog box to edit the individual value associated with each changing cell. When you have finished editing, click OK and then click Close.

▼ Quick Steps

Apply a Scenario
1. Click DATA tab.
2. Click What-If Analysis button.
3. Click *Scenario Manager* at drop-down list.
4. Click desired scenario name.
5. Click Show button.
6. Click Close button.

Deleting a Scenario

To delete a scenario, open the Scenario Manager dialog box, click the scenario you want to remove, and then click the Delete button. Click the Close button to close the Scenario Manager dialog box.

Project 3b   **Applying a Scenario's Values to a Worksheet**   Part 2 of 3

1. With **EL2-C5-P3-NationalBdgt.xlsx** open, apply the scenario that assumes the low inflation rate by completing the following steps:
   a. With DATA as the active tab, click the What-If Analysis button and then click *Scenario Manager* at the drop-down list.
   b. If necessary, drag the Scenario Manager dialog box to the right of the worksheet so you can see all of the values in Column D.
   c. Click *LowInflation* in the *Scenarios* list box and then click the Show button. Excel changes the values in the range C4:C7 to the values stored within the scenario. Notice that based on the assumption of a low inflation rate, the total cost of the new budget shown in cell D8 is $657,085.
2. With the Scenario Manager dialog box still open, change the worksheet to display the scenario that assumes a high inflation rate by clicking *HighInflation* in the *Scenarios* list box and then clicking the Show button. Notice that in this high-inflation scenario, the total cost of the new budget is $664,071.

Step 1c

	A	B	C	D	
1	**National Online Marketing Inc.**				
2	**Computing Services Department**				
3		**Current budget**	**Projected increase**	**New budget**	
4	Wages and benefits	371,875	15,224	387,099	Excel displays the
5	Computer supplies	150,350	2,765	153,115	worksheet with
6	Training and development	63,850	7,236	71,086	the high inflation
7	Other administrative costs	49,576	3,195	52,771	values applied in
8	Total costs:	635,651		664,071	Step 2.

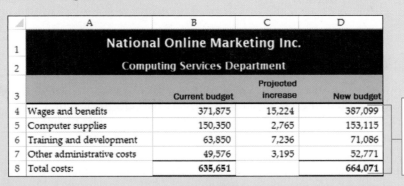

3. Show the worksheet with the data values from the *OriginalForecast* scenario.
4. Click the Close button to close the Scenario Manager dialog box.
5. Save **EL2-C5-P3-NationalBdgt.xlsx**.

Compiling a Scenario Summary Report

You can create a scenario summary report to compare scenarios side by side in a worksheet or PivotTable. At the Scenario Summary dialog box, shown in Figure 5.6, enter in the *Result cells* text box the formula cell or cells that change when you apply the data in various scenarios. Enter multiple cell addresses in this text box and use commas to separate them.

▼ **Quick Steps**

Create a Scenario Summary Report
1. Click DATA tab.
2. Click What-If Analysis button.
3. Click *Scenario Manager*.
4. Click Summary button.
5. If necessary, change cell address in *Result cells* text box.
6. Click OK.

Figure 5.6 Scenario Summary Dialog Box

Enter the address of the cell containing the total or other formula results impacted by the changing cells in each scenario. Enter multiple results cell addresses separated by commas.

Project 3c Generating a Scenario Summary Report

Part 3 of 3

1. With **EL2-C5-P3-NationalBdgt.xlsx** open, display a scenario summary report by completing the following steps:
   a. With DATA the active tab, click the What-If Analysis button and then click *Scenario Manager* at the drop-down list.
   b. Click the Summary button at the Scenario Manager dialog box.
   c. At the Scenario Summary dialog box, with the *Report type* set to *Scenario summary* and *Result cells* displaying the address D8, click OK.
2. Examine the Scenario Summary sheet added to the workbook. It displays each changing cell with the input for each scenario. Below the Changing Cells table, Excel displays the Result Cells, providing the value that results from each scenario's input.

Step 1c

In Step 2, Excel displays the Scenario Summary worksheet created in Step 1.

Scenario Summary				
	Current Values:	LowInflation	HighInflation	OriginalForecast
Changing Cells:				
WageInc	13,016	12,010	15,224	13,016
SuppliesInc	2,255	2,150	2,765	2,255
TrainingInc	6,385	5,276	7,236	6,385
AdminIncrease	2,479	1,998	3,195	2,479
Result Cells:				
TotalNewCosts	659,786	657,085	664,071	659,786
Notes: Current Values column represents values of changing cells at time Scenario Summary Report was created. Changing cells for each scenario are highlighted in gray.				

3. Print the Scenario Summary worksheet.
4. Save and then close **EL2-C5-P3-NationalBdgt.xlsx**.

Compare the Impacts of Various Inputs Related to Cost and Sales Pricing

2 Parts

Using one-variable and two-variable data tables, you will analyze the impact on the cost per unit and selling price per unit of a manufactured container.

Performing What-If Analysis Using Data Tables ■■■■■■

A *data table* is a range of cells that contains a series of input values. Excel calculates a formula substituting each input value in the data table range and places the result in the cell adjacent to the value. You can create a one-variable or a two-variable data table. A one-variable data table calculates a formula by modifying one input value in the formula. A two-variable data table calculates a formula substituting two input values. Using data tables provides a means to analyze various outcomes in a calculation that occur as a result of changing a dependent value without creating multiple formulas.

Creating a One-Variable Data Table

Design a one-variable data table with the variable input data values in a series down a column or across a row. Examine the worksheet shown in Figure 5.7. Assume that management wants to calculate the effects on the cost per unit for a variety of production volumes given a standard set of costs per factory shift. The worksheet includes the total costs for direct materials, direct labor, and overhead.

The formula in cell B8 sums the three cost categories. Based on a standard production volume of 500,000 units, the cost per unit is $3.21, calculated by dividing the total cost by the production volume (cell B8 divided by cell B10). In E6:E12, the factory manager has input varying levels of production. The manager would like to see the change in the cost per unit for each level of production volume, assuming the costs remain the same. In Project 4a, you will use a data table to show the various costs. This data table will manipulate one input value—production volume—so the table is a one-variable data table.

▼ **Quick Steps**

Create a One-Variable Data Table
1. Create variable data in column at right of worksheet.
2. Enter formula one row above and one cell right of variable data.
3. Select data range, including formula cell.
4. Click DATA tab.
5. Click What-If Analysis button.
6. Click *Data Table*.
7. Type cell address for variable data in source formula in *Column input cell* text box.
8. Press Enter or click OK.

Figure 5.7 Project 4a One-Variable Data Table

	A	B	C	D	E	F	G	H
1		**Precision Design and Packaging**						
2		**Cost Price Analysis**						
3		**"E" Container Bulk Cargo Box**						
4	Factory costs per shift				Variable unit production impact on cost			
5	Direct materials	$ 580,000						
6	Direct labor	880,552			425,000			
7	Overhead	145,350			450,000			
8	Total cost	$ 1,605,902			475,000			
9					500,000			
10	Standard production	500,000	units		525,000			
11					550,000			
12	Cost per unit	$ 3.21			575,000			

In this area of the worksheet, you can calculate the change in cost per unit based on varying the production volume using a data table.

1. Open **PreEBoxCost.xlsx**.
2. Save the workbook and name it **EL2-C5-P4-PreEBoxCost**.
3. Calculate the cost per unit for seven different production levels using a one-variable data table by completing the following steps:
   a. A data table requires that the formula for calculating the various outcomes be placed in the cell in the first row above and one column right of the table values. The data table values have been entered in E6:E12; therefore, make cell F5 active.
   b. The formula that calculates the cost per unit is =B8/B10. This formula has already been entered in cell B12. Link to the source formula by typing **=b12** and then pressing Enter.
   c. Select E5:F12.
   d. Click the DATA tab.
   e. Click the What-If Analysis button and then click *Data Table* at the drop-down list.

f. At the Data Table dialog box, click in the *Column input cell* text box, type **b10**, and then press Enter or click OK. At the Data Table dialog box, Excel needs to know which reference in the source formula is the address for which the variable data is to be inserted. (The production volume is cell B10 in the source formula.)

g. Click in any cell to deselect the range.
4. Print the worksheet.
5. Save and then close **EL2-C5-P4-PreEBoxCost.xlsx**.

Variable unit production impact on cost	
	3.21
425,000	3.78
450,000	3.57
475,000	3.38
500,000	3.21
525,000	3.06
550,000	2.92
575,000	2.79

The data table calculates costs at each production volume. Notice the costs are higher at lower volumes and decrease as production volume increases.

Creating a Two-Variable Data Table

Quick Steps

Create a Two-Variable Data Table

1. Create variable data at right of worksheet with one input series in column and another in row across top of table.
2. Enter formula in top left cell of table.
3. Select data table range.
4. Click DATA tab.
5. Click What-If Analysis button.
6. Click Data Table.
7. Type cell address for variable data in source formula in *Row input cell* text box.
8. Press Tab.
9. Type cell address for variable data in source formula in *Column input cell* text box.
10. Press Enter or click OK.

A data table can substitute two variables in a source formula. To modify two input cells, design the data table with a column along the left containing one set of variable input values and a row along the top containing the second set of variable input values. In a two-variable data table, the source formula is placed at the top left cell in the table. In the worksheet shown in Figure 5.8, the source formula will be inserted in cell E5, which is the top left cell in the data table.

Figure 5.8 Project 4b Two-Variable Data Table

This data table contains two input variables: production units and markup percentage. The data table will calculate a selling price at each production volume and at each markup percentage.

Project 4b **Creating a Two-Variable Data Table** **Part 2 of 2**

1. Open **PreEBoxSell.xlsx**.
2. Save the workbook and name it **EL2-C5-P4-PreEBoxSell**.
3. Calculate the selling price per unit for seven different production levels and three different markups using a two-variable data table by completing the following steps:
   a. In a two-variable data table, Excel requires that the source formula be placed in the top left cell in the data table; therefore, make cell E5 active.
   b. Type =b14 and press Enter. The formula that you want Excel to use to create the data table is in cell B14. The selling price per unit found in cell B14 is calculated by adding the cost per unit (cell B12) to the result of multiplying the cost per unit (cell B12) by the markup (cell B13).

c. Select E5:H12.

d. Click the DATA tab.

e. Click the What-If Analysis button and then click *Data Table* at the drop-down list.

f. At the Data Table dialog box with the insertion point positioned in the *Row input cell* text box, type **b13** and press Tab. Excel needs to know which reference in the source formula is the address relating to the variable data in the first row of the data table. (The markup value is in cell B13 in the source formula.)

g. Type **b10** in the *Column input cell* text box and then press Enter or click OK. As in Project 4a, Excel needs to know which reference relates to the production volume in the source formula.

h. Click in any cell to deselect the range.

Variable unit production impact on sell price			
$ 4.88	50%	52%	55%
425,000	5.67	5.74	5.86
450,000	5.35	5.42	5.53
475,000	5.07	5.14	5.24
500,000	4.82	4.88	4.98
525,000	4.59	4.65	4.74
550,000	4.38	4.44	4.53
575,000	4.19	4.25	4.33

Selling prices are calculated by the data table at each production volume and each percentage markup.

4. Print the worksheet.

5. Save and then close **EL2-C5-P4-PreEBoxSell.xlsx**.

Project 5 Audit a Worksheet to View and Troubleshoot Formulas   3 Parts

You will use buttons in the Formula Auditing group to view relationships between cells that comprise a formula, identify error codes in a worksheet, and troubleshoot errors using error checking tools.

Using Auditing Tools ■■■■■■■■■■■■■■■■■■■■■■■■■

The Formula Auditing group on the FORMULAS tab, shown in Figure 5.9, contains buttons that are useful for viewing relationships between cells in formulas. Checking a formula for accuracy can be difficult when the formula is part of a complex sequence of operations. Opening a worksheet created by someone else can also present a challenge in understanding the relationships between sets of data. When Excel displays an error message in a cell, viewing the relationships between the dependencies of cells assists with finding the source of the error.

Figure 5.9 Formula Auditing Group on FORMULAS Tab

Draw arrows to cells that provide data to the active cell.

Toggle between formula display and cell display.

Show error checking tools for the active cell.

Draw arrows to cells that use the data in the active cell.

Open a window in which to place cells for viewing while moving/editing within the worksheet.

Clear the arrows to/from the active cell.

Work through a formula value by value to determine how the result is calculated.

▼ **Quick Steps**

Trace Precedent Cells
1. Open worksheet.
2. Make desired cell active.
3. Click FORMULAS tab.
4. Click Trace Precedents button.
5. Continue clicking until all relationships are visible.

Trace Dependent Cells
1. Open worksheet.
2. Make desired cell active.
3. Click FORMULAS tab.
4. Click Trace Dependents button.
5. Continue clicking until all relationships are visible.

Trace Dependents

Remove Arrows

Show Formulas

Tracing Precedent and Dependent Cells

Precedent cells are cells that provide data to a formula cell. For example, if cell B3 contains the formula =B1+B2, then cell B1 and cell B2 are precedent cells. *Dependent cells* are cells that contain a formula that refers to other cells. In the previous example, cell B3 is the dependent cell to cells B1 and B2, since cell B3 relies on the data from cells B1 and B2. Click a cell and click the Trace Precedents button to draw tracer arrows that show direct relationships to cell(s) that provide data to the active cell. Click the button a second time to show indirect relationships to cell(s) that provide data to the active cell at the next level. Continue clicking the button until no further arrows are drawn. Excel will sound a beep when you click the button if no more relationships exist.

Click a cell and click the Trace Dependents button to draw tracer arrows that show direct relationships to other cell(s) in the worksheet that use the active cell's contents. As with the Trace Precedents button, click a second time to show the next level of indirect relationships and continue clicking the button until no further tracer arrows are drawn.

Excel draws blue tracer arrows if no error is detected in the active cell and red tracer arrows if an error condition is detected within the active cell.

Project 5a   **Viewing Relationships between Cells and Formulas**   Part 1 of 3

1. Open **EL2-C5-P4-PreEBoxSell.xlsx**.
2. View relationships between cells and formulas by displaying tracer arrows between cells by completing the following steps:
   a. Make cell B8 active.
   b. Click the FORMULAS tab.
   c. Click the Trace Precedents button in the Formula Auditing group. Excel draws a blue tracer arrow that shows the cells that provide data to cell B8.
   d. Click the Remove Arrows button in the Formula Auditing group. The blue tracer arrow leading to cell B8 is cleared.
   e. Make cell B14 active.

This blue precedent arrow is drawn to cell B8 in Step 2c.

4	Factory costs per shift		
5	Direct materials	$	580,000
6	Direct labor		880,552
7	Overhead		145,350
8	Total cost	$	1,605,902

Step 2a

f. Click the Trace Precedents button.

g. Click the Trace Precedents button a second time to show the next level of cells that provide data to cell B14.

h. Click the Trace Dependents button to view cell(s) dependent on cell B14.

3. Click the Remove Arrows button to clear all of the arrows.

4. Click the Show Formulas button to display cell formulas. Click the Show Formulas button again to turn off the display of formulas.

5. Close **EL2-C5-P4-PreEBoxSell.xlsx**. Click Don't Save when prompted to save changes.

Troubleshooting Formulas

Formulas in Excel can contain various types of errors. Some errors are obvious because Excel displays an error message such as *#VALUE!*. Other errors can occur that do not display error messages but are incorrect because the logic is flawed. For example, you could enter a formula in a cell that Excel does not flag as an error because the syntax is correct; however, the calculation could be incorrect for the data and the situation. Logic errors are difficult to find and require that you check a worksheet by entering proof formulas or by manually checking the accuracy of each formula.

A *proof formula* is a formula entered outside the main worksheet area that checks key figures within the worksheet. For example, in a payroll worksheet, a proof formula to check the total net pay column could add the total net pay to the totals of all of the deduction columns. The total displayed should be equal to the total gross pay amount in the worksheet.

Excel displays an error message code in a cell that is detected to have an error. Two types of error flags can occur. A green diagonal triangle in the upper left corner of a cell indicates an error condition. Activate the cell and an error checking button displays that you can use to access error checking tools. Errors can also be indicated with text entries, such as *#NAME?*. Figure 5.10 displays a portion of the worksheet you will use in Project 5b to troubleshoot errors. Table 5.1 describes the three error codes displayed in Figure 5.10.

Figure 5.10 Project 5b Partial Worksheet

	Model Number	Description	Base	East	West	North	South	Total			Sales Target Assumptions	
4	PD-1140	Gaylord with lid	2.75	#NAME?	#N/A	2.81	2.80	#NAME?		East	1.50%
5	PD-2185	Premium Gaylord with lid	2 14	#VALUE!	#VALUE!	#VALUE!	#VALUE!	#VALUE!		West	#N/A
6	PD-1150	Gaylord bottom	2.33	#NAME?	#N/A	2.38	2.37	#NAME?		North	2.15%
7	PD-1155	Gaylord lid	1.85	#NAME?	#N/A	1.89	1.88	#NAME?		South	1.75%
8	PD-3695	Telescoping top and bottom	2.45	#NAME?	#N/A	2.50	2.49	#NAME?			
9	PD-3698	Telescoping bottom	2.96	#NAME?	#N/A	3.02	3.01	#NAME?			

Precision Design and Packaging
Bulk Container 2014 Sales Target by Region (in millions)

Table 5.1 Error Codes in Figure 5.10 Worksheet

Error Code	Description of Error Condition
#N/A	A required value for the formula is not available.
#NAME?	The formula contains an unrecognized entry.
#VALUE!	A value within the formula is of the wrong type or otherwise invalid.

Error Checking

Evaluate Formula

The Error Checking button in the Formula Auditing group can be used to assist with finding the source of an error condition in a cell by displaying the Error Checking dialog box or drawing a red tracer arrow to locate the source cell that is contributing to the error. The Evaluate Formula button can be used to work through a formula value by value to determine the position within the formula where an error exists.

Project 5b Troubleshooting Formulas   Part 2 of 3

1. Open **PreSalesTrgt.xlsx**.
2. Save the workbook and name it **EL2-C5-P5-PreSalesTrgt**.
3. Solve the #N/A error by completing the following steps:
   a. Make cell E4 active.
   b. Point to the Trace Error button that displays next to the cell and read the ScreenTip that displays below the button.
   c. Look in the Formula bar at the formula that has been entered into the cell. Notice that the formula includes a reference to a named cell. You decide to use the tracer arrows to locate the source of the named cell.

d. Click the down-pointing arrow to the right of the Error Checking button in the Formula Auditing group on the FORMULAS tab and then click *Trace Error* at the drop-down list.

e. Excel moves the active cell to K5 and draws a red tracer arrow from cell K5 to cell E4. Look in the Formula bar and notice that *#N/A* displays as the entry in cell K5. Also notice the cell name *West* displayed in the Name box. Since a value does not exist in the cell named *West*, which is cell K5, the dependent cell E4 was not able to calculate its formula.

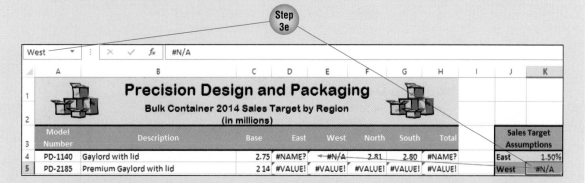

Step
3e

f. With cell K5 active, type 1.25% and press Enter. The red tracer arrow changes to blue now that the error is corrected and the #N/A error messages have disappeared.

g. Click the Remove Arrows button to clear the blue tracer arrow and then right-align the entry in cell K5.

4. Solve the #NAME? error by completing the following steps:

a. Make cell D4 active, point to the Trace Error button that appears, and then read the ScreenTip that appears. The message indicates that the formula contains unrecognized text.

b. Look at the entry in the Formula bar: *=C4+(C4*East)*. Notice the formula is the same as the formula you reviewed in Step 3c except that the named range is *East* instead of *West*. The formula appears to be valid.

c. Click the down-pointing arrow to the right of the Name box and view the range names in the drop-down list. Notice that a range named *East* is not in the list.

d. Click *North* at the Name box drop-down list. Cell K6 becomes the active cell. You know from this step and Step 3d that the named ranges should reference the percentage values within column K.

e. Make cell K4 active, type East in the Name box, and press Enter. The #NAME? error is resolved.

Step
4e

5. Solve the #VALUE! error by completing the following steps:

a. Make cell D5 active, point to the Trace Error button that appears, and then read the ScreenTip that appears. The message indicates that a value within the formula is of the wrong data type.

b. Click the Trace Precedents button in the Formula Auditing group on the FORMULAS tab to display tracer arrows showing the source cells that provide data to cell D5. Two blue arrows appear, indicating that two cells provide the source values: cells K4 and C5.

c. Make cell K4 active and look at the entry in the Formula bar: *1.5%*. This value is valid.

d. Make cell C5 active and look at the entry in the Formula bar: *2 14*. Notice there is a space instead of a decimal point between *2* and *1*.

e. Click in the Formula bar and then edit the formula to delete the space between *2* and *1* and type a period (inserting a decimal point). Press Enter. The #VALUE! error is resolved.

f. Click the Remove Arrows button to clear the blue tracer arrows.

6. Save **EL2-C5-P5-PreSalesTrgt.xlsx**.

▼ **Quick Steps**

Circle Invalid Data
1. Open worksheet containing validation rules.
2. Click DATA tab.
3. Click Data Validation button arrow.
4. Click *Circle Invalid Data*.

Watch a Formula Cell
1. Click FORMULAS tab.
2. Click Watch Window button.
3. Click Add Watch button.
4. Click desired cell.
5. Click Add button.

Watch Window

Data Validation

Circling Invalid Data

Recall from Chapter 3 that Data Validation is a feature used to restrict cell entries. If data validation rules are set up after data has been entered, existing values will not be tested against the new rules. In this situation, you can use the Circle Invalid Data feature, which draws red circles around the cells that do not conform to the new rule.

Watching a Formula Cell

In a large worksheet, a dependent cell may not always be visible while you are making changes to other cells that affect a formula. You can open a Watch Window and add a dependent cell to the window to view changes to the cell as you work within the worksheet. You can add multiple cells to the Watch Window to create a single window where you can keep track of the cells affected by key formulas within a large worksheet.

Consider assigning a name to a cell that you want to track using the Watch Window. At the Watch Window, the cell's name will appear in the *Name* column, providing a descriptive reference to the entry being watched. You can expand the width of the *Name* column if a range name is not entirely visible.

The Watch Window can be docked at the top, left, bottom, or right edge of the worksheet area by clicking the top edge of the window and dragging it to the desired edge of the screen. When the Watch Window is docked, Excel changes it to a Watch Window task pane.

1. With **EL2-C5-P5-PreSalesTrgt.xlsx** open, view the Data Validation rule in effect for column C by completing the following steps:

   a. If necessary, make any cell containing a value in column C active.

   b. Click the DATA tab.

   c. Click the top of the Data Validation button in the Data Tools group. (Do not click the down-pointing arrow on the button.) The Data Validation dialog box opens.

   d. Review the parameters for data entry in the Settings tab. Notice the restriction is that values should be greater than or equal to 1.57.

   e. Click OK.

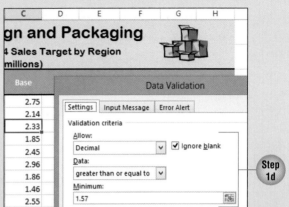

2. Click the Data Validation button arrow and then click *Circle Invalid Data* at the drop-down list. Three cells are circled in the worksheet: C11, C13, and C16.

3. Watch the total in cell H22 update as you correct the invalid data by completing the following steps:

   a. Make cell H22 active and then click the FORMULAS tab.

   b. Click the Watch Window button in the Formula Auditing group. A Watch Window opens.

   c. Click the Add Watch button in the Watch Window.

   d. At the Add Watch dialog box, move the dialog box out of the way if necessary to view cell H22. Notice that cell H22 is entered by default as the watch cell. Click the Add button.

   e. Scroll up the worksheet if necessary until you can view cell C11. If necessary, drag the Watch Window to an out-of-the-way location in the worksheet.

   f. Make cell C11 active, type 1.58, and press Enter. Notice that the red circle disappears, since you have now entered a value that conforms to the validation rule. Look at the value for cell H22 in the Watch Window. The new value is *153.67*.

g. Make cell C13 the active cell, type 1.61, and then press Enter. Look at the updated value for cell H22 in the Watch Window.

11	PD-4100	Additional lids for telescoping containers	1.58	1.60	1.60	1.61	1.61	6.43	
12	PD-4200	"D" 4-piece container	2.55						
13	PD-4415	"EO" container	1.61						
14	PD-5367	"EH" container	2.04						
15	PD-6418	"E" container	1.88						
16	PD-7459	Economy R.S.C.	1.54						
17	PD-8854	Premium R.S.C.	2.45						
18	PD-9101	Corrugated pads 15 x 15	2.69						
19	PD-9105	Corrugated pads 20 x 12	1.85						
20	PD-9110	Corrugated pads 24 x 18	1.77						

h. Make cell C16 active, type 1.57, and press Enter.

i. Click the Watch Window button in the Formula Auditing group on the FORMULAS tab to close the Watch Window.

4. Print the worksheet.

5. Save and then close **EL2-C5-P5-PreSalesTrgt.xlsx**.

Checking a worksheet for accuracy using auditing and error checking tools is an important skill to develop. Worksheets provide critical information to decision makers who rely on the validity of the data. After completing a worksheet, examine it carefully, looking for data entry mistakes, values that do not appear realistic, and other indications of potential errors that should be fixed.

Chapter Summary

- Open the Paste Special dialog box to paste attributes of the source cell(s) or perform a mathematical operation during the paste.

- Transposing data during a paste routine means that data arranged in columns is converted to rows and data arranged in rows is converted to columns.

- Click the Paste button arrow and then click *Paste Special* to access a gallery of different pasting options.

- The Goal Seek feature returns a value in a cell based on a target value you specify for another cell. The two cells must have a dependent relationship for Excel to calculate a value.

- Click the What-If Analysis button in the Data Tools group on the DATA tab to locate the Goal Seek, Scenario Manager, or Data Table command.

- Scenario Manager allows you to save multiple sets of values for key cells in a worksheet. Switch between scenarios to view the impact of changing the input cells on one of the worksheet's saved data sets.

- A scenario summary report presents the input data for each key cell in a scenario in tabular format with a results cell below each data set displaying the value if the data set is applied.

- A data table is a range of cells containing a series of input values with a calculated formula result adjacent to each input value.

- A one-variable data table modifies one input value within a formula.

- A two-variable data table modifies two input values within a formula.

- Design a one-variable data table with the input values in a columnar arrangement and the formula cell one row above and one column right of the input values.

- Design a two-variable data table with one set of input values in a columnar arrangement and the other set of input values starting in the first column right and first row above the first set of values. Add the formula cell to the top left cell within the input table.

- Buttons in the Formula Auditing group on the FORMULAS tab allow you to view relationships between cells and find and resolve errors.

- Use the Trace Precedents button to draw tracer arrows to cells that feed data into the active cell.

- Use the Trace Dependents button to draw tracer arrows to cells that use data from the active cell.

- Click the Trace Precedents or Trace Dependents button a second time to display an indirect set of relationship arrows at the next level.

- Logic errors occur when the formula is not correct for the data or situation.

- Reference errors occur when a formula points to the wrong data cell.

- Use proof formulas to test the accuracy of key figures in a worksheet. A proof formula is entered outside the main worksheet area and double-checks data within the worksheet.

- Excel displays two types of error flags in a cell in which an error has been detected.

- A green diagonal triangle in the upper left corner of the cell indicates an error is presumed. Click the active cell and use the Trace Error button to access error checking options.

- Error codes within a cell also indicate an error. For example, #NAME? means that the formula contains text that Excel cannot recognize.

- Other error codes include #VALUE!, which means a value within the formula is not valid, and #N/A, which means a value needed by the formula is not available.

- When a worksheet has data validation rules in force, data that existed before the rule was created is not tested. Use the Circle Invalid Data feature from the Data Validation button to place red circles around cells that do not test correct with the new rule.

- A Watch Window is a window that remains visible in the worksheet area while you scroll and edit other parts of a large worksheet. Add cells to the Watch Window that you want to observe while you make changes.

- After completing a worksheet, take time to examine the data carefully for data entry errors and logic errors that can impact the results.

Commands Review

FEATURE	RIBBON TAB, GROUP	BUTTON
circle invalid data	DATA, Data Tools	
data table	DATA, Data Tools	
Goal Seek dialog box	DATA, Data Tools	
Paste Special dialog box	HOME, Clipboard	
remove tracer arrow	FORMULAS, Formula Auditing	
Scenario Manager	DATA, Data Tools	
trace dependent cell	FORMULAS, Formula Auditing	
trace error	FORMULAS, Formula Auditing	
trace precedent cell	FORMULAS, Formula Auditing	
transpose	HOME, Clipboard	
Watch Window	FORMULAS, Formula Auditing	

Concepts Check Test Your Knowledge

Completion: In the space provided at the right, indicate the correct term, command, or number.

1. This option from the Paste drop-down gallery converts columns to rows and rows to columns. _____

2. Open this dialog box to perform a mathematical operation while pasting the copied range to the destination cells. _____

3. Use this feature if you know the result you want to obtain but are not sure what input value you need to achieve that result. _____

4. This feature allows you to store various sets of data for specified cells under a name. _____

5. This report compares various saved data sets side by side so you can view all of the results on one page. _____

6. In a one-variable data table, the source formula is entered at this location within the data table range. _____

7. The Data Table feature is accessed from this button. _____

8. In a two-variable data table, the source formula is entered at this location within the data table range. _____

9. Click this button to draw arrows to cells that feed data into the active cell. _____

10. Click this button to draw arrows to cells that use the data in the active cell. _____

11. Use this button in the Formula Auditing group to assist with locating the source cell that is causing an error code. _____

12. This type of formula is entered outside the main worksheet area and used to check key figures within the worksheet. _____

13. This error code indicates that a value needed by the formula to calculate the result is not available. _____

14. This type of error occurs when the formula has correct syntax but is not correct for the data or situation. _____

15. Use this feature to test existing data in a worksheet that has had a new data validation rule created. _____

Skills Check   Assess Your Performance

Assessment

1 CONVERT COLUMNS TO ROWS, ADD SOURCE CELLS TO DESTINATION CELLS, AND FILTER

1. Open **CRC.xlsx**.
2. Save the workbook and name it **EL2-C5-A1-CRC**.
3. Copy A4:F12, select cell A14, and paste the data so the columns become rows and vice versa.
4. Delete rows 4 through 13—the original source data rows from the worksheet.
5. Adjust the merging and centering of the title rows across the top of the worksheet. Apply bold formatting to B4:I4 and AutoFit all of the column widths.
6. Copy the values in the *Shipping* column. Paste the values into the *Total Cost* column using an Add operation so that the total cost now includes the shipping fee.
7. The values in the *Compact* column have a validation rule that you want to duplicate in the *Mid-size* and *SUV* columns. Copy the values in the *Compact* column and paste only the validation rule to the *Mid-size* and *SUV* columns.
8. Save, print, and then close **EL2-C5-A1-CRC.xlsx**.

2 USE GOAL SEEK

1. Open **NationalBdgt.xlsx**.
2. Save the workbook and name it **EL2-C5-A2-NationalBdgt**.
3. Make cell D8 the active cell and open the Goal Seek dialog box.
4. Find the projected increase for wages and benefits that will make the total cost of the new budget equal $655,000.
5. Accept the solution Goal Seek calculates.
6. Save, print, and then close **EL2-C5-A2-NationalBdgt.xlsx**.

3 USE SCENARIO MANAGER

1. Open **PreCdnTarget.xlsx**.
2. Save the workbook and name it **EL2-C5-A3-PreCdnTarget**.
3. Create scenarios to save various percentage data sets for the four regions using the following information:
   a. A scenario named *OriginalTarget* that stores the current values in K4:K7.
   b. A scenario named *LowSales* with the following values:

   East   0.20
   West   0.32
   Ontario 0.48
   Quebec   0.37

   c. A scenario named *HighSales* with the following values:

   East   0.36
   West   0.58
   Ontario 0.77
   Quebec   0.63

4. Show the LowSales scenario and then print the worksheet.
5. Create a scenario summary report displaying cell H18 as the result cell.
6. Print the Scenario Summary sheet.
7. Save and then close **EL2-C5-A3-PreCdnTarget.xlsx**.

4 CREATE A TWO-VARIABLE DATA TABLE

1. Open **NationalHlpDsk.xlsx**.
2. Save the workbook and name it **EL2-C5-A4-NationalHlpDsk**.
3. Create a two-variable data table that will calculate the average cost per call in the data table for each level of total call minutes logged and at each average cost per minute.
4. Save, print, and then close **EL2-C5-A4-NationalHlpDsk.xlsx**.

5 FIND AND CORRECT FORMULA ERRORS

1. Open **NationalCapital.xlsx**.
2. Save the workbook and name it **EL2-C5-A5-NationalCapital**.
3. Make cell D19 the active cell and use the Trace Error feature to draw red tracer arrows to find the source cell creating the #N/A error.
4. The Customer Service department manager has reported that the cost of a Pix firewall is $4,720. Enter this data in the appropriate cell to correct the #N/A error.
5. Remove the tracer arrows.
6. The worksheet contains a logic error in one of the formulas. Find and correct the error.
7. Save, print, and then close **EL2-C5-A5-NationalCapital.xlsx**.

Visual Benchmark   Demonstrate Your Proficiency

1 FIND THE BASE HOURLY RATE FOR DRUM LESSONS

1. Open **Lessons.xlsx**.
2. Save the workbook and name it **EL2-C5-VB1-Lessons**.
3. The current worksheet is shown in Figure 5.11 on the next page. The hourly rates in B5:B13 are linked to the cell named *BaseRate*, which is located in cell B16. Intermediate and advanced lessons have $4 and $8 added to the hourly base rate, respectively.
4. The drum teacher wants to earn $2,645.50 per month from drum lessons (instead of the current total of $2,292.00). Use the Goal Seek feature to change the base hourly rate to the required value needed to reach the drum teacher's target.
5. Save, print, and then close **EL2-C5-VB1-Lessons.xlsx**.

Figure 5.11 Visual Benchmark 1

	A	B	C	D
1	**THE DRUM STUDIO**			
2	**MONTHLY DRUM LESSON REVENUE**			
3				
4	**Class**	**Hourly Rate**	**Registered Students**	**Monthly Revenue**
5	Basic Drum Theory	18.00	10	180.00
6	Beginner Rock Drumming	18.00	15	270.00
7	Intermediate Rock Drumming	22.00	8	176.00
8	Advanced Rock Drumming	26.00	4	104.00
9	Beginner Jazz Drumming	18.00	18	324.00
10	Developing Jazz Style	22.00	10	220.00
11	Single Pedal Drum Beats	18.00	22	396.00
12	Single Pedal Drum Fills	18.00	15	270.00
13	Bass Drum Doubles	22.00	16	352.00
14	**TOTAL**			**2,292.00**
15				
16	Base hourly rate for all lessons:	18.00		

2 CREATE SCENARIOS FOR DRUM LESSON REVENUE

1. Open **Lessons.xlsx**.
2. Save the workbook and name it **EL2-C5-VB2-Lessons**.
3. The drum teacher has decided to create three models for an increase in the base hourly rate charged for drum lessons before deciding which base rate to use for next year. Examine the Scenario Summary report shown in Figure 5.12. Create three scenarios to save the hourly base rates shown: Low Rate Increase, Mid Rate Increase, and High Rate Increase.
4. Generate the Scenario Summary report to show the monthly revenue for each class at the three hourly base rates.
5. Format the report by changing the fill colors and font colors and adding the descriptive text in row 7. Use your best judgment in choosing colors that match those shown in Figure 5.12.
6. Edit the *Notes* text in cell B20 so that the sentence correctly references the highlighted color for changing cells.
7. Print the Scenario Summary worksheet.
8. Save and then close **EL2-C5-VB2-Lessons.xlsx**.

Figure 5.12 Visual Benchmark 2

	A	B	C	D	E	F	G
1							
2		Scenario Summary					
3				Current Values:	Low Rate Increase	Mid Rate Increase	High Rate Increase
5		Changing Cells:					
6		BaseRate		18.00	20.00	22.00	24.00
7		Result Cells:		*Monthly revenue for each lesson assuming no change in number of registered students*			
8		BasicTheory		180.00	200.00	220.00	240.00
9		BegRock		270.00	300.00	330.00	360.00
10		IntRock		176.00	192.00	208.00	224.00
11		AdvRock		104.00	112.00	120.00	128.00
12		BegJazz		324.00	360.00	396.00	432.00
13		DevJazz		220.00	240.00	260.00	280.00
14		SinglePedalBeats		396.00	440.00	484.00	528.00
15		SinglePedalFills		270.00	300.00	330.00	360.00
16		BassDoubles		352.00	384.00	416.00	448.00
17		MonthlyRevTotal		2,292.00	2,528.00	2,764.00	3,000.00
18		Notes: Current Values column represents values of changing cells at					
19		time Scenario Summary Report was created. Changing cells for each					
20		scenario are highlighted in green.					

Case Study   Apply Your Skills

Part 1

Yolanda Robertson is continuing her work on the marketing information package for prospective new franchise owners. She has sent you a workbook named **PBMStartup.xlsx**. The workbook contains information on the estimated capital investment required to start a new franchise, along with estimated sales and profits for the first year. The workbook calculates the number of months in which a new franchisee can expect to recoup his or her investment based on estimated sales and profits for the first year. Yolanda wants you to use the What-If Analysis tools to find out the value that is needed for projected sales in year 1 to pay back the initial investment in 12 months (instead of 17). Accept the proposed solution and save the revised workbook and name it **EL2-C5-CS-P1-PBMStartup**. Print the worksheet.

Part 2

After reviewing the printout from Part 1, Yolanda is concerned that the revised sales figure is not attainable in the first year. Restore the sales for year 1 to the original value of $485,000. Yolanda has created the following three models for the startup investment worksheet:

Item	Conservative	Optimistic	Aggressive
Projected Sales	$450,000	$590,000	$615,000
Profit Percent	20%	22%	18%

Yolanda would like you to set up the worksheet to save all three of these models. *Hint: Use a comma to separate two cell references as the changing cells.* Create a report that shows Yolanda the input variables for each model and how the model affects the number of months needed to recoup the initial investment. Save the revised workbook as **EL2-C5-CS-P2-PBMStartup**. Print the summary report. Switch to the worksheet and show the model that reduces the number of months to recoup the initial investment to the lowest value. Print the worksheet. Save **EL2-C5-CS-P2-PBMStartup**.

Part 3

Yolanda would like you to check all of the formulas in the worksheet to make sure they are accurate before submitting this worksheet to the client. Since you did not create this worksheet, you decide to check if there is a feature in Excel that navigates to formula cells automatically so you do not miss any calculated cells. Use the Help feature to find out how to select cells that contain formulas. Based on the information you learned in Help, select the cells within the worksheet that contain formulas and then review each formula cell in the Formula bar to ensure the formula is logically correct. *Hint: When the formula cells are selected as a group, press the Enter key to move to the next formula cell without losing the selection.* When you are finished reviewing the formula cells, type the name of the feature you used in a blank cell below the worksheet and then print the worksheet. Save the revised workbook and name it **EL2-C5-CS-P3-PBMStartup**.

Part 4

When meeting with prospective franchise owners, Yolanda expects that individuals who do not have excellent credit ratings will find it difficult to raise the money required for the initial capital investment. Assume that the owners of Pizza by Mario are willing to finance the initial investment. Search the Internet for the current lending rate for a secured credit line at the bank at which you have an account. In a new worksheet within the workbook, document the current loan rate you found and the URL of the bank website from which you obtained the rate. Add two percentage points to the lending rate to compensate the owners for the higher risk associated with financing the startup. Create a linked cell in the new worksheet to the Total Estimated Initial Investment in Sheet1. Calculate the monthly loan payment for a term of five years. Add appropriate labels to describe the data and format the worksheet as desired to improve its appearance. Save the revised workbook and name it **EL2-C5-CS-P4-PBMStartup**. Print the loan worksheet.

MICROSOFT EXCEL

Protecting and Sharing Workbooks

PERFORMANCE OBJECTIVES

Upon successful completion of Chapter 6, you will be able to:

- Add information to a workbook's properties
- Add comments containing additional information or other notes to the reader
- Share a workbook with other people and view other users who have the shared workbook open at the same time
- Edit a shared workbook and resolve conflicts with changes
- Print a history of changes made to a shared workbook
- Stop sharing a workbook
- Save and share a workbook using SkyDrive
- Protect cells within a worksheet to prevent changes
- Add a password to open a workbook
- Track changes made to a workbook
- Modify and resolve tracked changes

Tutorials

6.1 Inserting and Editing Comments
6.2 Adding Workbook Properties
6.3 Printing and Editing Comments
6.4 Sharing a Workbook
6.5 Resolving Conflicts in a Shared Workbook
6.6 Saving a Workbook to Windows SkyDrive, Inviting People to Share a Workbook, and Sending a Workbook via Email
6.7 Protecting and Unprotecting Worksheets
6.8 Protecting and Unprotecting the Structure of a Workbook
6.9 Adding Password Protection to a Workbook
6.10 Tracking Changes

In today's electronic business environment, collaborating with other people on an Excel workbook is becoming commonplace. Excel includes several features and tools that are useful for working in a collaborative environment. Adding information to a workbook's properties provides other editors with descriptive information about the nature and purpose of the workbook. Attaching a comment to a cell allows you to add explanatory information or ask questions when collaborating with others. Sharing a workbook, locking and unlocking worksheets and ranges, and tracking changes are all vital features for managing data that will be accessed by multiple individuals. By completing the projects in this chapter, you will learn how to use the collaborative tools in Excel. Model answers for this chapter's projects appear on the following page.

Note: Before beginning the projects, copy to your storage medium the EL2C6 subfolder from the EL2 folder on the CD that accompanies this textbook and then make EL2C6 the active folder.

Cell: C10
Comment: Student Name:
   Most competitors charge 168.99 for weekend rentals of luxury vehicles.

Cell: F10
Comment: Student Name:
   Last year this discount was 15%.

Project 1 Add Workbook Properties and Insert Comments

Project 1b, EL2-C6-P1-CRPricing.xlsx Comments Page

Action Number	Date	Time	Who	Change	Sheet	Range	New Value	Old Value	Action Type	Losing Action
1	3/20/2015	10:05 AM	Aaron Rubin	Cell Change	Sheet1	F5	12%	15%		
2	3/20/2015	10:05 AM	Aaron Rubin	Cell Change	Sheet1	B10	$95.99	$85.99		
3	3/20/2015	10:05 AM	Aaron Rubin	Cell Change	Sheet1	D10	$325.99	$299.99		
4	3/20/2015	10:09 AM	Chris Zajac	Cell Change	Sheet1	D10	$319.99	$325.99		

The history ends with the changes saved on 3/20/2015 at 10:09 AM.

Project 2 Sharing a Workbook

Project 2e, EL2-C6-P2-CRPricingShared.xlsx

CutRate Car Rentals
Estimated Monthly Revenue
West Region

Effective Date: May 1, 2015

Category	Weekday (Mo to Th)	Target Rentals	Target Revenue	Weekend (Fr to Su)	Target Rentals	Target Revenue	Weekly (*Min 5 days)	Target Rentals	Target Revenue	Monthly (*Min 21 days)	Target Rentals	Target Revenue
Compact	$ 35.99	362	$ 13,028	$ 55.99	173	$ 9,686	$ 175.99	33	$ 5,808	$ 675.99	11	$ 7,436
Mid-size	38.99	285	11,112	62.99	214	13,480	185.99	25	4,650	692.99	10	6,930
Full-size	40.99	175	7,173	65.99	75	4,949	215.99	30	6,480	775.99	8	6,208
Minivan	75.99	155	11,778	130.99	68	8,907	251.99	28	7,056	866.99	8	6,936
SUV	89.99	146	13,139	139.99	22	3,080	249.99	31	7,750	885.99	12	10,632
Luxury	99.99	55	5,499	155.99	30	4,680	329.99	10	3,300	999.99	5	5,000
TOTAL	Weekday:		$ 61,730	Weekend:		$ 44,782	Weekly:		$ 35,042	Monthly:		$ 43,141

TOTAL ESTIMATED MONTHLY REVENUE $ 184,696

*Days rented must be consecutive to qualify for weekly or monthly rate.

TOTAL ESTIMATED MONTHLY REVENUE BY CRITERIA

Compact	$ 35,958
Mid-size	36,172
Full-size	24,810
Minivan	34,677
SUV	34,600
Luxury	18,479
TOTAL	**$184,696**

Project 4 Track and Resolve Changes Made to a Workbook

Project 4c, EL2-C6-P4-CRWestReg.xlsx

Project 1 Add Workbook Properties and Insert Comments   **2 Parts**

You will add the author's name and other descriptive information in a workbook's properties and insert comments with explanatory information.

Adding Workbook Properties ■■■■■■■■■■■■■■■■■■■■■■

Workbook properties include information about the workbook such as the author's name, a title, a subject, a category to which the workbook is related (such as finance), and general comments about the workbook. This information can be added to the file at the Info backstage area, shown in Figure 6.1, or by using the document information panel, shown in Figure 6.2.

Some information is added to file properties automatically by Microsoft Excel. For example, Excel maintains workbook statistics such as the date the workbook was created, the date the workbook was last modified, and the name of the last person to save the workbook. Workbook properties are sometimes referred to as *metadata*—a term used to identify descriptive information about data.

To add an author's name or other descriptive information about a workbook, click the FILE tab. Excel displays the Info backstage area with the workbook's properties displayed at the right side of the screen. By default, Excel inserts in the *Author* property box the name of the computer user (as defined when Microsoft Office is installed) when a new workbook is created. To add another author or make a change to a workbook property (such as the title), click the mouse to open the text box next to the property's name. For example, click *Add a title* next to the Title property name. A text box opens in which you can type the desired title. Click outside the text box to end the entry. Properties that do not display with the message *Add a [property]* cannot be edited. Click the Show All Properties hyperlink at the bottom of the right section in the Info backstage area to add more properties to the view.

Figure 6.1 Properties in the Info Backstage Area

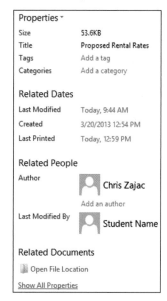

Properties ˅

Size	53.6KB
Title	Proposed Rental Rates
Tags	Add a tag
Categories	Add a category

Related Dates

Last Modified	Today, 9:44 AM
Created	3/20/2013 12:54 PM
Last Printed	Today, 12:59 PM

Related People

Author [ ] Chris Zajac

Add an author

Last Modified By [ ] Student Name

Related Documents

📄 Open File Location

Show All Properties

The document information panel, shown in Figure 6.2, displays between the ribbon and the worksheet. If you prefer to add or edit properties while viewing the worksheet, open the panel by clicking the Properties button at the top of the right section in the Info backstage area and then click *Show Document Panel* at the drop-down list.

In Chapter 8, you will learn how to strip metadata (including personal information) from a file if you do not want this information to be included when distributing a workbook outside your organization. Including personal information can be useful, however, when you are browsing a list of files. The words *Authors, Size,* and *Date Modified* appear in a ScreenTip when you hover the mouse pointer over a workbook name in the Open dialog box. This information helps you to select the correct file.

Figure 6.2 Document Information Panel

ⓘ Document Properties ▾					Location: G:\EL2C6\EL2-C6-P1-CRPricing.xlsx	⁂ Required field ✕
Author:	Title:	Subject:	Keywords:	Category:	Status:	
Chris Zajac	Proposed Rental Rates	Rental rates for May 2015	Rates, Proposed			
Comments:						
Proposed rental rates sent for review to regional managers.						

Project 1a Adding Information to Workbook Properties **Part 1 of 2**

1. Open **CRPricing.xlsx**.
2. Save the workbook and name it **EL2-C6-P1-CRPricing**.
3. Add an additional author's name, as well as a title, subject, and comments to be associated with the workbook, by completing the following steps:
   a. Click the FILE tab.
   b. At the Info backstage area, click *Add an author* below the current author's name in the *Related People* section to open an *Author* text box.
   c. Type Chris Zajac. If the message *We couldn't find the person you were looking for* displays, ignore it.
   d. Click outside the *Author* text box to close it.
   e. Click *Add a title* in the *Title* text box, type Proposed Rental Rates, and then click outside the text box.
   f. Click the Show All Properties hyperlink below the *Related Documents* section to display additional properties.
   g. Click *Specify the subject* in the *Subject* text box, type Rental rates for May 2015, and then click outside the text box.
   h. Click *Add comments* in the *Comments* text box, type Proposed rental rates sent for review to regional managers. and then click outside the text box.

4. Right-click *Paradigm Publishing Inc.* next to the *Author* text box and then click *Remove Person* at the shortcut menu.
5. Click the <u>Show Fewer Properties</u> hyperlink at the bottom of the properties.
6. Compare your properties with those shown in Figure 6.1 on page 187. Some of the dates may vary.
7. View the document information panel and add text to a workbook property by completing the following steps:

   a. Click the Properties button above the workbook properties and then click *Show Document Panel* at the drop-down list. The Info backstage area closes and the document information panel displays between the ribbon and the worksheet. Use this panel to view the worksheet while adding or modifying properties.
   b. Click in the *Keywords* text box, type Rates, Proposed, and then press Tab.
   c. Compare your document information panel with the one shown in Figure 6.2 on page 188.
   d. Click the Close button located in the top right corner of the document information panel. Be careful to click the Close button within the document information panel and not the Close button located at the top right of the ribbon.

8. Save **EL2-C6-P1-CRPricing.xlsx**.

Managing Comments

A *comment* is a pop-up box containing text that displays when you hover the mouse pointer over the cell to which it is attached. Use a comment to provide instructions, identify critical information, or add other explanatory information about a cell entry. Comments are also useful when you are collaborating with others to create or edit a worksheet. All of the reviewers can use comments to add feedback or pose questions about cell entries or layout.

Inserting a Comment

Insert a comment by clicking the REVIEW tab and then clicking the New Comment button in the Comments group. This displays a shaded box with the user's name inside. Type the comment text and then click in the worksheet area outside the comment box. You can also insert a comment by right-clicking a cell and then clicking *Insert Comment* at the shortcut menu.

Viewing a Comment

A small, red, diagonal triangle appears in the upper right corner of a cell to alert the reader that a comment exists. Hover the mouse pointer over a cell containing a

▼ **Quick Steps**

Insert a Comment
1. Make desired cell active.
2. Click REVIEW tab.
3. Click New Comment button.
4. Type comment text.
5. Click in worksheet area outside comment box.

New Comment

Show All Comments

Next

Previous

Edit Comment

Delete

comment and the comment box displays. Turn on the display of all comments by clicking the Show All Comments button in the Comments group on the REVIEW tab. Navigate to cells containing comments by clicking the Next button or the Previous button in the Comments group on the REVIEW tab.

Printing a Comment

By default, comments do not print. If you want comments printed with the worksheet, click the PAGE LAYOUT tab, click the Page Setup group dialog box launcher, and then click the Sheet tab at the Page Setup dialog box. Click the *Comments* option box arrow and then click *At end of sheet* to print the comments on a separate page after the cell contents or *As displayed on sheet* to print the comments as they appear within the worksheet area.

Editing and Deleting a Comment

To edit a comment, click the cell containing the comment and then click the Edit Comment button in the Comments group on the REVIEW tab. (The New Comment button changes to the Edit Comment button when the active cell contains a comment.) You can also edit a comment by right-clicking the cell containing the comment and then clicking *Edit Comment* at the shortcut menu. Insert or delete text as desired and then click in the worksheet area outside the comment box.

To delete a comment, click the cell containing the comment and then click the Delete button in the Comments group. You can also delete a comment by right-clicking the cell containing the comment and then clicking *Delete Comment* at the shortcut menu.

Copying and Pasting Comments

A comment that has been added to a cell can be copied and pasted to one or more cells. After copying the source cell, click the destination cell and then open the Paste Special dialog box. Click *Comments* in the *Paste* section and then click OK.

▼ **Quick Steps**

Copy and Paste Comments
1. Select source cell containing comment.
2. Click Copy button.
3. Click destination cell(s).
4. Click Paste button arrow.
5. Click *Paste Special.*
6. Click *Comments.*
7. Click OK.

Project 1b   Inserting, Editing, Pasting, Viewing, and Deleting Comments   **Part 2 of 2**

1. With **EL2-C6-P1-CRPricing.xlsx** open, insert comments by completing the following steps:
   a. Make cell C10 active.
   b. Click the REVIEW tab and then click the New Comment button in the Comments group. A tan shaded box with a green arrow pointing to cell C10 appears. The current user name is inserted in bold text at the top of the comment box followed by a colon. The insertion point is positioned at the left edge of the box on the second line.
   c. Type Most competitors charge 175.00 for weekend rentals of luxury vehicles.
   d. Click in the worksheet area outside the comment box. A small, red, diagonal triangle appears in the upper right corner of cell C10, indicating a comment exists for the cell.
   e. Right-click cell F8 and then click *Insert Comment* at the shortcut menu.

f. Type **Consider reducing the discount for minivans to 18%.** and then click in the worksheet area outside the comment box.

g. Right-click cell F9, click *Insert Comment* at the shortcut menu, type **Last year this discount was 12%.**, and then click in the worksheet area outside the comment box.

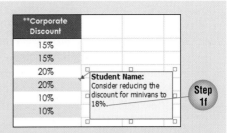

Step 1f

h. Right-click cell F9, click *Copy* at the shortcut menu, right-click cell F10, point to *Paste Special*, and then click *Paste Special* at the shortcut menu.

i. At the Paste Special dialog box, click the *Comments* option in the *Paste* section and then click OK.

j. Press the Esc key to remove the scrolling marquee from cell F9.

Step 1i

2. View comments by completing the following steps:

a. Hover the mouse pointer over cell C10. The comment box pops up and displays the comment text.

b. Hover the mouse pointer over cells F8, F9, and F10 (one after the other) to review the comments in those cells.

Step 2a

c. Press Ctrl + Home to make cell A1 active.

d. Click the Next button in the Comments group on the REVIEW tab. Excel displays the comment box in cell F8.

e. Click the Next button to display the comment box in cell F9.

f. Click the Next button to display the comment box in cell C10.

g. Click Next to display the comment box in cell F10. Consider using the Next button to view comments in a large worksheet to ensure you do not miss any comment cells.

Step 2d

h. Click the Show All Comments button in the Comments group on the REVIEW tab. All comment boxes display in the worksheet area.

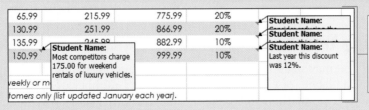

Clicking the Show All Comments button in Step 2h causes all of the comments in the worksheet to display.

i. Click the Show All Comments button again to turn off the display of all comments.

3. Edit and delete a comment by completing the following steps:

a. Right-click cell C10 and then click *Edit Comment* at the shortcut menu. The comment box pops up with the insertion point positioned at the end of the existing comment text.

b. Change *175.00* to *168.99* by moving the insertion point and then inserting and deleting text as required.

Step 3b

c. Click in the worksheet area outside the comment box.

d. Make cell F10 the active cell and then click the Edit Comment button in the Comments group on the REVIEW tab.

e. Change *12%* to *15%* and then click in the worksheet area outside the comment box.

f. Right-click cell F8 and then click *Delete Comment* at the shortcut menu.

g. Click cell F9 and then click the Delete button in the Comments group on the REVIEW tab.

4. Print the comments at the end of the worksheet by completing the following steps:

a. Click the FILE tab and then click the *Print* option.

b. At the Print backstage area, click the <u>Page Setup</u> hyperlink at the bottom of the *Settings* section.

c. At the Page Setup dialog box, click the Sheet tab.

d. Click the *Comments* option box arrow in the *Print* section and then click *At end of sheet* to print the comments on a separate sheet at the end of the document.

e. Click OK.

5. Print only the comments by printing only page 2.

6. Save and close **EL2-C6-P1-CRPricing.xlsx**.

Project 2 | Sharing a Workbook

7 Parts

You will share the workbook with other users for editing and viewing purposes.

Sharing Workbooks ■■■■■■■■■■■■■■■■■■■■

A workbook may need to be circulated among several people so they can review, add, delete, or edit data. Excel provides a number of options for sharing workbooks. One method for collaborating with other users is to share a workbook. A shared workbook can be saved to a network folder that is accessible by other individuals who need the file. Excel tracks each person's changes and displays a prompt if two people have the file open at the same time and attempt to make changes to the same data.

To share a workbook, click the REVIEW tab and then click the Share Workbook button in the Changes group. At the Share Workbook dialog box with the Editing tab active, as shown in Figure 6.3, click the *Allow changes by more than one user at the same time* check box.

Figure 6.3 Share Workbook Dialog Box with Editing Tab Selected

Clicking this check box allows more than one person to edit a workbook at the same time.

Click the Advanced tab in the Share Workbook dialog box to define the sharing options, as shown in Figure 6.4. A shared workbook should be saved to a network folder that is designated as a shared folder and is accessible to the other users. The network administrator is usually the person who creates a folder on a server designated with the read/write access rights for multiple accounts (referred to as a **network share**) and he or she can assist you with navigating to and saving to a network share. All individuals with access to the shared network folder will have full access to the shared workbook.

One drawback of using a shared workbook is that it cannot support all of Excel's features. If you need to use a feature that is unavailable or make a changes to a feature that is not allowed, you will first need to remove shared access. In a later section, you will learn how to lock and unlock worksheets and cells for editing if you want to protect the worksheet or sections of the worksheet from changes before you share the workbook.

Figure 6.4 Share Workbook Dialog Box with Advanced Tab Selected

Use the Advanced tab to select the options you want to use for tracking, updating, and resolving changes made to a shared workbook.

Quick Steps

View Other Users of a Shared Workbook
1. Open shared workbook.
2. Click REVIEW tab.
3. Click Share Workbook button.
4. Review names in *Who has this workbook open now* list box.
5. Click OK.

HINT

To instruct Excel not to display the Resolve Conflicts dialog box, open the Share Workbook dialog box, click the Advanced tab, and then select *The changes being saved win* in the *Conflicting changes between users* section.

1. Open **EL2-C6-P1-CRPricing.xlsx**, save the workbook and name it **EL2-C6-P2-CRPricingShared**.
2. Assume that you are Chris Zajac, regional manager of CutRate Car Rentals. You want feedback from another manager on the proposed rental rates. Share the workbook so that the other manager can make changes directly to the file by completing the following steps:
   a. If necessary, click the REVIEW tab.
   b. Click the Share Workbook button in the Changes group.
   c. At the Share Workbook dialog box with the Editing tab selected, click the *Allow changes by more than one user at the same time* check box to insert a check mark.

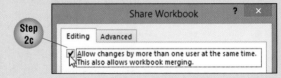

   d. Click OK.
   e. At the Microsoft Excel message box informing you that the workbook will now be saved and asking if you want to continue, click OK.

3. Notice that Excel adds *[Shared]* in the Title bar next to the workbook file name to indicate the workbook's status.

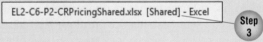

4. Close **EL2-C6-P2-CRPricingShared.xlsx**.

Changing the User Name

When a workbook is shared, Excel tracks the names of the users that edit it. User name information is entered when Microsoft Office is installed. You can change the user name associated with Excel by opening the Excel Options dialog box, selecting the existing text in the *User name* text box, typing the new user name, and then clicking OK.

Opening Multiple Instances of Excel

When multiple workbooks are opened in Excel 2013, the workbooks are opened in the same instance of the program. Excel does not open a new copy of the program every time you open a new workbook. Although working within the same instance of the program saves the computer's resources, at times you may prefer to have multiple instances open. To do this, press and hold Alt and then right-click the Excel icon in the Taskbar. Continue to hold Alt as you left-click *Excel 2013* at the shortcut menu. Release Alt and then click Yes to answer the question *Do you want to start a new instance of Excel?*.

1. At a blank Excel screen, change the user name on your computer to simulate an environment in which another manager is opening the shared workbook from a network share location by completing the following steps:
   a. Click the FILE tab.
   b. Click *Options*.
   c. At the Excel Options dialog box with *General* selected in the left pane, make a note of the existing entry in the *User name* text box in the *Personalize your copy of Microsoft Office* section, if the entry is a name other than your own. ***Note: You will restore the original user name in Project 4c.***
   d. Select the current entry in the *User name* text box, type Aaron Rubin, and then click OK.

2. Open **EL2-C6-P2-CRPricingShared.xlsx**.
3. Make the following changes to the proposed rental rates:
   a. Make cell F5 active and then change the entry from *15%* to *12%*.
   b. Make cell B10 active and then change the entry from *85.99* to *95.99*.
   c. Make cell D10 active and then change the entry from *299.99* to *325.99*.
4. Save **EL2-C6-P2-CRPricingShared.xlsx**.

---

1. Open a new instance of Excel by completing the following steps:
   a. Press and hold Alt and then right-click the Excel icon on the Taskbar.
   b. Continue to hold Alt as you left-click *Excel 2013* at the shortcut menu.
   c. Release Alt and then click Yes to answer the question *Do you want to start a new instance of Excel?* ***Note: You are opening another copy of Excel to simulate an environment in which multiple copies of the shared workbook are open. You will also change the user name to continue the simulation using a different identity.***

2. Click the Open Other Workbooks hyperlink at the bottom of the *Recent* section.
3. Click *Options* to open the Excel Options dialog box and then change the user name in the new copy of Excel to *Chris Zajac*. (Refer to Steps 1a–1d of Project 2b if you need assistance with this step.)
4. In the new copy of Excel, open **EL2-C6-P2-CRPricingShared.xlsx**.
5. View the names of the other users sharing the workbook by completing the following steps:
   a. Click the REVIEW tab.
   b. Click the Share Workbook button in the Changes group.
   c. At the Share Workbook dialog box with the Editing tab selected, look at the names in the *Who has this workbook open now* list box.
   d. Click OK.
6. Leave both copies of Excel open for the next project.

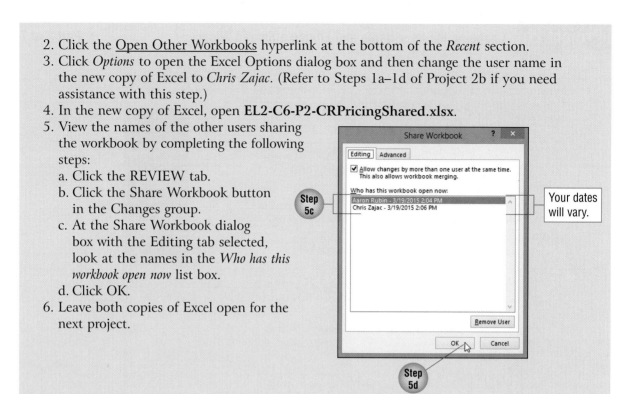

Resolving Conflicts in a Shared Workbook

When two users have copies of a shared workbook open and each user makes a change to the same cell, Excel prompts the second user to resolve the conflict by displaying the Resolve Conflicts dialog box, shown in Figure 6.5. The cell address, original entry, and revised entry are shown for each user. Click the Accept Mine button to save your revision or click the Accept Other button to remove your change and restore the cell to the entry made by the other user. Click the Accept All Mine button or Accept All Others button to avoid being prompted at each individual cell that has a conflict.

Figure 6.5 Resolve Conflicts Dialog Box

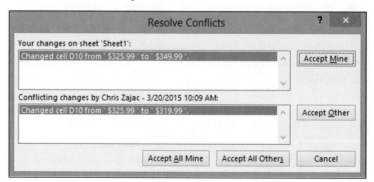

1. With **EL2-C6-P2-CRPricingShared.xlsx** open, assume that you are Chris Zajac and that you want to make a change to a proposed rental rate that will conflict with a change made by Aaron Rubin. Complete the following steps:
   a. Make sure the second copy of Excel you opened for Project 2c, in which you viewed the users with the shared workbook open, is active.
   b. Make cell D10 the active cell and then change *325.99* to *319.99*.
   c. Save **EL2-C6-P2-CRPricingShared.xlsx**.
2. Aaron Rubin has decided to change the weekly luxury rate again. Switch to the other copy of Excel to edit the worksheet and resolve the conflict by completing the following steps:
   a. Click the Excel icon on the Taskbar and then click the other copy of the shared workbook to make it active.
   b. Make cell D10 active and change the entry to *349.99*.
   c. Click the Save button. Since this change conflicts with the change made by Chris Zajac in Step 1b, Excel prompts the second user with the Resolve Conflicts dialog box.

   d. Click the Accept Other button to restore the cell to the value entered by Chris Zajac.

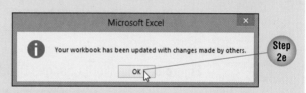

   e. At the Microsoft Excel message box informing you that the workbook has been updated with changes saved by other users, click OK.
3. Notice that cell D10 is displayed with a colored border, indicating that a change has been made. Hover the mouse pointer over cell D10 to view the pop-up box with the name, date, and time the cell change was saved as well as the original and revised entries.

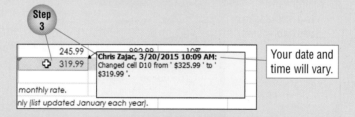

4. Exit the active copy of Excel.
5. With the other copy of Excel active, close **EL2-C6-P2-CRPricingShared.xlsx**.

Printing a History Sheet and Removing Shared Workbook Access

▼ **Quick Steps**

Print a History Sheet
1. Open shared workbook.
2. Click REVIEW tab.
3. Click Track Changes button.
4. Click *Highlight Changes*.
5. Change *When* to *All*.
6. If necessary, clear *Who* check box.
7. If necessary, clear *Where* check box.
8. Click *List changes on a new sheet* check box.
9. Click OK.
10. Print history sheet.

Stop Sharing a Workbook
1. Open shared workbook.
2. Click REVIEW tab.
3. Click Share Workbook button.
4. Remove check mark from *Allow changes by more than one user at the same time* check box.
5. Click OK.
6. Click Yes.

Track
Changes

H I N T

Before changing the status of a shared workbook to exclusive, make sure no one else is currently editing the workbook. Once you remove shared access, users that have the file open will not be able to save their changes.

Before changing the status of a shared workbook to an exclusive workbook, consider printing the change history so you have a record of the edits made by all of the users who worked on the file.

To do this, click the REVIEW tab, click the Track Changes button, and then click *Highlight Changes* at the drop-down list. At the Highlight Changes dialog box, shown in Figure 6.6, change *When* to *All*, remove the check marks from the *Who* and *Where* check boxes, click the *List changes on a new sheet* check box to insert a check mark, and then click OK.

By default, Excel displays a colored border around each changed cell. When you rest the mouse pointer over a cell with a colored border, Excel displays in a pop-up box the cell's change history. Remove the check mark from the *Highlight changes on screen* check box if you prefer not to highlight changed cells in the worksheet. Print the history sheet before you save the document, since this sheet does not save with the workbook.

To stop sharing a workbook, open the shared workbook, click the REVIEW tab, and then click the Share Workbook button. At the Share Workbook dialog box with the Editing tab selected, remove the check mark from the *Allow changes by more than one user at the same time* check box. When you click OK, Excel displays a message box informing you that changing the workbook to exclusive status will erase all of the change history in the workbook and prevent users who might have the workbook open from saving their changes. Consider copying and pasting the cells in the history sheet to a new workbook and saving the history as a separate file, since the history sheet will be removed when the shared workbook is saved.

Figure 6.6 Highlight Changes Dialog Box

Change this option to *All* to include in the history sheet changes made by all of the users who accessed the shared workbook.

By default, this option is selected, causing a colored border to display around each changed cell. Resting the mouse pointer over a highlighted cell causes a pop-up box to display with the change history.

Insert a check mark in this check box to create a sheet named *History* in the workbook with a list of changes made by each user.

1. Open **EL2-C6-P2-CRPricingShared.xlsx**.
2. Create a new sheet named *History* and print the record of changes made to the shared workbook by completing the following steps:
   a. If necessary, click the REVIEW tab.
   b. Click the Track Changes button in the Changes group and then click *Highlight Changes* at the drop-down list.
   c. At the Highlight Changes dialog box, click the *When* option box arrow and then click *All* at the drop-down list.
   d. If necessary, remove the check mark from the *Who* check box.
   e. If necessary, remove the check mark from the *Where* check box.
   f. Click the *List changes on a new sheet* check box to insert a check mark and then click OK.
   g. Print the history sheet.

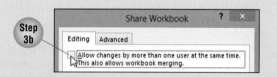

3. Stop sharing the workbook by completing the following steps:
   a. Click the Share Workbook button.
   b. Click the *Allow changes by more than one user at the same time* check box to remove the check mark.
   c. Click OK.
   d. At the Microsoft Excel message box informing you that the workbook will be removed from shared use, click Yes to make the workbook exclusive.

4. Close **EL2-C6-P2-CRPricingShared.xlsx**.

Sharing a Workbook on Windows SkyDrive

Another way to share workbooks is by using Windows SkyDrive. This Office 2013 feature allows you to save and share documents in a storage location on the Internet. You can save a workbook to your SkyDrive and then access the file from any other location where you have Internet access. Instructions for saving a document to your SkyDrive are provided on the next page, but SkyDrive is constantly changing, so the steps may vary.

HINT

If you have access to Microsoft SharePoint, a server application that allows you to share and collaborate on documents, you can save your workbook to a SharePoint library for others to view and/or edit.

Saving to your SkyDrive means you do not have to make a copy of the workbook on a USB drive or some other storage medium in order to edit the workbook at another location. After your workbook is saved to your SkyDrive, invite people to share your workbook with the *Invite People* option at the Share backstage area. When multiple people edit the workbook on SkyDrive, you do not need to manage multiple versions of the same file.

▼ **Quick Steps**

**Save a Workbook
to SkyDrive**
1. Open workbook.
2. Click FILE tab.
3. Click *Save As* option.
4. Click *SkyDrive*
   option.
5. Log in if necessary.
6. Click Browse button.
7. If necessary, select
   desired folder name.
8. Click Save button.

To save a workbook to SkyDrive, you need to have a Windows Live account. If you use Microsoft Hotmail or Messenger, the account you use to sign in to those applications is your Windows Live ID. If you do not already have a Windows Live user name and password, you can sign up for a free account at login.live.com by clicking the Sign up now button. SkyDrive is free and includes 25 gigabytes (GB) of storage on the SkyDrive server.

To save a workbook to your SkyDrive, click the *Share* option and then click the Save to Cloud button at the Share backstage area. At the Save As backstage area with your SkyDrive selected in the *Places* section, click the Browse button. At the Save As dialog box, choose the folder within your SkyDrive, type the file name, and then click Save.

To invite people to view and/or edit your workbook, click the *Share* option. In the *Invite People* section, shown in Figure 6.7, type the names or email addresses of people you want to view and/or edit the workbook or click the Address Book icon

Figure 6.7 Share Backstage Area with *Invite People* Option Selected

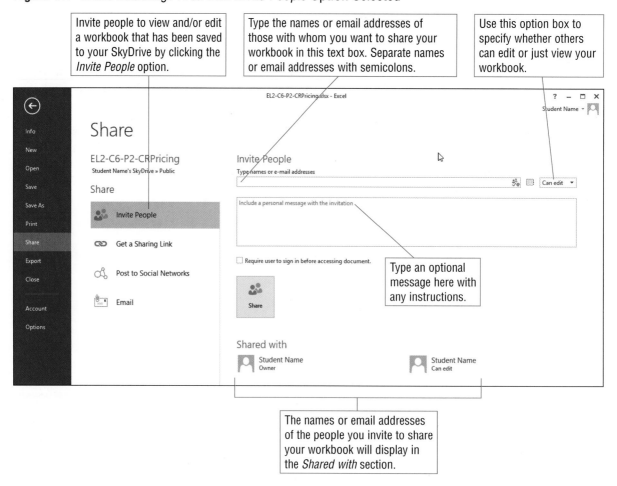

Invite people to view and/or edit a workbook that has been saved to your SkyDrive by clicking the *Invite People* option.

Type the names or email addresses of those with whom you want to share your workbook in this text box. Separate names or email addresses with semicolons.

Use this option box to specify whether others can edit or just view your workbook.

Type an optional message here with any instructions.

The names or email addresses of the people you invite to share your workbook will display in the *Shared with* section.

to the right of the *Type names or e-mail addresses* text box and choose people from your contacts. The option box to the right of the Address Book icon offers the options *Can edit* and *Can view*. If you want to allow people to view the workbook but do not want to allow them to make changes, ensure that you change this option from the default *Can edit* to *Can view*. You must send separate invitations if you want to invite certain people to edit and others only to view. After you type a personal message with the invitation, click the Share button. Emails are sent to the people you invited and their names or email addresses will appear in the *Shared with* section.

At the Share backstage area, you can also get a sharing link, post your workbook to your social networks, or email your workbook. Place the sharing link in a Word document or PowerPoint presentation and use it as a hyperlink to your workbook saved on SkyDrive.

To stop sharing a workbook with someone else, right-click the person's name in the *Shared with* section and then click *Remove User* at the shortcut menu. To remove the sharing link, click the Disable Link button at the Share backstage area.

▼ **Quick Steps**

Share a Workbook Saved on SkyDrive
1. Click FILE tab.
2. Click *Share* option.
3. Type names or addresses.
4. Choose *Can edit* or *Can view* option.
5. Type optional message.
6. Click Share button.

Share

| Project 2f | Optional: Saving and Sharing a Workbook Using Windows SkyDrive | Part 6 of 7 |

Note: Complete this project only if you have a Windows Live ID.

1. Open **EL2-C6-P2-CRPricingShared.xlsx** and save the workbook to your SkyDrive by completing the following steps. *Note: If you already save your work to your SkyDrive, skip to Step 2.*
   a. Click the FILE tab and then click the *Save As* option.
   b. Click *SkyDrive* at the Save As backstage area. Log in to your SkyDrive account or click the Browse button if you are already logged in. *Note: SkyDrive is constantly changing, so these steps may vary.*

   c. Navigate to the public folder, if necessary, and then click Save.

2. To invite people to share your workbook, complete the following steps:
   a. Click the FILE tab and then click the *Share* option.
   b. At the Share backstage area, click in the *Type names or e-mail addresses* text box and then type the email address of your instructor or a classmate.
   c. Click the down-pointing arrow at the right side of the option box containing the text *Can edit* and then click *Can view*.
   d. Click in the *Include a personal message with the invitation* text box and type Please review proposed rate changes.
   e. Click the Share button. An email is sent to the person you invited and his or her name displays in the *Shared with* section of the Share backstage area.

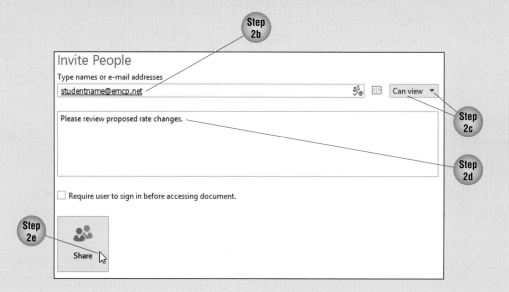

3. Check with your instructor or classmate to see if he or she received your email with the hyperlink to your workbook.
4. Stop sharing the workbook with your instructor or classmate by right-clicking the name in the *Shared with* section and then clicking *Remove User* at the shortcut menu.

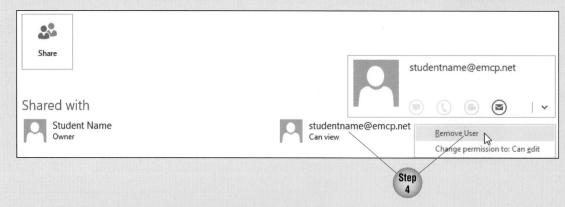

5. Save and close **EL2-C6-P2-CRPricingShared.xlsx**.

Sending a Workbook via Email

A workbook can be sent to others as a file attached to an email message. You can attach the workbook using your email program's file attachment feature or you can initiate the message using Excel. To do this, click the FILE tab and then click the Share option. At the Share backstage area with *Email* selected in the *Share* section, click the Send as Attachment button located in the *Email* section. The default email program, Microsoft Outlook, launches an email message window with the workbook file already attached and the file name inserted in the *Subject* text box. Type the recipient's email address in the *To* text box, type the message text in the message window, and then click the Send button. The message is moved to Outlook's Outbox folder and is then sent out to the recipient.

The *Email* section of the Share backstage area also contains buttons to attach the workbook to an email message as a portable document format (PDF) or as an XML paper specification (XPS) document instead of the default workbook file format. In addition to sending the workbook as an attachment, you can also send a link to the workbook in an email or send the workbook as an Internet fax.

▼ **Quick Steps**

Send a Workbook via Email
1. Open workbook.
2. Click FILE tab.
3. Click *Share*.
4. Click *Email*.
5. Click Send as Attachment button.
6. Type recipient's email address in *To* text box.
7. If necessary, edit text in *Subject* text box.
8. Type message in message window.
9. Click Send.

Project 2g | **Optional: Sending a Workbook via Email** | **Part 7 of 7**

Note: Complete this project only if you use Microsoft Outlook as your email provider.

1. Open **CRFinalPrices.xlsx**.
2. Save the workbook and name it **EL2-C6-P2-CRFinalPrices**.
3. Send the workbook as a file attached to an email message by completing the following steps:
   a. Click the FILE tab and then click the *Share* option.
   b. Click *Email* in the *Share* section and then click the Send as Attachment button in the *Email* section.

c. With the insertion point positioned in the *To* text box at the message window, type your own email address.

d. Click in the message window and then type the following text:

Here are the new rental rates that are effective May 1, 2015. Please ensure that everyone is using these rates for any rentals after April 30, 2015. Target revenues are on the second sheet.

e. Click the Send button. The message is sent and the message window closes.

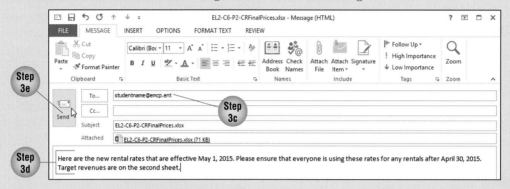

4. Open Outlook.

5. Check your inbox for the new message and then open and view the message. *Note: Depending on your mail server, you may need to wait a few seconds for the message to be processed.*

6. Close the message and then exit Outlook.

7. Close **EL2-C6-P2-CRFinalPrices.xlsx**.

Project 3   Lock and Unlock a Workbook, Worksheet, and Ranges   4 Parts

You will protect a worksheet, unlock ranges, prevent changes to the structure of a workbook, and add a password to open a workbook.

Protecting and Unprotecting Worksheets ■■■■■■■■■■

Protect
Sheet

Quick Steps

Protect a Worksheet
1. Open workbook.
2. Activate desired sheet.
3. Click REVIEW tab.
4. Click Protect Sheet button.
5. Type password.
6. Choose allowable actions.
7. Click OK.
8. Retype password.
9. Click OK.

Protecting a worksheet prevents other users from editing cells that you do not want accidentally deleted or modified or otherwise changed. By default, when a worksheet is protected, each cell in it is locked. This means that no one can insert, delete, or modify the content. In most cases, some cells within a worksheet contain data that you want to allow other users to be able to change. Therefore, in a collaborative environment, protecting a worksheet generally involves two steps:

1. Clear the lock attribute on those cells that you will allow to be edited.
2. Protect the worksheet.

To clear the lock attribute for (unlock) the cells that you will allow to be modified, select the cells, click the HOME tab, and then click the Format button in the Cells group. Click *Lock Cell* in the *Protection* section of the drop-down list to turn off the lock attribute. Next, turn on worksheet protection by clicking the REVIEW tab and then clicking the Protect Sheet button in the Changes group. At the Protect Sheet dialog box, as shown in Figure 6.8, select the actions you want to allow and then click OK. You can also choose to assign a password to unprotect the sheet. Be cautious if you add a password to remove protection, since you will not be able to unprotect the worksheet if you forget the password. If necessary, write down the password and store it in a secure location.

▼ **Quick Steps**

Unlock a Cell
1. Select cell(s) to be unlocked.
2. Click HOME tab.
3. Click Format button.
4. Click *Lock Cell*.
5. Deselect cell(s).

Figure 6.8 Protect Sheet Dialog Box

You can choose to add a password that must be entered to unprotect the worksheet.

Use this list box to select the actions that users of the protected worksheet can perform.

Format

Project 3a **Protecting an Entire Worksheet**   **Part 1 of 4**

1. Open **CRFinalPrices.xlsx**.
2. Save the workbook and name it **EL2-C6-P3-CRFinalPrices**.
3. Protect the entire FinalPrices worksheet by completing the following steps:
   a. Make sure FinalPrices is the active sheet.
   b. Click the REVIEW tab.
   c. Click the Protect Sheet button in the Changes group.
   d. At the Protect Sheet dialog box with the insertion point positioned in the *Password to unprotect sheet* text box, type e**L2-C6** and then click OK.
   e. At the Confirm Password dialog box with the insertion point positioned in the *Reenter password to proceed* text box, type e**L2-C6** and then press Enter or click OK.
   f. Make any cell active in the FinalPrices sheet and attempt to delete the data or type new data. Since the entire worksheet is now protected, all cells are locked and Excel displays a message that the worksheet is protected. Click OK at the Microsoft Excel message indicating that you need to unprotect the sheet to modify the cell.

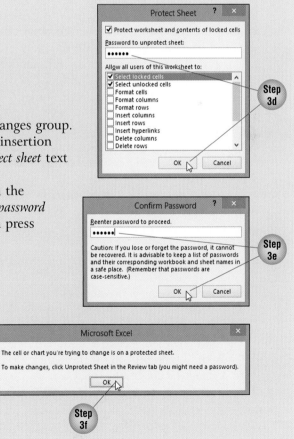

4. Notice the Protect Sheet button changes to the Unprotect Sheet button when a worksheet has been protected.
5. Save **EL2-C6-P3-CRFinalPrices.xlsx**.

Project 3b **Unlocking Cells and Protecting a Worksheet**   Part 2 of 4

1. With **EL2-C6-P3-CRFinalPrices.xlsx** open, make TargetRevenue the active sheet.
2. Unlock the weekday target rental data cells for editing by completing the following steps:
   a. Select C5:C10.
   b. Click the HOME tab.
   c. Click the Format button in the Cells group.
   d. At the Format button drop-down list, look at the icon next to *Lock Cell* in the *Protection* section. The highlighted icon indicates the lock attribute is turned on.
   e. Click *Lock Cell* at the Format button drop-down list to turn the lock attribute off for the selected range.
   f. Click in any cell within the range C5:C10 and then click the Format button in the Cells group. Look at the icon next to *Lock Cell* in the drop-down list. The icon is no longer highlighted, which indicates the cell is unlocked.
   g. Click within the worksheet area to close the drop-down list.

Highlighted icon indicates lock attribute is active.

Step 2d

Nonhighlighted icon indicates lock attribute is not active.

Step 2f

3. Unlock the remaining target rental ranges for editing by completing the following steps:
   a. Select F5:F10, hold down the Ctrl key, and then select I5:I10 and L5:L10.
   b. Press the F4 key to repeat the command to unlock the cells or click the Format button in the Cells group and then click *Lock Cell* at the drop-down list.
   c. Click in any cell to deselect the ranges.
4. Protect the TargetRevenue worksheet by completing the following steps:
   a. Click the REVIEW tab.
   b. Click the Protect Sheet button in the Changes group.
   c. Type eL2-C6 in the *Password to unprotect sheet* text box.
   d. Click OK.
   e. Type eL2-C6 in the *Reenter password to proceed* text box and then press Enter or click OK.
5. Save **EL2-C6-P3-CRFinalPrices.xlsx**.
6. Test the worksheet protection applied to the TargetRevenue sheet by completing the following steps:
   a. Make cell B8 active and then press the Delete key.
   b. Click OK at the Microsoft Office Excel message box that indicates the protected cell cannot be changed.
   c. Make cell C8 active and then press the Delete key. Since cell C8 is unlocked, its contents are deleted and its dependent cells are updated.
   d. Click the Undo button on the Quick Access toolbar to restore the contents of cell C8.
7. Save and then close **EL2-C6-P3-CRFinalPrices.xlsx**.

Step 6c

4	Category	Weekday (Mo to Th)		Target Rentals	Target Revenue
5	Compact	$	36	675	$ 24,293
6	Mid-size		38.99	880	34,311
7	Full-size		40.99	425	17,421
8	Minivan		75.99		-
9	SUV		89.99	198	17,818
10	Luxury		99.99	86	8,599
11	TOTAL			Weekday:	$ 102,442

When a worksheet has protection turned on, the Protect Sheet button in the Changes group on the REVIEW tab changes to the Unprotect Sheet button. To remove worksheet protection, click the Unprotect Sheet button or click the Unprotect hyperlink in the Info backstage area in the *Protect Workbook* section. If a password was entered when the worksheet was protected, the Unprotect Sheet dialog box, shown in Figure 6.9, appears. Type the password and then press Enter or click OK.

Unprotect
Sheet

Figure 6.9 Unprotect Sheet Dialog Box

Protecting and Unprotecting the Structure of a Workbook

Use the Protect Workbook button in the Changes group on the REVIEW tab to prevent changes to the structure of a workbook, such as inserting a new sheet, deleting a sheet, or unhiding a hidden worksheet. At the Protect Structure and Windows dialog box, shown in Figure 6.10, you can also turn on protection for the workbook's windows. Click the *Windows* check box to prevent a user from resizing or changing the position of the windows in the workbook. As you did to protect a worksheet, you can enter an optional password that will protect the workbook in the future.

Figure 6.10 Protect Structure and Windows Dialog Box

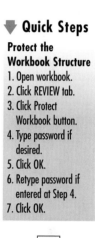

▼ **Quick Steps**

**Protect the
Workbook Structure**
1. Open workbook.
2. Click REVIEW tab.
3. Click Protect
   Workbook button.
4. Type password if
   desired.
5. Click OK.
6. Retype password if
   entered at Step 4.
7. Click OK.

Protect
Workbook

Project 3c   **Protecting the Structure of a Workbook**   **Part 3 of 4**

1. Open **EL2-C6-P3-CRFinalPrices.xlsx**.
2. Protect the workbook structure by completing the following steps:
   a. If necessary, click the REVIEW tab.
   b. Click the Protect Workbook button in the Changes group.
   c. At the Protect Structure and Windows dialog box with the insertion point positioned in the *Password (optional)* text box, type eL2-C6 and then press Enter or click OK.

Step
2c

d. At the Confirm Password dialog box with the insertion point positioned in the *Reenter password to proceed* text box, type **eL2-C6** and press Enter or click OK.

3. To test the workbook protection, attempt to insert a new worksheet by completing the following steps:

   a. Right-click the TargetRevenue sheet tab.

   b. Look at the shortcut menu. Notice that all of the options related to managing worksheets are dimmed, which means the options are unavailable.

   c. Click within the worksheet area to close the shortcut menu.

4. Save **EL2-C6-P3-CRFinalPrices.xlsx**.

Unprotecting a Workbook

Protect Workbook

When the structure of a workbook has been protected, the Protect Workbook button in the Changes group on the REVIEW tab displays with a green, shaded background. To remove workbook protection, click the Protect Workbook button. If a password was entered when the workbook was protected, the Unprotect Workbook dialog box, shown in Figure 6.11, appears. Type the password and then press Enter or click OK.

Figure 6.11 Unprotect Workbook Dialog Box

Adding and Removing a Password in a Workbook ■ ■ ■ ■ ■

▼ **Quick Steps**

Add a Workbook Password
1. Open workbook.
2. Click FILE tab.
3. Click Protect Workbook button.
4. Click *Encrypt with Password*.
5. Type password.
6. Press Enter or click OK.
7. Retype password.
8. Press Enter or click OK.
9. Save workbook.

You can prevent unauthorized access to Excel data by requiring a password to open a workbook. The password to open a workbook is encrypted. In an *encrypted password*, the plain text you type is converted into a scrambled format called *ciphertext*, which prevents unauthorized users from retrieving the password. To add an encrypted password to an open workbook, click the FILE tab. At the Info backstage area, as shown in Figure 6.12, click the Protect Workbook button in *Protect Workbook* section. Click *Encrypt with Password* at the drop-down list to open the Encrypt Document dialog box, shown in Figure 6.13.

When you create a password, it is good practice to include a combination of four types of characters: uppercase letters, lowercase letters, symbols, and numbers. Passwords constructed using these elements are considered secure and more difficult to crack. Note that if you forget the password, you will not be able to open the workbook. If necessary, write down the password and store it in a secure location.

Figure 6.12 Info Backstage Area with Protect Workbook Drop-down List

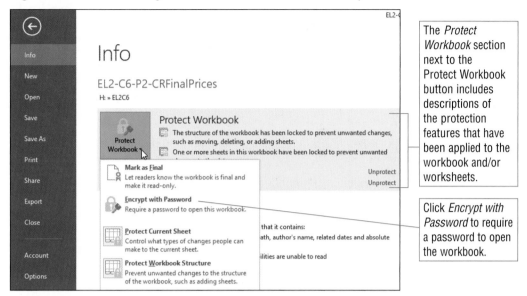

The *Protect Workbook* section next to the Protect Workbook button includes descriptions of the protection features that have been applied to the workbook and/or worksheets.

Click *Encrypt with Password* to require a password to open the workbook.

Figure 6.13 Encrypt Document Dialog Box

Project 3d Adding a Password to Open a Workbook   **Part 4 of 4**

1. With **EL2-C6-P3-CRFinalPrices.xlsx** open, add a password to open the workbook by completing the following steps:
   a. Click the FILE tab. The backstage area opens with the *Info* option selected.
   b. Read the information in the *Protect Workbook* section. Since this workbook has protection features already applied, the existing features are described and a hyperlink is provided to unprotect each protected worksheet. In a workbook with no pre-existing protection, the *Permissions* section displays the text *Control what types of changes people can make to this workbook.*
   c. Click the Protect Workbook button.

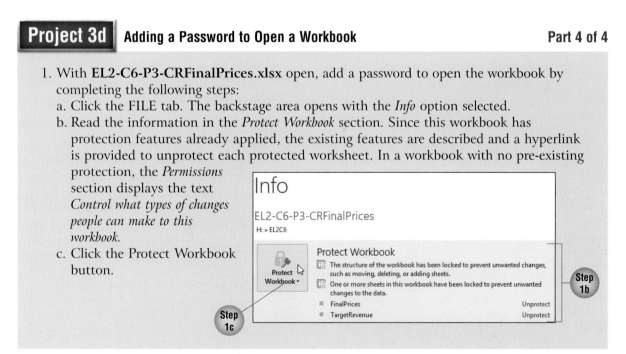

d. Click *Encrypt with Password* at the drop-down list.

e. At the Encrypt Document dialog box with the insertion point positioned in the *Password* text box, type **eL2-C6** and then press Enter or click OK.

f. Type **eL2-C6** at the Confirm Password dialog box with the insertion point positioned in the *Reenter password* text box and then press Enter or click OK.

g. Notice that Excel has added to the first line of the *Protect Workbook* section next to the Protect Workbook button the text *A password is required to open this workbook*.

h. Click the Back button to return to the worksheet.

2. Save and then close **EL2-C6-P3-CRFinalPrices.xlsx**.

3. Test the password security on the workbook by completing the following steps:

a. Open **EL2-C6-P3-CRFinalPrices.xlsx**.

b. At the Password dialog box with the insertion point positioned in the *Password* text box, type a password that is incorrect for the file and then press Enter.

c. At the Microsoft Excel message box indicating that the password you supplied is not correct, click OK.

d. Open **EL2-C6-P3-CRFinalPrices.xlsx**.

e. Type **eL2-C6** in the *Password* text box and then press Enter or click OK.

4. Close **EL2-C6-P3-CRFinalPrices.xlsx**.

To remove a password from a workbook, open the workbook using your password. At the Info backstage area, click the Protect Workbook button in the *Protect Workbook* section. Click *Encrypt with Password* at the drop-down list to open the Encrypt Document dialog box. Delete the password and then click OK.

You will begin tracking changes made to a workbook, view changes made by two users, and accept and reject changes.

Tracking Changes to a Workbook ■■■■■■■■■■■■■■■■■

As you learned in Project 1, Excel automatically tracks changes made by individuals who share a workbook. As you saw with the history sheet in Project 2e, you can display and print a record of the changes. If a workbook is not shared, you can turn on the Track Changes feature and Excel will automatically share the workbook. To do this, click the Track Changes button in the Changes group on the REVIEW tab and then click *Highlight Changes* at the drop-down list. At the Highlight Changes dialog box, click the *Track changes while editing* check box and then click OK.

As the owner of a shared workbook, you might want to view the worksheet with all of the cells highlighted in which changes have been made to the data. Figure 6.14 displays the worksheet you will edit in Project 4 with all of the changes highlighted. As you hover the mouse pointer over a highlighted cell, a pop-up box displays the name of the person who changed the cell, along with the date, time, original entry, and revised entry.

▼ **Quick Steps**

Track Changes
1. Open workbook.
2. Click REVIEW tab.
3. Click Track Changes button.
4. Click *Highlight Changes.*
5. Click *Track changes while editing* check box.
6. Click OK twice.

Highlight Changes
1. Open tracked workbook.
2. Click REVIEW tab.
3. Click Track Changes button.
4. Click *Highlight Changes.*
5. Change *When* to *Not yet reviewed.*
6. Make sure *Who* is set to *Everyone.*
7. Click OK.

Figure 6.14 Project 4 Worksheet with Changes Highlighted

The pop-up box displays the name, date, time, original entry, and revised entry.

Changed cells in a shared workbook can be displayed with a colored border to identify which cells were changed. Each person's changes are identified with a different color.

Accepting and Rejecting Tracked Changes

▼ Quick Steps

Accept and Reject Changes

1. Open tracked workbook.
2. Click REVIEW tab.
3. Click Track Changes button.
4. Click *Accept/Reject Changes.*
5. Make sure *When* is set to *Not yet reviewed.*
6. Make sure *Who* is set to *Everyone.*
7. Click OK.
8. Click Accept or Reject button at each change.

In addition to displaying the worksheet with the changes highlighted, you can navigate to each change and accept or reject it. To do this, click the Track Changes button in the Changes group on the REVIEW tab and then click *Accept/Reject Changes* at the drop-down list. At the Select Changes to Accept or Reject dialog box, as shown in Figure 6.15, define which changes you want to review and then click OK.

Excel navigates to the first changed cell and displays the Accept or Reject Changes dialog box, shown in Figure 6.16. Review the information in the dialog box and click the Accept button or the Reject button. If you reject a change, the cell is restored to its original value. After you respond to each changed cell, the colored border is removed since the cell has been reviewed. The dialog box also includes an Accept All button and a Reject All button, which you can use to make a global review decision, if desired. Be careful when accepting and rejecting changes, since Undo is not available after you review the cells.

Figure 6.15 Select Changes to Accept or Reject Dialog Box

You can choose to navigate to changes not yet reviewed or made after a specific date.

You can restrict the review to changes made by a specific user.

Figure 6.16 Accept or Reject Changes Dialog Box

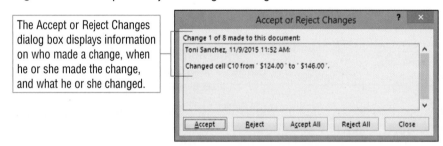

The Accept or Reject Changes dialog box displays information on who made a change, when he or she made the change, and what he or she changed.

Project 4a Tracking Changes Made to a Workbook   Part 1 of 3

1. Open **CRWestReg.xlsx**.
2. Save the workbook and name it **EL2-C6-P4-CRWestReg**.
3. Begin tracking changes by completing the following steps:
   a. If necessary, click the REVIEW tab.
   b. Click the Track Changes button in the Changes group.
   c. Click *Highlight Changes* at the drop-down list.

d. At the Highlight Changes dialog box, click the *Track changes while editing* check box to insert a check mark. Notice that turning on the Track Changes feature automatically shares the workbook.

e. With *When* set to *All* and *Who* set to *Everyone* by default, click OK.

f. At the Microsoft Excel message box indicating that this action will now save the workbook, click OK to continue.

4. Close **EL2-C6-P4-CRWestReg.xlsx**.

Project 4b **Editing a Tracked Workbook** **Part 2 of 3**

1. Assume that you are Toni Sanchez, the SUV rental manager for the West region at CutRate Car Rentals. You have been asked to edit the target rental values for SUVs. At a blank Excel window, change the user name to *Toni Sanchez*. (Refer to Project 2b, Step 1 if you need assistance changing the user name.) You will return to the original user name in Project 4c.

2. Open **EL2-C6-P4-CRWestReg.xlsx**.

3. Edit the cells that contain the SUV target data as follows:

C10:	from	*124*	to	*146*
F10:	from	*22*	to	*47*
I10:	from	*22*	to	*31*
L10:	from	*8*	to	*12*

4. Save and then close **EL2-C6-P4-CRWestReg.xlsx**.

5. Assume that you are Sam Forwell, the compact rental manager for the West region at CutRate Car Rentals. You have been asked to edit the target rental values for compact cars. At a blank Excel window, change the user name to *Sam Forwell*.

6. Open **EL2-C6-P4-CRWestReg.xlsx**.

7. Edit the cells that contain the compact target data as follows:

C6:	from	*362*	to	*391*
F6:	from	*165*	to	*173*
I6:	from	*33*	to	*46*
L6:	from	*15*	to	*11*

8. Save and then close **EL2-C6-P4-CRWestReg.xlsx**.

1. Assume that you are the operations manager for the West region at CutRate Car Rentals. You decide to review the changes made by Toni Sanchez and Sam Forwell. At a blank Excel window, change the user name back to the original user name for the computer you are using.
2. Open **EL2-C6-P4-CRWestReg.xlsx**.
3. Highlight all cells with changes that have not yet been reviewed by completing the following steps:
   a. Click the Track Changes button in the Changes group on the REVIEW tab.
   b. Click *Highlight Changes* at the drop-down list.
   c. At the Highlight Changes dialog box, click the down-pointing arrow at the right of the *When* option box and then click *Not yet reviewed* at the drop-down list.
   d. With *Who* set to *Everyone* by default, click OK.

4. Accept and reject changes as you navigate through the worksheet by completing the following steps:
   a. Press Ctrl + Home to make cell A1 active.
   b. Click the Track Changes button and then click *Accept/Reject Changes* at the drop-down list.
   c. At the Select Changes to Accept or Reject dialog box with *When* set to *Not yet reviewed* and *Who* set to *Everyone*, click OK.
   d. Excel moves the active cell to cell C10, where the first change was made, and displays the Accept or Reject Changes dialog box. Click the Accept button to leave cell C10 at *$146.00*.

   e. Excel makes cell F10 the active cell. Click the Reject button to restore cell F10 to the original value of *$22.00*. **Note: If necessary, drag the Accept or Reject Changes dialog box out of the way to see the cell being reviewed in the worksheet area.**
   f. Respond to the remaining changes to the cells as follows:

      I10:   Accept
      L10:   Accept
      C6:   Reject
      F6:   Accept
      I6:   Reject
      L6:   Accept
5. Save the worksheet.
6. Print and then close **EL2-C6-P4-CRWestReg.xlsx**.

Turning Off Track Changes

When you no longer need to track the changes made to a workbook, click the Track Changes button and then click *Highlight Changes* at the drop-down list. At the Highlight Changes dialog box, click the *Track changes while editing* check box to remove the check mark and then click OK. Excel displays the warning message that the workbook will no longer be shared and that the change history will be erased. Click Yes to complete the action.

If you have not reviewed all of the changes made to the workbook, consider printing a copy of the history sheet before turning off the Track Changes feature. (Refer to Project 2e, Step 2, for assistance with printing a history sheet.)

Excel provides several methods to share and collaborate data with other users of Excel. The method that you choose depends on factors such as the availability of a network share folder, need to protect ranges or otherwise restrict access to sensitive data, and resources available by the users who will receive the data. In Chapter 8, you will explore other features that are important to consider when distributing a workbook, such as restricting access and removing personal information.

▼ **Quick Steps**

Turn Off Track Changes
1. Open tracked workbook.
2. Click REVIEW tab.
3. Click *Highlight Changes*.
4. Click *Track changes while editing check box* check box to remove check mark.
5. Click OK.
6. Click Yes.

Chapter Summary

- Workbook properties include descriptive information about the workbook, such as the author's name and the workbook title, subject, or comments.

- Workbook properties are sometimes referred to as *metadata*.

- Display the Info backstage area or open the document information panel to add information to a workbook's properties.

- Comments display text in a pop-up box when the cell pointer is hovering over a cell to which a comment has been attached.

- Comments are useful for adding explanatory notes, descriptions, or questions about a cell entry when a workbook is being created, edited, or shared with other reviewers.

- Insert, edit, view, or delete a comment using buttons in the Comments group on the REVIEW tab. Comment text can be copied and pasted to another cell using the Paste Special dialog box.

- Sharing a workbook generally involves turning on the sharing feature and saving the workbook to a folder on a networked server that is accessible to the other users who need the file.

- Use the Share Workbook button in the Changes group on the REVIEW tab to turn on the sharing feature.

- When Microsoft Office is installed, a user name is defined for the computer onto which the software has been copied. Excel automatically inserts this name in the *Author* workbook property when a new workbook is created.

- Change the user name at the Excel Options dialog box.

- View other users who have a shared workbook open at the Share Workbook dialog box.

- When a workbook is shared, Excel automatically tracks the changes made by all of the individuals who access the file.

- If two users have a shared workbook open at the same time and each one makes a change to the same cell, a Resolve Conflicts dialog box appears when the second user saves the workbook.

- At the Resolve Conflicts dialog box, the second user can choose to accept the change he or she made or restore the cell to the entry made by the last person to save the file.

- Print a history sheet to provide a detailed record of all of the changes made to a shared workbook before removing shared access to the workbook.

- When a shared workbook is changed to an exclusive workbook, all of the change history is removed from the file.

- You can save workbook to a folder in your own storage location on Windows Live SkyDrive, where you can retrieve it from any location with Internet access.

- Invite people to edit or view the workbooks that you have saved to your SkyDrive folders or SharePoint library.

- An email message with the current workbook added as a file attachment can be generated from Excel using the Share backstage area. You can attach the workbook in the default Excel (.xlsx) format, as a portable data format (PDF) document, or as an XML paper specification (XPS) document.

- You can protect an entire worksheet to prevent another person from accidentally inserting or deleting or otherwise changing data that you do not want modified.

- Protect a worksheet using the Protect Sheet button in the Changes group on the REVIEW tab.

- You can add a password that is required to unprotect a worksheet.

- Each cell in a worksheet has a lock attribute that activates when the worksheet is protected.

- To allow individual cells in a protected worksheet to be editable, select the cells and turn off the lock attribute before protecting the worksheet.

- The Protect Workbook button in the Changes group on the REVIEW tab is used to protect a workbook from a user inserting, deleting, renaming, or otherwise managing worksheets in it.

- You can prevent unauthorized access to an Excel workbook by adding an encrypted password to open and/or modify the workbook.

- At the Info backstage area, click the Protect Workbook button and then click *Encrypt with Password* to add a workbook password. Save the workbook after typing and confirming the password.

- Turn on or off the Track Changes feature or display changes in a shared workbook by opening the Highlight Changes dialog box.

- The Accept/Reject Changes feature is used to navigate to each changed cell in a worksheet and then accept or reject the revision.

Commands Review

FEATURE	RIBBON TAB, GROUP/OPTION	BUTTON	KEYBOARD SHORTCUT
accept/reject changes	REVIEW, Changes		
add comment	REVIEW, Comments		Shift + F2
add password	FILE, *Info*		
change user name	FILE, *Options*		
delete comment	REVIEW, Comments		
document information panel	FILE, *Info*	Properties ▾	
edit comment	REVIEW, Comments		
highlight changes	REVIEW, Changes		
paste copied comment	HOME, Clipboard		Ctrl + Alt + V
protect workbook	REVIEW, Changes		
protect worksheet	REVIEW, Changes		
share workbook	REVIEW, Changes		
track changes	REVIEW, Changes		
unlock cells	HOME, Format		

Concepts Check   Test Your Knowledge

Completion: In the space provided at the right, indicate the correct term, command, or number.

1. Open this view to add descriptive information about a workbook, such as a title or subject heading. _____

2. This panel displays the workbook's properties between the ribbon and worksheet. _____

3. A small, red, diagonal triangle in the upper right corner of a cell indicates that this box will pop up when the mouse pointer rests on the cell. _____

4. Open this dialog box to turn on the feature that allows changes to be made by more than one user at the same time. _____

5. Change the user name for the computer that you are using by opening this dialog box. _____

6. When two users have the same workbook open at the same time and both make changes to the same cell, this dialog box appears when the second person saves the workbook. _____

7. Open this dialog box to create a history sheet, which includes a record of all of the changes made to a shared workbook. _____

8. Select a cell that you want to allow changes to and then click this button and menu option to unlock the cell before protecting the worksheet. _____

9. At this dialog box, you can add a password that is required to unprotect a worksheet. _____

10. Prevent users from inserting or deleting worksheets in a workbook by opening this dialog box. _____

11. Click this option from the Protect Workbook drop-down list at the Info backstage area view to assign a password to open a workbook. _____

12. Turn on this feature and Excel automatically changes the workbook to a shared workbook, if it is not already shared. _____

13. Excel applies this formatting to cells in a shared workbook that have been modified to make the revised cells stand out. _____

14. Use this feature to navigate to each changed cell in a shared workbook and decide whether to keep the change or restore the cell back to its previous value. _____

15. This feature is not available to restore cells to their previous values after you have finished reviewing tracked changes. _____

Skills Check Assess Your Performance

Assessment

1 ENTER AND DISPLAY WORKBOOK PROPERTIES AND INSERT COMMENTS

1. Open **NationalLicenses.xlsx**.
2. Save the workbook and name it **EL2-C6-A1-NationalLicenses**.
3. Type the following text in the appropriate workbook properties:

Add an Author	Wendy Cheung
Title	MSO 2013 License Chargeback
Subject	Journal entry by department
Categories	JE supporting document
Status	Posted
Comments	Audit worksheet for Office 2013 site license with internal chargebacks

4. Remove the existing author, *Paradigm Publishing Inc.*
5. Display the document information panel.
6. Insert a screen image of the worksheet showing the document information panel in a new Microsoft Word document using Print Screen with Paste or the Screenshot feature in Word (INSERT tab, Screenshot button in Illustrations group). Type your name a few lines below the screen image.
7. Save the Microsoft Word document and name it **EL2-C6-A1-NationalLicenses.docx**.
8. Print **EL2-C6-A1-NationalLicenses.docx** and then exit Word.
9. At the Microsoft Excel worksheet, close the document information panel.
10. Make cell B8 active and insert a new comment. Type Check this quantity with Marty. The number seems high. in the comment box.
11. Make cell B14 active and insert a new comment. Type Make a note in the budget file for next year. This quantity will increase by 5. in the comment box.
12. Print the worksheet with the comments at the end of the sheet.
13. Save and close **EL2-C6-A1-NationalLicenses.xlsx**.

Assessment

2 SHARE A WORKSHEET, EDIT A SHARED WORKBOOK, AND PRINT A HISTORY SHEET

1. Open **PreMfgTargets.xlsx**.
2. Save the workbook and name it **EL2-C6-A2-PreMfgTargets**.
3. Share the workbook.
4. Change the user name to *Lorne Moir* and then edit the following cells:
   C11:   from   *4,352*   to   *5520*
   C18:   from   *15,241*   to   *15960*
5. Save the workbook.
6. Open a new instance of Excel. ***Note: Refer to Project 2c to open a new instance of Excel.***

7. Change the user name to *Gerri Gonzales,* open **EL2-C6-A2-PreMfgTargets.xlsx,** and then edit the following cells:

    F4: from *3,845* to *5126*
    F9: from *7,745* to *9320*

8. Save the workbook.
9. Create a history sheet with a record of the changes made to the data by all of the users.
10. Print the history sheet. *Note: If you submit your assignment work electronically, create a copy of the history sheet in a new workbook, since the history sheet is automatically deleted when the file is saved.*
11. Save and then close both instances of **EL2-C6-A2-PreMfgTargets.xlsx.**
12. Change the user name back to the original user name for the computer you are using.

Assessment

3 REMOVE SHARED ACCESS

1. Open **EL2-C6-A2-PreMfgTargets.xlsx.**
2. Save the workbook and name it **EL2-C6-A3-PreMfgTargets.**
3. Remove the shared access to the workbook.
4. Close **EL2-C6-A3-PreMfgTargets.xlsx.**

Assessment

4 PROTECT AN ENTIRE WORKSHEET AND ADD A PASSWORD TO A WORKBOOK

1. Open **EL2-C6-A1-NationalLicenses.xlsx.**
2. Save the workbook and name it **EL2-C6-A4-NationalLicenses.**
3. Protect the entire worksheet using the password *eL2-A4* to unprotect.
4. Add the password *eL2-A4* to open the workbook.
5. Save and close **EL2-C6-A4-NationalLicenses.xlsx.**
6. Open **EL2-C6-A4-NationalLicenses.xlsx** and test the password to open the workbook.
7. Close **EL2-C6-A4-NationalLicenses.xlsx.**

Assessment

5 UNLOCK CELLS AND PROTECT A WORKSHEET AND PROTECT WORKBOOK STRUCTURE

1. Open **PreMfgTargets.xlsx.**
2. Save the workbook and name it **EL2-C6-A5-PreMfgTargets.**
3. Select C4:F21 and unlock the cells.
4. Deselect the range and then protect the worksheet using the password *eL2-A5* to unprotect.
5. Rename Sheet1 as *2015MfgTargets.*
6. Protect the workbook structure to prevent users from inserting, deleting, or renaming sheets using the password *eL2-A5* to unprotect.
7. Save and then close **EL2-C6-A5-PreMfgTargets.xlsx.**

Assessment

6 TRACK CHANGES, ACCEPT/REJECT CHANGES, AND PRINT A HISTORY SHEET

1. Open **EL2-C6-A5-PreMfgTargets.xlsx**.
2. Save the workbook and name it **EL2-C6-A6-PreMfgTargets**.
3. Unprotect the workbook structure so that new sheets can be added, deleted, renamed, or copied.
4. Turn on the Track Changes feature.
5. Change the user name to *Grant Antone* and then edit the following cells:

    D4:   from   *3,251*   to   *3755*
    D17:   from   *5,748*   to   *6176*

6. Save the workbook, change the user name to *Jean Kocsis*, and then edit the following cells:

    E6:   from   *6,145*   to   *5748*
    E11:   from   *2,214*   to   *3417*

7. Save the workbook and then change the user name back to the original user name for the computer you are using.
8. Accept and Reject the changes in the cells as follows:

    D4:   Accept
    D17:   Reject
    E6:   Reject
    E11:   Accept

9. Create and print a history sheet of the changes made to the worksheet. ***Note: If you submit your assignment work electronically, create a copy of the history sheet in a new workbook, since the history sheet is automatically deleted when the file is saved.***
10. Print the 2015MfgTargets worksheet.
11. Save and then close **EL2-C6-A6-PreMfgTargets.xlsx**

    Optional: Open **EL2-C6-A6-A6-PreMfgTargets.xlsx** and email the workbook to yourself. Compose an appropriate message within the message window, as if you are an employee of Precision Design and Packaging sending the file to the office manager. Open the message window from the inbox in your email program and print the message. Close the message window and exit your email program.

Visual Benchmark   Demonstrate Your Proficiency

TRACK CHANGES; INSERT COMMENTS

1. Open **PawsParadise.xlsx**.
2. Save the workbook and name it **EL2-C6-VB-PawsParadise**.
3. Figure 6.17 illustrates the worksheet after the owner/operator reviewed the worksheet created by the kennel manager. While reviewing the service price list, the owner made comments and changed cells. Using Figure 6.17 and Figure 6.18, make the same changes to your copy of the worksheet, ensuring that the changes are associated with the owner's name.

4. Create and print a history sheet scaled to fit on one page. *Note: If you submit your assignment work electronically, create a copy of the sheet in a new workbook, since the history sheet is automatically deleted when the file is saved.*

5. Print the worksheet with the changes highlighted and the comments as displayed on the worksheet.

6. Save and then close **EL2-C6-VB-PawsParadise.xlsx**.

7. Change the user name back to the original user name for the computer you are using.

Figure 6.17 Visual Benchmark Worksheet with Comments

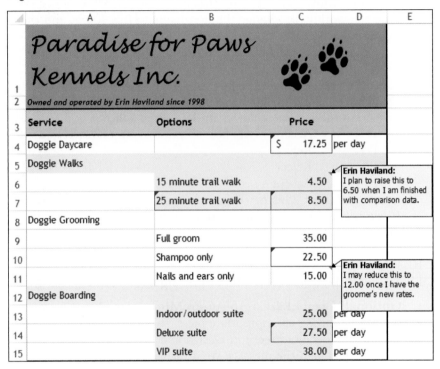

Figure 6.18 Visual Benchmark History Worksheet

Action Number	Date	Time	Who	Change	Sheet	Range	New Value	Old Value	Action Type	Losing Action
1	11/11/2015	4:03 PM	Erin Haviland	Cell Change	Sheet1	C4	$17.25	$16.50		
2	11/11/2015	4:03 PM	Erin Haviland	Cell Change	Sheet1	C7	$8.50	$8.25		
3	11/11/2015	4:03 PM	Erin Haviland	Cell Change	Sheet1	C10	$22.50	$20.00		
4	11/11/2015	4:03 PM	Erin Haviland	Cell Change	Sheet1	C14	$27.50	$28.50		
5	11/11/2015	4:03 PM	Erin Haviland	Cell Change	Sheet1	B7	25 minute trail walk	30 minute trail walk		

The history ends with the changes saved on 11/11/2015 at 4:03 PM.

Case Study   Apply Your Skills

Part 1

Yolanda Robertson of NuTrends Market Research is working with Nicola Carlucci of Pizza by Mario on a workbook with projected franchise startups for 2015. The workbook is currently in draft format in a file named **PBMNewFranchises.xlsx**. Open the workbook and save the document as **EL2-C6-CS-P1-PBMNewFranchises**. Add an appropriate title and subject to the workbook's properties and include comment text to explain that the draft workbook was created in consultation with Nicola Carlucci. Yolanda has asked for your assistance with protecting the workbook to prevent accidental data modifications or erasures when the workbook is shared with others. Yolanda and Nicola have agreed that the city, state, and store numbers should be protected; however, the month a new store is planned to open and names of prospective franchisees can change. Share the workbook. Yolanda and Nicola have agreed on the following passwords:

- Password to unprotect the worksheet is *eL2-CS1*.
- Password to open the workbook is *eL2-CS1*.

Part 2

Save the workbook and name it **EL2-C6-CS-P2-PBMNewFranchises**. Yolanda has reviewed her research files and meeting notes and would like the following changes made to the data. Make sure the user name is correct so that the following changes are associated with Yolanda:

    Store 138: Franchisee is Jae-Dong Han
    Store 149: Franchisee is Leslie Posno

Save the workbook. Nicola is in charge of logistics planning and has two changes to make to the months that stores are scheduled to open. Make sure the user name is correct so that the following changes are associated with Nicola:

    Store 135: Open in February
    Store 141: Open in December

Save the workbook and then display the worksheet with all of the changes made by Yolanda and Nicola highlighted. Create a history sheet. Print the worksheet with the cells highlighted and also print the history sheet. *Note: If you submit your assignment work electronically, create a copy of the history sheet in a new workbook, since the history sheet is automatically deleted when the file is saved.* Restore the worksheet to exclusive use. Close **EL2-C6-CS-P2-PBMNewFranchises.xlsx**. Change the user name back to the original user name for the computer you are using.

Part 3

Yolanda will be sending the shared workbook from Part 1 to Leonard Scriver, a colleague at the Michigan office of NuTrends Market Research. Yolanda wants Leonard to review the data and add his recommendations; however, Yolanda would prefer that Leonard save his copy using a different name so that the original shared version is not changed. Open **EL2-C6-CS-P1-PBMNewFranchises.xlsx**. Unprotect the worksheet, remove the password to open the workbook, and then save the workbook using the name **EL2-C6-CS-P3-PBM-LScriver**. Based on Leonard's experience with franchise startups, he has the following recommendations, which he prefers to show in comments within the worksheet. Make sure the user name is correct so that the comment boxes display Leonard's name:

Store 136: Opening a second store in Chicago is more likely to occur in April.

Store 144: Move this opening to June, as resources at the head office will be stretched in May.

Store 152: Try to open this franchise at the same time as store 151.

Show all comments within the worksheet and then print the worksheet, making sure the comments print as displayed. Save and then close **EL2-C6-CS-P3-PBM-LScriver.xlsx**. Change the user name back to the original user name for the computer that you are using.

Part 4

Mario Carlucci has commented that the password to open the workbook is not intuitive for him and he has had trouble remembering it. He wants to change the workbook password to something more user friendly, such as *Target14*. Yolanda and Nicola chose the passwords they have used in the workbook carefully based on their understanding of strong passwords that are difficult to crack by unauthorized users. Yolanda has asked you to assist with a training package for Mario that will educate him on strong passwords. Conduct research on the Internet to find guidelines for creating strong passwords. Based on what you have learned from your research, create a document in Microsoft Word that highlights the components of a strong password. Include a table of do's and don'ts for creating strong passwords in a user-friendly, easy-to-understand format for Mario. Finally, create a minimum of three examples that show weak passwords improved by stronger passwords. Include a suggestion for how to use the phrasing technique to create strong passwords so they are easier to remember. Save the document and name it **EL2-C6-CS-P4-PBMPasswords**. Print and then close **EL2-C6-CS-P4-PBMPasswords.docx**.

EXCEL

Automating Repetitive Tasks and Customizing Excel

CHAPTER 7

PERFORMANCE OBJECTIVES

Upon successful completion of Chapter 7, you will be able to:

- Record, run, and edit a macro
- Save a workbook containing macros as a macro-enabled workbook
- Create a macro that is run using a shortcut key combination
- Pin and unpin a frequently used file to the Recent Workbooks list
- Customize the display options for Excel
- Hide the ribbon to increase space in the work area
- Customize the ribbon by creating a custom tab and adding buttons
- Add and remove buttons for frequently used commands to the Quick Access toolbar
- Create and apply custom views
- Create and use a template
- Customize save options for AutoRecover files

Tutorials

7.1 Using Macros
7.2 Editing a Macro
7.3 Managing Macros
7.4 Pinning Workbooks to the Recent Workbooks List
7.5 Customizing the Work Area
7.6 Customizing the Ribbon
7.7 Customizing the Quick Access Toolbar
7.8 Using Custom Templates

Automating and customizing the Excel environment to accommodate your preferences can increase your efficiency. For example, create a macro when you find yourself repeating the same task frequently to save time and ensure consistency. Add a button for a frequently used command to the Quick Access toolbar to provide single-click access to the feature. Other ways to customize Excel include pinning frequently used files to the Recent Workbooks list; creating a custom template, ribbon tab, or view; and modifying display and save options. Through completing the projects in this chapter, you will learn how to effectively automate and customize the Excel environment. Model answers for this chapter's projects appear on the following page.

Note: Before beginning the projects, copy to your storage medium the EL2C7 subfolder from the EL2 folder on the CD that accompanies this textbook and then make EL2C7 the active folder.

Student Name

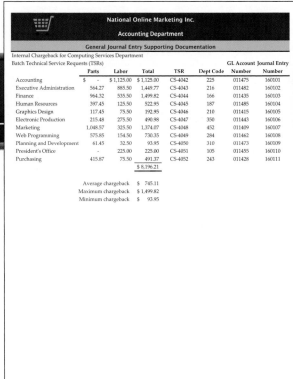

Project 2 Customize the Excel Work Environment

Project 2e, EL2-C7-P2-NationalJE.docx

Project 2e, EL2-C7-P2-NationalJE.xlsx

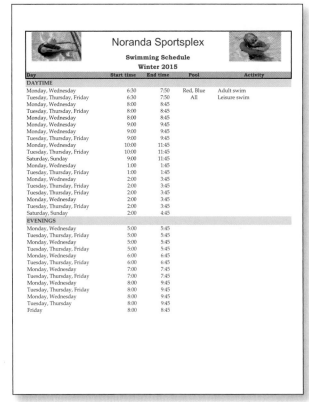

Project 3 Save a Workbook as a Template

Project 3b, EL2-C7-P3-SwimSchWinter2015.xlsx

> You will create, edit, run, and delete macros to automate tasks, including assigning a macro to a shortcut key and storing frequently used macros in a macro workbook.

Automating Tasks Using Macros ■■■■■■■■■■■■■■■■

A *macro* is a series of instructions stored in a sequence that can be recalled and carried out whenever the need arises. You might consider creating a macro when you find yourself repeatedly performing the same task without variation. Saving the instructions for a task in a macro not only saves time—it also ensures that the steps are performed consistently every time, which can prevent errors in data entry, formatting, or other worksheet options.

Before you record a new macro, take a few moments to plan the steps you need to perform. Also consider if the active cell location at the time the macro is run will be a factor. For example, will the first step in the macro involve making a specific cell active? If so, you can position the active cell using a shortcut key or Go To command during the recording.

To create a macro, begin by turning on the macro recorder, which opens the Record Macro dialog box, shown in Figure 7.1. Identify your macro by assigning a unique name to the steps that will be saved. A macro name must begin with a letter and can be a combination of letters, numbers, and underscore characters. A macro name cannot include spaces; use the underscore character if you want to separate words in a macro name. You also use the Record Macro dialog box, to choose the location in which to save the macro. By default, Excel saves the macro within the current workbook.

A macro can be assigned to a Ctrl shortcut key combination, which allows the user to run the macro more quickly by pressing Ctrl plus the chosen lowercase or uppercase letter. Entering a description of the macro's purpose provides information to other users who might use or edit the macro. In a macro workbook that will be shared, also consider entering the creator's name and the date into

Quick Steps

Record a Macro
1. Click VIEW tab.
2. Click Macros button arrow.
3. Click *Record Macro*.
4. Type macro name.
5. Click in *Description* text box and type description text.
6. Click OK.
7. Perform desired actions.
8. Click Stop Recording button.

Macros

H I N T

When recording a macro, your mouse clicks to select tabs within the ribbon are not saved.

Figure 7.1 Record Macro Dialog Box

Macro names begin with a letter and can include a combination of letters, numbers, and underscore characters.

Assigning a macro to a Ctrl key combination enables you to quickly run the macro by pressing Ctrl plus the letter.

Use this option box to choose the location in which to save the macro.

Including a description of the macro's purpose, the name of the person who created the macro, and the date it was recorded is useful for others who might need to run or edit the macro.

Record Macro

Macro name:
Macro1

Shortcut key:
Ctrl+

Store macro in:
This Workbook

Description:

OK   Cancel

Stop Recording

the description box for reference purposes. Click OK when you are finished identifying the macro and the recorder will begin saving the text and/or steps that you perform. Do not be concerned if you make a typing mistake or have to cancel a dialog box while recording a macro. Correct your mistakes as you go, since only the result will be saved. Once you have completed the tasks you want saved, click the Stop Recording button on the Status bar to end the recording.

Saving Workbooks Containing Macros

When a macro is created in Excel, the commands are written and saved in a language called *Microsoft Visual Basic for Applications (VBA)*. A workbook that contains a macro should be saved using the macro-enabled file format. The default format for extensible markup language (XML) files, .xlsx, cannot store the macro code. The macro recorder that you use when creating a macro converts your actions to VBA statements behind the scenes. You can view and edit the VBA code or you can create macros from scratch by using the VBA Editor in Microsoft Visual Basic for Applications. In Project 1e, you will look at the VBA statements created when the AcctgDocumentation macro was recorded and edit an instruction.

To save a new or existing workbook as a macro-enabled workbook, perform one of the following actions:

- *New workbook*. Click the Save button on the Quick Access toolbar or click the FILE tab and then click the *Save As* option. At the Save As backstage area, click the desired location in the *Places* section. Click the Browse button to display the Save As dialog box. Type the file name and then change the *Save as type* option to *Excel Macro-Enabled Workbook (*.xlsm)*. Click the Save button.

- *Existing workbook*. Click the FILE tab and then click the *Save As* option. At the Save As backstage area, click the desired location in the *Places* section. Click the Browse button to display the Save As dialog box. Type the file name and then change the *Save as type* option to *Excel Macro-Enabled Workbook (*.xlsm)*. Click the Save button.

▼ **Quick Steps**

Save a Macro-Enabled Workbook
1. Click FILE tab.
2. Click *Save As*.
3. If necessary, click desired place.
4. Click Browse button.
5. Type file name in *File name* text box.
6. Click *Save as type* list arrow.
7. Click *Excel Macro-Enabled Workbook (*.xlsm)*.
8. Click Save.

Project 1a **Creating a Macro and Saving a Workbook as a Macro-Enabled Workbook**   **Part 1 of 4**

1. You work in the Accounting department at a large company. The company has a documentation standard for all Excel workbooks that requires each worksheet to show the department name, author's name, creation date, and revision history. To standardize the documentation, you decide to create a macro that will insert row labels for this data. Begin by opening a new blank workbook.

2. Create the documentation macro by completing the following steps:
    a. Make cell C4 the active cell and then click the VIEW tab. (You are making a cell other than cell A1 active because you want to move the active cell to the top left cell in the worksheet during the macro.)
    b. Click the Macros button arrow in the Macros group.
    c. Click *Record Macro* at the drop-down list.

d. At the Record Macro dialog box, with the insertion point positioned in the *Macro name* text box, type AcctgDocumentation.

e. Click in the *Description* text box and then type Accounting department documentation macro. Created by [Student Name] on [Date]. Substitute your name for *[Student Name]* and the current date for *[Date]*.

f. Click OK. The macro recorder is now turned on, as indicated by the Stop Recording button in the Status bar (which displays as a white square next to *READY*).

g. Press Ctrl + Home to move the active cell to cell A1. Including this command in the macro ensures that the documentation will begin at cell A1 in every workbook.

h. Type Accounting department and then press Enter.

i. With cell A2 active, type Author and then press Enter.

j. With cell A3 active, type Date created and then press Enter.

k. With cell A4 active, type Revision history and then press Enter three times to leave two blank rows before the start of the worksheet.

l. Click the Stop Recording button located at the left side of the Status bar, next to *READY*.

3. Save the workbook as a macro-enabled workbook by completing the following steps:

a. Click the Save button on the Quick Access toolbar.

b. At the Save As backstage area, click the desired location in the *Places* section and then click the Browse button.

c. At the Save As dialog box, navigate to the EL2C7 folder in the Navigation pane and then double-click the *EL2C7* folder that displays in the Content pane.

d. Click in the *File name* text box and then type EL2-C7-P1-Macros.

e. Click the *Save as type* option box, scroll up or down the pop-up list, and then click *Excel Macro-Enabled Workbook (*.xlsm)*.

f. Click the Save button.

Running a Macro

▼ **Quick Steps**

Run a Macro
1. Click VIEW tab.
2. Click Macros button.
3. Double-click macro name.

Running a macro is also sometimes referred to as *playing a macro*. Since a macro is a series of recorded tasks, running a macro involves instructing Excel to *play back* the recorded tasks. Think of a macro as a video you have made. When you play the video, the same thing happens every time. To run (play) a macro, view a list of macros by clicking the Macros button in the Macros group on the VIEW tab. This opens the Macro dialog box, as shown in Figure 7.2. Click the name of the macro you want to run and then click the Run button, or double-click the name of the macro in the *Macro name* list box.

Figure 7.2 Macro Dialog Box

By default, all macros in all open workbooks are displayed in this list box. Double-click the macro name to run it.

If the currently selected macro contains a description, the text displays here.

Click this button to run the currently selected macro.

Change the list of macros you want to view using this option box. You can view macros contained in all open workbooks, in only the current workbook, or in another specific open workbook.

Project 1b **Running a Macro** **Part 2 of 4**

1. With **EL2-C7-P1-Macros.xlsm** open, run the AcctgDocumentation macro to test that it works correctly by completing the following steps:
   a. Select A1:A4 and press Delete to erase the cell contents.
   b. To test the Ctrl + Home command in the macro, you need to make sure cell A1 is not active when the macro begins playing. Click any cell in the worksheet other than cell A1 to deselect the range.
   c. Click the Macros button in the Macros group on the VIEW tab. Make sure to click the button and not the button arrow.
   d. At the Macro dialog box with *AcctgDocumentation* already selected in the *Macro name* list box, click the Run button.
2. Save and then close **EL2-C7-P1-Macros.xlsm**.

Assigning a Macro to a Shortcut Key

When recording a macro, you have the option to assign the macro to a Ctrl key combination. A macro that is assigned to a keyboard shortcut can be run without displaying the Macro dialog box. You can choose any lowercase or uppercase letter for a macro's keyboard shortcut. Excel distinguishes the case of the letter you choose when you type the letter in the *Shortcut key* text box at the Record Macro dialog box. For example, if you type an uppercase O, Excel defines the shortcut key as *Ctrl + Shift + O*, as shown in Figure 7.3.

If an Excel feature is already assigned to the key combination you choose, your macro will override the existing Excel feature. For example, pressing Ctrl + p in Excel causes the Print backstage area to display. If you create a macro and assign it to Ctrl + p, pressing that keyboard shortcut will now run your macro instead of displaying the Print dialog box. You can view a list of Excel-assigned keyboard shortcuts in Help by typing *keyboard shortcuts* in the search box in the Excel Help window. Select *Keyboard shortcuts in Excel 2013* in the Results list.

Quick Steps

Assign a Macro to a Shortcut Key
1. Click VIEW tab.
2. Click Macros button arrow.
3. Click *Record Macro*.
4. Type macro name.
5. Click in *Shortcut key* text box.
6. Type desired letter.
7. Click in *Description* text box.
8. Type description text.
9. Click OK.
10. Perform desired actions.
11. Click Stop Recording button.

Record Macro

Figure 7.3 Record Macro Dialog Box with Shortcut Key Assigned

Typing an uppercase letter in the *Shortcut key* text box defines the shortcut key as Ctrl + Shift + the letter; typing a lowercase letter defines the shortcut key as Ctrl + the letter.

Project 1c **Creating and Running a Macro Using a Shortcut Key** **Part 3 of 4**

1. Open **EL2-C7-P1-Macros.xlsm**.
2. The default security setting when opening any workbook that contains a macro is *Disable all macros with notification*. This causes a security warning to appear in the message bar (between the ribbon and the formula bar) notifying you that macros have been disabled. Enable the macros in the workbook by clicking the Enable Content button.

3. Create a macro that changes print options for a worksheet and assign it to a keyboard shortcut by completing the following steps:

a. Once a macro has been recorded and stopped in an Excel session, the Stop Recording button in the Status bar changes to the Record New Macro button. Click the Record New Macro button located at the left side of the Status bar next to *READY*. If you exited Excel before starting this project, start a new macro by clicking the VIEW tab, clicking the down-pointing arrow on the Macros button, and then clicking *Record Macro*.

b. Type LandscapeScaled1Pg in the *Macro name* text box.

c. Click in the *Shortcut key* text box, hold down the Shift key, and then type the letter o.

d. Click in the *Description* text box and then type Change orientation to landscape and scale to 1 page wide by 1 page tall. Created by [Student Name] on [Date]. Substitute your name for *[Student Name]* and the current date for *[Date]*.

e. Click OK.

f. Click the PAGE LAYOUT tab.

g. Click the Page Setup dialog box launcher located at the bottom right of the Page Setup group.

h. At the Page Setup dialog box with the Page tab selected, click *Landscape* in the *Orientation* section.

i. Click *Fit to* in the *Scaling* section to scale the printout to 1 page wide by 1 page tall.

j. Click OK.

k. Click the Stop Recording button.

4. Press Ctrl + N to open a new blank workbook.
5. Press Ctrl + Shift + o to run the LandscapeScaled1Pg macro.
6. Type your name in cell A1, press Enter, and then press Ctrl + F2 to display the worksheet in the Print backstage area. Notice in the Print Preview that the page orientation is landscape. Review the options in the Settings category. Notice that *Landscape Orientation* and *Fit Sheet on One Page* have been selected by the macro.
7. Click the Back button to return to the worksheet and then close the workbook. Click Don't Save when prompted to save changes.
8. Save **EL2-C7-P1-Macros.xlsm**.

Editing a Macro

The actions that you perform while recording a macro are stored in Visual Basic for Applications (VBA) program code. Each macro is saved as a separate module within a VBAProject for the workbook. A *module* can be described as a receptacle for the macro instructions. Figure 7.4 displays the window containing the VBA code module for the macro created in Project 1a.

You can use the module to edit a macro if the change you need to make is easy to decipher within the VBA statements. If you need to make several changes to a macro, or if you do not feel comfortable with the VBA code, you can re-record the macro. When you record a new macro that has the same name as an existing macro, Excel prompts you to replace the existing macro. You can then record the correct steps by overwriting the original macro.

▼ **Quick Steps**

Edit a Macro
1. Open workbook containing macro.
2. Click VIEW tab.
3. Click Macros button.
4. Click desired macro name.
5. Click Edit button.
6. Make desired changes in VBA code window.
7. Click Save button.
8. Click File.
9. Click *Close and Return to Microsoft Excel.*

Figure 7.4 Microsoft Visual Basic for Applications Window for Project 1a AcctgDocumentation Macro

A line of text that appears in green and is preceded with an apostrophe is a comment. Comments are explanatory text and are ignored when the macro is run.

The actions performed by the macro are saved in this section. Each action is provided in a separate line.

1. With **EL2-C7-P1-Macros.xlsm** open, edit the AcctgDocumentation macro to leave only one blank row after the last entry by completing the following steps:

   a. If necessary, click the VIEW tab.

   b. Click the Macros button in the Macros group.

   c. At the Macro dialog box with *AcctgDocumentation* already selected in the *Macro name* list box, click the Edit button. A Microsoft Visual Basic for Applications window opens with the program code displayed for EL2-C7-P1-Macros.xlsm - [Module1 (Code)].

   d. Read the statements between the *Sub* and *End Sub* statements. *Sub* indicates the beginning of the procedure and *End Sub* indicates the end of the procedure. A ***procedure*** is a set of VBA statements that perform actions. The name of the procedure is placed after the opening *Sub* statement and is the macro name. Each line beginning with a single apostrophe (') is a comment. A comment is used in programming to insert explanatory text that describes the logic or purpose of a statement. Statements that begin with apostrophes are ignored when the macro is run. The commands that are executed when the macro is run are the indented lines of text below the comment lines.

   e. The last statement before *End Sub* reads *Range("A7").Select.* This is the last action in the macro and it makes cell A7 active. Notice that the entry two lines above this final action reads *Range("A4").Select.* To edit the macro to leave only one blank row, change the address in the last statement from *A7* to *A6.* To do this, position the insertion point between the *A* and the *7* and then click the left mouse button. Press Delete and then type 6.

   f. Click the Save button on the toolbar.

2. Click File and then click *Close and Return to Microsoft Excel*.
3. Test the edited macro to make sure only one blank row is left before the active cell by completing the following steps:
   a. Select the range A1:A4 and then press Delete.
   b. Make any cell other than cell A1 active.
   c. Click the Macros button in the Macros group on the VIEW tab. Make sure to click the button and not the button arrow.
   d. At the Macro dialog box, double-click *AcctgDocumentation* in the *Macro name* list box.
4. Save and then close **EL2-C7-P1-Macros.xlsm**.

Deleting a Macro

If you no longer need a macro, you can delete it at the Macro dialog box. Open the Macro dialog box, select the macro name in the *Macro name* list box, and then click the Delete button.

▼ **Quick Steps**
Delete a Macro
1. Open Macro dialog box.
2. Click macro name.
3. Click Delete button.
4. Click Yes.

Managing Macros

By default, a macro is stored within the workbook that is active when the macro is recorded. When you close the workbook, the macros within the file are no longer available. For example, if you close the EL2-C7-P1-Macros.xlsm file, the AcctgDocumentation macro you created will not be available to you in a new workbook. If you want to use the macros you have created in other workbooks, leave the workbook containing the macros open, since the Macro dialog box displays macros for all open workbooks in the *Macro name* list box by default.

Consider creating a macros workbook with a set of standard macros that you want to use in any file, similar to the macros workbook you created in Projects 1a through 1d. Open this workbook whenever you are working in Excel and the macros stored within it will be available to you for all of the files that you create or edit during an Excel session. When you create a macros workbook, you can also copy it to any other computer so that a set of standard macros can be distributed to others for their use.

Project **2** **Customize the Excel Work Environment**   **8 Parts**

You will customize the Excel environment by pinning a frequently used workbook to the Recent Workbooks list, minimizing the ribbon to create more space in the work area, changing display options, importing and exporting custom settings for the Quick Access toolbar and ribbon, creating a custom ribbon tab, adding buttons to the Quick Access toolbar to make features more accessible, and creating custom views.

Pin a Workbook to
the Recent
Workbooks List
1. Make sure workbook
   has been opened
   recently.
2. Click FILE tab.
3. If necessary, click
   Open.
4. Position mouse over
   workbook name and
   click pin icon.

Unpin a Workbook
from the Recent
Workbooks List
1. Click FILE tab.
2. If necessary, click
   Open.
3. Click down-pointing
   pin icon next to
   workbook name.

Pinning Workbooks to the Recent Workbooks List ■■■■

The Recent Workbooks list at the Open backstage area displays the file names and locations of the 25 most recently opened workbooks by default. To open a workbook you used recently, click the workbook name in the Recent Workbooks list.

A workbook that you use frequently can be permanently added, or *pinned*, to the Recent Workbooks list. To do this, make sure you have recently opened the workbook, click the FILE tab, click the *Open* option, and, if necessary, click *Recent Workbooks* in the *Places* section. Hover your mouse over the desired workbook and then click the pin icon to the right of the workbook name. A workbook that is permanently pinned to the list displays with a down-pointing pin icon. Click the down-pointing pin icon to unpin a workbook from the list.

To change the number of workbooks shown in the Recent Workbooks list, open the Excel Options dialog box and then click *Advanced* in the left pane. In the *Display* section, change the number in the *Show this number of Recent Documents* text box to the desired value.

Project 2a **Pinning a Frequently Used Workbook to the Recent Workbooks List**   **Part 1 of 8**

1. Open **NWinterSch.xlsx**.
2. Scroll down the worksheet to review the winter swimming schedule and then close the workbook.
3. At a blank Excel screen, pin two workbooks to the Recent Workbooks list by completing the following steps:
   a. Click the FILE tab.
   b. By default, the Open backstage area displays if no workbooks are currently open.
   c. Position your mouse over **NWinterSch.xlsx** in the Recent Workbooks list and then click the pin icon located at the right.

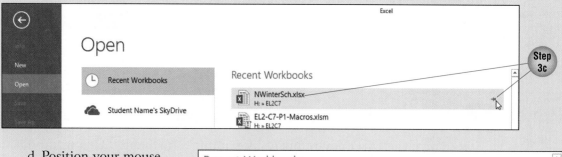

   d. Position your mouse over **EL2-C7-P1-Macros.xlsm** and then click the pin icon located at the right.
   e. Press Esc to close the backstage area.

4. Click the FILE tab and then click **EL2-C7-P1-Macros.xlsm** in the Recent Workbooks list to open the workbook.
5. Close **EL2-C7-P1-Macros.xlsm**.
6. Unpin the two workbooks by completing the following steps:
   a. Click the FILE tab.
   b. Click the down-pointing pin icon to the right of **EL2-C7-P1-Macros.xlsm**.
   c. Click the down-pointing pin icon to the right of **NWinterSch.xlsx**.
   d. Press Esc to close the Open backstage area.

Changing Display Options to Customize the Work Area

When the default display options in Excel do not suit your needs, the Excel Options dialog box contains many options for customizing the environment. As shown in Figure 7.5, Excel groups options that affect the display by those that are global settings, those that affect the entire workbook, and those that affect only the active worksheet. Changes to workbook and/or worksheet display options are saved with the workbook.

▼ **Quick Steps**

Customize Display Options
1. Click FILE tab.
2. Click *Options*.
3. Click *Advanced* in left pane.
4. Change display options as required.
5. Click OK.

Figure 7.5 Excel Options Dialog Box with Display Options Shown

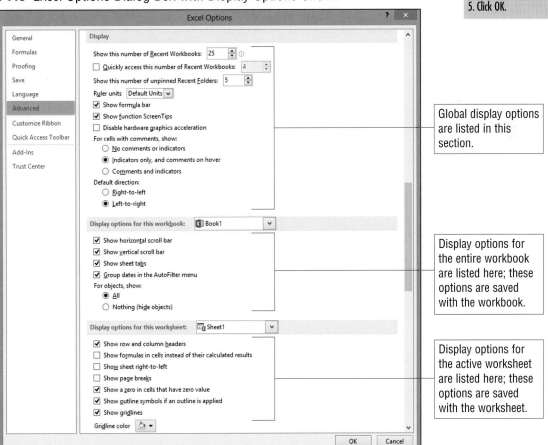

Global display options are listed in this section.

Display options for the entire workbook are listed here; these options are saved with the workbook.

Display options for the active worksheet are listed here; these options are saved with the worksheet.

Minimizing the Ribbon ■■■■■■■■■■■■■■■■■■■■■

Quick Steps

Minimize the Ribbon
Press Ctrl + F1.
OR
1. Click Ribbon Display Options button.
2. Click Show Tabs.
OR
Click Collapse the Ribbon button.

Collapse   Ribbon
the Ribbon   Display
          Options

When you are working with a large worksheet, you may find it easier to work with the ribbon minimized, which creates more space within the work area. Figure 7.6 on the next page shows the worksheet you will use in Project 2b to customize the display options and minimize the ribbon.

One way to minimize the ribbon is to click the Collapse the Ribbon button. With the ribbon minimized, clicking a tab temporarily redisplays it to allow you to select a feature. After you select the feature, the ribbon returns to the minimized state. Press Ctrl + F1 or double-click the ribbon to toggle the ribbon on or off.

Another way to minimize the ribbon, new in Excel 2013, is to click the Ribbon Display Options button. This button remains in the upper right corner of the screen and allows you to quickly hide the ribbon (including the tabs), show tabs, or show just the tabs and commands.

Project 2b   Customizing Display Options and Minimizing the Ribbon   Part 2 of 8

1. Open **NWinterSch.xlsx**.
2. Save the workbook and name it **EL2-C7-P2-NWinterSch**.
3. Turn off the display of the Formula bar (since no formulas exist in the workbook), turn off the display of sheet tabs (since only one sheet exists in the workbook), and turn off the display of row and column headers and gridlines by completing the following steps:
   a. Click the FILE tab.
   b. Click *Options*.
   c. Click *Advanced* in the left pane.
   d. Scroll down the Excel Options dialog box to the *Display* section and then click the *Show formula bar* check box to remove the check mark.
   e. Scroll down to the *Display options for this workbook* section and then click the *Show sheet tabs* check box to remove the check mark.
   f. Scroll down to the *Display options for this worksheet* section and then click the *Show row and column headers* check box to remove the check mark.
   g. Click the *Show gridlines* check box to remove the check mark.
   h. Click OK.
4. Press Ctrl + F1 to hide the ribbon.
5. Compare your screen with the one shown in Figure 7.6 on the next page.
6. Save and then close **EL2-C7-P2-NWinterSch.xlsx**.

Figure 7.6 Project 2b Worksheet with Customized Display Options and Minimized Ribbon

Double-click a tab to show or hide the ribbon.

Day	Start time	End time	Pool	Activity
DAYTIME				
Monday, Wednesday	6:30	7:50	All	Adult swim
Tuesday, Thursday, Friday	6:30	7:50	All	Moms & tots swim
Monday, Wednesday	8:00	8:45	Blue, Green	Beginner aquafit
Tuesday, Thursday, Friday	8:00	8:45	Blue, Green	Adult swim
Monday, Wednesday	8:00	8:45	Red	Deep water aquafit
Monday, Wednesday	9:00	9:45	Blue, Green	Intermediate aquafit
Monday, Wednesday	9:00	9:45	Red	Senior aquafit
Tuesday, Thursday, Friday	9:00	9:45	Red	Beginner aquafit
Monday, Wednesday	10:00	11:45	All	Leisure swim
Tuesday, Thursday, Friday	10:00	11:45	Blue, Green	Senior aquafit
Saturday, Sunday	9:00	11:45	All	Swimming lessons
Monday, Wednesday	1:00	1:45	Blue	Moms & tots swim
Tuesday, Thursday, Friday	1:00	1:45	Red, Green	Intermediate aquafit
Monday, Wednesday	2:00	3:45	All	Leisure swim
Tuesday, Thursday, Friday	2:00	3:45	Blue, Green	Private bookings
Tuesday, Thursday, Friday	2:00	3:45	Red	Diving club
Monday, Wednesday	2:00	3:45	Blue, Green	Intermediate aquafit
Tuesday, Thursday, Friday	2:00	3:45	Blue, Green	Beginner aquafit
Saturday, Sunday	2:00	4:45	All	Family swim
EVENINGS				
Monday, Wednesday	5:00	5:45	Blue, Green	Swimming lessons
Tuesday, Thursday, Friday	5:00	5:45	Blue, Green	Swimming lessons
Monday, Wednesday	5:00	5:45	Red	Beginner aquafit
Tuesday, Thursday, Friday	5:00	5:45	Red	Deep water aquafit
Monday, Wednesday	6:00	6:45	All	Swimming lessons

Noranda Sportsplex

Winter Swimming Schedule

Project 2c | **Restoring Default Display Options** | Part 3 of 8

1. Press Ctrl + N to open a new blank workbook.
2. Notice that the workbook and worksheet display options that were changed in Project 2b are restored to the default options. The Formula bar remains hidden (since this is a global display option) and the ribbon remains minimized (since the display of the ribbon is a toggle on/off option).
3. Open **EL2-C7-P2-NWinterSch.xlsx**.
4. Notice that the sheet tabs, row and column headers, and gridlines are hidden (since these display option settings are saved with the workbook).
5. Close **EL2-C7-P2-NWinterSch.xlsx** without saving it.
6. Click the Ribbon Display Options button next to the Minimize button in the upper right corner of the screen and then click *Show Tabs and Commands* at the drop-down list.

Step 6

7. Redisplay the Formula bar by completing the following steps:
   a. Open the Excel Options dialog box.
   b. Click *Advanced* in the left pane.
   c. Scroll down the Excel Options dialog box to the *Display* section, click the *Show formula bar* check box to insert a check mark, and then click OK.
8. Close the workbook without saving it.

Customizing Ribbons and the Quick Access Toolbar ▪▪▪▪

As you work with Excel, you may find that you prefer to access frequently used features from the Quick Access toolbar or in a new group within an existing or new ribbon. You will learn how to customize both the ribbon and the Quick Access toolbar in Projects 2e and 2f.

You or your instructor may already have taken the time to customize a ribbon or the Quick Access toolbar on the computers in your institution's computer lab. To be able to restore these customizations after you make changes in the upcoming projects, you will learn how to save (export) them in Project 2d. You will then learn how to reinstall (import) them in Project 2g.

To save your current ribbon and Quick Access toolbar settings, click the FILE tab and then click *Options*. At the Excel Options dialog box, click *Customize Ribbon* in the left pane. The dialog box will display as shown in Figure 7.7 on the next page.

Click the Import/Export button in the lower right corner of the Excel Options dialog box. Click *Export all customizations* to save the file with the custom settings. You can then use this file to reinstall the saved settings in Project 2g or install customized settings on a different computer. Click the Import/Export button and then click *Import customization file*. Locate the file and reinstall the customized settings.

Project 2d **Exporting Customizations** **Part 4 of 8**

1. Press Ctrl + N to open a new blank workbook.
2. Save the current ribbon and Quick Access toolbar settings to the desktop by completing the following steps:
   a. Click the FILE tab and then click *Options*.
   b. Click *Customize Ribbon* in the left pane of the Excel Options dialog box.
   c. Click the Import/Export button located at the bottom right of the Excel Options dialog box.
   d. Click *Export all customizations* at the drop-down list.
   e. Click *Desktop* in the *Favorites* list at the left of the File Save dialog box.
   f. Change the file name to **EL2-C7-P2-ExcelCustomizations** and then click the Save button. The file saves with the name **EL2-C7-P2-ExcelCustomizations.exportedUI**.
   g. Click OK.
   h. Close the workbook. Click Don't Save if prompted to save changes.

Step 2c

Step 2d

H I N T # Customizing the Ribbon

To save mouse clicks used when switching tabs and choosing options from drop-down lists, consider creating a custom tab with the buttons you use on a regular basis.

To customize the ribbon by adding a new tab, group, or button, click the FILE tab and then click *Options*. At the Excel Options dialog box, click *Customize Ribbon* in the left pane. The dialog box will display as shown in Figure 7.7.

The commands shown in the left list box are dependent on the current option in the *Choose commands from* option box. Click the down-pointing arrow at the right of the current option (*Popular Commands*) to select from a variety of command lists, such as *Commands Not In the Ribbon* and *All Commands*. The tabs shown in

Figure 7.7 Excel Options Dialog Box with *Customize Ribbon* Selected

the right list box are dependent on the current option in the *Customize the Ribbon* option box. Click the down-pointing arrow at the right of the current option (*Main Tabs*) to select *All Tabs*, *Main Tabs*, or *Tool Tabs*.

You can create a new group in an existing tab and add buttons within the new group, or you can create a new tab, create a new group within the tab, and then add buttons to the new group.

Creating a New Tab

To create a new tab, in the *Main Tabs* list box, click the tab name after which you want the new tab positioned and then click the New Tab button located below the *Main Tabs* list box. This inserts a new tab in the list box along with a new group below the new tab, as shown in Figure 7.8. If you selected the wrong tab name before clicking the *New Tab* button, you can move the new tab up or down the list box by clicking *New Tab (Custom)* and then clicking the Move Up button or Move Down button at the right side of the dialog box.

Adding Buttons to a Group

Add commands to a tab by clicking the group name within the tab, clicking the desired command in the list box at the left, and then clicking the Add button that displays between the two list boxes. Remove commands in a similar manner: click the command you want to remove from the tab group and then click the Remove button that displays between the two list boxes.

▼ Quick Steps

Create a New Tab and Group
1. Click FILE tab.
2. Click *Options*.
3. Click *Customize Ribbon* in left pane.
4. Click tab name to precede new tab.
5. Click New Tab button.

Add a New Group to an Existing Tab
1. Click FILE tab.
2. Click *Options*.
3. Click *Customize Ribbon* in left pane.
4. Click tab name on which to add new group.
5. Click New Group button.

Add Buttons to a Group
1. Click FILE tab.
2. Click *Options*.
3. Click *Customize Ribbon* in left pane.
4. Click group name in which to insert new button.
5. Change *Choose commands from* to desired command list.
6. Click desired command.
7. Click Add button.

Figure 7.8 New Tab and Group Created in the Customize Ribbon Pane at the Excel Options Dialog Box

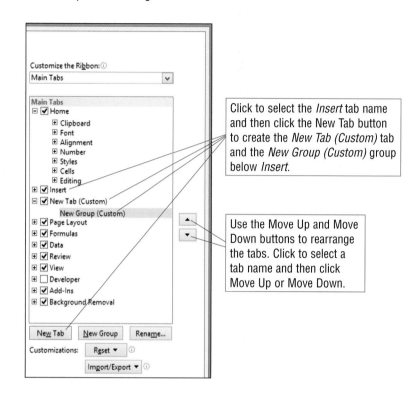

Click to select the *Insert* tab name and then click the New Tab button to create the *New Tab (Custom)* tab and the *New Group (Custom)* group below *Insert*.

Use the Move Up and Move Down buttons to rearrange the tabs. Click to select a tab name and then click Move Up or Move Down.

▼ Quick Steps

Rename a Tab or Group
1. Click FILE tab.
2. Click *Options*.
3. Click *Customize Ribbon* in left pane.
4. Click tab or group to be renamed.
5. Click Rename button.
6. Type new name.
7. Press Enter or click OK.

Renaming a Tab, Group, or Command

Rename a tab by clicking the tab name in the *Main Tabs* list box and then clicking the Rename button located below the *Main Tabs* list box. At the Rename dialog box, type the desired name for the tab and then press Enter or click OK. You can also display the Rename dialog box by right-clicking the tab name and then clicking *Rename* at the shortcut menu.

Complete similar steps to rename a group or command. The Rename dialog box for a group or command name contains a *Symbol* list as well as the *Display name* text box. Type the new name for the group in the *Display name* text box and then press Enter or click OK. The symbols are useful for identifying new buttons.

Project 2e | Customizing the Ribbon   Part 5 of 8

1. Open **NationalJE.xlsx**.
2. Save the workbook and name it **EL2-C7-P2-NationalJE**.
3. Customize the ribbon by adding a new tab and two new groups within the tab by completing the following steps. ***Note: The ribbon will be reset to its original settings in Project 2g.***
   a. Click the FILE tab and then click *Options*.
   b. Click *Customize Ribbon* in the left pane of the Excel Options dialog box.

c. Click to select *Insert* in the *Main Tabs* list box located at the right of the dialog box.

d. Click the New Tab button located below the list box. (This inserts a new tab below the Insert tab and a new group below the new tab.)

e. With *New Group (Custom)* selected below *New Tab (Custom)*, click the New Group button that displays below the list box. (This inserts another new group on the new tab.)

4. Rename the tab and groups by completing the following steps:

   a. Click to select *New Tab (Custom)* in the *Main Tabs* list box.

   b. Click the Rename button that displays below the list box.

   c. At the Rename dialog box, type your first and last names in all caps and then press Enter or click OK.

   d. Click to select the first *New Group (Custom)* group name that displays below the new tab.

   e. Click the Rename button.

   f. At the Rename dialog box, type Borders in the *Display name* text box and then press Enter or click OK. (The Rename dialog box for a group or button displays symbols in addition to the *Display name* text box. You will apply a symbol to a button in a later step.)

   g. Right-click the *New Group (Custom)* group name below *Borders (Custom)* and then click *Rename* at the shortcut menu.

   h. Type Statistics in the *Display name* text box at the Rename dialog box and then press Enter or click OK.

5. Add buttons to the *Borders (Custom)* group by completing the following steps:

   a. Click to select *Borders (Custom)* in the *Main Tabs* list box.

   b. Click the down-pointing arrow at the right of the *Choose commands from* option box (which currently displays *Popular Commands*) and then click *All Commands* at the drop-down list.

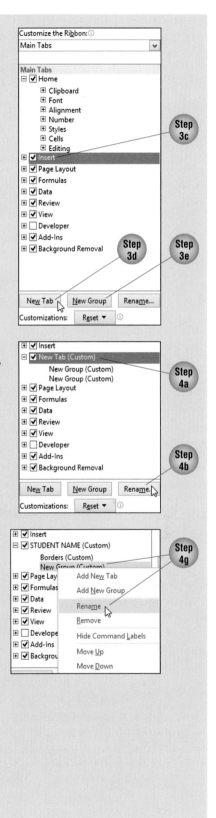

c. Scroll down the *All Commands* list box (the list displays alphabetically), click *Thick Bottom Border*, and then click the Add button located between the two list boxes. (This inserts the command below the *Borders (Custom)* group name.)

Step 5c

d. Scroll down the *All Commands* list box, click *Top and Double Bottom Border*, and then click the Add button.
6. Add buttons to the *Statistics (Custom)* group by completing the following steps:
   a. Click to select *Statistics (Custom)* in the *Main Tabs* list box.
   b. Scroll up the *All Commands* list box, click *Average*, and then click the Add button.

Step 6a

Step 6b

c. Scroll down the *All Commands* list box, click *Max*, and then click the Add button.
d. Scroll down the *All Commands* list box, click *Min*, and then click the Add button.
7. Change the symbol for the Average, Max, and Min buttons by completing the following steps:
   a. Right-click *Average* below *Statistics (Custom)* in the *Main Tabs* list box and then click *Rename* at the shortcut menu.
   b. At the Rename dialog box, click the calculator icon in the *Symbol* list box (fifth row, second column) and then click OK.
   c. Change the symbol for *Max* and *Min* to the calculator symbol by completing actions similar to those in Step 7b.

Step 7b

8. Click OK to close the Excel Options dialog box.

9. Use buttons in the custom tab to format and add formulas to the worksheet by completing the following steps:

   a. Make cell A3 the active cell, click the custom tab with your name, and then click the Thick Bottom Border button in the Borders group.

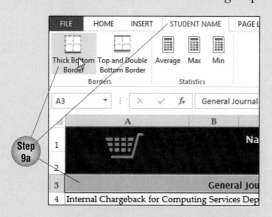

   b. Select B6:H6 and then click the Thick Bottom Border button in the Borders group.

   c. Make cell D18 the active cell and then click the Top and Double Bottom Border button in the Borders group.

   d. Make cell D20 the active cell and then click the Average button in the Statistics group.

   e. With D7:D19 selected in the formula *=AVERAGE(D7:D19)*, drag to select D7:D17 and then press Enter.

   f. With cell D21 active, click the Max button in the Statistics group, drag to select D7:D17, and then press Enter.

   g. With cell D22 active, click the Min button in the Statistics group, drag to select D7:D17, and then press Enter.

10. Save **EL2-C7-P2-NationalJE.xlsx**.

11. In a new Word document, insert a screenshot of the worksheet showing the custom tab using either Print Screen with Paste or the Screenshot feature (INSERT tab, Screenshot button in Illustrations group). Type your name a few lines below the screenshot.

12. Save the Microsoft Word document and name it **EL2-C7-P2-NationalJE**.

13. Print **EL2-C7-P2-NationalJE.docx** and then exit Word.

14. Print and then close **EL2-C7-P2-NationalJE.xlsx**.

Customizing the Quick Access Toolbar

Click the Customize Quick Access Toolbar button located at the right side of the Quick Access toolbar to open the Customize Quick Access Toolbar drop-down list, as shown in Figure 7.9. Click *More Commands* at the drop-down list to open the Excel Options dialog box with *Quick Access Toolbar* selected in the left pane, as shown in Figure 7.10. Change the list of commands shown in the left list box by clicking the down-pointing arrow to the right of *Choose commands from* and then clicking the desired category. Scroll down the list box to locate the command and then double-click the command name to add it to the Quick Access toolbar.

Customize Quick Access Toolbar

A few less popular features in Excel are available only by adding buttons to the Quick Access toolbar. If a feature you are trying to locate is not available in any tab on the ribbon, search for it in the *All Commands* list.

Add a Button to the Quick Access Toolbar
1. Click Customize Quick Access Toolbar button.
2. Click desired button.
OR
1. Click Customize Quick Access Toolbar button.
2. Click *More Commands*.
3. Click down-pointing arrow at right of *Choose commands from*.
4. Click desired category.
5. Double-click desired command in commands list box.
6. Click OK.

Remove a Button from the Quick Access Toolbar
1. Click Customize Quick Access Toolbar button.
2. Click desired command.
OR
1. Click Customize Quick Access Toolbar button.
2. Click *More Commands*.
3. Click desired command in right list box.
4. Click Remove button.
5. Click OK.

Figure 7.9 Customize Quick Access Toolbar Drop-down List

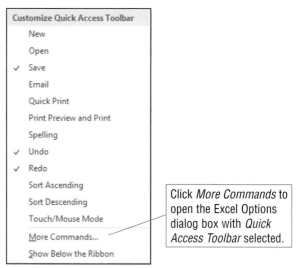

Click *More Commands* to open the Excel Options dialog box with *Quick Access Toolbar* selected.

Figure 7.10 Excel Options Dialog Box with *Quick Access Toolbar* Selected

Begin by selecting the category from which to choose commands.

Next, double-click the command you want to add in this list box.

1. Press Ctrl + N to open a new blank workbook and then add the Print Preview and Print and Sort commands to the Quick Access toolbar by completing the following steps. *Note: You will reset the Quick Access toolbar to the original settings in Project 2g.*

    a. Click the Customize Quick Access Toolbar button located at the right side of the Quick Access toolbar.

    b. Click *Print Preview and Print* at the drop-down list. The Print Preview and Print button is added to the end of the Quick Access toolbar. *Note: Skip to Step 1d if the Print Preview and Print button is already present on your Quick Access toolbar.*

    c. Click the Customize Quick Access Toolbar button.

    d. Click *More Commands* at the drop-down list.

    e. At the Excel Options dialog box with *Quick Access Toolbar* selected in the left pane, click the *Choose commands from* option box arrow and then click *All Commands*.

    f. Scroll down the *All Commands* list box and then double-click the second *Sort* option, which displays the ScreenTip *Data Tab | Sort & Filter | Sort....* *(SortDialog). Note: The commands are organized in alphabetical order; you will need to scroll far down the list to find this option.*

    g. Click OK. The Sort button is added to the end of the Quick Access toolbar.

2. Type your name in cell A1, press Enter, and then click the Print Preview and Print button on the Quick Access toolbar to display the Print backstage area.

3. Press Esc to close the Print backstage area.

4. Click the Sort button on the Quick Access toolbar to open the Sort dialog box.

5. Click the Cancel button at the Sort dialog box.

6. Close the workbook. Click Don't Save when prompted to save changes.

You can delete a button from the Quick Access Toolbar by clicking the Customize Quick Access Toolbar button and then clicking the command at the drop-down list. If the command is not in the drop-down list, click the *More Commands* option. At the Excel Options dialog box, click the desired command in the right list box and then click the Remove button.

Resetting the Ribbons and the Quick Access Toolbar

Restore the original ribbons and Quick Access toolbar that came with Excel 2013 by clicking the Reset button that displays below the *Main Tabs* list box in the Excel Options dialog box with *Customize Ribbon* selected. Clicking the Reset button displays two options: *Reset only selected Ribbon tab* and *Reset all customizations*. Click *Reset all customizations* to restore the ribbons and Quick Access toolbar to their original settings and then click Yes at the message box that displays *Delete all Ribbon and Quick Access Toolbar customizations for this program?* If you want to remove a tab that you previously created, right-click the tab and then click *Customize the Ribbon*. Right-click the tab in the *Main Tabs* list box and then click *Remove*.

To restore the ribbons and Quick Access toolbar to your institution's original settings, you will need to import the settings you exported in Project 2d. Click the Import/Export button in the lower right corner of the Excel Options dialog box and then click *Import customization file*. Locate the file and reinstall the customized settings.

Project 2g   **Importing Ribbon and Quick Access Toolbar Customizations**   **Part 7 of 8**

1. Import the ribbon and Quick Access Toolbar customizations you saved in Project 2d to reset your institution's original settings by completing the following steps:
   a. Press Ctrl + N to open a new blank workbook.
   b. Click the FILE tab and then click *Options*.
   c. Click *Customize Ribbon* in the left pane of the Excel Options dialog box.
   d. Click the Import/Export button located at the bottom right of the Excel Options dialog box.
   e. Click *Import customization file* at the drop-down list.
   f. Click *Desktop* in the *Favorites* list at the left of the File Open dialog box.
   g. Click **EL2-C7-P2-ExcelCustomizations.exportedUI**.
   h. Click Open.
   i. Click Yes at the message asking if you want to replace all existing ribbon and Quick Access Toolbar customizations for this program.
   j. Click OK.
2. Close the workbook. Click Don't Save if prompted to save changes.

▼ **Quick Steps**

Create a Custom View
1. Change display and print settings as desired.
2. Click VIEW tab.
3. Click Custom Views.
4. Click Add.
5. Type name for view.
6. Choose desired *Include in view* options.
7. Click OK.

Apply a Custom View
1. Click VIEW tab.
2. Click Custom Views.
3. Click desired view name.
4. Click Show.

Custom Views

Creating and Applying a Custom View ▪■▪■▪■▪■▪■▪▪■

A *custom view* saves display and print settings for the active worksheet. These settings can include column widths, row heights, hidden rows and/or columns, filter settings, cell selections, windows settings, page layout options, and print areas. You can create multiple custom views for the same worksheet and access stored views using the Custom Views dialog box. In Project 2h, you will create three custom views that store display settings, hidden rows, and a row height for a swimming schedule. You will switch between views to show different portions of the worksheet, such as only the daytime swimming activities.

Begin creating a custom view by applying the desired settings to the active worksheet, clicking the cell you want to be active, and displaying the rows and columns you want shown on the screen. When you are finished, click the VIEW tab, click the Custom Views button in the Workbook Views group, click the Add button, type a name for the custom view, and then click OK.

Change a worksheet to display a custom view's settings by opening the Custom Views dialog box, selecting the desired view name in the *Views* list box, and then clicking the Show button. You can also double-click the desired view name to apply the saved display and print settings to the worksheet. If a worksheet other than the one in which the view was created is active, you will be switched to the worksheet for which the view applies.

HINT

You can only apply a custom view to the worksheet in which it was created.

Project 2h   **Creating and Applying Custom Views**   Part 8 of 8

1. Open **EL2-C7-P2-NWinterSch.xlsx**.
2. Save the workbook, name it **EL2-C7-P2-NWinterSch-CV**, and redisplay the row and column headers in the worksheet. Refer to Project 2c if you need assistance with this step.
3. Create a custom view with display settings for all swimming sessions by completing the following steps:
   a. Select rows 4 through 37, click the Format button in the Cells group on the HOME tab, click *Row Height* at the drop-down list, type **20** in the *Row height* text box at the Row Height dialog box, and then press Enter or click OK.
   b. Press Ctrl + Home.
   c. Click the VIEW tab.
   d. Click the Custom Views button in the Workbook Views group.
   e. Click the Add button at the Custom Views dialog box.
   f. With the insertion point positioned in the *Name* text box at the Add View dialog box, type **AllSessions**.
   g. Make sure that the *Print settings* and *Hidden rows, columns and filter settings* check boxes contain check marks and then click OK.
4. Create a second custom view to display the daytime swimming activities and hide the evening activities by completing the following steps:
   a. Select rows 24 through 37, click the HOME tab, click the Format button in the Cells group, point to *Hide & Unhide* in the *Visibility* section, and then click *Hide Rows*.
   b. Press Ctrl + Home.
   c. Click the VIEW tab and then click the Custom Views button in the Workbook Views group.
   d. At the Custom Views dialog box, click the Add button.
   e. At the Add View dialog box, type **DaytimeSessions** in the *Name* text box.
   f. Make sure that the *Print settings* and *Hidden rows, columns and filter settings* check boxes contain check marks and then click OK.
5. Click the Custom Views button in the Workbook Views group. With *AllSessions* selected in the *Views* list box, click the Show button to apply the custom view.

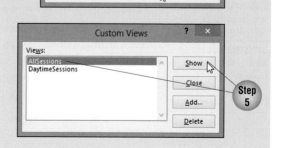

6. Create a third custom view to show only the evening swimming sessions by completing the following steps:
   a. Select rows 4 through 23 and hide the rows by completing a step similar to Step 4a.
   b. Create a custom view named *EveningSessions* by completing steps similar to Steps 4b–4f.
7. Click the Custom Views button and then double-click *DaytimeSessions* in the *Views* list box at the Custom Views dialog box.
8. Show the *EveningSessions* custom view.
9. Show the *AllSessions* custom view.
10. Save and then close **EL2-C7-P2-NWinterSch-CV.xlsx**.

Custom views cannot be created for any worksheet in which a table resides.

If you no longer need a custom view you previously created, delete it by opening the Custom Views dialog box, selecting the custom view name in the *Views* list box, and then clicking the Delete button.

Project 3 Save a Workbook as a Template　　　　　　　　2 Parts

You will modify an existing workbook and save the revised version as a template.

Saving a Workbook as a Template ■■■■■■■■■■■■■■■

▼ **Quick Steps**

Save a Workbook as a Template
1. Open workbook.
2. Make desired changes.
3. Click FILE tab.
4. Click *Save As*.
5. Click Browse button.
6. Change *Save as type* to *Excel Template (*.xltx)*.
7. Type desired file name.
8. Click OK.

If macros exist in the template workbook, change the *Save as type* option to *Excel Macro-Enabled Template (*.xltm)*.

Templates are workbooks with standard text, formulas, and formatting. Cell entries are created and formatted for all of the data that does not change. Cells that will contain variable information have formatting applied, but are left empty since they will be filled in when the template is used to generate a worksheet. Examples of worksheets that are well suited to templates include invoices, purchase orders, time cards, and expense forms. These types of worksheets are usually filled in with the same kinds of data, but the data itself varies.

Several templates have already been created and are installed on your computer or can be installed after they are downloaded. If you want to use a template to create a worksheet, first check the New backstage area to see if a template already exists that is suited to your purpose. You can also search online for templates using categories such as *Budget, Invoice, Calendars,* and *Expenses.* Once you have selected a topic in Suggested Searches, you can either download one of the templates shown or choose another topic from the Category task pane.

If none of the existing templates meet your needs, you can create your own custom template. To do this, create a workbook that contains all of the standard data, formulas, and formatting. Leave cells empty for any information that is variable; however, format those cells as required. When you are ready to save the workbook as a template, use the Save As dialog box and change the *Save as type* option to *Excel Template (*.xltx)*. Before saving it as a template, consider protecting the worksheet by locking all of the cells except those that will hold variable data.

1. Open **EL2-C7-P2-NWinterSch.xlsx**.
2. Redisplay the row and column headers in the worksheet. Refer to Project 2c if you need assistance with this step.
3. Assume that you work at the Noranda Sportsplex, which publishes swimming schedules on a continual basis. The sportsplex manager never changes the days or times the pool operates, but the activities and assigned pools often change. You decide to modify this workbook and then save it as a template to be reused whenever the schedule changes. To begin, make the following changes to the worksheet:
   a. Clear the cell contents for the ranges D5:E23 and D25:E37.
   b. Make cell A2 the active cell and then delete *Winter* in *Winter Swimming Schedule* so that the subtitle reads *Swimming Schedule*.
   c. Insert a new row between rows 2 and 3 and merge and center the cells in the new row to match the subtitle. (This will be used later to enter the timeframe for the new schedule.)

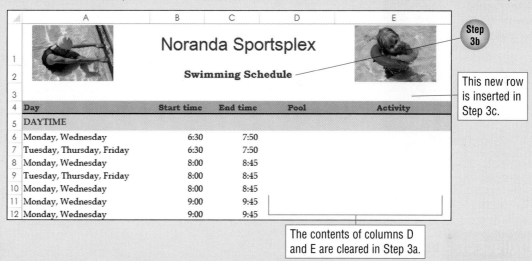

Step 3b

This new row is inserted in Step 3c.

The contents of columns D and E are cleared in Step 3a.

   d. Select and turn off the lock attribute for cell A3 and the ranges D6:E24 and D26:E38. Deselect the range.
   e. Protect the worksheet. Do not assign a password to unprotect.
4. Save the revised workbook as a template by completing the following steps:
   a. Click the FILE tab.
   b. Click *Save As*.
   c. Click the Browse button.
   d. Click *Save as type* and then click *Excel Template (*.xltx)* at the pop-up list.
   e. Select the current text in the *File name* text box and then type SwimSchTemplate-StudentName, substituting your name for *StudentName*.
   f. Click the Save button.

Step 4e

Step 4d

Step 4f

5. Close **SwimSchTemplate-StudentName.xltx**.

Using a Custom Template

Quick Steps

Use a Custom Template
1. Click FILE tab.
2. Click *New*.
3. Click *PERSONAL*.
4. Double-click desired template.

To use a template that you created yourself, click the FILE tab and then click *New*. At the New backstage area, click *PERSONAL*. This opens the PERSONAL template section, as shown in Figure 7.11. Double-click the name of the desired template to open it. A workbook (.xlsx) opens with the name of the template followed by a *1*. You can then save the document with a more descriptive name. In Project 3b you will create a new workbook using the template created in Project 3a, add information for the Winter 2015 schedule, and then save the workbook as EL2-C7-P3-SwimSchWinter2015.

HINT

By default, custom template workbook files are stored in the path [c:\]\Users*username*\ My Documents\Custom Office Templates.

Figure 7.11 New Backstage Area

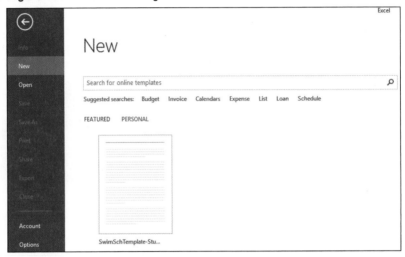

Project 3b **Using a Custom Template** **Part 2 of 2**

1. At a blank Excel screen, open the template created in Project 3a by completing the following steps:
   a. Click the FILE tab.
   b. Click *New*.
   c. At the New backstage area, click *PERSONAL*.
   d. In the PERSONAL template section, double-click *SwimSchTemplate-StudentName.xltx.* (Your template will have your name in place of *StudentName*.)
2. Look at the workbook name in the title bar. Notice that Excel has added *1* to the end of the name.
3. Make cell A3 the active cell and then type Winter 2015.

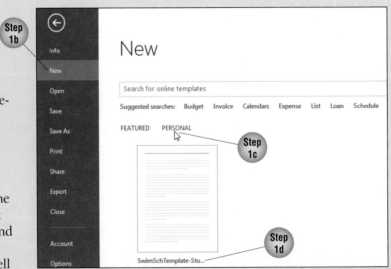

Step 1b

Step 1c

Step 1d

---

4. Enter data for the first two rows in the *Daytime* section by making up a pool name and activity for each row.
5. Click the Save button on the Quick Access toolbar.
6. Excel opens the Save As dialog box and automatically changes the *Save as type* option to *Excel Workbook (*.xlsx)*. Navigate to the EL2C7 folder on your storage medium, type EL2-C7-P3-SwimSchWinter2015 in the *File name* text box, and then click the Save button.
7. Print and then close **EL2-C7-P3-SwimSchWinter2015.xlsx**.

Deleting a Custom Template

To delete a custom template, use the Open dialog box to navigate to [c:]\Users\ *username*\My Documents\Custom Office Templates. Right-click the name of the template you want to delete and then click *Delete* at the shortcut menu. Click Cancel to close the Open dialog box.

▼ **Quick Steps**

Delete a Custom Template
1. Click FILE tab.
2. Click *Open*.
3. Click *Computer*.
4. Click Browse button.
5. Navigate to [c:]\ Users*username*\My Documents\Custom Office Templates.
6. Right-click desired template name.
7. Click *Delete*.
8. Click Cancel.

Project ▪4▪ Managing Excel's Save Options   2 Parts

You will review Excel's current save options, modify the AutoRecover options, and recover an unsaved workbook.

Customizing Save Options ■■■■■■■■■■■■■■■■■■■■■■

The *AutoRecover* feature saves versions of your work at a specified time interval so that you can restore all or part of your data should you forget to save or if you experience a situation that causes Excel to close unexpectedly (such as a power outage). When you restart Excel, the opening screen displays a *Recovered* section above the Recent files list. Click the <u>Show Recovered Files</u> hyperlink and the Document Recovery task pane opens with a list of workbooks for which an AutoRecover file exists.

By default, Excel's AutoRecover feature is turned on and will automatically save AutoRecover information every 10 minutes. You can adjust the time interval to meet your needs. Keep in mind that data loss can still occur even with AutoRecover turned on. For example, suppose the time interval is 20 minutes and a power outage occurs. Depending on when the power outage occurred, when you restart Excel, the recovered file may not contain the last 19 minutes of work if you did not save manually.

In conjunction with AutoRecover, Excel includes the *AutoSave* feature, which keeps the last version of a workbook saved in a temporary file. If you close a workbook without saving or want to return to an earlier version of the file, you can recover the AutoSaved version. At the bottom of the Recent Workbooks list, click the Recover Unsaved Workbooks button to view a list of AutoSaved files.

Open the Excel Options dialog box and select *Save* in the left pane to view and/or change the AutoRecover and AutoSave options.

▼ **Quick Steps**

Customize Save Options
1. Click FILE tab.
2. Click *Options*.
3. Click *Save* in left pane.
4. Change save options as desired.
5. Click OK.

Do not rely on AutoRecover and AutoSave as you work. Saving regularly to minimize data loss and protect against unforeseen events is the best practice.

1. At a blank Excel screen, click the FILE tab and then click *Options* to open the Excel Options dialog box.
2. Click *Save* in the left pane of the Excel Options dialog box.
3. Take note of the current settings for *Save AutoRecover information every [ ] minutes* and *Keep the last autosaved version if I close without saving*. By default, both check boxes should be checked and the time interval should be 10 minutes; however, the settings may have been changed on the computer you are using. In that case, write down the options so that you can restore the program to its original state once you are finished.
4. If necessary, click the two check boxes to turn on the AutoRecover and AutoSave features.
5. Select the current value in the *Save AutoRecover information every [ ] minutes* text box and then type 2 to change the time interval to 2 minutes.
6. Click OK.

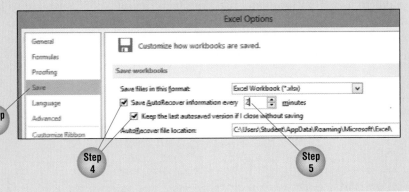

1. Open **EL2-C7-P2-NationalJE.xlsx**.
2. Save the workbook and name it **EL2-C7-P4-NationalJE**.
3. Note the system time in the bottom right corner of the screen. You will use this time to make sure that more than two minutes elapse before you interrupt the Excel session.
4. Make the following changes to the worksheet:
   a. Select A7:A17 and apply the Dark Red font color (first color in the *Standard Colors* section of the drop-down color palette).
   b. Select E7:E17 and apply the Dark Red font color.
   c. Delete rows 20 through 22 to remove the data from the workbook.

The data in rows 20–22 is deleted in Step 4c.

6		Parts	Labor	Total	TSR	Dept Code	Number	Number
7	Accounting	$ -	$ 1,125.00	$ 1,125.00	CS-4042	225	011475	160101
8	Executive Administration	564.27	885.50	1,449.77	CS-4043	216	011482	160102
9	Finance	964.32	535.50	1,499.82	CS-4044	166	011435	160103
10	Human Resources	397.45	125.50	522.95	CS-4045	167	011485	160104
11	Graphics Design	117.45	75.50	192.95	CS-4046	210	011415	160105
12	Electronic Production	215.48	275.50	490.98	CS-4047	350	011443	160106
13	Marketing	1,048.57	325.50	1,374.07	CS-4048	452	011409	160107
14	Web Programming	575.85	154.50	730.35	CS-4049	284	011462	160108
15	Planning and Development	61.45	32.50	93.95	CS-4050	310	011473	160109
16	President's Office	-	225.00	225.00	CS-4051	105	011455	160110
17	Purchasing	415.87	75.50	491.37	CS-4052	243	011428	160111
18				$ 8,196.21				
19								
20								
21								
22								

5. Make sure more than two minutes have elapsed since you checked the system time in Step 3. If necessary, wait until you are sure an AutoRecover file has been saved.

6. Press Alt + Ctrl + Delete.

7. At the Windows screen, select *Task Manager*.

8. At the Task Manager dialog box, click *Microsoft Excel (32 bit)* in the task list box and then click the End task button.

9. Close the Task Manager dialog box.

10. Restart Microsoft Excel. At the opening screen, click the <u>Show Recovered Files</u> hyperlink in the *Recovered* section. There are two available files: the original version of the file used in this project and the AutoRecovered version.

11. Point to the first file in the Document Recovery task pane. A ScreenTip displays to inform you that the first file is the AutoRecover version.

12. Point to the second file in the Document Recovery task pane. A ScreenTip displays to inform you that the second file is the original workbook.

13. Click the first file in the Document Recovery task pane. Notice that the edited version of the file appears. Look at the additional information displayed next to the file name in the Title bar. Excel includes *(version 1)* and *[Autosaved]* in the file name. Notice also that the Autosaved file has the file extension *.xlsb*.

14. Click *Recovered* next to *Ready* in the task bar at the bottom of the screen to redisplay the Document Recovery task pane.

15. Click the second file in the Document Recovery task pane. Notice that the original workbook opens and the message *[Last saved by user]* is added to the file name in the Title bar.

16. Close both workbooks. Click Save when prompted to save changes and then click *Save* at the Save As dialog box to accept the default name *EL2-C7-P4-NationalJE (Autosaved).xlsx*.

17. Open the Excel Options dialog box. The time interval changed back to 10 minutes when you clicked End task in Project 4b Step 8. If necessary, restore the Save options to the settings you wrote down in Project 4a. Close the Excel Options dialog box.

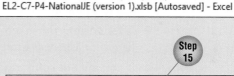

The Save options at the Excel Options dialog box also allow you to specify the drive and/or folder in which to store AutoRecovered files, as well as the default file location for all new workbooks.

At the Recent backstage view, click the Recover Unsaved Workbooks button at the bottom of the Recent Places pane to view a list of Autosaved files.

Chapter Summary

- Create a macro for a task that you repeat frequently and for which the steps do not vary.

- Start creating a new macro by clicking the VIEW tab, clicking the Macros button arrow in the Macros group, and then clicking *Record Macro*.

- At the Record Macro dialog box, you can assign a name, an optional shortcut key, and a description to the macro.

- The macro recorder is turned on after you click OK to close the Record Macro dialog box. All commands and keystrokes will be recorded until you click the Stop Recording button.

- Workbooks that contain macros are saved in the *Excel Macro-Enabled Workbook (*.xlsm)* file format.

- Run a macro by opening the Macro dialog box and double-clicking the macro name.

- A macro assigned to a shortcut key can be run by pressing Ctrl + the assigned letter.

- Excel differentiates the case of the letter typed in the *Shortcut key* text box at the Record Macro dialog box. An uppercase letter is assigned with the shortcut key Ctrl + Shift + the assigned letter.

- If you assign a shortcut key to a macro that is the same as a shortcut key assigned to an Excel feature, the macro overrides the Excel feature.

- The instructions for a macro are recorded in Visual Basic for Applications (VBA) program code. To edit a macro, open the Macro dialog box, click the macro name to be edited, and then click the Edit button. A Microsoft Visual Basic for Applications window opens, displaying a code module in which you can edit the macro's program code.

- After editing the macro, save the changes, click File, and then click *Close and Return to Microsoft Excel*.

- If you are not comfortable with editing a macro in VBA, you can record a new macro with the correct steps and then save it with the same name to replace the existing macro.

- Delete a macro at the Macro dialog box.

- Macros are stored in the workbook in which they are created. When you open the Macro dialog box, all macros from all open workbooks are accessible. Therefore, to use a macro stored in another workbook, you will need to open that workbook first.

- Another option for making macros accessible to other workbooks is to create a macros workbook with all of your standard macros and then open the macros workbook each time you start Excel.

- Pin a workbook that you want to make permanently available in the Recent Workbooks list at the Open backstage area.

- A pinned workbook displays with a down-pointing pin icon. Clicking the icon unpins the workbook from the list.

- Add buttons to or delete buttons from the Quick Access toolbar using the Customize Quick Access Toolbar button. To locate a feature you want to add to the Quick Access toolbar, click *More Commands* at the drop-down list to open the Excel Options dialog box with *Quick Access Toolbar* selected.

- Display options in Excel are grouped by global display options, options that affect the current workbook, and options that affect the current worksheet.

- Customized workbook and worksheet display options are saved with the file.

- Minimize the ribbon to provide more space in the work area when working with a large worksheet. Clicking a tab temporarily redisplays the ribbon to allow you to select a feature.

- You can customize the ribbon by creating a new tab, creating a new group within the new tab, and/or adding buttons within the new group.

- To customize the ribbon, open the Excel Options dialog box and then click *Customize Ribbon* in the left pane.

- Create a new ribbon tab by clicking the tab name that will precede the new tab and then clicking the New Tab button. A new group is automatically added with the new tab.

- Rename a custom tab by selecting the tab name, clicking the Rename button, typing a new name, and then pressing Enter or clicking OK. Rename a group or command using a similar process.

- Add buttons to a group by clicking the group name, selecting the desired command in the commands list box, and then clicking the Add button located between the two list boxes.

- Export and import customizations to save and restore previous settings on the ribbon(s) and Quick Access toolbar.

- A custom view saves display settings so that you can apply the saved settings to a worksheet when needed. Multiple custom views can be created for the same worksheet at the Custom Views dialog box. Open this dialog box by clicking the Custom Views button in the Workbook Views group on the VIEW tab.

- Templates are workbooks with standard text, formatting, and formulas.

- You can create a custom template from an existing workbook by selecting *Excel template (*.xltx)* in the *Save as type* option box in the Save As dialog box.

- To use a custom template, open the New backstage area, click *PERSONAL* to display the templates, and then double-click the custom template name.

- By default, Excel saves your work every 10 minutes to an AutoRecover file. If your Excel session is unexpectedly terminated or you close the file without saving, you can recover the file when you restart Excel at the Document Recovery task pane.

Commands Review

FEATURE	RIBBON TAB, GROUP/OPTIONS	BUTTON	KEYBOARD SHORTCUT
customize display options	FILE, *Options*		
customize Quick Access toolbar	FILE, *Options*		
customize ribbons	FILE, *Options*		
customize save options	FILE, *Options*		
custom views	VIEW, Workbook Views		
delete macro	VIEW, Macros		Alt + F8
edit a macro	VIEW, Macros		Alt + F8
minimize the ribbon			Ctrl + F1
record a macro	VIEW, Macros	OR	
ribbon display options			Ctrl + F1
save as a macro-enabled workbook	FILE, *Save As*		F12
use a custom template	FILE, *New*		

Concepts Check   Test Your Knowledge

Completion: In the space provided at the right, indicate the correct term, command, or number.

1. A macro name must begin with a letter and can contain a combination of letters, numbers, and this character. _____

2. Click this button to indicate that you have finished the tasks or keystrokes you want saved in the macro. _____

3. A workbook containing a macro is saved in this file format. _____

4. A macro can be assigned to a shortcut key that is a combination of a lowercase or uppercase letter and this key. _____

5. Macro instructions are stored in this program code. _____

6. A workbook that you use frequently can be permanently added to the Recent Workbooks list by clicking this icon next to the workbook name. _____

7. Display options are shown in the Excel Options dialog box with this option selected in the left pane. _____

8. Click this button to minimize the ribbon and provide more space in the work area. _____

9. Click this option in the left pane at the Excel Options dialog box to create a custom ribbon tab. _____

10. Click this option at the Customize Quick Access Toolbar drop-down list to locate a feature to add to the toolbar from the commands list box. _____

11. Click this button at the Custom Views dialog box to create a new custom view that will save the current display settings for the active worksheet. _____

12. Change *Save as type* to this option at the Save As dialog box to save the current workbook as a standard workbook that can be opened from the New dialog box. _____

13. This task pane opens when Excel is restarted after the previous session ended abnormally. _____

Skills Check   Assess Your Performance

Assessment

1 CREATE MACROS

SNAP Grade It

1. At a new blank workbook, create the following two macros:
   a. Create a macro named *Landscape* that changes the page orientation to landscape, sets custom margins (top = 1 inch; bottom, left, and right = 0.5 inch), and centers the worksheet horizontally. Assign the macro to the shortcut key Ctrl + Shift + Q. Enter an appropriate description that includes your name and the date the macro was created.
   b. Create a macro named *Ion* that applies the Ion theme and turns off the display of gridlines in the active worksheet. Assign the macro to the shortcut key Ctrl + t. Enter an appropriate description that includes your name and the date the macro was created.
2. Save the workbook as a macro-enabled workbook named **MyMacros-StudentName**, with your name substituted for *StudentName*.
3. Leave the **MyMacros-StudentName.xlsm** workbook open for the next assessment.

Assessment

2 RUN MACROS

1. Open **NationalCS.xlsx**.
2. Save the workbook and name it **EL2-C7-A2-NationalCS**.
3. Press Ctrl + t to run the Ion macro.
4. Press Ctrl + Shift + Q to run the Landscape macro.
5. Save, print, and then close **EL2-C7-A2-NationalCS.xlsx**.
6. Close **MyMacros-StudentName.xlsm**.

Assessment

3 CREATE MACROS; SAVE AS A MACRO-ENABLED WORKBOOK

 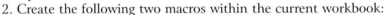

1. Open **EL2-C7-A2-NationalCS.xlsx**.
2. Create the following two macros within the current workbook:
   a. Create a macro named *FormulaBarOff* that turns off the display of the Formula bar and protects the worksheet. Do not enter a password to unprotect the sheet. Assign the macro to the shortcut key Ctrl + Shift + M. Enter an appropriate description that includes your name and the date the macro was created.
   b. Create a macro named *FormulaBarOn* that turns on the display of the Formula bar and unprotects the worksheet. Assign the macro to the shortcut key Ctrl + Shift + B. Enter an appropriate description that includes your name and the date the macro was created.
3. Test each macro to make sure the shortcut key runs the correct commands.
4. Save the revised workbook as a macro-enabled workbook and name it **EL2-C7-A3-NationalCS**.
5. Close **EL2-C7-A3-NationalCS.xlsm**.

Assessment

4 PRINT MACROS

1. Open **EL2-C7-A3-NationalCS.xlsm** and enable the content.
2. Open the Macro dialog box and edit the FormulaBarOff macro.
3. At the Microsoft Visual Basic for Applications window with the insertion point blinking in the code window, click File on the Menu bar and then click *Print*. At the Print - VBAProject dialog box, click OK. ***Note: The FormulaBarOn macro code will also print, since both macros are stored within the VBAProject.***
4. Click File on the Menu bar and then click *Close and Return to Microsoft Excel*.
5. Close **EL2-C7-A3-NationalCS.xlsm**.
6. Open **MyMacros-StudentName.xlsm** and enable the content.
7. Open the Macro dialog box and edit the Landscape macro.
8. At the Microsoft Visual Basic for Applications window with the insertion point blinking in the code window, click File on the Menu bar and then click *Print*. At the Print - VBAProject dialog box, click OK. ***Note: The Ion macro code will also print, since both macros are stored within the VBAProject.***
9. Click File on the Menu bar and then click *Close and Return to Microsoft Excel*.
10. Close **MyMacros-StudentName.xlsm**.

Assessment

5 CUSTOMIZE THE EXCEL ENVIRONMENT

1. Open **BillingsDec18.xlsx**.
2. Save the workbook and name it **EL2-C7-A5-BillingsDec18**.
3. Make the following changes to the display options:
   a. Turn off the horizontal scroll bar.
   b. Turn off sheet tabs.
   c. Turn off row and column headers.
   d. Turn off gridlines.
4. Change the current theme to the Wisp theme.
5. Freeze the first four rows in the worksheet.
6. Create a screen image of the worksheet with the modified display options and paste the image into a new Word document. Type your name a few lines below the screen image.
7. Save the Word document and name it **EL2-C7-A5-BillingsDec18**.
8. Print **EL2-C7-A5-BillingsDec18.docx** and then exit Word.
9. Save and close **EL2-C7-A5-BillingsDec18.xlsx**.

Assessment

6 CREATE CUSTOM VIEWS

1. Open **BillingsDec18.xlsx**.
2. Save the workbook and name it **EL2-C7-A6-BillingsDec18**.
3. Select A4:I23 and custom sort the cells in ascending order by attorney and then by the client's last name.
4. With A4:I23 still selected, turn on filter arrows.
5. Deselect the range and then filter the *Attorney* column to show only those rows with attorney Kyle Williams.
6. Press Ctrl + Home and create a custom view named *Williams* to save the filter settings.
7. Clear the filter in the *Attorney* column.
8. Filter the list by the attorney name *Marty O'Donovan*.
9. With cell A1 still selected, create a custom view named *O'Donovan* to save the filter settings.
10. Clear the filter in the *Attorney* column.
11. Create a custom view named *Martinez* by completing steps similar to those in Steps 8 and 9 and then clear the filter from the *Attorney* column.
12. Create a custom view named *Sullivan* by completing steps similar to those in Steps 8 and 9 and then clear the filter from the *Attorney* column.
13. Open the Custom Views dialog box. If necessary, drag the Custom Views dialog box Title bar to move the dialog box to the right of the worksheet. Create a screen image of the worksheet with the dialog box open and paste the image into a new Word document. Type your name a few lines below the screen image.
14. Save the Word document and name it **EL2-C7-A6-BillingsDec18**.
15. Print **EL2-C7-A6-BillingsDec18.docx** and then exit Word.
16. Close the Custom Views dialog box and then save and close **EL2-C7-A6-BillingsDec18.xlsx**.

7 CREATE AND USE A TEMPLATE

1. Open **EL2-C7-A5-BillingsDec18.xlsx** and turn on the display of row and column headers.
2. Make the following changes to the workbook:
   a. Select and delete all of the data below the column headings in row 4.
   b. Delete the text in cell A3.
   c. Edit the subtitle in cell A2 to *Associate Weekly Billing Summary*.
3. Save the revised workbook as a template named **Billings-StudentName**, with your name substituted for *StudentName*.
4. Close **Billings-StudentName.xltx**.
5. Start a new workbook based on the **Billings-StudentName.xltx** template.
6. Type November 16 to 20, 2015 in cell A3.
7. Enter the two billings shown in Figure 7.12.
8. Save the worksheet as an Excel workbook named **EL2-C7-A7-Billings**.
9. Print and then close **EL2-C7-A7-Billings.xlsx**.
10. Copy **Billings-StudentName.xltx** from [c]\Users\username\My Documents\ Custom Office Templates folder to the *EL2C7* folder on your storage medium. Close the Computer window.

Figure 7.12 Assessment 7

| IN-774 | 10665 | 11/16/2015 | Rankin | Jan | Maureen Myers | Insurance | 4.50 | 100.00 |
| EP-895 | 10996 | 11/17/2015 | Knox | Velma | Rosa Martinez | Estate | 3.50 | 100.00 |

Visual Benchmark   Demonstrate Your Proficiency

1 CUSTOMIZE THE RIBBON

1. Create the custom tab including the groups and buttons shown in Figure 7.13. Substitute your name for *STUDENT NAME* in the tab. You can locate all of the buttons using the *All Commands* list.
2. Insert a screen image in a new Word document that shows the ribbon with the custom tab displayed in Microsoft Excel.
3. Save the Word document and name it **EL2-C7-VB1-MyRibbon**.
4. Print **EL2-C7-VB1-MyRibbon.docx** and then exit Word.
5. Remove the STUDENT NAME tab.

2 CREATE A CUSTOM TEMPLATE

1. Create a custom template that can be used to generate a sales invoice similar to the one shown in Figure 7.14. Use your best judgment to match the column widths, row heights, and color formatting. The font used in cell A1 is 36-point Footlight MT Light, and Garamond is used for the remaining cells (18-point in cell A2 and 12-point elsewhere). Substitute an appropriate clip art image if the one shown is not available on the computer you are using. (Recall that a template should contain only text, formulas, and formatting that does not change from one invoice to another.)
2. Save the workbook as a template and name it **EL2-C7-VB2-AudennitaSalesInv**.
3. Using the template, fill out a sales invoice using the data shown in Figure 7.14.
4. Save the completed invoice and name it **EL2-C7-VB2-AudennitaInvToVanderwyst**.
5. Print the invoice and then close **EL2-C7-VB2-AudennitaInvToVanderwyst.xlsx**.
6. Make a copy of the custom template at the New dialog box, saving the copy to your storage medium in the EL2C7 folder.

Figure 7.13 Visual Benchmark 1

Figure 7.14 Visual Benchmark 2

Case Study   Apply Your Skills

Part 1

Yolanda Robertson of NuTrends Market Research would like you to help her become more efficient by creating macros for the frequently performed tasks in the list below. To share the macros with colleagues in the office, you decide to save all of the macros in a macro-enabled workbook named **EL2-C7-CS-P1-NuTrendMacros**. Rename Sheet1 to *MacroDocumentation*. Document the macros in the workbook by typing the macro names, shortcut keys assigned to each macro, and descriptions of the actions each macro performs. This documentation will assist your colleagues in using the macros in the file. For example, in column A, type the name of the macro; in column B, type the macro's shortcut key; and in column C, enter a description of the actions that the macro performs.

Create a separate macro for each of the following tasks. At the Record Macro dialog box, type your name and the current date in the *Description* text box for each macro.

- Apply the Organic theme and show all comments.
- Set the active column's width to 20 characters.
- Apply conditional formatting to highlight the top 10 in a selected list. Accept the default formatting options.
- Apply the Accounting format with no places after the decimal point.
- Create a footer that prints your name centered at the bottom of the worksheet.

Print the MacroDocumentation worksheet. Open the Macro dialog box and edit the first macro. At the Microsoft Visual Basic for Applications window, print the macros in the VBAProject. Close the Visual Basic for Applications window to return to the worksheet. Save **EL2-C7-CS-P1-NuTrendsMacros.xlsm**.

Part 2

Yolanda has received the file named **PBMNewFranchiseRev.xlsx** from Nicola Carlucci. She wants you to format the workbook using the macros created in Part 1. Open the workbook save it using the name **EL2-C7-CS-P2-PBMNewFranchiseRev**. Run each macro created in Part 1 using the following information:

- Set all of the column widths to 20 characters except column C.
- Run the number formatting and conditional formatting with the values in column E selected.
- Run the theme and footer macros.

Print the worksheet making sure the comments print as displayed. Save and then close **EL2-C7-CS-P2-PBMNewFranchiseRev.xlsx**. Close **EL2-C7-CS-P1-NuTrendsMacros.xlsm**.

Part 3

Yolanda would like to customize the Quick Access toolbar but finds the process using the Excel Options dialog box to locate commands cumbersome. Use Excel Help to learn how to add a button to the Quick Access toolbar directly from the ribbon. Test the information you learned by adding two buttons of your choosing to the Quick Access toolbar using the ribbon. For example, add the Orientation button from the PAGE LAYOUT tab and the New Comment button from the REVIEW tab. Using Microsoft Word, compose a memo to Yolanda that describes the steps for adding a button to the Quick Access toolbar directly from the ribbon. Insert a screen image of the Quick Access toolbar in Excel that displays the buttons you added below the memo text. Save the Word memo and name it **EL2-C7-C5-P3-CustomizeQATMemo**. Print **EL2-C7-CS-P3-CustomizeQATMemo.docx** and then exit Word. Remove the two buttons you added to the Quick Access toolbar.

Part 4

Yolanda has mentioned that she sometimes sees a *Recovered* section above the *Recent* files list when she starts Excel. She has asked you to explain why this appears and what she should do when she sees it. Compose a memo to Yolanda using Microsoft Word in which you explain the AutoRecover and AutoSave features in your own words. Include an explanation that the *Recovered* section appears in the opening screen after Excel has not been properly closed and provide advice for Yolanda on how to review the files in the Document Recovery task pane to make sure she has not lost data.

MICROSOFT
EXCEL®

Importing, Exporting, and Distributing Data

PERFORMANCE OBJECTIVES

Upon successful completion of Chapter 8, you will be able to:

- Import data from an Access table, website, and text file
- Append data from an Excel worksheet to an Access table
- Embed and link data in an Excel worksheet to a Word document
- Copy and paste data in an Excel worksheet to a PowerPoint presentation
- Export data as a text file
- Scan and remove private or confidential information from a workbook
- Mark a workbook as final
- Check a workbook for features incompatible with earlier versions of Excel
- View Trust Center settings
- Save an Excel workbook as a PDF or XPS file
- Save an Excel worksheet as a web page

Tutorials

8.1 Importing Data from Access, a Text File, or a Website
8.2 Exporting Data from Excel
8.3 Copying and Pasting Worksheet Data between Programs
8.4 Copying and Pasting Worksheet Data to a Word Document
8.5 Exporting Data as a Text File
8.6 Preparing a Worksheet for Distribution
8.7 Converting a Workbook to a Different Format
8.8 Viewing Trust Center Settings
8.9 Creating a PDF/XPS Copy of a Workbook
8.10 Publishing a Worksheet as a Web Page

Exchanging data contained in one program with another by importing or exporting eliminates duplication of effort and reduces the likelihood of data errors or missed entries that would arise if the data was retyped. One of the advantages of working with a suite of programs such as Word, Excel, Access, and PowerPoint is being able to easily integrate data from one program to another. In this chapter, you will learn how to bring data into an Excel worksheet from sources external to Excel and how to export data in a worksheet for use with other programs. You will also learn to use features that allow you to send Excel data using a variety of distribution methods. Model answers for this chapter's projects appear on the following pages.

Excel
EL2C8

Note: Before beginning the projects, copy to your storage medium the EL2C8 subfolder from the EL2 folder on the CD that accompanies this textbook and then make EL2C8 the active folder.

NuTrends Market Research
US Population Estimates by State

Source: US Census Bureau

ID	State	July2011	July2010	July2009	July2008
1	Alabama	4,802,740	4,779,736	4,708,708	4,677,464
2	Alaska	722,718	710,231	698,473	688,125
3	Arizona	6,482,505	6,392,017	6,595,778	6,499,377
4	Arkansas	2,937,979	2,915,918	2,889,450	2,867,764
5	California	37,691,912	37,253,956	36,961,664	36,580,371
6	Colorado	5,116,796	5,029,196	5,024,748	4,935,213
7	Connecticut	3,580,709	3,574,097	3,518,288	3,502,932
8	Delaware	907,135	897,934	885,122	876,211
9	District of Columbia	617,996	601,723	599,657	590,074
10	Florida	19,057,542	18,801,310	18,537,969	18,423,878
11	Georgia	9,815,210	9,687,653	9,829,211	9,697,838
12	Hawaii	1,374,810	1,360,301	1,295,178	1,287,481
13	Idaho	1,584,985	1,567,582	1,545,801	1,527,506
14	Illinois	12,869,257	12,830,632	12,910,409	12,842,954
15	Indiana	6,516,922	6,483,802	6,423,113	6,388,309
16	Iowa	3,062,309	3,046,355	3,007,856	2,993,987
17	Kansas	2,871,238	2,853,118	2,818,747	2,797,375
18	Kentucky	4,369,356	4,339,367	4,314,113	4,287,931
19	Louisiana	4,574,836	4,533,372	4,492,076	4,451,513
20	Maine	1,328,188	1,328,361	1,318,301	1,319,691
21	Maryland	5,828,289	5,773,552	5,699,478	5,658,655
22	Massachusetts	6,587,536	6,547,629	6,593,587	6,543,595
23	Michigan	9,846,187	9,883,640	9,969,727	10,002,486
24	Minnesota	5,344,861	5,303,925	5,266,214	5,230,567
25	Mississippi	2,978,512	2,967,297	2,951,996	2,940,212
26	Missouri	6,010,688	5,988,927	5,987,580	5,956,335
27	Montana	998,199	989,415	974,989	968,035
28	Nebraska	1,842,641	1,826,341	1,796,619	1,781,949
29	Nevada	2,723,322	2,700,551	2,643,085	2,615,772
30	New Hampshire	1,318,194	1,316,470	1,324,575	1,321,872
31	New Jersey	8,821,155	8,791,894	8,707,739	8,663,398
32	New Mexico	2,082,224	2,059,179	2,009,671	1,986,763
33	New York	19,465,197	19,378,102	19,541,453	19,467,789
34	North Carolina	9,656,401	9,535,483	9,380,884	9,247,134
35	North Dakota	683,932	672,591	646,844	641,421
36	Ohio	11,544,951	11,536,504	11,542,645	11,528,072
37	Oklahoma	3,791,508	3,751,351	3,687,050	3,644,025
38	Oregon	3,871,859	3,831,074	3,825,657	3,782,991
39	Pennsylvania	12,742,886	12,702,379	12,604,767	12,566,368
40	Rhode Island	1,051,302	1,052,567	1,053,209	1,053,502
41	South Carolina	4,679,230	4,625,364	4,561,242	4,503,280
42	South Dakota	824,082	814,180	812,383	804,532
43	Tennessee	6,403,353	6,346,105	6,296,254	6,240,456
44	Texas	25,674,681	25,145,561	24,782,302	24,304,290
45	Utah	2,817,222	2,763,885	2,784,572	2,727,343
46	Vermont	626,431	625,741	621,760	621,049
47	Virginia	8,096,604	8,001,024	7,882,590	7,795,424
48	Washington	6,830,038	6,830,038	6,664,195	6,566,073
49	West Virginia	1,855,364	1,852,994	1,819,777	1,814,873
50	Wisconsin	5,711,767	5,686,986	5,654,774	5,627,610
51	Wyoming	568,158	563,626	544,270	532,981
52	Puerto Rico	3,706,690	3,725,789	3,967,288	3,954,553

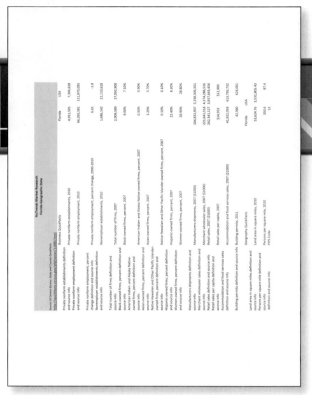

Project 1 Import Data from External Sources to Excel

Project 1a, EL2-C8-P1-NuTrendsCensusData.xlsx with
PopulationEstimates Worksheet

Project 1b, EL2-C8-P1-NuTrendsCensusData.xlsx with
FloridaGeographicData Worksheet

Housing Unit Estimates
100 Fastest Growing Counties
Change between April 1, 2010 and July 1, 2011

Source: Population Division, US Census Bureau (HU-EST2005-06)

Rank	Geographic Area	Housing Unit Estimates		Change, 2010 to 2011	
		1-Apr-10	1-Jul-11	Number	Percent
1	Long County, GA	6,030	6,412	382	6.3
2	Fort Bend County, TX	197,031	208,696	11,665	5.9
3	Sumter County, FL	53,026	55,988	2,962	5.6
4	Rockwall County, TX	27,939	29,306	1,367	4.9
5	Matanuska-Susitna Borough, AK	41,329	43,242	1,913	4.6
6	Taney County, MO	29,255	30,605	1,350	4.6
7	Madison County, MT	6,940	7,253	313	4.5
8	Lincoln County, SD	17,875	18,665	790	4.4
9	McIntosh County, GA	9,220	9,615	395	4.3
10	Lamar County, MS	24,070	25,083	1,013	4.2
11	Campbell County, WY	18,955	19,743	788	4.2
12	Telfair County, GA	7,297	7,597	300	4.1
13	Hays County, TX	59,416	61,821	2,405	4
14	White County, GA	16,062	16,685	623	3.9
15	Dooly County, GA	6,328	6,573	245	3.9
16	Hancock County, MS	21,840	22,658	818	3.7
17	Faulkner County, AR	46,612	48,325	1,713	3.7
18	Wilson County, TX	16,765	17,377	612	3.7
19	Guadalupe County, TX	50,015	51,815	1,800	3.6
20	Hoke County, NC	18,211	18,858	647	3.6
21	Williamson County, TX	162,773	168,515	5,742	3.5
22	Columbia County, GA	48,626	50,331	1,705	3.5
23	Blanco County, TX	5,532	5,725	193	3.5
24	Parker County, TX	46,628	48,241	1,613	3.5
25	Sevier County, TN	55,917	57,804	1,887	3.4
26	Sublette County, WY	5,770	5,963	193	3.3
27	Summit County, UT	26,544	27,407	863	3.3
28	Nye County, NV	22,350	23,068	718	3.2
29	Onslow County, NC	68,226	70,366	2,140	3.1
30	Denton County, TX	256,139	264,071	7,932	3.1
31	Harrison County, MS	85,181	87,773	2,592	3
32	Limestone County, AL	34,977	36,019	1,042	3
33	Hood County, TX	24,951	25,694	743	3
34	Fredericksburg city, VA	10,467	10,777	310	3
35	Dallas County, IA	27,260	28,065	805	3
36	Franklin County, WA	24,423	25,120	697	2.9
37	Livingston Parish, LA	50,195	51,607	1,412	2.8
38	Kane County, UT	5,815	5,978	163	2.8
39	Sweetwater County, WY	18,735	19,258	523	2.8
40	Sequatchie County, TN	6,368	6,545	177	2.8

Page 1

177,650	182,513	4,863	2.7
13,313	13,671	358	2.7
9,493	9,745	252	2.7
19,303	19,813	510	2.6
125,470	128,777	3,307	2.6
38,323	39,320	997	2.6
6,678	6,850	172	2.6
13,137	13,472	335	2.6
7,161	7,343	182	2.5
17,444	17,887	443	2.5
55,186	56,576	1,390	2.5
109,442	112,189	2,747	2.5
46,963	48,141	1,178	2.5
106,772	109,440	2,668	2.5
10,379	10,637	258	2.5
73,372	75,194	1,822	2.5
32,137	32,932	795	2.5
40,321	41,308	987	2.4
24,669	25,269	600	2.4
10,464	10,717	253	2.4
22,547	23,090	543	2.4
21,011	21,513	502	2.4
67,938	69,560	1,622	2.4
30,578	31,308	730	2.4
21,114	21,616	502	2.4
5,147	5,269	122	2.4
12,928	13,233	305	2.4
17,195	17,598	403	2.3
40,757	41,702	945	2.3
41,783	42,740	957	2.3
13,291	13,593	302	2.3
13,868	14,183	315	2.3
32,687	33,429	742	2.3
12,780	13,070	290	2.3
61,938	63,343	1,405	2.3
22,730	23,242	512	2.3
189,896	194,138	4,242	2.2
94,196	96,281	2,085	2.2
14,517	14,837	320	2.2
11,413	11,663	250	2.2
93,084	95,116	2,032	2.2
26,740	27,323	583	2.2
70,099	71,622	1,523	2.2
28,212	28,820	608	2.2
113,958	116,403	2,445	2.1
300,960	307,353	6,393	2.1
5,055	5,162	107	2.1

Page 2

8,285	8,460	175	2.1
8,085	8,252	167	2.1
44,812	45,737	925	2.1
49,351	50,369	1,018	2.1
159,222	162,504	3,282	2.1
11,788	12,028	240	2
28,151	28,721	570	2
25,728	26,248	520	2
146,447	149,385	2,938	2
29,315	29,895	580	2
45,810	46,715	905	2
17,462	17,802	340	1.9
50,739	51,726	987	1.9

...se reflects changes to the 2010 Census housing units from
...her geographic program revisions. It does not reflect
...ram. All geographic boundaries for the 2011 housing unit

...t Growing Counties With 5,000 or More Housing Units in
...)

Page 3

Project 1c, EL2-C8-P1-NuTrendsCensusData.xlsx with
HousingUnitData Worksheet

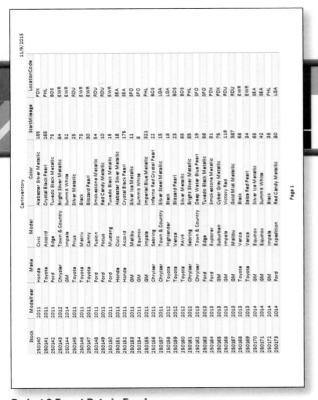

Project 2 Export Data in Excel

Project 2a, CarInventory Datasheet from CRInventory.accdb

Project 2b, EL2-C8-P2-CRCarRpt.docx

Project 2c, EL2-C8-P2-CRCarRptLinked.docx

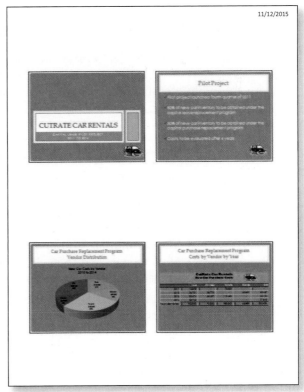

Project 2e, EL2-C8-P2-CRCarRpt.pptx

EL2-C8-P2-CRInventory.csv

```
CutRate Car Rentals,,,,,,
New Car Inventory,,,,,,
,,,,,,
Stock,ModelYear,Make,Model,Color,StartMileage,LocationCode
250145,2011,Toyota,Prius,Silver Metallic,25,RDU
250146,2011,Toyota,Matrix,Black,75,EWR
250147,2011,Toyota,Camry,Blizzard Pearl,30,EWR
250148,2011,Ford,Fusion,Smokestone Metallic,54,RDU
250149,2011,Ford,Focus,Red Candy Metallic,10,RDU
250150,2011,Ford,Mustang,Tuxedo Black Metallic,15,EWR
250151,2011,Honda,Civic,Alabaster Silver Metallic,18,SEA
250152,2011,Honda,Accord,Crystal Black Pearl,175,SEA
250153,2011,GM,Malibu,Silver Ice Metallic,11,SFO
250154,2011,GM,Equinox,Summit White,8,SFO
250155,2011,GM,Impala,Imperial Blue Metallic,321,PHL
250156,2011,Chrysler,Sebring,Inferno Red Crystal Pearl,22,BOS
250157,2011,Chrysler,Town & Country,Silver Steel Metallic,15,LGA
250158,2012,Toyota,Highlander,Black,18,LGA
250159,2012,Toyota,Venza,Blizzard Pearl,23,BOS
250160,2012,Toyota,RAV4,Silver Metallic,65,BOS
250161,2012,Chrysler,Sebring,Bright Silver Metallic,85,PHL
250162,2013,Chrysler,Town & Country,Deep Water Blue Pearl,19,SFO
250163,2013,Ford,Edge,Tuxedo Black Metallic,56,SFO
250164,2013,Ford,Explorer,Smokestone Metallic,81,PDX
250165,2013,GM,Suburban,Cyber Gray Metallic,75,PDX
250166,2013,GM,Impala,Victory Red,119,RDU
250167,2013,GM,Malibu,Gold Mist Metallic,387,RDU
250168,2013,Toyota,Venza,Black,68,EWR
250169,2013,Toyota,Venza,Salsa Red Pearl,34,EWR
250170,2014,GM,Equinox,Silver Ice Metallic,65,SEA
250171,2014,GM,Equinox,Summit White,42,SEA
250172,2014,GM,Impala,Black,38,PHL
250173,2014,Ford,Expedition,Red Candy Metallic,80,LGA
```

Page 1

Project 2f, EL2-C8-P2-CRInventory.csv

Compatibility Report for CRBuyLeaseAnalysis.xlsx
Run on 11/12/2012 22:27

The following features in this workbook are not supported by earlier versions of Excel. These features may be lost or degraded when opening this workbook in an earlier version of Excel or if you save this workbook in an earlier file format.

Significant loss of functionality	# of occurrences	Version
One or more cells in this workbook contain a conditional formatting type that is not supported in earlier versions of Excel, such as data bars, color scales, or icon sets.	1	
Sheet1!D13:Q16		Excel 97-2003
Some cells contain conditional formatting with the 'Stop if True' option cleared. Earlier versions of Excel do not recognize this option and will stop after the first true condition.	1	
Sheet1!B5:K8		Excel 97-2003

Minor loss of fidelity

	# of occurrences	Version
A table style is applied to a table in this workbook. Table style formatting cannot be displayed in earlier versions of Excel.	1	
Sheet1!A4:K9		Excel 97-2003
Some cells or styles in this workbook contain formatting that is not supported by the selected file format. These formats will be converted to the closest format available.	18	Excel 97-2003

Project 3 Prepare a Workbook for Distribution

Project 3c, EL2-C8-P3-CRBuyLeaseAnalysisCompChk.xlsx

Project 1 — Import Data from External Sources to Excel — 3 Parts

You will import US Census Bureau data related to a market research project from an Access database, the US Census Bureau website, and a text file previously downloaded from the Census Bureau.

Importing Data into Excel ▪▪▪▪▪▪▪▪▪▪▪▪▪▪▪▪▪▪▪▪

The Get External Data group on the DATA tab contains buttons for importing data from external sources into an Excel worksheet. During an import or export routine, the program containing the original data is called the *source* and the program to which the data source is being copied, embedded, or linked is called the *destination*. To import data, make active the cell where you want the imported data to start and then click the button representing the source application or click the From Other Sources button to select the source from a drop-down list.

A connection can be established to an external data source to avoid having to repeat the import process each time you need to analyze the data in Excel. Once a connection has been created, you can repeat the import in another worksheet by simply clicking the connection file in the Existing Connections dialog box.

Importing Data from Access

Exchanging data between Access and Excel is a seamless process since data in an Access datasheet is structured in the same row and column format as an Excel worksheet. You can import the Access data as an Excel table, PivotTable Report, or PivotChart. The imported data can be appended to an existing worksheet or placed in a new worksheet.

To import an Access table, click the DATA tab and then click the From Access button in the Get External Data group. At the Select Data Source dialog box, navigate to the drive and/or folder in which the source database resides and then double-click the Access database file name in the file list. If the source database contains more than one table, the Select Table dialog box opens so you can choose the table containing the data you want to import. If the source database contains only one table, you will not be prompted to select a table name. Once the table is identified, the Import Data dialog box appears, as shown in Figure 8.1. Choose how you want to view the data, select the location to begin the import, and then click OK.

Quick Steps

Import an Access Table
1. Make active cell at which to begin import.
2. Click DATA tab.
3. Click From Access button.
4. Navigate to drive and/or folder.
5. Double-click source database file name.
6. If necessary, click desired table name and then OK.
7. Select desired view format.
8. Click OK.

From Access

HINT

Only one table can be imported at a time. To import all of the tables in the source database, repeat the import process for each table.

Figure 8.1 Import Data Dialog Box

Choose the format in which you want the Access table imported in this section.

Choose where to place the imported data in this section.

Project 1a **Importing Data from an Access Database** Part 1 of 3

1. Open **NuTrendsCensus.xlsx**.
2. Save the workbook and name it **EL2-C8-P1-NuTrendsCensus**.
3. Import four years of US state population estimates, which have been compiled by the US Census Bureau and stored in an Access database, and append it to an existing worksheet by completing the following steps:
   a. With PopulationEstimates the active worksheet, make cell A5 active.
   b. Click the DATA tab.
   c. Click the From Access button in the Get External Data group.
   d. At the Select Data Source dialog box, navigate to the EL2C8 folder on your storage medium and then double-click **NuTrendsCensus.accdb**.

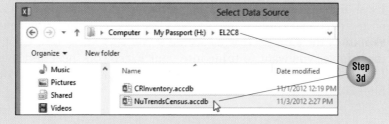

e. Since the source database contains more than one table, the Select Table dialog box appears. Click *PopByState* in the *Name* column and then click OK.

f. At the Import Data dialog box with *Table* selected in the *Select how you want to view this data in your workbook* section and the cell reference *=$A$5* in the *Existing worksheet* text box in the *Where do you want to put the data?* section, click OK.

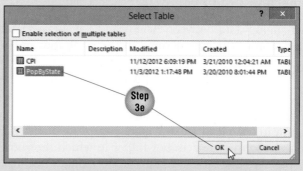

4. Scroll down the imported table data. Notice that the data is formatted as a table with filter arrows.

5. With the TABLE TOOLS DESIGN tab active, make the following changes to the worksheet:

a. Remove the filter arrows.

b. Change the table style to *Table Style Medium 1* (first column in the first row of the *Medium* section).

c. Make the HOME tab active and apply comma formatting with no places after the decimal point.

d. Adjust the widths of columns C through F to 15 characters.

e. Center-align the labels in C5:F5.

6. Print the PopulationEstimates worksheet scaled to fit one page in width and height and centered horizontally between the left and right margins.

7. Save **EL2-C8-P1-NuTrendsCensus.xlsx**.

Importing Data from a Website

Quick Steps

Import Data from a Website
1. Make cell active at which to begin import.
2. Click DATA tab.
3. Click From Web button.
4. Navigate to desired web page.
5. Click arrows next to tables to import.
6. Click Import button.
7. Click OK.

From Web

Tables in a website can be downloaded directly using the New Web Query dialog box, as shown in Figure 8.2. Make active the cell at which you want to begin the import, click the DATA tab, and then click the From Web button in the Get External Data group. Use the Address bar and web navigation buttons to go to the page containing the data you want to use in Excel. At the desired page, Excel displays black right-pointing arrows inside yellow boxes next to elements on the page that contain importable tables. Point to an arrow and a blue border surrounds the data Excel will capture if you click the arrow. Click the arrow for those tables you want to bring into your Excel worksheet and then click the Import button. In Project 1b, you will import multiple sections of data about Florida from the US Census Bureau QuickFacts web page.

Figure 8.2 New Web Query Dialog Box

> Navigate to the desired website, as you would in a browser window.

> Point to an arrow in a yellow box to display a blue border around a table on the web page. Click the arrow to select the table and then click the Import button to copy the data into the active cell.

| **Project 1b** | **Importing a Table from a Web Page** | **Part 2 of 3** |

1. With **EL2-C8-P1-NuTrendsCensus.xlsx** open, make FloridaGeographicData the active worksheet.
2. Import statistics related to Florida from the US Census Bureau QuickFacts web page by completing the following steps. *Note: During any part of this project, if a Script Error dialog box displays, click Yes to continue running scripts on the page*.
   a. Make cell A6 active.
   b. Click the From Web button in the Get External Data group on the DATA tab.
   c. At the New Web Query dialog box, select the current entry in the *Address* text box, type http://www.census.gov, and then press Enter.
   d. Point to the Data tab located near the top of the web page and then click *Quick Facts* at the drop-down list.

e. Resize the New Web Query dialog box until you can see the entire map of the United States.

f. Click the state of Florida in the map.

g. At the Florida QuickFacts page, notice the black right-pointing arrows inside yellow boxes along the left edge of the page. Point to one of the arrows to see the yellow box change to green and a blue border surround the data that will be imported into Excel if you click the arrow.

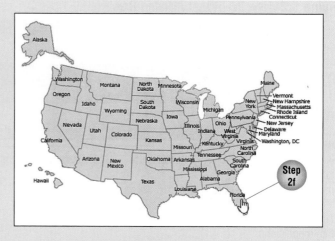

Step 2f

h. Scroll down the page to the section titled *Business QuickFacts*.

i. Click the black right-pointing arrow next to *Business QuickFacts* to select the table. The arrow changes to a check mark inside a green box when the table is selected for import.

j. Click the arrow next to *Geography QuickFacts* to select the table.

k. Click the Import button.

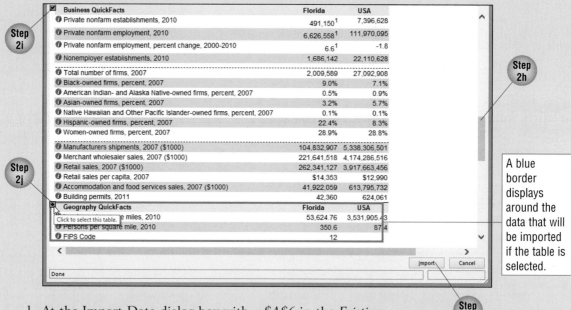

Business QuickFacts	Florida	USA
Private nonfarm establishments, 2010	491,150[1]	7,396,628
Private nonfarm employment, 2010	6,626,558[1]	111,970,095
Private nonfarm employment, percent change, 2000-2010	6.6[1]	-1.8
Nonemployer establishments, 2010	1,686,142	22,110,628
Total number of firms, 2007	2,009,589	27,092,908
Black-owned firms, percent, 2007	9.0%	7.1%
American Indian- and Alaska Native-owned firms, percent, 2007	0.5%	0.9%
Asian-owned firms, percent, 2007	3.2%	5.7%
Native Hawaiian and Other Pacific Islander-owned firms, percent, 2007	0.1%	0.1%
Hispanic-owned firms, percent, 2007	22.4%	8.3%
Women-owned firms, percent, 2007	28.9%	28.8%
Manufacturers shipments, 2007 ($1000)	104,832,907	5,338,306,501
Merchant wholesaler sales, 2007 ($1000)	221,641,518	4,174,286,516
Retail sales, 2007 ($1000)	262,341,127	3,917,663,456
Retail sales per capita, 2007	$14,353	$12,990
Accommodation and food services sales, 2007 ($1000)	41,922,059	613,795,732
Building permits, 2011	42,360	624,061
Geography QuickFacts	**Florida**	**USA**
e miles, 2010	53,624.76	3,531,905.43
Persons per square mile, 2010	350.6	87.4
FIPS Code	12	

Click to select this table.

Step 2i

Step 2j

Step 2h

A blue border displays around the data that will be imported if the table is selected.

Import   Cancel

Done

Step 2k

l. At the Import Data dialog box with =$A$6 in the *Existing worksheet* text box in the *Where do you want to put the data?* section, click OK. Excel imports the data from the web page into the Excel worksheet starting in cell A6.

3. Make the following changes to the worksheet:

a. Decrease the width of column A to 35 characters.

b. Select the cells in column A that contain imported text, click the HOME tab, and then click the Wrap Text button in the Alignment group.

Import Data

Where do you want to put the data?
● Existing worksheet:
=SAS6
○ New worksheet
☐ Add this data to the Data Model

Properties...   OK   Cancel

Step 2l

c. With the cells in column A still selected, click the Format button in the Cells group on the HOME tab and then click *AutoFit Row Height* at the drop-down list.

d. Center-align the text in the range C6:D6.

e. Change the page orientation to landscape.

4. Print the FloridaGeographicData worksheet scaled to fit on one page and centered between the left and right margins.

5. Save **EL2-C8-P1-NuTrendsCensus.xlsx**.

Importing Data from a Text File

A *text file* is often used to exchange data between dissimilar programs since the file format is recognized by nearly all applications. Text files contain no formatting and consist only of letters, numbers, punctuation symbols, and a few control characters. Two commonly used text file formats separate fields with either tab characters (*delimited file format*) or commas (*comma separated file format*). The text file you will use in Project 1c is shown in a Notepad window in Figure 8.3. If necessary, you can view and edit a text file in Notepad prior to importing it.

To import a text file into Excel, use the From Text button in the Get External Data group on the DATA tab and then select the source file at the Import Text File dialog box. Excel displays in the file list any file in the active folder that ends with the file extension *.prn, .txt,* or *.csv*. Once the source file is selected, Excel begins the Text Import Wizard, which guides you through the import process using three dialog boxes.

▼ **Quick Steps**

Import Data from a Comma Separated Text File
1. Make active cell at which to begin import.
2. Click DATA tab.
3. Click From Text button.
4. Double-click .csv file name.
5. Click Next.
6. Click *Comma* check box.
7. Click Next.
8. Click Finish.
9. Click OK.

From Text

HINT

Most programs can export data in a text file. If you need to use data from a program that is not compatible with Excel, check the source program's export options for a text file format.

Figure 8.3 Project 1c Text File Contents

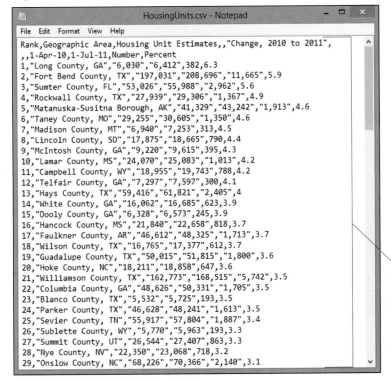

Text files contain no formatting codes. In a comma separated file (.csv), commas separate the fields. During the import, Excel starts a new column at each comma. Notice also that quotes surround text data. Excel strips the quotes from the data upon importing it.

Non-native files including, but not limited to, web pages, XML files, text files and data sources can also be opened directly in Excel. To open a non-native file directly in Excel, click the FILE tab and then click the *Open* option. Click the file location and then click the Browse button to display the Open dialog box. Navigate to the specific folder and then click the *File Type* option box to display a drop down list of all the different file types that can be opened in Excel. Click the specific file type and then double-click the file name. If you are not sure of the exact file type, select *All Files (*.*)* to display all of the available files. Save the file as an Excel workbook or, if changes were made, resave it as a text file, noting that some features might be lost.

Project 1c   Importing Data from a Comma Separated Text File   Part 3 of 3

1. With **EL2-C8-P1-NuTrendsCensus.xlsx** open, make HousingUnitData the active worksheet.
2. Import statistics related to the top-growing US counties based on changes in housing units, which have been downloaded from the US Census Bureau website and saved in a text file, by completing the following steps:
   a. Make cell A6 active.
   b. Click the DATA tab.
   c. Click the From Text button in the Get External Data group.
   d. At the Import Text File dialog box, double-click **HousingUnits.csv** in the file list.
   e. At the Text Import Wizard - Step 1 of 3 dialog box, with *Delimited* selected in the *Original data type* section, click the *My data has headers* check box to insert a check mark and then click Next. Notice that the preview window in the lower half of the dialog box displays a sample of the data in the source text file. Delimited files use commas or tabs as separators, while fixed-width files use spaces.
   f. At the Text Import Wizard - Step 2 of 3 dialog box, click the *Comma* check box in the *Delimiters* section to insert a check mark and then click Next. Notice that after you select the comma as the delimiter character, the data in the *Data preview* section updates to show the imported data arranged in columns.

Step 2e

Step 2f

g. Click Finish at the Text Import Wizard - Step 3 of 3 dialog box to import all of the columns using the default *General* format. Formatting can be applied after the data has been imported into the worksheet.

h. At the Import Data dialog box with =$A$6 in the *Existing worksheet* text box in the *Where do you want to put the data?* section, click OK.

3. Scroll down the worksheet and view the imported data. The text file contained the top 100 counties in the United States ranked by change in housing units from 2010 to 2011. The number of housing units and the percent change are included for each county.

4. Make the following changes to the data:
   a. Change the width of column A to 5 characters and columns C, D, and E to 14 characters.
   b. Select C6:D6, click the HOME tab, and then click the Merge & Center button in the Alignment group.
   c. Merge and center E6:F6.
   d. Right-align the data in cell E7.
   e. Scroll to the bottom of the list. Using features in the Alignment and Cells groups on the HOME tab, adjust the notes so that they fit between columns A through F.
5. Print the HousingUnitData worksheet centered between the left and right margins.
6. Save and then close **EL2-C8-P1-NuTrendsCensus.xlsx**.
7. The workbook **EL2-C8-P1-NuTrendsCensus** required three worksheets. If you require only one worksheet in your workbook, you can open the .csv file directly in Excel by completing the following steps:
   a. Click the FILE tab and then click the *Open* option. At the Open backstage area, click your SkyDrive or *Computer* to locate your data files.
   b. Click the Browse button and then navigate to your EL2C8 folder.
   c. Click the *File Type* option box and then click *Text Files (*.prn, *.txt, *.csv)*.
   d. Double-click **HousingUnits.csv** in the file list.
8. Close the workbook without saving.

You will copy and paste data related to car inventory from an Excel worksheet to integrate with an Access database, Word report, and PowerPoint presentation. You will also save a worksheet as a comma separated text file for use in a non-Microsoft program.

Exporting Data from Excel ■■■■■■■■■■■■■■■■■■■■■■■

Excel data can be exported for use in other programs by copying the cells to the Clipboard task pane and then pasting them into the destination document, or by saving the worksheet as a separate file in another file format.

To use Excel data in Word, PowerPoint, or Access, use the copy and paste method, since the programs within the Microsoft Office suite are designed for integration. To export Excel data for use in another program, open the Save As dialog box and then change the *Save as type* option to the desired file format. If the file format for the destination program that you want to use does not appear in the *Save as type* list, try copying and pasting the data or go to the Microsoft Office Online website and search for a file format converter that you can download and install.

Another way to save the current worksheet in a different file format is to click the FILE tab and then click the *Export* option at the backstage area. At the Export backstage area, click *Change File Type* in the center section. In the *Change File Type* section at the right, click the desired file format in the *Workbook File Types* or *Other File Types* section and then click the Save As button. If necessary, navigate to the desired drive and/or folder in the Save As dialog box. Type the desired file name and then click the Save button.

Quick Steps

Append Excel Data to an Access Table
1. Select cells.
2. Click Copy button.
3. Start Access.
4. Open database.
5. Open table in Datasheet view.
6. Click Paste button arrow.
7. Click *Paste Append.*
8. Click Yes.
9. Deselect pasted range.

Copying and Pasting Worksheet Data to an Access Table

Data in an Excel worksheet can be copied and pasted into an Access table datasheet, query, or form using the Clipboard task pane. To paste data into a table datasheet, make sure that the column structures in the two programs match. If the Access datasheet already contains records, you can choose to replace the existing records or append the Excel data to the end of the table. If you want to export Excel data to an Access database that does not have an existing table in which to receive the data, perform an import routine from Access. To do this, start Access, open the desired database, click the EXTERNAL DATA tab, and then click the Import Excel spreadsheet button.

Project 2a   Copying and Pasting Excel Data to an Access Datasheet   **Part 1 of 6**

1. Open **CRInventory.xlsx**.
2. Copy and paste the rows in the Inventory worksheet to the bottom of an Access table by completing the following steps:
   a. Make sure Inventory is the active worksheet.
   b. Select A5:G33 and then click the Copy button in the Clipboard group on the HOME tab.
   c. Start Microsoft Access 2013.

d. At the Access 2013 opening screen, click the *Open Other Files* option.

e. At the Open backstage area, click the desired location in the *Places* section and then click the Browse button. At the open dialog box, navigate to the EL2C8 folder on your storage medium and then double-click ***CRInventory.accdb***. If a security warning message displays below the ribbon stating that active content has been disabled, click the Enable Content button.

f. Double-click the object named *CarInventory* in the Tables group in the Navigation pane at the left side of the Access window. This opens the CarInventory table in Datasheet view. Notice that the structure of the columns in the datasheet is the same as in the source worksheet in Excel.

g. With the table open in Datasheet view, click the down-pointing arrow on the Paste button in the Clipboard group and then click *Paste Append* at the drop-down list.

h. At the Microsoft Access message box informing you that you are about to paste 29 records and asking if you are sure, click Yes.

i. Click in any cell within the datasheet to deselect the pasted records.

Stock	ModelYear	Make	Model	Color	StartMileage	LocationCode
250140	2011	Honda	Civic	Alabaster Silver Metallic	185	PDX
250141	2011	Toyota	Accord	Crystal Black Pearl	165	PHL
250142	2011	Ford	Edge	Tuxedo Black Metallic	75	BOS
250143	2012	Chrysler	Town & Country	Bright Silver Metallic	84	EWR
250144	2014	GM	Impala	Summit White	52	EWR
250145	2011	Toyota	Prius	Silver Metallic	25	RDU
250146	2011	Toyota	Matrix	Black	75	EWR
250147	2011	Toyota	Camry	Blizzard Pearl	30	EWR
250148	2011	Ford	Fusion	Smokestone Metallic	54	RDU
250149	2011	Ford	Focus	Red Candy Metallic	10	RDU
250150	2011	Ford	Mustang	Tuxedo Black Metallic	15	EWR
250151	2011	Honda	Civic			
250152	2011	Honda	Accord			
250153	2011	GM	Malibu			
250154	2011	GM	Equinox			
250155	2011	GM	Impala			
250156	2011	Chrylser	Sebring			

Step 2h

Microsoft Access
You are about to paste 29 record(s).
Are you sure you want to paste these records?
Yes   No

3. Print the Access datasheet in landscape orientation by completing the following steps:

a. Click the FILE tab, click the *Print* option, and then click Print Preview.

b. Click the Landscape button in the Page Layout group on the PRINT PREVIEW tab.

c. Click the Page Setup button in the Page Layout group.

Step 3b   **Step 3c**

d. At the Page Setup dialog box with the Print Options tab selected, change the top and bottom margins to 0.5 inch. The left and right margins should already be set to 1 inch. Click OK.

e. Click the Print button in the Print group and then click OK at the Print dialog box.

f. Click the Close Print Preview button in the Close Preview group.

Step 3d

Page Setup
Print Options | Page
Margins (inches)   Sample
Top: 0.5
Bottom: 0.5
Left: 1
Right: 1

4. Click the Close button in the upper right corner to close Access.

5. Click in any cell to deselect the range in the Inventory worksheet and then press Esc to remove the scrolling marquee.

6. Leave the **CRInventory.xlsx** workbook open for the next project.

Copying and Pasting Worksheet Data to a Word Document

Using a process similar to the one in Project 2a, you can copy and paste Excel data, copy and embed Excel data as an object, or copy and link Excel data as an object in a Word document. Use the copy and paste method if the data being brought into Word will not likely be updated or require editing after the source cells are pasted in the Word document. Copy and embed the data if you want to be able to edit the data in Word using Excel's editing tools and features. Copy and link the data if the information being pasted into Word will likely be changed in the future and you want the document in Word updated if the data in the source file changes.

▼ **Quick Steps**

Embed Excel Data in a Word Document
1. Select cells.
2. Click Copy button.
3. Open Word document.
4. Position insertion point at desired location.
5. Click Paste button arrow.
6. Click *Paste Special*.
7. Click *Microsoft Excel Worksheet Object*.
8. Click OK.

Link Excel Data to a Word Document
1. Select cells.
2. Click Copy button.
3. Open Word document.
4. Position insertion point at desired location.
5. Click Paste button arrow.
6. Click *Paste Special*.
7. Click *Microsoft Excel Worksheet Object*.
8. Click Paste link.
9. Click OK.

Embedding Excel Data into a Word Document

To embed copied Excel data into a Word document, open the desired Word document, move the insertion point to the location at which you want to insert the copied Excel data, and then open the Paste Special dialog box. At the Paste Special dialog box, click *Microsoft Excel Worksheet Object* in the *As* list box and then click OK.

To edit an embedded Excel object in Word, double-click the embedded cells to open them for editing in a worksheet. Word's ribbon is temporarily replaced with Excel's ribbon. Click outside the embedded object to restore Word's ribbon and close the worksheet object in Word.

Linking Excel Data to a Word Document

Linking Excel data to a Word document means that the source data exists only in Excel. Word places a shortcut to the source data file name and range in the document. When you open a Word document containing one or more links, Word prompts you to update the links. Since the data resides in the Excel workbook only, be careful not to move or rename the original workbook from which you copied the cells. If you do so, the link in the document will no longer work.

To paste copied Excel data as a link in a Word document, open the desired Word document, move the insertion point to the location at which you want to link the cells, open the Paste Special dialog box, click *Microsoft Excel Worksheet Object* in the *As* list box, click *Paste link*, and then click OK.

Project 2b | **Embedding Excel Data in a Word Document** | Part 2 of 6

1. With **CRInventory.xlsx** open, copy and embed the data in the CarCosts worksheet to a Word document by completing the following steps:
   a. Make CarCosts the active worksheet.
   b. Select the range A4:F9.
   c. Click the Copy button in the Clipboard group.
   d. Start Microsoft Word 2013.
   e. Open **CRCarRpt.docx** from the EL2C8 folder on your storage medium. If a security warning displays in the message bar below the ribbon stating that the document is in Protected View, click the Enable Editing button.
   f. Save the document and name it **EL2-C8-P2-CRCarRpt**.

g. Press Ctrl + End to move the insertion point to the end of the document.

h. Click the Paste button arrow in the Clipboard group and then click *Paste Special* at the drop-down list.

i. At the Paste Special dialog box, click *Microsoft Excel Worksheet Object* in the *As* list box and then click OK.

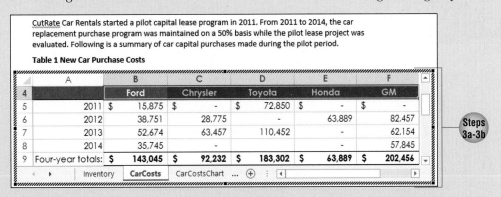

2. Save **EL2-C8-P2-CRCarRpt.docx**.

3. When you use Paste Special, the copied cells are embedded as an object in the Word document. Edit the embedded object using Excel's editing tools by completing the following steps:

a. Double-click any cell in the embedded worksheet object. The object is surrounded with a border and Excel's column and row headers appear. Word's ribbon is temporarily replaced with Excel's ribbon.

b. Select the range B4:F4 and then click the Center button in the Alignment group.

c. Click in the document outside the embedded object to close the object and restore Word's ribbon. Excel becomes the active application.

4. Double-click Word in the Taskbar. Save and then print **EL2-C8-P2-CRCarRpt.docx**.

5. Close Word.

6. Click in any cell to deselect the range in the CarCosts worksheet and leave the **CRInventory.xlsx** workbook open for the next project.

1. With **CRInventory.xlsx** open, copy and link the data in the CarCosts worksheet to a Word document by completing the following steps:
   a. With CarCosts the active worksheet, select the range A4:F9 and then click the Copy button.
   b. Start Microsoft Word 2013.
   c. Open **CRCarRpt.docx**.
   d. Save the document and name it **EL2-C8-P2-CRCarRptLinked**.
   e. Press Ctrl + End to move the insertion point to the end of the document.
   f. Click the Paste button arrow and then click *Paste Special* at the drop-down list.
   g. At the Paste Special dialog box, click *Microsoft Excel Worksheet Object* in the *As* list box and then click the *Paste link* option.
   h. Click OK.

2. Save and then close **EL2-C8-P2-CRCarRptLinked.docx**. When data is linked, the data exists only in the source program. In the destination document, Word inserts a shortcut to the source range. Edit the source range and view the update to the Word document by completing the following steps:
   a. Click the button on the Taskbar representing the Excel workbook **CRInventory.xlsx**.
   b. With CarCosts the active worksheet, press Esc to remove the scrolling marquee (if necessary) and then click in any cell to deselect the copied range.
   c. Make cell E5 active, type 85000, and then press Enter.
   d. Click the button on the Taskbar representing Word.
   e. Open **EL2-C8-P2-CRCarRptLinked.docx**.
   f. At the Microsoft Word message box asking if you want to update the document with data from the linked files, click Yes.

3. Notice that the data inserted in the Excel worksheet is also shown in the linked Word document.
4. Save and then print **EL2-C8-P2-CRCarRptLinked.docx**.
5. Exit Word.
6. With CarCosts the active worksheet in **CRInventory.xlsx**, delete the contents of cell E5 and leave the workbook open for a later project.

Breaking a Link to an Excel Object

If you link Excel data to a Word document and later decide you no longer need the data to be linked, you can break the connection between the source and destination files so that you are not prompted to update the object each time you open the document. Breaking the link means that the data in the Word document will no longer be connected to the data in the Excel workbook. If you make a change to the original data in Excel, the Word document will not reflect the updated information.

To break a link, open the document, right-click the linked object, point to *Linked Worksheet Object,* and then click *Links* at the shortcut menu. This opens the Links dialog box. If more than one linked object exists in the document, click the source object for the link you want to break and then click the Break Link button. At the message box that appears, click Yes to confirm you want to break the link.

▼ **Quick Steps**

Break a Link to an Excel Object
1. Open document.
2. Right-click linked object.
3. Point to *Linked Worksheet Object.*
4. Click *Links.*
5. Click Break Link button.
6. Click Yes.
7. Save document.

Project 2d **Breaking a Link**   **Part 4 of 6**

1. Start Word and open **EL2-C8-P2-CRCarRptLinked.docx**.
2. At the message asking if you want to update links, click No.
3. Break the link between the Excel workbook and the linked object by completing the following steps:
   a. Right-click the linked Excel worksheet object.
   b. Point to *Linked Worksheet Object* and then click *Links* at the shortcut menu.

   c. At the Links dialog box, with the linked object file name selected in the *Source file* list box, click the Break Link button.

   d. At the Microsoft Word dialog box asking if you are sure you want to break the selected link, click Yes.

4. Save **EL2-C8-P2-CRCarRptLinked.docx** and then exit Word.

Copying and Pasting Worksheet Data to a PowerPoint Presentation

Embed Excel Data in a PowerPoint Presentation
1. Select cells.
2. Click Copy button.
3. Open PowerPoint presentation.
4. Make desired slide active.
5. Click Paste button arrow.
6. Click *Paste Special*.
7. Make sure *Microsoft Excel Worksheet Object* is selected in *As* list box.
8. Click OK.

As with Word, you can copy and paste, copy and embed, or copy and link Excel data to slides in a PowerPoint presentation. Presentations often incorporate charts to visually depict numerical data in a graph format that is easy to understand. Although you can create tables and charts in a PowerPoint slide, you may prefer to use Excel for these tasks and then copy and paste the data in to PowerPoint. In the Office 2013 suite, the charting system is fully integrated within Word, Excel, and PowerPoint. A chart inserted in a Word document or PowerPoint presentation is created as an embedded object with the source data used to generate the chart stored in an Excel worksheet; the Excel worksheet with the source data becomes part of the document or presentation file.

Since the chart feature is fully integrated within Word, Excel, and PowerPoint, you can edit a chart in a PowerPoint presentation using the same techniques you learned to edit a chart in Excel. Clicking a chart in a PowerPoint slide causes the contextual CHART TOOLS DESIGN and CHART TOOLS FORMAT tabs to become active with the same groups and buttons available as in Excel. Three new buttons—Chart Elements, Chart Styles and Chart Filter—are also available for editing.

Project 2e   **Embedding Excel Data in a PowerPoint Presentation**   Part 5 of 6

1. With **CRInventory.xlsx** open, copy and embed the chart in the CarCostsChart worksheet to a slide in a PowerPoint presentation by completing the following steps:
   a. Make CarCostsChart the active worksheet.
   b. Click the HOME tab and then click the Copy button.
   c. Start Microsoft PowerPoint 2013.
   d. Open **CRCarRpt.pptx**.
   e. Save the presentation and name it **EL2-C8-P2-CRCarRpt**.
   f. Click Slide 3 in the slide thumbnails pane.
   g. Click in the *Click to add text* placeholder and then click the Paste button in the Clipboard group. Since all charts are embedded by default, you do not need to use Paste Special.
2. Change the chart colors by clicking the Chart Styles button and then clicking the COLOR tab. Click the *Color 2* option from the *Colorful* section of the color palette.

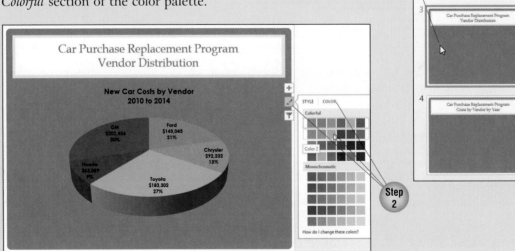

3. Copy and embed the table used to generate the chart in the CarCosts worksheet to the next slide in the PowerPoint presentation by completing the following steps:

a. Click Slide 4 in the slide thumbnails pane.

b. Click the button on the Taskbar representing the Excel workbook **CRInventory.xlsx**.

c. Make CarCosts the active worksheet, select the range A1:F9, and then click the Copy button.

d. Click the button on the Taskbar representing the PowerPoint presentation **EL2-C8-P2-CRCarRpt.pptx**.

e. Click the Paste button arrow and then click *Paste Special* at the drop-down list.

f. With *Microsoft Excel Worksheet Object* selected in the *As* list box, click OK.

4. Resize and position the embedded table to the approximate height, width, and position shown at the right.

5. Click the FILE tab and then click the *Print* option. At the Print backstage area, click the button in the *Settings* category that currently reads *Full Page Slides* and then click *4 Slides Horizontal* at the drop-down list. Click the Print button.

6. Save **EL2-C8-P2-CRCarRpt.pptx** and then exit PowerPoint.

7. Press Esc to remove the scrolling marquee and then click in any cell to deselect the range in the CarCosts worksheet. Leave the **CRInventory.xlsx** workbook open for the next project.

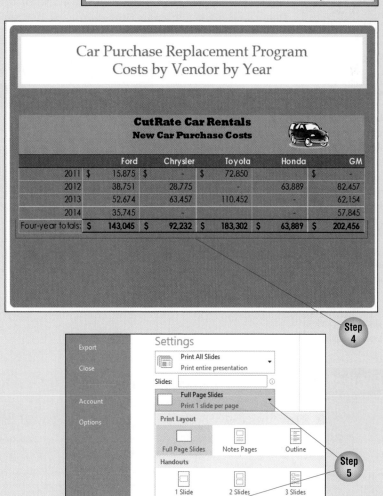

Exporting Excel Data as a Text File

▼ Quick Steps

Export a Worksheet as a Text File
1. Make desired sheet active.
2. Click FILE tab.
3. Click *Export* option.
4. Click *Change File Type*.
5. Click desired text file type in *Other File Types* section.
6. Click Save As button.
7. If necessary, navigate to desired drive and/or folder.
8. Type file name.
9. Click Save button.
10. Click OK.
11. Click Yes.

If you need to exchange Excel data with someone who is not able to import a Microsoft Excel worksheet or cannot copy and paste using the Clipboard task pane, you can save the data as a text file. Excel provides several text file options, including file formats suitable for computers that use the Macintosh operating system, as shown in Table 8.1. To save a worksheet as a text file, open the Save As dialog box and change the file type to the desired option. Type a file name for the text file and then click the Save button. Click OK at the message box that informs you that only the active worksheet will be saved and then click Yes at the next message box to confirm that you want to save the data as a text file.

Another way to save the current worksheet in a text file format is to click the FILE tab and then click the *Export* option. At the Export backstage area, click *Change File Type*. In the *Change File Type* section at the right, click *Text (Tab delimited) (*.txt)*, *CSV (Comma delimited) (*.csv)*, or *Formatted Text (Space delimited) (*.prn)* in the *Other File Types* section and then click the Save As button. If necessary, navigate to the desired drive and/or folder in the Save As dialog box. Type the desired file name and then click the Save button.

H I N T

Why are there so many text file formats? Although all systems support text files, differences occur across platforms. For example, a Macintosh computer denotes the end of a line in a text file with a carriage return character, Unix uses a linefeed character, and DOS inserts both a linefeed and a carriage return character code at the end of each line.

Table 8.1 Supported Text File Formats for Exporting

Text File Format Option	File Extension
text (tab delimited)	.txt
unicode text	.txt
CSV (comma delimited)	.csv
formatted text (space delimited)	.prn
text (Macintosh)	.txt
text (MS-DOS)	.txt
CSV (Macintosh)	.csv
CSV (MS-DOS)	.csv

Project 2f   **Exporting a Worksheet as a Text File**   **Part 6 of 6**

1. With **CRInventory.xlsx** open, export the Inventory worksheet data as a text file by completing the following steps:
   a. Make Inventory the active worksheet.
   b. Click the FILE tab and then click *Export* option.

c. Click *Change File Type* at the Export backstage area.
d. Click *CSV (Comma delimited) (*.csv)* in the *Other File Types* section.
e. Click the Save As button.

f. Type EL2-C8-P2-CRInventory in the *File name* text box.
g. Click the Save button.

h. Click OK to save only the active sheet at the Microsoft Excel message box that informs you the selected file type does not support workbooks that contain multiple sheets.

i. Click Yes to save the workbook in this format at the next message box that informs you **EL2-C8-P2-CRInventory.csv** may contain features that are not compatible with CSV (comma delimited).

2. Close **EL2-C8-P2-CRInventory.csv**. Click Don't Save when prompted to save changes. (You do not need to save the file, because you have not made any changes since you changed the file type.)

3. Open Notepad and view the text file created in Step 1 by completing the following steps:
   a. Click the Start button. At the Start screen, start typing notepad. When *Notepad* appears in the *Apps* area, press Enter. (Depending on your operating system, these steps may vary.)
   b. Click File on the Notepad Menu bar and then click *Open*.
   c. Navigate to the EL2C8 folder on your storage medium.

   d. Click the Text Documents (*.txt) button and then click *All Files (*.*)* at the drop-down list.
   e. Double-click **EL2-C8-P2-CRInventory.csv**.
   f. If necessary, scroll down to view all of the data in the text file. Notice that commas have been inserted between the columns' data.

4. Click File on the Notepad Menu bar and then click *Print*. Click the Print button at the Print dialog box.

5. Exit Notepad.

Project 3   Prepare a Workbook for Distribution   4 Parts

You will remove confidential information from a workbook and mark the workbook as final to prepare it for distribution. In another workbook, you will check for compatibility issues with earlier versions of Excel before sending the workbook to someone who uses Excel 2003. You will also explore the default settings in the Trust Center.

Preparing a Workbook for Distribution ▪■▪■■■■▪■■▪■

In today's workplace, you often work as part of a team both within and outside of your organization. Excel workbooks are frequently exchanged between workers via email message attachments; by saving to a shared network folder, a document management server, or a company website; or by other means of electronic distribution. Prior to making a workbook available for others to open, view, and edit, Excel provides several features that allow you to protect and/or maintain confidentiality.

Removing Information from a Workbook before Distributing

Before distributing a workbook electronically to others, you should consider using the ***Document Inspector*** to scan the workbook for personal data or other hidden information that you would not want others to view. Recall from Chapter 6 that a workbook's properties, sometimes referred to as ***metadata***, include information that is tracked automatically by Excel, such as the names of the individuals that accessed and edited a workbook. If a workbook will be sent electronically by email or made available on a document management server or other website, consider the implications of recipients of that workbook being able to look at some of this hidden information. Ask yourself if this information should remain confidential and, if so, remove sensitive data and/or metadata before distributing the file. To do this, click the FILE tab. At the Info backstage area, click the Check for Issues button in the *Inspect Workbook* section and then click *Inspect Document* at the drop-down list. This opens the Document Inspector dialog box shown in Figure 8.4. By default, all check boxes are selected. Clear the check boxes for those items that you do not need or want to scan for and/or remove and then click the Inspect button.

Before removing sensitive data, you can save a copy of the original file that retains all content using password protection or other security measures to limit access. In addition, you can use the Document Inspector to reveal the presence of headers, footers, hidden items, or other invisible data in a workbook of which you are not the original author.

The Document Inspector scans the workbook for the existence of any of the checked items. When completed, a dialog box like the one in Figure 8.5 appears. Excel displays check marks in the sections for which no items were found and red exclamation marks in the sections in which items were detected within the workbook. Click the Remove All button in the section that contains content you decide you want to remove. Click OK when finished and then distribute the workbook as needed.

▼ Quick Steps

Use the Document Inspector to Remove Private Information
1. Open workbook.
2. Click FILE tab.
3. Click Check for Issues button.
4. Click *Inspect Document.*
5. Clear check boxes for those items you do not want to scan and remove.
6. Click Inspect button.
7. Click Remove All button in those sections with items you want removed.
8. Click Close button.

Inspect

Figure 8.4 Document Inspector Dialog Box

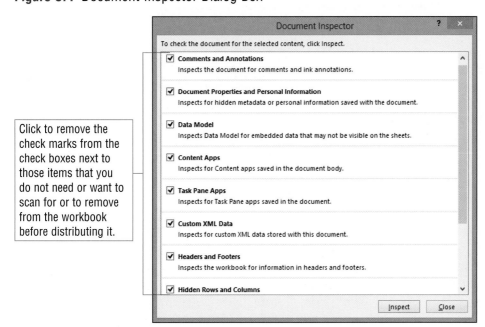

Click to remove the check marks from the check boxes next to those items that you do not need or want to scan for or to remove from the workbook before distributing it.

Figure 8.5 Document Inspector Dialog Box with Inspection Results Shown

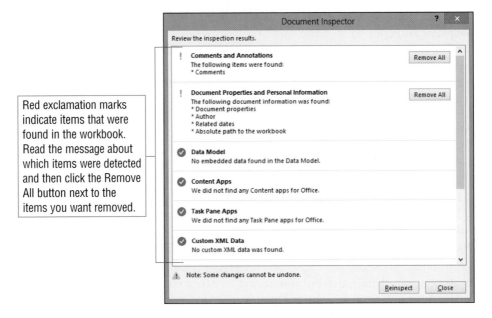

Red exclamation marks indicate items that were found in the workbook. Read the message about which items were detected and then click the Remove All button next to the items you want removed.

Project 3a Removing Private and Confidential Data from a Workbook **Part 1 of 4**

1. Open **CRPilotPrjRpt.xlsx**.
2. Save the workbook and name it **EL2-C8-P3-CRPilotPrjRpt**.
3. Examine the workbook for private and other confidential information by completing the following steps:
   a. Click the FILE tab.
   b. Read the property information in the fields in the *Properties* section located at the right side of the screen.
   c. Click the Properties button and then click *Advanced Properties* at the drop-down list.
   d. Click the Custom tab in the **EL2-C8-P3-CRPilotPrjRpt.xlsx** Properties dialog box.
   e. Position the mouse pointer on the right column boundary for the *Value* column in the *Properties* list box until the pointer changes to a left-and-right-pointing arrow with a vertical line in the middle and then drag the column width to the right until you can read all of the text in the column.
   f. Notice that the extra information added to the workbook properties contains names and other data that you might not want widely circulated.
   g. Click OK.
   h. Press Esc or click the Back button.

Step 3c

Step 3d

Step 3e

i. Click the REVIEW tab and then click the Show All Comments button in the Comments group.

j. Read the two comments displayed in the worksheet area.

Lease Toyota	Buy Honda	Lease Honda	Buy GM	Lease GM	
$ 71,856	$ -		-	$ -	
-	63,889	**Francis Geddes:** Let's try to negotiate a better lease contract with Toyota.	82,457	75,128	**Whitney Simms:** This was high due to excessive mileage. We can mitigate this in the future via earlier returns.
90,653	-		62,154	36,412	
	-		57,845	158,745	
$ 162,509	$ 63,889		202,456	$ 270,285	

Step 3j

4. Use the Document Inspector to scan the workbook for other confidential information by completing the following steps:

a. Click the FILE tab, click the Check for Issues button in the *Inspect Workbook* section at the Info backstage area, and then click *Inspect Document* at the drop-down list.

b. At the message box indicating that the file contains changes that have not been saved, click Yes to save the file now.

c. At the Document Inspector dialog box with all of the check boxes selected, click the Inspect button to check for all of the items.

d. Read the messages in each section of the Document Inspector dialog box that displays with a red exclamation mark.

e. Click the Remove All button in the *Document Properties and Personal Information* section. Excel deletes the metadata and the section now displays with a check mark indicating the information has been removed.

Step 4e

f. Notice that the inspection results indicate that a header and three hidden rows were found. You decide to review these items before removing them. Click the Close button to close the Document Inspector dialog box.

5. Display the worksheet in Page Layout view and view the header.

6. Look at the row numbers in the worksheet area. Notice that after row 10, the next row number is 14. Select row numbers 10 and 14, right-click the selected rows, and then click *Unhide* at the shortcut menu to display rows 11 through 13.

Step 6

7. Click in any cell to deselect the range. Review the information in the rows that were hidden.

8. You decide that the rows that were initially hidden should remain displayed, but you want to prevent reviewers of the workbook from seeing the header and comments. Use the Document Inspector to remove these items by completing the following steps:

a. Click the FILE tab, click the Check for Issues button, click *Inspect Document* at the drop-down list, and then click Yes to save the changes to the workbook.

b. Remove the check marks from all of the check boxes except those next to *Comments and Annotations* and *Headers and Footers*.

c. Click the Inspect button.

d. Click the Remove All button in the *Comments and Annotations* section.

e. Click the Remove All button in the *Headers and Footers* section.

f. Click the Close button.

9. Notice that the comments and header have been deleted from the worksheet. Switch back to Normal view.

10. Click the Show All Comments button in the Comments group on the REVIEW tab to turn off the feature.

11. Save and then close **EL2-C8-P3-CRPilotPrjRpt.xlsx**.

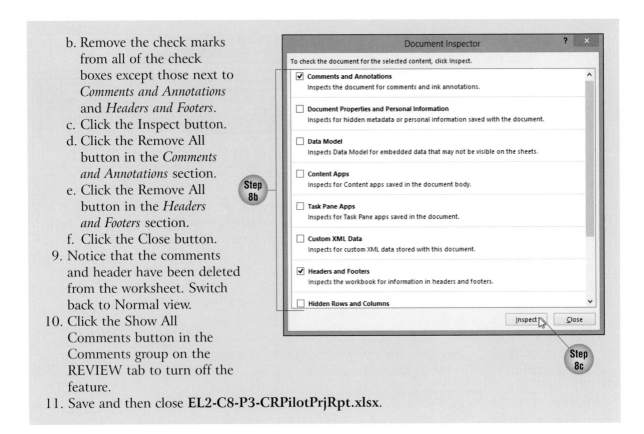

Step 8b

Step 8c

Marking a Workbook as Final

▼ Quick Steps

Mark a Workbook as Final
1. Open workbook.
2. Click FILE tab.
3. Click Protect Workbook button.
4. Click *Mark as Final*.
5. Click OK twice.

Mark as Final

A workbook that will be distributed to others can be marked as final, which means it is protected from additions, deletions, and modifications. When a workbook is marked as final, it is changed to read-only and the status property is set to *Final*. In addition to protecting it, marking a workbook as final also serves to indicate to the recipient(s) of the workbook that you consider the content complete. To mark a workbook as final, click the FILE tab. At the Info backstage area, click the Protect Workbook button and then click *Mark as Final* at the drop-down list. (Note that marking a workbook as final should not be considered as secure as using password-protected, locked ranges.)

A workbook marked as final displays with the ribbon minimized and a message above the Formula bar that informs the reader that an author has marked the workbook as final to discourage editing. You can click the Edit Anyway button in the message bar to remove the Mark as Final feature, redisplay the ribbon, and make changes to the workbook.

1. Open **EL2-C8-P3-CRPilotPrjRpt.xlsx**.
2. Save the workbook and name it **EL2-C8-P3-CRPilotPrjRptFinal**.
3. Mark the workbook as final to prevent changes and set the Status property to *Final* by completing the following steps:
   a. Click the FILE tab, click the Protect Workbook button in the *Protect Workbook* section of the Info backstage area, and then click *Mark as Final*.

   b. Click OK at the message box that says the workbook will be marked as final and then saved.

   c. Click OK at the second message box that says the workbook has been marked as final to indicate that editing is complete and this is the final version of the document. ***Note: If this message box does not appear, it has been turned off by a previous user who clicked the* Don't show this message again *check box.***

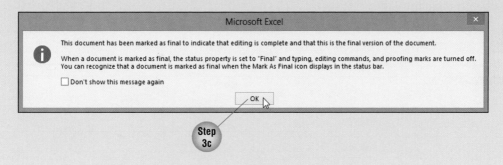

4. Click the FILE tab and notice that the *Protect Workbook* section of the Info backstage area displays in yellow and with a message indicating the workbook has been marked as final. Click the Back button and notice also the addition of *[Read-Only]* next to the file name in the Title bar.

5. The ribbon is minimized and a marked as final message displays above the Formula bar, indicating that the workbook has been marked as final to discourage editing. Additionally, a *Marked as Final* icon displays in the Status bar next to *Ready*.

The ribbon is minimized and a marked as final message displays as described in Step 5.

6. Make any cell active and attempt to insert or delete text in the cell. Since the workbook is now read-only, you cannot open the cell for editing or delete the contents.

7. Close **EL2-C8-P3-CRPilotPrjRptFinal.xlsx**.

Using the Compatibility Checker

▼ Quick Steps

Check a Workbook for Compatibility
1. Open workbook.
2. Click FILE tab.
3. Click Check for Issues button.
4. Click *Check Compatibility*.
5. Read information in *Summary* list box.
6. If desired, click *Copy to New Sheet* button.
OR
Click Close.

Check Compatibility

If you have a workbook that will be exchanged with other individuals who do not have Excel 2007, Excel 2010, or Excel 2013, you can save the workbook in the Excel 97-2003 file format. When you save the file in the earlier version's file format, Excel automatically does a compatibility check and prompts you with information about loss of functionality or fidelity. If you prefer, you can use the Compatibility Checker feature before you save the workbook so that you know in advance areas of the worksheet that may need changes prior to saving in order to maintain backward compatibility.

In the *Summary* list box at the Microsoft Excel - Compatibility Checker dialog box, if an issue displays a Fix hyperlink, click Fix to resolve the problem. If you want more information about a loss of functionality or fidelity, click the Help hyperlink next to the issue. To return to the worksheet with the cells selected that are problematic for earlier Excel versions, click the Find hyperlink next to the issue.

1. Open **CRBuyLeaseAnalysis.xlsx**.
2. Run the Compatibility Checker to check the workbook before you save in an earlier Excel file format by completing the following steps:
   a. Click the FILE tab.
   b. Click the Check for Issues button in the Info backstage area.
   c. Click *Check Compatibility* at the drop-down list.
   d. At the Microsoft Excel - Compatibility Checker dialog box, read the information in the *Summary* box in the *Significant loss of functionality* section.
   e. Scroll down and read the information displayed in the *Minor loss of fidelity* section.
   f. Scroll back up to the top of the *Summary* box.
   g. Click the Copy to New Sheet button.
3. At the Compatibility Report sheet, read the information in the box with the hyperlink <u>Sheet1'!D13:D16</u> and then click the hyperlink. Sheet1 becomes active with the cells selected that have conditional formatting applied that is not supported in the earlier version of Excel (D13:D16).
4. Make the Compatibility Report sheet active and then print the worksheet with the worksheet scaled to *Fit Sheet on One Page*.
5. Save the revised workbook and name it **EL2-C8-P3-CRBuyLeaseAnalysisCompChk**.
6. Make Sheet1 the active worksheet and deselect the range.
7. To save the workbook in an earlier version of Excel, click the FILE tab, click the *Export* option, click *Change File Type*, click *Excel 97-2003 Workbook (*.xls)* in the *Workbook File Types* section, and then click the Save As button. Click the Save button at the Save As dialog box to accept the default file name. Click the Continue button at the Compatibility Checker dialog box.
8. Close **EL2-C8-P3-CRBuyLeaseAnalysisCompChk.xls**.

Step 2b

Step 2c

Step 2d

Step 2g

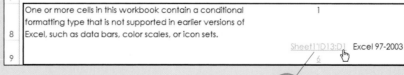

Step 3

Viewing Trust Center Settings for Excel ■■■■■■■■■■■■

▼ Quick Steps

View Trust Center Options
1. Click FILE tab.
2. Click *Options*.
3. Click *Trust Center* in left pane.
4. Click Trust Center Settings button.
5. Click desired trust center category in left pane.
6. View and/or modify options as desired.
7. Click OK twice.

Changing the macro security setting in Excel does not affect the macro security setting in other Microsoft programs such as Word or Access.

In Excel, the Trust Center is responsible for blocking unsafe content when you open a workbook. You may recall the security warning that sometimes appears in the message bar when you open a workbook—this warning is generated by the Trust Center, and it can be closed by clicking the Enable Content button. The Trust Center also allows you to view and/or modify the security options that are in place to protect your computer from malicious content.

The Trust Center maintains a Trusted Locations list that keeps track of locations from which content can be considered trusted. When you add a location to the Trusted Locations list, Excel will treat any files opened from that location as safe. Workbooks opened from trusted locations do not cause a security warning to display in the message bar and none of their content will be blocked.

If a workbook contains macros, the Trust Center checks for a valid and current digital signature from an entity in the Trusted Publishers list before it enables the macros. The Trusted Publishers list is maintained by you on the computer you are using. You can add a publisher to the Trusted Publishers list by enabling content from that publisher and then clicking the *Trust all content from this publisher* option.

Depending on the active macro security setting, if the Trust Center cannot match the digital signature information with an entity in the Trusted Publishers list or the macro does not contain a digital signature, a security warning displays in the message bar. The default macro security setting is *Disable all macros with notification*. Table 8.2 describes the four options for macro security. In some cases, you may decide to change the default macro security setting, and you can do so at the Trust Center dialog box. You will explore the Trust Center in Project 3d.

Table 8.2 Macro Security Settings for Workbooks Not Opened from a Trusted Location

Macro Setting	Description
Disable all macros without notification	All macros are disabled; security alerts will not appear.
Disable all macros with notification	All macros are disabled; security alerts appear with the option to enable content if you trust the source of the file. This is the default setting.
Disable all macros except digitally signed macros	A macro that does not contain a digital signature is disabled; security alerts do not appear. If the macro is digitally signed by a publisher in your Trusted Publishers list, the macro is allowed to run. If the macro is digitally signed by a publisher not in your Trusted Publishers list, a security alert appears.
Enable all macros (not recommended, potentially dangerous code can run)	All macros are allowed; security alerts do not appear.

1. To explore current settings in the Trust Center, complete the following steps:
   a. Click the FILE tab and then click *Options*.
   b. Click *Trust Center* in the left pane of the Excel Options dialog box.
   c. Click the Trust Center Settings button in the *Microsoft Excel Trust Center* section.

   d. At the Trust Center dialog box, click *Macro Settings* in the left pane.
   e. Review the options in the *Macro Settings* section. Note which option is active on the computer you are using. The default option is *Disable all macros with notification*. **Note: The security setting on the computer you are using may be different than the default option. Do not change the security setting without your instructor's permission.**
   f. Click *Trusted Publishers* in the left pane. If any publishers have been added to the list on the computer you are using, their names will be shown in the list box. If the list box is empty, no trusted publishers have been added.

   g. Click *Trusted Locations* in the left pane. Review the paths and descriptions of any folders in the trusted locations list. By default, Excel adds the folder created upon installation that contains the templates provided by Microsoft. Additional folders that have been added by a system administrator or network administrator may also appear.
   h. Click OK to close the Trust Center dialog box.
2. Click OK to close the Excel Options dialog box.

Project 4 Distributing Workbooks

3 Parts

You will publish a workbook as a PDF document, and an XPS document. You will also publish a worksheet as a web page.

Distributing Workbooks ■■■■■■■■■■■■■■■■■■■■■■■■■

Many organizations that need to make documents accessible to several users create a document management server or network share folder from which users can retrieve files. Recall from Chapter 6 that if you do not have access to these resources, you can send a workbook via an email message by attaching the file to the message. You can attach the workbook using your email program's file attachment feature or you can initiate the email attachment feature directly from Excel.

A popular method of distributing documents that travel over the Internet is to publish the workbook as a PDF or XPS document. A workbook can also be published as a web page to make the content available on the Internet.

Publishing a Workbook as a PDF Document

▼ **Quick Steps**

Publish a Workbook as a PDF Document
1. Open workbook.
2. Click FILE tab.
3. Click *Export*.
4. Click Create PDF/XPS button.
5. Click Publish button.

A PDF document is a workbook saved in a fixed-layout format known as *portable document format*. The PDF standard was developed by Adobe and has become a popular choice for sharing files with people outside an organization. By creating a PDF copy of the workbook, you ensure that the workbook will look the same on most computers with all fonts, formatting, and images preserved. You do not need to be concerned if the recipient of the file has Microsoft Excel on his or her computer in order to read the file.

To open and view a PDF file, the recipient of the file must have Adobe Reader installed on his or her computer. The reader is a free application available from Adobe and can be downloaded and installed if the computer being used does not currently have the reader installed. Go to www.adobe.com and click Get Adobe Reader to download and install the latest version of the reader software. You can also open a PDF file with Word 2013. Word 2013 converts your PDF to an editable document, with any formulas converted to values and any charts converted to objects. It may not look exactly like the original PDF, however.

H I N T

You can publish a multi-sheet workbook as a multi-page PDF document by clicking the Options button in the Publish as PDF or XPS dialog box and then clicking *Entire workbook* in the *Publish what* section of the Options dialog box.

1. Open **EL2-C8-P3-CRPilotPrjRpt.xlsx**.
2. Publish the workbook as a PDF document by completing the following steps:
   a. Click the FILE tab.
   b. Click the *Export* option.
   c. With *Create PDF/XPS Document* selected in the Export backstage area, click the Create PDF/XPS button.

d. Insert a check mark in the *Open file after publishing* check box at the bottom of the Publish as PDF or XPS dialog box.
e. With *PDF(*.pdf)* in the *Save as type* text box and *EL2-C8-P3-CRPilotPrjRpt.pdf* in the *File name* text box, click the Publish button.

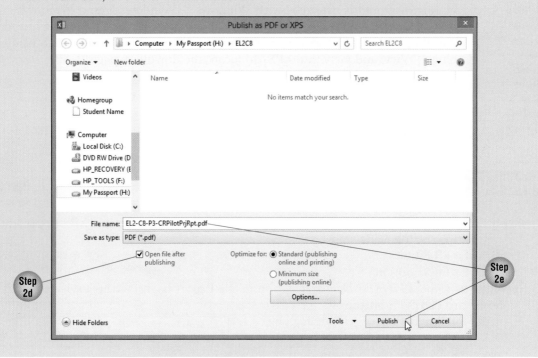

3. An Adobe Reader (or Adobe Acrobat) application window opens with the published workbook displayed. Notice that the workbook has retained all of the Excel formatting and other visual features.

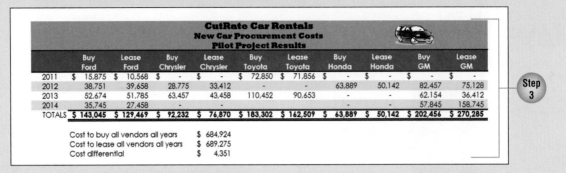

	Buy Ford	Lease Ford	Buy Chrysler	Lease Chrysler	Buy Toyota	Lease Toyota	Buy Honda	Lease Honda	Buy GM	Lease GM
2011	$ 15,875	$ 10,568	$ -	$ -	$ 72,850	$ 71,856	$ -	$ -	$ -	$ -
2012	38,751	39,658	28,775	33,412	-	-	63,889	50,142	82,457	75,128
2013	52,674	51,785	63,457	43,458	110,452	90,653	-	-	62,154	36,412
2014	35,745	27,458	-	-			-	-	57,845	158,745
TOTALS	$ 143,045	$ 129,469	$ 92,232	$ 76,870	$ 183,302	$ 162,509	$ 63,889	$ 50,142	$ 202,456	$ 270,285

Cost to buy all vendors all years $ 684,924
Cost to lease all vendors all years $ 689,275
Cost differential $ 4,351

Step 3

4. Close the Adobe application window.
5. Return to Excel and leave the **EL2-C8-P3-CRPilotPrjRpt.xlsx** workbook open for the next project.

Publishing a Workbook as an XPS Document

▼ **Quick Steps**

Publish a Workbook as an XPS Document
1. Open workbook.
2. Click FILE tab.
3. Click *Export*.
4. Click Create PDF/XPS button.
5. Click Save as type option box.
6. Click *XPS Document (*.xps)*.
7. Click Publish button.

XPS stands for *XML paper specification*, which is another fixed-layout format with all of the same advantages as a PDF document. XPS was developed by Microsoft with the Office 2007 suite. Similar to PDF files, which require Adobe Reader to view documents, XPS documents require the XPS viewer. The viewer is provided by Microsoft and is packaged with Windows 8, Windows 7, and Windows Vista. However, to view an XPS document using Windows XP, you may need to download the viewer application. Go to www.microsoft.com and search using the phrase "View and Generate XPS" to locate the download page.

Project 4b Publishing a Workbook as an XPS Document   Part 2 of 3

1. With **EL2-C8-P3-CRPilotPrjRpt.xlsx** open, publish the workbook as an XPS document by completing the following steps:
   a. Click the FILE tab.
   b. Click the *Export* option.
   c. With the *Create PDF/XPS Document* option in the Export backstage area selected, click the Create PDF/XPS button.
   d. At the Publish as PDF or XPS dialog box, click the *Save as type* option box located below the *File name* text box and then click *XPS Document (*.xps)* at the drop-down list.

File name: EL2-C8-P3-CRPilotPrjRpt.pdf
Save as type: PDF (*.pdf)
PDF (*.pdf)
XPS Document (*.xps)
publishing

Step 1d

e. With a check mark in the *Open file after publishing* check box and *EL2-C8-P3-CRPilotPrjRpt.xps* in the *File name* text box, click the Publish button.

2. The XPS Viewer application window opens with the published worksheet displayed. Notice that similar to the PDF document format, the XPS document format has retained all of the Excel formatting and other visual features.
3. Close the XPS Viewer application window.

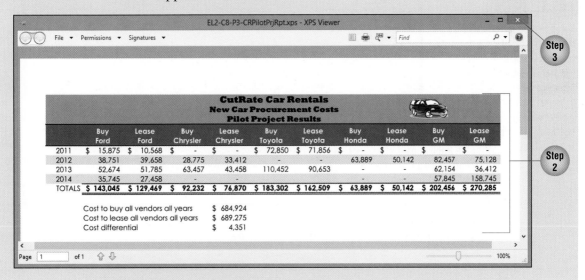

	Buy Ford	Lease Ford	Buy Chrysler	Lease Chrysler	Buy Toyota	Lease Toyota	Buy Honda	Lease Honda	Buy GM	Lease GM
2011	$ 15,875	$ 10,568	$ -	$ -	$ 72,850	$ 71,856	$ -	$ -	$ -	$ -
2012	38,751	39,658	28,775	33,412	-	-	63,889	50,142	82,457	75,128
2013	52,674	51,785	63,457	43,458	110,452	90,653	-	-	62,154	36,412
2014	35,745	27,458	-	-	-	-	-	-	57,845	158,745
TOTALS	$ 143,045	$ 129,469	$ 92,232	$ 76,870	$ 183,302	$ 162,509	$ 63,889	$ 50,142	$ 202,456	$ 270,285

CutRate Car Rentals
New Car Procurement Costs
Pilot Project Results

Cost to buy all vendors all years $ 684,924
Cost to lease all vendors all years $ 689,275
Cost differential $ 4,351

4. Leave **EL2-C8-P3-CRPilotPrjRpt.xlsx** open for the next project.

Publishing a Worksheet as a Web Page

▼ Quick Steps

Publish a Worksheet as a Web Page
1. Open workbook.
2. Click FILE tab.
3. Click *Export*.
4. Click *Change File Types*.
5. Click *Save as Another File Type* option.
6. Click Save As button.
7. Click *Save as type* option box.
8. Click *Single File Web Page (*.mht; *.mhtml)*.
9. If necessary, change the drive, folder, and/or file name.
10. Click Change Title button, type title, and then click OK.
11. Click Publish button.
12. Set desired options.
13. Click Publish.

You can publish a worksheet as a single web page by changing the *Save as type* option to *Single File Web Page (*.mht; *.mhtml)*. In this format, all of the data in the worksheet, such as graphics and other supplemental data, is saved in a single file that can be uploaded to a web server. Alternatively, you can publish the worksheet in the traditional html (hypertext markup language) file format for web pages by changing the *Save as type* option to *Web Page (*.htm; *.html)*. In the *html* option, Excel creates additional files for supplemental data and saves the files in a subfolder.

When you choose a web page option at the *Save as type* list, the Save As dialog box changes, as shown in Figure 8.6. At this dialog box, specify whether you want to publish the entire workbook or only the active sheet. Click the Change Title button if you want to add a title to the web page. The page title displays in the Title bar of the browser window and on the Internet Explorer tab when the page is viewed on the Internet. Click the Publish button and the Publish as Web Page dialog box appears as shown in Figure 8.7, with additional publishing options.

H I N T

Not all browsers support the single file (.mht) web page format. If you or others will not be viewing the page in Internet Explorer, consider using the traditional .htm or .html web page format.

Figure 8.6 Save As Dialog Box with File Type Changed to *Single File Web Page (*.mht; *.mhtml)*

Click here to open the Publish as Web Page dialog box with advanced options.

Click here to enter a page title for the web page.

Figure 8.7 Publish as Web Page Dialog Box

1. With **EL2-C8-P3-CRPilotPrjRpt.xlsx** open, publish the worksheet as a single file web page by completing the following steps:
   a. Click the FILE tab.
   b. Click the *Export* option.
   c. Click the *Change File Type* option and then click the *Save as Another File Type* option in the Other File Types section.
   d. Click the Save As button.
   e. Click the *Save as type* option box and then click *Single File Web Page (*.mht; *.mhtml)* at the pop-up list.
   f. Click the Change Title button.

   g. At the Enter Text dialog box, type Cut Rate Car Rentals Pilot Project Report in the *Page title* text box and then click OK.

   h. Click the Publish button.
   i. At the Publish as Web Page dialog box, click the *Open published web page in browser* check box to insert a check mark and then click the Publish button. (This automatically displays the worksheet in your default web browser.)

2. After viewing the web page, close the browser window.
3. Save and close **EL2-C8-P3-CRPilotPrjRpt.xlsx**.

Chapter Summary

- The Get External Data group in the DATA tab contains buttons to use for importing data into an Excel worksheet from Access, the Web, or a text file.

- Only one Access table can be imported at a time.

- Tables in a website can be imported to Excel using the New Web Query dialog box.

- Text files are often used to exchange data between different programs, since the file format is recognized by nearly all applications.

- Text files generally separate data between fields with either a tab character or a comma.

- The Text Import Wizard guides you through the process of importing a text file through three dialog boxes, where you define the source file as delimited and select the delimiter character.

- Data in an Excel worksheet can be copied and pasted or copied and appended to an existing Access table.

- Worksheet data can be embedded or linked to a Word document. Embedding inserts a copy of the source data in the Word document and allows the object to be edited using Excel's tools within the Word environment, whereas linking the object inserts a shortcut to the Excel workbook from which the source data is retrieved.

- Breaking a link involves removing the connection between the source program and destination program so that the object is no longer updated in the destination document when the source data changes.

- You can embed and link objects to slides in a PowerPoint presentation using the same techniques you would use to embed or link cells to a Word document.

- In Office 2013, the charting tools are fully integrated. A chart copied and pasted from Excel to a PowerPoint presentation or Word document is embedded by default.

- Save a worksheet as a text file by changing the file type at the Export backstage area.

- Excel includes several text file formats to accommodate differences across operating systems, which configure text files using various end of line character codes.

- The Document Inspector feature allows you to search for personal or hidden information and review and remove it, if desired, before distributing a file.

- Once the workbook has been inspected, Excel displays a red exclamation mark in each section in which Excel detected the presence of the requested item. Clicking the Remove All button deletes the items from the workbook.

- Mark a workbook as final to change it to a read-only file with the status property set to *Final*.

- Run the Compatibility Checker feature before saving a workbook in an earlier version of Excel to determine if a loss of functionality or fidelity will occur.

- The results of the compatibility check can be copied to a new worksheet for easy referencing and documentation purposes.

- A workbook can be saved in PDF or XPS format, which are fixed-layout formats that preserve all of the Excel formatting and layout features.

- Adobe Reader or Word 2013 is required to open and view a workbook saved as a PDF file.

- The XPS Viewer is included automatically with Windows Vista and Windows 7 or Windows 8.

- If necessary, Adobe Reader or the XPS Viewer application can be downloaded from the Adobe or Microsoft websites. Both readers are free.

- Open the Save As dialog box and change the *Save as type* option to either *Single File Web Page* or *Web Page* to publish the current worksheet as a web page.

Commands Review

FEATURE	RIBBON TAB, GROUP/OPTION	BUTTON, OPTION	KEYBOARD SHORTCUT
Compatibility Checker	FILE, *Info*		
copy	HOME, Clipboard		Ctrl + C
Document Inspector	FILE, *Info*		
import from Access table	DATA, Get External Data		
import from text file	DATA, Get External Data		
import from web page	DATA, Get External Data		
mark workbook as final	FILE, *Info*		
Paste Special	HOME, Clipboard	, *Paste Special*	Ctrl + Alt + V
save as	FILE, *Save As*		F12
save as PDF/XPS	FILE, *Export* OR FILE, *Save As*		
save as web page	FILE, *Export* OR FILE, *Save As*		F12

Concepts Check

Completion: In the space provided at the right, indicate the correct term, command, or number.

1. This group on the DATA tab contains buttons for importing data from Access.

   _____

2. If the source database used to import data contains more than one table, this dialog box appears after you select the data source to allow you to choose the desired table.

   _____

3. To import tables from a web page, open this dialog box to browse to the website and click arrows next to tables on the page that you want to import.

   _____

4. These are the two commonly used delimiter characters in delimited text file formats.

   _____

5. To add to the bottom of the active Access datasheet cells that have been copied to the Clipboard task pane, click this option at the Paste button drop-down list.

   _____

6. Choosing *Microsoft Excel Worksheet Object* at the Paste Special dialog box in a Word document and then clicking OK inserts the copied cells as this type of object.

   _____

7. If the Excel data you are pasting into a Word document will likely be updated in the future and you will want the Word document to reflect the updated values, paste the data as this type of object.

   _____

8. A chart copied from Excel and pasted to a slide in a PowerPoint presentation is pasted as this type of object by default.

   _____

9. Click this option in the *Other File Types* section of the Export backstage area to select the CSV file format to export the active worksheet as a text file.

   _____

10. This feature scans the open workbook for personal and hidden information and provides you with the opportunity to review and remove the items.

    _____

11. A workbook that has been marked as final is changed to this type of workbook to prevent additions, deletions, and modifications to cells.

    _____

12. Use this feature to check the current workbook for formatting or features that are not available with versions of Excel prior to Excel 2007 and that could cause loss of functionality if saved in the earlier file format.

    _____

13. Save a workbook in either of these fixed-layout formats, which preserve Excel's formatting and layout features while allowing distribution of the file to others who may not have Excel installed on their computers. _____

14. Click this button in the Save As dialog box once the *Save as type* option has been changed to a web page file format to type a page title. _____

Skills Check   Assess Your Performance

Assessment

1   IMPORT DATA FROM ACCESS AND A TEXT FILE

1. Open **HRS.xlsx**.
2. Save the workbook and name it **EL2-C8-A1-HRS**.
3. Make cell A6 active in the CPIData worksheet. Import the CPI table from the Access database named ***NuTrendsCensus.accdb***.
4. Make the following changes to the worksheet:
   a. Apply the Table Style Medium 15 table style to the imported cells.
   b. Format the values in all columns *except* column A to have one place after the decimal point.
   c. Remove the filter arrows and then center the column headings.
   d. If necessary, adjust the column widths to accommodate the data.
5. Print the CPIData worksheet.
6. Make UIRateMI the active worksheet.
7. Make cell A6 active. Import the comma delimited text file named ***UIRateMI.csv***.
8. Make the following changes to the data:
   a. Change the width of column B to 8 characters.
   b. Change the width of columns C to F to 15 characters.
9. Print the UIRateMI worksheet.
10. Save and then close **EL2-C8-A1-HRS.xlsx**.

Assessment

2   LINK DATA TO A WORD DOCUMENT

1. Open **HROctSalesByDateByRep.xlsx**.
2. Save the workbook and name it **EL2-C8-A2-HROctSalesByDateByRep**.
3. With SalesByDate the active worksheet, link A3:G27 at the end of the Word document named **HROctRpt.docx**.
4. Change the margins in the Word document to *Narrow* (top, bottom, left, and right to 0.5 inch).
5. Use Save As to name the revised Word document **EL2-C8-A2-HROctRpt.docx**.
6. Switch to Excel and then press Esc to remove the scrolling marquee and then deselect the range.
7. Change the value in cell F4 to *525000*.

8. Change the value in cell F5 to *212000*.
9. Save **EL2-C8-A2-HROctSalesByDateByRep.xlsx**.
10. Switch to Word, right-click the linked object, and then click *Update Link* at the shortcut menu.
11. Print the Word document.
12. Break the link in the Word document.
13. Save **EL2-C8-A2-HROctRpt.docx** and then exit Word.
14. Save and then close **EL2-C8-A2-HROctSalesByDateByRep.xlsx**.

Assessment

3 EMBED DATA IN A POWERPOINT PRESENTATION

1. Open **HROctSalesByDateByRep.xlsx**.
2. Save the workbook and name it **EL2-C8-A3-HROctSalesByDateByRep**.
3. Make SalesByRep the active worksheet.
4. Display the worksheet at outline level 2 so that only the sales agent names, sale prices, and commissions display.
5. Create a column chart in a separate sheet to graph the sales commissions earned by each sales agent. You determine an appropriate chart style, title, and other chart elements.
6. Start PowerPoint and open **HROctRpt.pptx**.
7. Save the presentation with Save As and name it **EL2-C8-A3-HROctRpt**.
8. Embed the chart created in Step 5 on Slide 3 of the presentation. Resize the chart if necessary.
9. Print the presentation as Handouts with three slides per page.
10. Save **EL2-C8-A3-HROctRpt.pptx** and then exit PowerPoint.
11. Save and then close **EL2-C8-A3-HROctSalesByDateByRep.xlsx**.

Assessment

4 EXPORT DATA AS A TEXT FILE

1. Open **HROctSalesByDateByRep.xlsx**.
2. With SalesByDate the active worksheet, save the worksheet as a CSV (Comma delimited) (*.csv) text file named **EL2-C8-A4-HROctSalesByDateByRep**.
3. Close **EL2-C8-A4-HROctSalesByDateByRep.csv**. Click Don't Save when prompted to save changes.
4. Start Notepad and open **EL2-C8-A4-HROctSalesByDateByRep.csv**.
5. Delete the first two lines at the beginning of the file that contain the title text from the top of the worksheet. The first words in the file that should be deleted begin the heading *Hillsdale Realtors* and end with *Commission*.
6. Delete the bottom row in the file that contains the commas and the total commission value.
7. Print the document.
8. Save **EL2-C8-A4-HROctSalesByDateByRep.csv** and then exit Notepad.

Assessment

5 PREPARE A WORKBOOK FOR DISTRIBUTION

1. Open **HR2015Sales.xlsx**.
2. Save the workbook and name it **EL2-C8-A5-HR2015Sales**.
3. Display the Info backstage area and show all properties. Read the information in the *Author, Title,* and *Subject* property text boxes. Open the Properties dialog box (by clicking *Advanced Properties* from the Properties button drop-down list) and read the information in the Statistics and Custom tabs. Close the Properties dialog box. Click the Back button and click the REVIEW tab.
4. Turn on the display of all comments and then read the comments that appear.
5. Change to Page Layout view and check for a header or footer in the workbook.
6. Use the Document Inspector feature to check the workbook for private and hidden information. Leave all options selected at the Document Inspector dialog box.
7. Remove all items that display with red exclamation marks and then close the dialog box.
8. Click the REVIEW tab, turn off the Show All Comments feature, and switch to Normal view.
9. Click the FILE tab. With the Info backstage area displayed showing all properties, paste a screen image into a new Word document using the Print Screen with Paste or the Screenshot feature. Type your name a few lines below the screen image. Print the Word document and then exit Word without saving.
10. Run the Compatibility Feature to check for loss of functionality or fidelity in the workbook if saved in an earlier Excel version. Save the Summary report to a new sheet and then print the Compatibility Report sheet on one page.
11. Mark the workbook as final.
12. Close **EL2-C8-A5-HR2015Sales.xlsx**.

Assessment

6 PREPARE AND DISTRIBUTE A WORKBOOK

1. Open **HR2015Sales.xlsx**.
2. Save the workbook and name it **EL2-C8-A6-HR2015Sales**.
3. Use the Document Inspector feature to remove comments and annotations.
4. Publish the workbook as a PDF file named **EL2-C8-A6-HR2015Sales.pdf**.
5. Publish the worksheet as a single file web page named **EL2-C8-A6-HR2015Sales.mht** with a page title *Hillsdale Realtors*.
6. Save and close **EL2-C8-A6-HR2015Sales.xlsx**.
7. Display the contents of the EL2C8 folder on your storage medium. Make sure the folder is displaying file extensions. Paste a screen image of the folder's contents into a new Word document using the Print Screen with Paste or the Screenshot feature. Type your name a few lines below the screen image. Print the Word document and then exit Word without saving. Close the Computer or Documents window.

Visual Benchmark   Demonstrate Your Proficiency

IMPORT, ANALYZE, AND EXPORT POPULATION DATA

1. Look at the data in the worksheet shown in Figure 8.8. Create this worksheet by importing the PopByState table from the Access database named ***NuTrendsCensus.accdb*** into a new worksheet. Once imported, the rows and columns included in the database but not shown in the figure were deleted and the filter arrows removed. The Table Style Light 2 style has been applied to the worksheet. Add the title rows at the top of the imported data and change the title in cell B4 as shown. Use your best judgment to match other formatting characteristics, such as column width, row height, number formatting, alignment, and fill color.
2. Rename the worksheet *PopulationTable* and then print it.
3. Select A4:B19 and create the chart shown in Figure 8.9 in a new sheet named *PopulationChart*. The chart has the Style 12 style applied. The *Rounded Rectangle* in the Insert Shapes group on the CHART TOOLS FORMAT tab was used to insert the source information. Use the Shape Effects button in the Shape Styles group to apply the shadow. Use your best judgment to match the other chart options and formatting with the chart shown.
4. Save the workbook and name it **EL2-C8-VB-PBMPopData**.
5. Start Microsoft Word and then open **PBMReport.docx**. Rename the workbook **EL2-C8-VB-PBMReport**. Change *Student Name* on page 1 to your name. Copy and paste the Excel chart, positioning the chart between the last two paragraphs on page 2 of the document. Make any formatting adjustments to the chart you think are necessary once the chart has been inserted. Save, print, and then close **EL2-C8-VB-PBMReport.docx**.
6. Close **EL2-C8-VB-PBMPopData.xlsx**.

Figure 8.8 Visual Benchmark PopulationTable Worksheet

	A	B
1	U.S. Population Estimates as of July 1, 2011	
2	US Census Bureau	
3	States Selected for Franchise Expansion	
4	State	Population
5	Illinois	12,869,257
6	Indiana	6,516,922
7	Iowa	3,062,309
8	Kansas	2,871,238
9	Kentucky	4,369,356
10	Michigan	9,846,187
11	Minnesota	5,344,861
12	Missouri	6,010,688
13	Montana	998,199
14	Nebraska	1,842,641
15	North Dakota	683,932
16	Ohio	11,544,951
17	South Dakota	824,082
18	Wisconsin	5,711,767
19	Wyoming	568,158

Figure 8.9 Visual Benchmark PopulationChart Chart

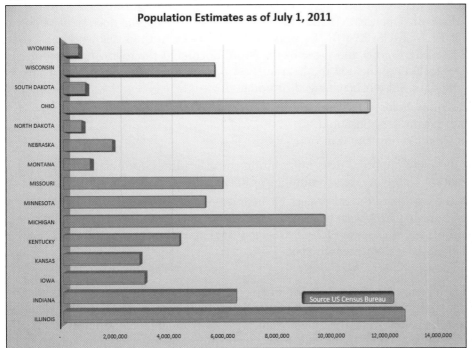

Population Estimates as of July 1, 2011

Case Study   Apply Your Skills

Part 1

Yolanda Robertson of NuTrends Market Research would like new research data from the US Census Bureau for her Pizza by Mario franchise expansion project. The franchise expansion is planned for the states of Illinois, Indiana, and Kentucky. Start a new workbook and set up three worksheets named using the state names. In each sheet, using the New Web Query feature, display the web page http://quickfacts.census.gov/qfd/ and import the People Quickfacts table for the state. Once the data is imported, delete column A, which is the definitions information. Add an appropriate title, merged and centered above the imported data, and apply formatting enhancements to improve the appearance of the column headings. Save the workbook and name it **EL2-C8-CS-P1-PBMResearch**. Print all three worksheets.

Part 2

To prepare for an upcoming meeting with Mario and Nicola Carlucci of Pizza by Mario, Yolanda would like you to copy selected information from each state to a Word report. Open **PBMExpansionResearch.docx**. Save the document and name it **EL2-C8-CS-P2-PBMExpansionResearch**. From the Excel workbook you created in Part 1, copy and paste to the Word document the following data for each state. (Do not include the data in the *USA* column.) Do not embed or link, since the data will not be changed or updated.

> Households
> Persons per household
> Median household income

If the data you imported does not contain these headings, locate and copy information closely related to number of households and income for the state.

At the bottom of the document, create a reference for the data from the US Census Bureau. Check with your instructor for the preferred format for the reference. Save, print, and then close **EL2-C8-CS-P2-PBMExpansionResearch.docx**. Close **EL2-C8-CS-P1-PBMResearch.xlsx**.

Part 3

Yolanda has noticed that when she opens the workbook created in Part 1, a message appears in the message bar that says *Data connections have been disabled*. Yolanda has asked what this message means and wonders what circumstances are acceptable to click the Enable Content button. Research in Help how to manage connections to external data using the Workbook Connections dialog box. Since the data that was imported does not need to be refreshed in the future, you decide to remove the connections so that Yolanda does not see the security message in the future. Open **EL2-C8-CS-P1-PBMResearch.xlsx** and click the Enable Content button that appears in the message bar. Open the Workbook Connections dialog box and using the information you learned in Help, remove all of the connections. Save the revised workbook as **EL2-C8-CS-P3-PBMResearch** and then close the workbook.

Compose a memo to Yolanda using Microsoft Word that provides a brief explanation of why the security warning message about data connections appears when a workbook is opened that contains external content. Base the memo on the information you learned in Help, making sure that you compose the explanation using your own words. Explain that you have created a new copy of the workbook with the connections removed. Save the Word memo and name it **EL2-C8-CS-P3-DataConnectionsMemo**. Print and then close **EL2-C8-CS-P3-DataConnectionsMemo.docx** and then exit Word.

Part 4

Yolanda noticed that you can save a workbook as a web page (*.htm,*.html). Research in Excel Help the different options in the Browser View Options dialog box. Next, search the Internet for at least two web-hosting providers. Using Microsoft Word, compose a memo to Yolanda that briefly explains the options in the Browser View Options dialog box in Excel, making sure you compose the explanation using your own words. Include in the memo the URLs of the two web-hosting providers you visited and add your recommendation for the provider you want to use. Save the memo and name it **EL2-C8-CS-P4-WebMemo**. Print and then close **EL2-C8-CS-P4-WebMemo.docx** and then exit Word.

MICROSOFT® EXCEL® Performance Assessment

Note: Before beginning unit assessments, copy to your storage medium the EL2U2 subfolder from the EL2 folder on the CD that accompanies this textbook and then make EL2U2 the active folder.

Assessing Proficiency ■■■■■■■■■■■■■■■

In this unit, you learned to use features in Excel that facilitate performing what-if analysis, identifying relationships between worksheet formulas, collaborating with others by sharing and protecting workbooks, and automating repetitive tasks using macros. You also learned how to customize the Excel environment to suit your preferences and to integrate Excel data by importing from and exporting to external resources. Finally, you learned how to prepare and distribute a workbook to others by removing items that are private or confidential, marking the workbook as final, checking for features incompatible with earlier versions of Excel, and saving and sending a worksheet in various formats.

Assessment 1 Use Goal Seek and Scenario Manager to Calculate Investment Proposals

1. Open **HillsInvtPlan.xlsx**.
2. Save the workbook and name it **EL2-U2-A1-HillsInvtPlan**.
3. Use Goal Seek to find the monthly contribution amount the client must make to increase the projected value of the plan to $65,000 at the end of the term. Accept the solution Goal Seek calculates.
4. Assign the range name *AvgReturn* to cell E8.
5. Create three scenarios for changing cell E8 as follows:

Scenario name	Interest rate
Moderate	5.5%
Conservative	4.0%
Aggressive	12.5%

6. Apply the Aggressive scenario and then print the worksheet.
7. Change the Moderate scenario's interest rate to 8.0% and then apply the scenario.
8. Create and then print a scenario summary report.
9. Save and then close **EL2-U2-A1-HillsInvtPlan.xlsx**.

Assessment 2 Calculate Investment Outcomes for a Portfolio Using a Two-Variable Data Table

1. Open **HillsResearchInvtTbl.xlsx**.
2. Save the workbook and name it **EL2-U2-A2-HillsResearchInvtTbl**.
3. Create a two-variable data table that calculates the projected value of the investment plan at the end of the term for each monthly contribution payment and at each interest rate in the range A11:G20.
4. Apply comma formatting to the projected values in the table and adjust the column widths as necessary.
5. Make cell E8 active and display precedent arrows.
6. Make cell A11 active and display precedent arrows.
7. Remove the arrows.
8. Save, print, and then close **EL2-U2-A2-HillsResearchInvtTbl.xlsx**.

Assessment 3 Solve an Error and Check for Accuracy in Investment Commission Formulas

1. Open **HillsModPortfolio.xlsx**.
2. Save the workbook and name it **EL2-U2-A3-HillsModPortfolio**.
3. Solve the #VALUE! error in cell E19. Use formula auditing tools to help find the source cell containing the invalid entry.
4. Check the logic accuracy of the formula in cell E19 by creating proof formulas below the worksheet as follows:
   a. In row 21, calculate the amount from the customer's deposit that would be deposited into each of the six funds based on the percentages in column B. For example, in cell B21, create a formula to multiply the customer's deposit in cell B19 ($5,000.00) by the percentage recommended for investment in the DW Bond fund in cell B5 (40%). Create similar formulas for the remaining funds in C21:G21.
   b. In row 22, multiply the amount deposited to each fund by the fund's commission rate. For example, in cell B22, create a formula to multiply the value in cell B21 ($2,000.00) by the commission rate paid by the DW Bond fund in cell B17 (1.15%). Create similar formulas for the remaining funds in C22:G22.
   c. In cell B23, use the SUM function to calculate the total of the commissions for the six funds in B22:G22.
   d. Add appropriate labels next to the values created in rows 21 through 23.
5. Save, print, and then close **EL2-U2-A3-HillsModPortfolio.xlsx**.

Assessment 4 Document and Share a Workbook and Manage Changes in an Investment Portfolio Worksheet

1. Open **EL2-U2-A3-HillsModPortfolio.xlsx**.
2. Save the workbook and name it **EL2-U2-A4-HillsModPortfolio**.
3. Type the following data into the workbook properties. *Note: If any of the properties currently contains text, replace it with the entries indicated below*.

Author	Logan Whitmore
Title	Recommended Moderate Portfolio
Comments	Proposed moderate fund
Subject	Moderate Investment Allocation

4. In a new Word document, paste a screenshot of the Info backstage area with all properties visible. Type your name a few lines below the image, print the document, and then close Word without saving.
5. Click the REVIEW tab and then share the workbook.
6. Change the user name to *Carey Winters* and then edit the cells as follows:
   - B7: from *10%* to *15%*
   - B8: from *15%* to *10%*
7. Save **EL2-U2-A4-HillsModPortfolio.xlsx**.
8. Change the user name to *Jodi VanKemenade* and then edit the cells as follows:
   - D17: from *2.15%* to *2.32%*
   - E17: from *2.35%* to *2.19%*
9. Save **EL2-U2-A4-HillsModPortfolio.xlsx**.
10. Create and then print a History sheet. *Note: If you are to submit your assignment electronically, create a copy of the History worksheet in a new workbook named EL2-U2-A4-HillsModPortfolioHistory.*
11. Change the user name back to the original name on the computer you are using.
12. Accept and reject changes made to the cells in the ModeratePortfolio worksheet as follows:
    - B7: Reject
    - B8: Reject
    - D17: Accept
    - E17: Reject
13. Save, print, and then close **EL2-U2-A4-HillsModPortfolio.xlsx**.

Assessment 5 Insert Comments and Protect a Confidential Investment Portfolio Workbook

1. Open **EL2-U2-A4-HillsModPortfolio.xlsx**.
2. Save the workbook and name it **EL2-U2-A5-HillsModPortfolio.xlsx**.
3. Remove the shared access to the workbook.
4. Hide rows 20 through 23.
5. Make cell B17 the active cell and insert a comment. Type Commission rate to be renegotiated in 2015 in the comment box.
6. Copy the comment in cell B17 and paste it to cells D17 and G17. Press the Esc key to remove the scrolling marquee from cell B17.
7. Edit the comment in cell G17 to change the year from *2015* to *2016*.
8. Protect the worksheet to only allow editing in cell B19. Assign the password *eL2-U2* to unprotect the worksheet.
9. Encrypt the workbook with the password *eL2-U2*.
10. Save and close **EL2-U2-A5-HillsModPortfolio.xlsx**.
11. Test the security features added to the workbook by opening **EL2-U2-A5-HillsModPortfolio.xlsx** using the password created in Step 9. Try to change one of the values in the range B5:B10 and in the range B17:G17.
12. Make cell B19 active and then change the value to *10000*.
13. Display all of the comments in the worksheet and then print the worksheet with the comments displayed and with the worksheet scaled to fit on one page.
14. Save and then close **EL2-U2-A5-HillsModPortfolio.xlsx**.

Assessment 6 Automate and Customize an Investment Portfolio Workbook

1. Open **EL2-U2-A5-HillsModPortfolio.xlsx**.
2. Unprotect the worksheet, turn off the display of all comments, and then delete the comments in cells B17, D17, and G17.
3. Display the Custom Views dialog box. When a workbook has been shared, Excel automatically creates a custom view (with the label *Personal View*) for each person who accessed the file and for the original worksheet state before sharing was enabled. Delete all of the custom views in the dialog box and then add a new custom view named *ModeratePortfolioOriginalView*.
4. Create two macros to be stored in the active workbook as follows:
   a. Create a macro named *CustomDisplay* that applies the Metropolitan theme and turns off the display of gridlines and row and column headers in the current worksheet. Assign the macro to the shortcut key Ctrl + Shift + T. Enter an appropriate description that includes your name and the date the macro was created.
   b. Create a macro named *CustomHeader* that prints the text *Private and Confidential* at the left margin in the header. Assign the macro to the shortcut key Ctrl + Shift + H. Enter an appropriate description that includes your name and the date the macro was created.
5. Test the macros by opening **EL2-U2-A1-HillsInvtPlan.xlsx**. Make InvestmentPlanProposal the active worksheet and then run the two macros created in Step 4. View the worksheet in the Print backstage area. Close the Print backstage area and then close **EL2-U2-A1-HillsInvtPlan.xlsx** without saving the changes.
6. Print the VBA program code for the two macros and then close the Microsoft Visual Basic for Applications window and return to Excel.
7. Create a custom view named *ModeratePortfolioTemplateView*.
8. Save the revised workbook as a macro-enabled workbook named **EL2-U2-A6-HillsModPortfolio.xlsm** and remove the password to open the workbook.
9. Print the worksheet.
10. Display the Custom Views dialog box. Paste a screenshot of the worksheet with the Custom Views dialog box open into a new Word document. Type your name a few lines below the image, print the document, and then exit Word without saving.
11. Close the Custom Views dialog box and then close **EL2-U2-A6-HillsModPortfolio.xlsm**.

Assessment 7 Create and Use an Investment Planner Template

1. Open **EL2-U2-A2-HillsResearchInvtTbl.xlsx**.
2. Make the following changes to the worksheet:
   a. Change the label in cell A3 to *Investment Planner*.
   b. Change the font color of cell A11 to white. This will make the cell appear to be empty. (You want to disguise the entry in this cell because you think displaying the value at the top left of the data table will confuse Hillsdale customers.)
   c. Clear the contents of E5:E7.
   d. Protect the worksheet so that editing is allowed only in E5:E7. Assign the password *eL2-U2* to unprotect the worksheet.
3. Save the revised workbook as a template named **HillsInvPlan-StudentName** with your name substituted for *StudentName*.

4. Close **HillsInvPlan-StudentName.xltx**.
5. Start a new workbook based on the **HillsInvPlan-StudentName.xltx** template.
6. Type the following information in the appropriate cells:
   Monthly contribution: -475
   Number of years to invest: 5
   Forecasted annual interest rate: 4.75%
7. Save the workbook as an Excel workbook named **EL2-U2-A7-HillsInvPlan**.
8. Print and then close **EL2-U2-A7-HillsInvPlan.xlsx**.
9. Copy the template created in this assessment to the EL2U2 folder on your storage medium.

Assessment 8 Export a Chart and Prepare and Distribute an Investment Portfolio Worksheet

1. Open **EL2-U2-A6-HillsModPortfolio.xlsm**. If a security warning appears, enable the content.
2. Start Microsoft PowerPoint 2013 and then open **HillsPortfolios.pptx**.
3. Save the presentation and name it **EL2-U2-A8-HillsPortfolios**.
4. Copy the pie chart from the Excel worksheet to Slide 7 in the PowerPoint presentation.
5. Resize the chart on the slide and edit the legend if necessary to make the chart consistent with the other charts in the presentation.
6. Print the PowerPoint presentation as a handout with nine slides printed horizontally on the page.
7. Save **EL2-U2-A8-HillsPortfolios.pptx** and then exit PowerPoint.
8. Deselect the chart in the Excel worksheet.
9. Inspect the document, leaving all items checked at the Document Inspector dialog box.
10. Remove all items that display with red exclamation marks and then close the dialog box.
11. Change the file type to a workbook with an .xlsx file extension and name it **EL2-U2-A8-HillsModPortfolio**. Click Yes at the message stating that the file cannot be saved with the VB Project. Click OK at the privacy warning message box.
12. Mark the workbook as final. Click OK if the privacy warning message box reappears.
13. Send the workbook to yourself as an XPS document in an email initiated from Excel. Include an appropriate message in the message window, assuming you work for Hillsdale Financial Services and are sending the portfolio file to a potential client. Open the message window from the inbox in your email program and print the message. Close the message window and exit your email program.
14. Display the Info backstage area and make sure all properties are visible. Take a screenshot and paste it into a new Word document. Type your name a few lines below the image, print the document, and then exit Word without saving.
15. Close **EL2-U2-A8-HillsModPortfolio.xlsx**.

Writing Activities ▪▪▪▪▪▪▪▪▪▪▪▪▪▪▪

The following activities give you the opportunity to practice your writing skills while demonstrating an understanding of some of the important Excel features you have mastered in this unit. Use appropriate word choices and correct grammar, capitalization, and punctuation when setting up new worksheets. Labels should clearly describe the data that is presented.

Create a Computer Maintenance Template

The Computing Services department of National Online Marketing Inc. wants to create a computer maintenance template for Help Desk employees to complete electronically and save to a document management server. This system will make it easy for a technician to check the status of any employee's computer from any location within the company. Help Desk employees perform the following computer maintenance tasks at each computer twice annually:

- Delete temporary Internet files
- Delete temporary document files that begin with a tilde (~)
- Update hardware drivers
- Reconfirm all serial numbers and asset records
- Have employee change password
- Check that automatic updates for the operating system are active
- Check that automatic updates for virus protection are active
- Confirm that automatic backup to the computing services server is active
- Confirm that the employee is archiving all email messages
- Clean the computer's screen, keyboard, and system unit

In a new workbook, create a template that can be used to complete the maintenance form electronically. The template should include information that identifies the workstation by asset ID number, the department in which the computer is located, the name of the employee using the computer, the name of the technician that performs the maintenance, and the date the maintenance is performed. In addition, include a column next to each task with a drop-down list containing these options: *Completed*, *Not Completed*, and *Not Applicable*. Next to this column, include a column in which the technician can type notes. At the bottom of the template, include a text box and type the following message inside it:

Save using the file naming standard CM-StationID##-yourinitials, where ## is the asset ID. Example: CM-StationID56-JW

Protect the worksheet, leaving unlocked the cells that the technician will fill in as he or she completes a maintenance visit. Do not include a password for unprotecting the sheet. Save the template and name it **NationalCMForm-StudentName** with your name substituted for *StudentName*. Start a new workbook based on the custom template. To test the template's organization and layout, fill out a form as if you are a technician working on your own computer. Save the completed form as an Excel workbook named **EL2-U2-Act1-NationalCMForm**. Print the form scaled to fit on one page. Copy the **NationalCMForm-StudentName.xltx** template file to your storage medium.

Internet Research ▪■■■■■■▪■■▪■■▪■■■

Apply What-If Analysis to a Planned Move

Following graduation, you plan to move out of the state/province for a few years to live on your own. Create a new workbook to use as you plan this move to develop a budget for expenses in the first year. Research typical rents for apartments in the city in which you want to find your first job. Estimate other living costs in the city including transportation, food, entertainment, clothes, telephone, cable/satellite, cell phone, Internet, and so on. Calculate total living costs for an entire year. Next, research annual starting salaries for your chosen field of study in the same area. Estimate the take-home pay at approximately 70% of the annual salary you decide to use. Using the take-home pay and the total living costs for the year, calculate whether you will have enough money to cover your expenses.

Next, assume you want to save money to go on a vacation at the end of the year. Use Goal Seek to find the take-home pay you need to earn to have $2,000 left over at the end of the year. Accept the solution that Goal Seek provides and then create two scenarios in the worksheet, as follows:

- A scenario named *LowestValues,* in which you adjust each value down to the lowest amount you think is reasonable
- A scenario named *HighestValues,* in which you adjust each value up to the highest amount you think is reasonable

Apply each scenario and watch the impact on the amount left over at the end of the year. Display the worksheet in the *HighestValues* scenario and then create a scenario summary report. Print the worksheet, applying print options as necessary to minimize the pages required. Print the scenario summary report. Save the workbook as **EL2-U2-Act2-MyFirstYearBudget.** Close **EL2-U2-Act2-MyFirstYearBudget.xlsx.**

Research and Compare Smartphones

You work for an independent marketing consultant who travels frequently in North America and Europe for work. The consultant, Lindsay Somers, would like to purchase a smartphone. While traveling, Lindsay will use the smartphone for conference calls, sending email, web browsing, text messaging, and modifying PowerPoint presentations, Word documents, and Excel worksheets. Using the Internet, research the latest smartphones from three different manufacturers. Prepare a worksheet that compares the three smartphones, organizing the information so the main features are shown along the left side of the page by category and each phone's specifications for those features are set in columns. At the bottom of each column, provide the hyperlink to the phone's specifications on the Web. Based on your perception of the best value, select one of the phones as your recommendation and use a comment box in the worksheet to note the phone you think Lindsay should select. In the comment box, provide a brief explanation of why you chose this phone. Make sure comments are displayed in the worksheet. Save the worksheet and name it **EL2-U2-Act3-Smartphones.** Publish the worksheet as a single file web page, accepting the default file name and changing the page title to *Smartphone Feature and Price Comparison.* Print the web page from the Internet Explorer window. Close Internet Explorer and then close **EL2-U2-Act3-Smartphones.xlsx.**

Job Study ■■■■■■■■■■■■■■■■■■■■■■■■■■■■

Prepare a Wages Budget and Link the Budget to a Word Document

You work at a small, independent, long-term care facility named Gardenview Place Long-Term Care. As assistant to the business manager, you are helping with the preparation of next year's hourly wages budget. Create a worksheet to estimate next year's hourly wage expenses using the average wage costs in Table U2.1 and the following information about hourly paid workers:

- The facility runs three 8-hour shifts, 7 days per week, 52 weeks per year: 6 a.m. to 2 p.m., 2 p.m. to 10 p.m., and 10 p.m. to 6 a.m.

- Each shift requires two registered nurses, four licensed practical nurses, and two health-care aid workers.

- On each shift, one of the registered nurses is designated as the charge nurse and is paid a premium of 15% his or her regular hourly rate.

- The shifts from 6 a.m. to 2 p.m. and 2 p.m. to 10 p.m. require one custodian; the shift from 10 p.m. to 6 a.m. requires two custodians.

- Each shift requires the services of an on-call physician and on-call pharmacist. Budget for the physician and pharmacist at 4 hours per shift.

- Add 14% to each shift's total wage costs to cover the estimated costs of benefits such as vacation pay, holiday pay, and medical care coverage plans for all workers *except* the on-call physician and on-call pharmacist, who do not receive these benefits.

Make use of colors, themes, and table features to make the budget calculations workbook easy to read. Save the workbook and name it **EL2-U2-JS-GardenviewWageBdgt**. Print the worksheet, adjusting print options as necessary to minimize the pages required. Create a chart in a separate sheet to show the total hourly wages budget by worker category. You determine the chart type and chart options to use in presenting the information.

Start Word and open the document named **GardenviewOpBdgt.docx**. Change the year on the title page to the current year. Change the name and date at the bottom of the title page to your name and the current date. Link the chart created in the Excel worksheet to the end of the Word document. Save the revised document as **EL2-U2-JS-GardenviewOpBdgt**. Print and then close **EL2-U2-JS-GardenviewOpBdgt.docx**. Deselect the chart and close it.

Table U2.1 Average Hourly Wage Rates

Wage Category	Average Wage Rate
registered nurse	29.64
licensed practical nurse	18.63
health-care aid worker	14.05
custodian	10.96
on-call physician	66.00
on-call pharmacist	48.00

removing information before, 289–292
document information panel, 187, 188
Document Inspector, 289–292

E

Edit Anyway button, 292
Edit Comment button, 190
editing
    comments, 190–191
    conditional formatting rules, 10–12
    macro, 233–235
    range name, 51–52
    Scenario Manager, 163
    source data, 111–113
    tracked workbook, 213
Edit Links button, 111
Edit Links dialog box, 111–112
Edit the Rule Description section, 8–9
email, sending workbook by, 203–204
embedding Excel data
    in PowerPoint presentation, 284–285
    in Word document, 280–281
Encrypt Document dialog box, 208, 209
encrypted passwords, 208
error alert messages, 85
Error Checking button, 172
errors
    error codes, 171–172
    logic errors, 171
    troubleshooting formulas, 171–174
Evaluate Formula button, 172
Existing Connections dialog box, 270
exponential notation, 16–17
exporting data, 278–288
    breaking link to Excel object, 283
    copying and pasting worksheet data to
        Access, 278–279
        PowerPoint, 284–285
        Word, 280–282

as text file, 286–288
EXTERNAL DATA tab, 278
external reference
    editing source data and updating external link, 111–113
    point-and-click approach to creating, 110
    removing, 113–114

F

field names row, 74
fields, defined, 74
Field Settings button, 126
files
    comma separated file format, 275
    delimited file format, 275
    importing data from text file, 275–277
FILE tab, 187
filtering
    by font color, 30
    by icon set, 29
    PivotTables
        overview, 121–122
        using Slicers, 122–124
        using Timelines, 124–126
    tables, 78–79
    using conditional formatting or cell attributes, 29–31
    worksheet using Custom AutoFilter, 27–28
Financial button, 56, 57
financial functions, 56–57
    IPMT function, 56
    PMT function, 56
    PPMT function, 56–57
Flash Fill, populating data using, 81–82
folder, shared, 193
Format as Table button, 74
Format button, 204, 205
Format Cells dialog box, 16–17, 18–19
formatting
    conditional, 6–16
    custom number formats, 20–22
    filtering and sorting using conditional formatting, 29–31

fraction, 16–18
    PivotTables, 121–122
    scientific, 16–18
    special number, 18–19
    table, 76–78
    with text functions, 23–26
Formula Auditing group, 169–176
    circling invalid data, 174–176
    tracing precedent and dependent cells, 170
    troubleshooting formulas, 171–174
    viewing relationships between cells and formulas, 170–171
    watching formula cell, 174–176
formulas
    array formula, 15
    auditing tools for, 169–176
    conditional formatting using, 15–16
    one-variable data table, 166–167
    proof formula, 171
    range names for, 41–42, 51–52
    referencing cell in separate worksheet, 106–109
    standard, 41
    3-D formulas, 106
    two-variable data table, 168–169
    viewing relationships between cells and formulas, 170–171
FORMULAS tab, 23, 51, 106, 169
fraction formatting, 16–18
From Access button, 271
From Other Sources button, 270
From Text button, 275
From Web button, 272
function formula
    argument in, 39
    creating range name, 41–42
    editing and deleting range name, 51–52
    standard, 41
    structure of, 39

Excel 2013 Feature	Ribbon Tab, Group/Option	Button	Keyboard Shortcut
Accounting format	HOME, Number		
align text left, center, or right	HOME, Alignment		
align text top, middle, or bottom	HOME, Alignment		
bold text	HOME, Font	B	Ctrl + B
borders	HOME, Font		
cell styles	HOME, Styles		
change file type	FILE, Export		
close Excel			Alt + F4
close workbook	FILE, Close		Ctrl + F4
Comma format	HOME, Number		
comments	REVIEW, Comments		
conditional formatting	HOME, Styles		
Consolidate	DATA, Data Tools		
convert text to columns	DATA, Data Tools		
copy selected cells	HOME, Clipboard		Ctrl + C
cut selected cells	HOME, Clipboard		Ctrl + X
data table	DATA, Data Tools		
data validation	DATA, Data Tools		
decrease decimal places	HOME, Number		
decrease indent	HOME, Alignment		Ctrl + Alt + Shift + Tab
delete cells, rows, or columns	HOME, Cells		
display formulas	FORMULAS, Formula Auditing		Ctrl + `

Excel 2013 Feature	Ribbon Tab, Group/Option	Button	Keyboard Shortcut
fill color	HOME, Editing		
financial functions	FORMULAS, Function Library		
Find & Select	HOME, Editing		Ctrl + E
Flash Fill	DATA, Data Tools		
font color	HOME, Font		
Format Cells dialog box	HOME, Number		
Format Painter	HOME, Clipboard		
Goal Seek	DATA, Data Tools		
group and ungroup	DATA, Outline		Shift + Alt + Right Arrow key, Shift + Alt + Left Arrow Key
header and footer	INSERT, Text		
Help			F1
hyperlink	INSERT, Links		Ctrl + K
import from Access, web page, or text file	DATA, Get External Data		
increase decimal places	HOME, Number		
increase indent	HOME, Alignment		
inspect workbook	FILE, Info		
insert cells, rows, or columns	HOME, Cells		
Insert Chart dialog box	INSERT, Charts		
Insert Function dialog box	FORMULAS, Function Library	fx	Shift + F3
italicize text	HOME, Font	I	Ctrl + I
logical functions	FORMULAS, Function Library		

Excel 2013 Feature	Ribbon Tab, Group/Option	Button	Keyboard Shortcut
lookup and reference functions	FORMULAS, Function Library		
macros	VIEW, Macros		Alt + F8
mark workbook as final	FILE, Info		
math and trigonometry functions	FORMULAS, Function Library		
merge and center cells	HOME, Alignment		
Name Manager dialog box	FORMULAS, Defined Names		Ctrl + F3
New backstage area	FILE, New		
number format	HOME, Number	General	
online pictures	INSERT, Illustrations		
Open backstage area	FILE, Open		Ctrl + O
Orientation	HOME, Alignment		
page orientation	PAGE LAYOUT, Page Setup		
paste selected cells	HOME, Clipboard		Ctrl + V
Percent format	HOME, Number	%	Ctrl + Shift + %
PivotTable or PivotChart	INSERT, Tables, INSERT Charts, or PIVOTTABLE TOOLS ANALYZE, Tools		
Print backstage area	FILE, Print		Ctrl + P
protect worksheet	REVIEW, Changes		
recommended chart	INSERT, Charts		Alt + F1
remove duplicates	DATA, Data Tools or TABLE TOOLS DESIGN, Tools		
Save As backstage area	FILE, Save As		
save as PDF/XPS	FILE, Export		Ctrl + S, F12
Scenario Manager	DATA, Data Tools		
screenshot	INSERT, Illustrations		

Excel 2013 Feature	Ribbon Tab, Group/Option	Button	Keyboard Shortcut
share workbook	REVIEW, Changes		
Slicer	INSERT, Filters or TABLE TOOLS DESIGN, Tools or PIVOTTABLE TOOLS ANALYZE, Filter		
SmartArt graphic	INSERT, Illustrations		
sort and filter data	HOME, Editing		
Sparklines: Line, Column, Win/Loss	INSERT, Sparklines		
spelling checker	REVIEW, Proofing		F7
statistical functions	FORMULAS, Function Library		
subtotals	DATA, Outline		
SUM function	HOME, Editing OR FORMULAS, Function Library		Alt + =
Symbol dialog box	INSERT, Symbols		
table	INSERT, Table		
text box	INSERT, Text		
text functions	FORMULAS, Function Library		
themes	PAGE LAYOUT, Themes		
Timeline	INSERT, Filters or PIVOTTABLE TOOLS ANALYZE, Filter		
trace dependents or trace precedents	FORMULAS, Auditing		
Track Changes	REVIEW, Changes		
underline text	HOME, Font		Ctrl + U
unlock cells	HOME, Cells		
update formulas	FORMULAS, Calculation		F9
wrap text	HOME, Alignment		